CW00767384

BUSINESS LAW AND PRACTICE

BUSINESS LAW AND PRACTICE

Trevor Adams BSc, PhD, Solicitor

Alexis Longshaw MA (Oxon), Solicitor

Christopher Morris BA, Solicitor

Published by

College of Law Publishing,
Braboeuf Manor, Portsmouth Road, St Catherines, Guildford GU3 1HA

© The College of Law 2009

All rights reserved.

No part of this publication may be reproduced, stored in a retrieval system, or transmitted in any way or by any means, including photocopying or recording, without the written permission of the copyright holder, application for which should be addressed to the publisher.

British Library Cataloguing-in-Publication Data
A catalogue record for this book is available from the British Library.

ISBN 978 1 905391 75 2

Typeset by Style Photosetting Ltd, Mayfield, East Sussex
Printed in Great Britain by Ashford Colour Press Ltd, Gosport, Hampshire

Preface

In writing this book, we have set out to describe the forms of business organisation most commonly encountered in practice in the context of their 'internal' concerns, their relations with outsiders and their possible tax liabilities. It is intended to be a comprehensive guide to the whole field of advising people who run small businesses, whatever the chosen form of organisation.

The style which we have adopted has been chosen in the hope that the contents will be readily understood and appreciated by someone who is totally unacquainted with the subject as well as by someone with some prior knowledge. In so far as this style necessitates a less detailed treatment of topics than some textbooks adopt, we hope that the inclusion of statutory references in the text will encourage the reader to consult the original source materials whenever further research into a topic is required. To this end, we have prepared a companion volume, *Business and Company Legislation*, which contains the up-to-date text of the key legislation referred to in the book. In addition, we have listed below a few of the many textbooks which the reader may find useful for further study.

Company Law

Alcock, A, Birds, J and Gale, S, *Companies Act 2006* (1st edn, 2007)

Birds, J, Boyle, A, Ferran, E and Villiers, C, *Boyle and Birds' Company Law* (6th edn, 2007)

Boyle, A, *Gore-Browne on Companies* (44th edn, 2008)

Ferran, E, *Company Law and Corporate Finance* (1999)

FL Memo, *Company Law* (2009)

Fuller, G, *Corporation Borrowing Law and Practice* (3rd edn, 2006)

Mayson, S, French, D and Ryan, C, *Company Law* (25th edn, 2008)

Morse, G, *Palmer's Company Law*

Competition Law

Whish, R, *Whish: Competition Law* (6th edn, 2008)

Lindrup, G, *Butterworths Competition Law Handbook* (8th edn, 2002)

Insolvency

Davies, S, *Insolvency and the Enterprise Act 2002* (2003)

Keay, A and Walton, P, *Insolvency Law* (2008)

Milman, D and Durrant, C, *Corporate Insolvency* (3rd edn, 1999)

Partnership

Morse, G, *Partnership Law* (6th edn, 2006)

Lindley, N and Banks, RC L'Anson, *Lindley and Banks on Partnership* (18th edn, 2005)

Taxation

Revenue Law Principles and Practice (24th edn, 2006)

The law is stated as at 1 October 2009.

In the interests of brevity, we have used the masculine pronoun throughout to include the feminine.

Similarly, in the interests of brevity, we have used the following abbreviations:

BNA 1985	Business Names Act 1985
CA 1985	Companies Act 1985
CA 2006	Companies Act 2006
CAA 2001	Capital Allowances Act 2001
CDDA 1986	Company Directors Disqualification Act 1986
CPA 2004	Civil Partnership Act 2004
CTA 2009	Corporation Tax Act 2009
DRO	Debt relief order
EA 2002	Enterprise Act 2002
ERA 1996	Employment Rights Act 1996
FA	Finance Act (various years)
HMRC	HM Revenue and Customs
GAAP	Generally Accepted Accounting Practice
IA 1986	Insolvency Act 1986
IAS	International Accounting Standards
ICTA1998	Income and Corporation Taxes Act 1988
IHTA1984	Inheritance Tax Act 1984
ITA 2007	Income Tax Act 2007
ITEPA 2003	Income Tax (Earnings and Pensions) Act 2003
ITTOIA 2005	Income Tax (Trading and Other Income) Act 2005
LLPA 2000	Limited Liability Partnership Act 2000
PA 1890	Partnership Act 1890
SGA 1979	Sale of Goods Act 1979
SGSA 1982	Supply of Goods and Services Act 1982
SSGA 1982	Sale and Supply of Goods Act 1994
TCGA 1992	Taxation of Chargeable Gains Act 1992
TMA 1970	Taxes Management Act 1970
UCTA 1977	Unfair Contract Terms Act 1977

Preface to this Edition

Note from Trevor Adams

I am grateful to Debbie Woods, my colleague at Chester and an expert in employment law, for kindly updating the provisions on employment law.

Chris Morris has revised the chapters on taxation, overcoming the usual problems that the timing of the Budget causes him.

Alexis Longshaw remains responsible for Chapters 34, 35 and 36.

Lesley King wrote the material for Appendix 3 on interpretation of company accounts.

The process of implementation of the Companies Act 2006 has started and will, it is hoped, be complete by October 2009, on the current timetable. In this edition, we have assumed that this is the case.

Sadly, this edition of the book has gone to press without the input of our publisher, Alistair MacQueen, who passed away in September 2008. His ebullient enthusiasm will be sadly missed by all who knew him in his long publishing career.

My thanks to David Stott for all his help with this edition.

TREVOR ADAMS
Rhos on Sea

Introduction to the Companies Act 2006

The Companies Act 2006 has been the biggest change in company legislation in more than 20 years. It primarily deregulates various aspects of the requirements affecting private companies. However, the provisions on directors' duties will have an impact all companies, though probably more on large plcs than on small family companies.

The following areas are the main ones affected:

- directors
- consequences of breach of duty and derivative claims
- miscellaneous provisions on directors
- shareholder communications
- meetings
- constitutional changes
- share capital and capital maintenance
- company secretary and company records
- company names
- directors' annual reports and
- auditors.

Other areas include some revision of the controls on political donations, and bringing the audit requirements for charitable companies into line with the general requirements on companies.

Companies Act 2006: Commencement Dates

The Government announced details of the final commencement timetable for the 2006 Act by Written Statement on 13 December 2007. The Statement is available as a link from the BERR website.

Unless otherwise stated in the table, provisions relating to accounts and reports will be commenced for financial years beginning on or after the relevant date (eg paragraph 43 in Schedule 3 to the Third Commencement Order provides that 'Section 417 of the Companies Act 2006 (contents of directors' report: business review) applies to directors' reports for financial years beginning on or after 1st October 2007').

Some provisions (eg definitions) may initially be brought into force only so far as necessary for the purposes of provisions which are being commenced before October 2009.

	Part	Commencement Date
1	General introductory provisions (1–6) Section 2: 6 April 2007	1 October 2009
2	Company formation (7–16)	1 October 2009
3	A company's constitution (17–38) Sections 29 & 30: 1 October 2007	1 October 2009
4	A company's capacity and related matters (39–52) Section 44: 6 April 2008	1 October 2009
5	A company's name (53–85) Sections 69 to 74: 1 October 2008 Sections 82 to 85: 1 October 2008	1 October 2009
6	A company's registered office (86–88)	1 October 2009
7	Re-registration as a means of altering a company's status (89–111)	1 October 2009
8	A company's members (112–144) Sections 116 to 119: 1 October 2007 Sections 121 & 128: 6 April 2008	1 October 2009
9	Exercise of members' rights (145–153)	1 October 2007
10	A company's directors (154–259) Sections 155 to 159: 1 October 2008 Sections 162 to 167: 1 October 2009 Sections 175 to 177: 1 October 2008 Sections 180(1), (2)(in part), & (4)(b), and 181(2) & (3): 1 October 2008 Sections 182 to 187: 1 October 2008 Sections 240 to 247: 1 October 2008	1 October 2007
11	Derivative claims and proceedings by members (260–269)	1 October 2007
12	Company secretaries (270–280) Section 270(3)(b)(ii): 1 October 2009 Sections 275 to 279: 1 October 2009	6 April 2008
13	Resolutions and meetings (281–361) Sections 308 & 309: 20 January 2007 Section 333: 20 January 2007 Sections 327(2)(c) & 330(6)(c) are not being commenced for the time being.	1 October 2007
14	Control of political donations and expenditure (362–379) Provisions relating to independent election candidates: 1 October 2008 Part 14 comes into force in Northern Ireland on 1 November 2007, except for provisions relating to independent election candidates.	1 October 2007

	Part	Commencement Date
15	Accounts and reports (380–474)	6 April 2008
	Section 417: 1 October 2007 Section 463: 20 January 2007 for reports and statements first sent to members and others after that date	
16	Audit (475–539)	6 April 2008
	Sections 485 to 488: 1 October 2007	
17	A company's share capital (540–657)	1 October 2009
	Section 544: 6 April 2008 Sections 641(1)(a) & (2)–(6), 642, 643 & 652: 1 October 2008 Section 654: 1 October 2008	
18	Acquisition by limited company of its own shares (658–737)	1 October 2009
	Repeal of the restrictions under the Companies Act 1985 on financial assistance for acquisition of shares in private companies, including the 'whitewash' procedure: 1 October 2008	
19	Debentures (738–754)	6 April 2008
20	Private and public companies (755–767)	6 April 2008
21	Certification and transfer of securities (768–790)	6 April 2008
22	Information about interests in a company's shares (791–828)	20 January 2007
	Sections 811(4), 812, 814: 6 April 2008	
23	Distributions (829–853)	6 April 2008
24	A company's annual return (854–859)	1 October 2009
25	Company charges (860–894)	1 October 2009
26	Arrangements and reconstructions (895–901)	6 April 2008
27	Mergers and divisions of public companies (902–941)	6 April 2008
28	Takeovers etc (942–992)	6 April 2007
29	Fraudulent trading (993)	1 October 2007
30	Protection of members against unfair prejudice (994–999)	1 October 2007
31	Dissolution and restoration to the register (1000–1034)	1 October 2009
32	Company investigations: amendments (1035–1039)	1 October 2007
33	UK companies not formed under the Companies Acts (1040–1043)	1 October 2009
	Section 1043: 6 April 2007	
34	Overseas companies (1044–1059)	1 October 2009
35	The registrar of companies (1060–1120)	1 October 2009
	Section 1063 (in respect of England, Wales and Scotland): 6 April 2007 Section 1068(5): 1 January 2007 Sections 1077 to 1080: 1 January 2007 Sections 1085 to 1092: 1 January 2007 Sections 1102 to 1107: 1 January 2007 Section 1111: 1 January 2007	
36	Offences under the Companies Acts (1121–1133)	With relevant provisions
	Section 1124: 1 October 2007	
37	Companies: supplementary provisions (1134–1157)	With relevant provisions
	Section 1137(1), (4), (5)(b) and (6): 30 September 2007 Sections 1143 to 1148: 20 January 2007 Section 1157: 1 October 2008	
38	Companies: interpretation (1158–1174)	With relevant provisions
	Section 1170: 6 April 2007 Section 1172: 6 April 2008	

	Part	Commencement Date
39	Companies: minor amendments (1175–1181)	6 April 2007
	Section 1175 (only for Part 1 of Schedule 9): 1 April 2008 Section 1180: 1 October 2009 Section 1181: 1 October 2009	
40	Company directors: foreign disqualification etc (1182–1191)	1 October 2009
41	Business names (1192–1208)	1 October 2009
42	Statutory auditors (1209–1264)	6 April 2008
43	Transparency obligations and related matters (1265–1273)	Royal Assent
44	Miscellaneous provisions (1274–1283)	
	Sections 1274 and 1276: Royal Assent Sections 1277 to 1280: 1 October 2008 Section 1281: 6 April 2007 Section 1282: 6 April 2008 Section 1283: 1 October 2009	
45	Northern Ireland (1284–1287)	With relevant provisions
46	General supplementary provisions (1288–1297)	Royal Assent
	Section 1295: With relevant provisions	
47	Final provisions (1298–1300)	Royal Assent

Contents

Table of Cases

V

W

Y

Table of Statutes

Table of Secondary Legislation

Codes

Rules

Accounting Standards

Table of European Legislation

Part I

STARTING A BUSINESS

Part I aims to introduce the reader to the common forms of business organisation from which the new business person(s) might choose, namely sole trader, partnership and limited company.

Chapter 1

Introduction to Common Forms of Business Organisation

1.1 Introduction

There are various forms of business organisation in which a person or persons may choose to operate a business, each of which may offer a number of advantages and disadvantages compared with alternative forms of business organisation. In ascending order of complexity, the most common forms are: sole trader, partnership, limited liability partnership, private limited company and public limited company. Their respective merits and demerits are considered in **Part VI**. The essential features of these forms of business organisation are given below.

1.2 Sole trader

A sole trader is someone who is in business on his own as a self-employed person. He may have employees but he is the person running the business. This could be a corner sweet shop owner, or a plumber, or a solicitor who is a sole practitioner.

A sole trader earns his income from the money received from customers/clients and pays income tax as a self-employed person under Schedule D. He can claim various allowances against tax.

A sole trader is personally liable for all the debts of the business, so could go bankrupt if the business goes badly, and lose his savings, house and other possessions.

When the sole trader retires or dies, the business ceases (though the assets and goodwill may be sellable).

Thus, a sole trader is a person who alone:

(a) has the right to make all decisions affecting the business;

(b) owns all the assets of the business;

(c) is responsible for paying income tax on all the profits of the business; and

(d) is responsible for the debts and obligations of the business without any limit.

1.3 Partnership

A partnership is where a number of individuals are in business together as equals in the business (as opposed to employer and employee). The governing legislation is the Partnership Act 1890.

The partners will divide the profits, and losses, of the business between them. The business could be a trade such as plumbing, or a profession such as surveying.

The major disadvantage of a partnership is unlimited liability for the debts of the partnership both jointly and severally. The partners could thus become bankrupt and lose their possessions because their partners are unable to pay the debts of the business.

A partnership may find it harder to raise capital as it cannot issue debentures (a type of 'IOU') or create floating charges; see **Chapters 11** and **12**. Partners will have to contribute personally to any capital demands on the partnership.

When a partner leaves, he will be bought out by the remaining partners, who have to raise the money themselves.

Overall, there are few formalities, so there is less expense and publicity than in the case of a company. The advantages of a partnership are that it has *no*:

(a)   formality in setting it up;

(b)   memorandum and articles;

(c)   registration;

(d)   publicly available accounts or other details;

(e)   need for a written agreement;

(f)   prescribed roles of 'director' or 'member', so internal management is fluid;

(g)   huge raft of rules, unlike a company, for example, on maintaining capital.

Thus, a partnership consists of two or more persons who, on the basis of a contract between them (which need not be a written contract):

(a)   share the right to take part in making decisions which affect the business or the business assets, although they may have agreed that this right shall be limited in relation to one or more of their number (for example, a 'sleeping partner' may have agreed not to be involved in day-to-day matters while reserving the right to be consulted on fundamental matters such as borrowing);

(b)   share the ownership of the assets of the business, although they may have agreed that the firm will use an asset which is owned by one of the partners individually;

(c)   share the net profits of the business, although the contract need not provide for equal shares; and

(d)   share responsibility for the debts and obligations of the business without any limit, although if one does not pay then the others must pay his share.

1.4   Private limited company

The big advantage of a limited company is the limited liability it allows the members, and consequent protection for shareholders and directors, at least when acting honestly. (A company also has a distinct identity in law, unlike a partnership.)

The downside is increased formality, but there have been various moves over the last 15 years or so to decrease formality for small companies – the typical family business. This has made the limited company even more attractive. Formality has been decreased further by the Companies Act 2006.

A business which is run as a private limited company will be owned and operated by the company itself. The company is recognised in law as having an existence which is separate from the person or persons who formed the company and from the directors and shareholders (see **Chapter 2**).

Decisions affecting the business, the company or its assets are made either by directors or by shareholders (ie members). The division of powers between board meetings (by which, generally, decisions of directors are made) and general meetings (by which, generally, decisions of shareholders are made) is a fundamental aspect of company law. It imposes on a company a degree of formality which is absent from the running of a business by a sole trader or a partnership. In many private companies, the same persons hold the positions of directors and shareholders so that it may seem pointless to make any distinction between these roles. Nevertheless, this distinction must be observed since the validity of many decisions may be in question if the appropriate formality has not been observed.

A company has freedom to operate anywhere within the EU even though it is formed in a Member State other than the one where it conducts its business: *Centros v Erhvervs-OG Selskabsstyrelsen* [2000] 2 WLR 1048, which concerned an English company formed by Danes but operating only in Denmark. A similar situation occurred in *Ueberseering BV v Nordic Construction Company Baumanagement GmbH* [2002] OJ C323/12. The European Court of Justice (ECJ) held that the company was deemed under German law to have de facto moved its administration centre to Germany. However, Articles 43 and 49 on the right to provide services and the right of establishment prevented Germany discriminating against it on the basis that it was a non-national company. On the negative side, an English company can be sued in England in respect of operations even outside the EU: *Lubbe v Cape plc* [2000] 1 WLR 1545.

It is worth mentioning in passing that there is a special type of private company which is usually used for mutual insurance companies, members clubs (eg sports clubs), professional societies, and charities, in particular. It is a company limited by guarantee. The members guarantee, in the event of the liquidation of the company, that they will pay a specified sum to the creditors, usually £1. Their liability is limited to that amount. Thus, in this case the members are not 'shareholders', as there are no shares and no share capital. The members do not receive any dividend. The 'benefit' to the member is therefore not a direct financial one of receiving dividends, but the broader one of being a member of the sports club, or whatever the organisation is, and at the same time being protected by limited liability.

1.5 Public limited company

Whether a company is a public limited company or a private limited company depends essentially on its constitution. To be a public company, the company's constitution must state that it is a public company, must include the words 'public limited company' (or the abbreviation 'plc') at the end of the company's name and satisfy requirements as to the minimum amount of its share capital. Any company which is not a public company is a private company.

As with a private company, the business will be owned and operated by the company broadly as described in **1.4** and **2.7**, but there are important differences between public companies and private companies, some derived from statute, others derived from practice. Some of these differences are described in **1.5.2** and **1.5.3**.

1.5.1 Dealings in shares of public companies

A public company may (but need not) apply to have its shares listed on the Stock Exchange or on the Alternative Investment Market (AIM). In each case this means that a price will be quoted at which dealings in the company's shares will take place.

1.5.1.1 The Official List

In general, only a large public company which has traded for at least three years can apply for its shares to be listed on the Stock Exchange. The company must comply with the initial and on-going requirements of the Financial Services Authority as to publication of information about the company's affairs. These requirements are contained in a volume called the Listing

Rules, available from the Financial Services Authority website at http://fsahandbook.info/FSA/ html/handbook/LR. Listing on the Stock Exchange means that the company's shares are among the most marketable of all shares. Only around 3,000 of the UK's companies are listed on the Stock Exchange, compared with a total of over 1,000,000 companies registered in the UK.

1.5.1.2   The Alternative Investment Market (AIM)

The Alternative Investment Market, which was set up in June 1995, is less stringently regulated than the Stock Exchange. The AIM deals in the shares of smaller and growing companies, and provides a market-place with lower costs and less regulation than the Stock Exchange. There are no minimum capital requirements, no minimum number of shares required to be in public hands and no requirements for a minimum trading record. Currently, around 1,500 companies are listed on the AIM. There are special tax breaks for investors putting money into AIM shares.

1.5.1.3   Regulation of financial services

The Financial Services and Markets Act 2000 provides the framework for the increased powers of the Financial Services Authority (FSA). The FSA has become the competent authority to maintain the official list of securities, in place of the London Stock Exchange. The 2000 Act deals with many areas of financial services and is beyond the scope of this book.

1.5.2   Companies Acts requirements

Although, in general, the Companies Acts apply to both public and private companies, there are many differences of detail.

(a)   A private company is not obliged to have a secretary.

(b)   A private company can have just one director who may also be the only shareholder; a public company must have at least two directors and at least two shareholders.

(c)   A private company can buy back the shares of a member who wishes to leave the company even if the company's accumulated profits are not sufficient so that it is necessary to use capital for the purchase.

(d)   A private company is prohibited from offering to issue its shares to the public at large.

(e)   There are fewer provisions regulating directors' dealings with their company if the company is a private company.

(f)   Private companies up to a certain size may be permitted to file abbreviated accounts with the Registrar of Companies.

(g)   Only a private company may be exempt from the statutory obligation to have its year-end accounts audited.

(h)   Only a private company is not obliged to hold an annual general meeting.

(i)   Only a private company can dispense with the formality of holding general meetings by having all its shareholders sign resolutions in writing.

(j)   A public company must have a trading certificate under s 761 of the Companies Act 2006, before it can commence business.

(k)   A public company must have allotted share capital of £50,000 (CA 2006, s 763), at least one quarter of which must be paid up (CA 2006, s 761).

1.5.3   Differences in practice

In a private company, the directors and shareholders are often substantially the same persons. In a public company, there will usually be a significant difference in personnel between the shareholders (who are likely to include institutional investors) and the directors (whose position is more like that of employees who are paid to manage the business).

In a private company, the shareholders cannot easily sell their shares because the articles of association usually contain restrictions on transfer (often in the form of directors' power of veto on the registration of the transfer) and because of difficulties of valuation, given that there is no ready 'market' for the shares. In a public company, there is less likely to be any restriction on transfer. If the shares are listed on the Stock Exchange or the AIM, there can be no restriction.

A private company may, or may not, choose to pay dividends to its shareholders. Many private companies pay no dividend at all. In practice, a public company needs to have a record of paying dividends every year in order to encourage investors to buy shares in that company.

1.6 Limited liability partnership (LLP)

This is a new business format created by the Limited Liability Partnerships Act 2000. An LLP is a hybrid between a partnership and a limited company. It is intended to offer the protection from liability of a limited company and the informality of a partnership. Most LLPs are professional firms who converted to this format from partnership to protect themselves from personal liability. See **Chapter 18** for further details. (*Note*: An LLP should not be confused with a 'limited partnership' under the Limited Partnerships Act 1907 – see **1.7** below.)

1.7 Limited partnership

These are formed under the Limited Partnerships Act 1907. The Act requires that there be at least one general partner who has unlimited liability for all the debts of the partnership. However, it does permit a limited partner whose liability is limited to the amount contributed provided that he takes no part in running the partnership. The structure is sometimes used for joint ventures. It is also used for investment funds, for example that invest in companies or in property.

1.8 European economic interest grouping (EEIG)

These stem from European Regulation 2137/85 ([1985] OJ L199/1) and from the European Economic Interest Grouping Regulations 1989 (SI 1989/638). The intention is to facilitate cross-border alliances. However, EEIGs can be used only where the purpose is not to make profits. They are used for alliances between accountancy firms, solicitors firms, and research and development collaborations. For example, three diesel engine manufacturers have entered into an EEIG that is to last until 2010 and which is to develop new types of diesel engines.

1.9 European company

The European Company Statute establishes the first pan-European company structure. These companies will be known as *Societas Europaea* (SEs).

In future, a single company, or a group of companies, operating in different EU Member States will be able to operate as a single corporate entity subject to one set of rules valid in all Member States. The requirement is that the company has adopted the company statute and has a paid-up share capital of €120,000. It must already have a two-year trading record.

The legislation setting up the European company is Regulation 2157/2001 (OJ L294/1). Directive 2001/86/EC (OJ L294/22) deals with employee rights. The European Regulation came into effect on 8 October 2004. Where the Regulation is silent on a particular aspect of company law, then the national law of the Member State of incorporation is used. The European Public Limited Liability Company Regulations 2004 (SI 2004/2326) control how the European company is governed. The European company structure may find a use as a common vehicle where there is a joint venture or takeover which crosses national borders. An SE registered under the Regulation has to be registered in the Member State where it has its administrative head office. It can operate throughout the EU with one set of rules and reporting system. The disadvantage is that the SE is subject to both the Regulation and to the law of the Member State, or States, in which it operates. This could make life rather difficult for the SE.

1.10 A purely contractual relationship

This will often be a simple sharing of costs and resources between two or more parties, usually companies. The reasons for this can include:

(a)   for the purposes of research and development;

(b)   exploration for natural resources; or

(c)   bidding for a particular project (eg Private Finance Initiative/Public Private Partnership projects).

The advantages include a lack of formality and the fact that the terms can be kept confidential.

The disadvantages include a lack of identity, a lack of organisational structure and the danger of it becoming a partnership by fulfilling the criteria under s 1 of the Partnership Act 1890 (PA 1890).

1.11 Community interest companies

This is a new form of company, intended for organisations that wish to use their profits and assets for the public good. The relevant legislation is the Companies (Audit, Investigations and Community Enterprise) Act 2004. These companies do not have charitable status. It remains to be seen how popular they will be.

Chapter 2

Introduction to the Company

2.1 The key concepts

It is essential to realise at the outset of studying company law that there are two key features of a company which are its important characteristics for the businessman. They are:

(a)   the distinct legal personality of the company; and

(b)   that only a company permits limited liability.

These key features have been so successful for companies that they have been borrowed to create the new hybrid structure, the Limited Liability Partnership (see **Chapter 18**). However, for the moment we are concentrating on looking at companies.

2.1.1 The key properties of a company

The key properties of a company are that:

(a)   it has its own legal identity separate from that of the human beings who are involved in the company;

(b)   the owners of the company have limited liability;

(c)   there is separation of ownership (the members) and control (the directors);

(d)   all the assets are owned by the company;

(e)   contracts are conducted or defended in the company's name, not that of the humans who are involved;

(f)   all debts and obligations owed to third parties are owed by the company itself, not by the members or directors;

(g)   there is transferability of ownership (shares can be bought and sold);

(h)   there is perpetual succession – the company can outlive the humans involved;

(i)   it can raise money by borrowing; and

(j)   it can create 'floating' charges over the company's assets which enable it to borrow when a partnership or sole trader could not (see **12.3.3**).

2.2 What is the point of being able to trade as a company?

The net result of the properties outlined in **2.1.1** is that trading as a company has the following benefits:

(a)   it promotes business, as entrepreneurs are more likely to take on speculative business ventures if they know that their personal assets are protected if the company goes insolvent;

(b)   investors can find out what they are investing in, because the company is obliged to submit records, including accounts, to Companies House; and

(c)   third parties trading with a company can access the public records at Companies House to see who is behind the company and what its financial position is.

2.3   How did we get to the point of the modern company?

At common law, the Crown had always had the right of granting charters of incorporation. The right was used to create commercial corporations at the beginning of the seventeenth century, eg the East India Company, and the Hudson's Bay Company. These corporations were legal entities quite separate from their members. Common law took the view that the members were not liable for the debts of the corporation.

Towards the end of the seventeenth century the joint stock company emerged. This is the type of company which is common today. This is where the company acts as a single person with stock, ie capital, which is contributed by its members. These companies could be formed only by Act of Parliament or by charter. These methods proved to be expensive and slow.

A new form of company grew up based on contract. The contract regulated the dealings of the members between themselves and provided for the transfer of shares. However, in the eyes of the law this was only a partnership, and liability of the members was therefore *unlimited*.

The Bubble Companies Act 1825 allowed the Crown to decide the extent of personal liability of members in granting future charters. This was the beginning of limited liability. The Chartered Companies Act 1837 allowed the Crown to grant the advantages of incorporation without granting a charter. They could be granted limited liability where they registered a deed dividing the capital into shares and providing for its transfer. The Joint Stock Companies Registration Act 1844 allowed incorporation by registration without the need for royal charter or Act of Parliament. The Limited Liability Act 1835 and Joint Stock Companies Act 1856 allowed for a member's liability to be limited to the amount unpaid on shares, and substituted the memorandum and articles for the deed of settlement.

The Companies Act 1907 allowed the formation of *private* limited companies for the first time.

2.4   Corporate personality: *Salomon v Salomon*

In *Salomon v Salomon* [1897] AC 22, the House of Lords held that a company's acts were its own acts, not those of Mr Salomon personally. This was the case even though he was in effect the only person involved in running the company, and was the major shareholder. He was therefore not personally liable for the company's debts. In that case, Lord Halsbury said: 'the [Companies] Act appears to me to give a company a legal existence with, as I have said, rights and liabilities of its own, whatever may have been the ideas or schemes of those who brought it into existence.'

The principle that a company is a distinct legal entity from its members is applied strictly by the courts whenever, for example, a third party is attempting to make the shareholders liable for the liabilities of the company. This is the 'veil of incorporation'. In practice the courts will only look behind the veil in cases of fraud or deliberate breach of trust.

There are also personal liabilities for directors who act improperly – banning orders under the Company Directors Disqualification Act 1986, and wrongful and fraudulent trading actions under the Insolvency Act 1986 (see **Chapter 6**). They cannot therefore rely totally on the protection of the veil (see **3.1**).

2.5 Principles of company law

These principles arise from the above concepts. They are enshrined in legislation, primarily the Companies Act 2006 (CA 2006), but also arise in common law and equity. The principles that have emerged include:

(a) the maintenance of capital, as a fund for the company's creditors;

(b) the ultra vires doctrine (largely substituted by provisions of the CA 1985, the remains of which have been removed by the CA 2006);

(c) publicly available accounts;

(d) division of powers between directors and shareholders;

(e) duties imposed on directors;

(f   rights of shareholders;

(g) the position of creditors, ie they can only sue the company; and

(h) financing the company – shares or borrowing.

2.6 Legislative control of companies

The government body that holds company records is Companies House, located in Cardiff.

The principal legislation controlling companies is the CA 2006. The framework of the Act is as follows:

1.   Company formation ss 7–16

2.   Articles of association ss 18–27

3.   Company's constitution ss 29–38

4.   Power to make contracts and doing business generally ss 39–52

5.   Name and type of company ss 53–85

6.   Registered office ss 86–88

7.   Company's members ss 112–128, 145–153

8.   Directors ss 154–246

9.   Company secretary ss 270–289

10. Resolutions and meetings ss 281–361

11. Accounts and reports ss 380–484

12. Auditors ss 485–539

13. Shares and share capital ss 540–732

14. Distribution of profits ss 829–853

15. Company charges ss 860–877

2.7 The directors and the members: who decides what?

2.7.1 Decisions of directors

The directors manage the company and its day-to-day affairs. Typically, the directors will be responsible for making the following decisions, although this list is not exhaustive:

(a) entering into contracts (including sales and purchases, borrowing, contracts of employment);

(b) other matters of day-to-day management of the business;

(c) calling general meetings;

(d) taking legal proceedings in the company's name; and

(e) approving the registration of the transfer of shares (and thus changes in membership).

Typically, the directors will also have limited authority for the following decisions in the sense that they must first seek approval from the shareholders in a general meeting:

(a)   issuing new shares in the company (see CA 2006 , s 549);

(b)   entering into contracts with individual directors by which the company will buy from or sell to that director something of significant value (see CA 2006, ss 190–196); or

(c)   awarding to individual directors service contracts of significant duration (see CA 2006, ss 188, 189).

Decisions of the directors will normally be made at a board meeting on the basis of one vote per director and a simple majority will suffice.

The board of directors will generally be able to delegate its decision-making to one or more individual director(s). The most common example of this is delegation of wide managerial authority to a managing director, but many companies have directors, or committees of directors, to whom more specific functions have been delegated by the board, for example, sales director, finance director, personnel director.

Directors can appoint a new director (model articles for private companies, art 17; see further **4.7.2** below).

2.7.2   Decisions of shareholders (the members)

The shareholders are the owners of the company. In order to protect their position as owners, the law gives them the right to make some decisions affecting those rights, and to change the directors.

Shareholders will be responsible for making the following decisions, although this list is not exhaustive:

(a)   altering any aspect of the company's constitution, eg its name (CA 2006, s 77–81) or its regulations (CA 2006, s 21));

(b)   dismissing a director from the board (CA 2006, s 168);

(c)   appointing a director to the board (model articles for private companies, art 17); or

(d)   condoning any breach of duty to the company by its directors (by ordinary resolution).

Shareholders will also be responsible for authorising the directors to make the following decisions (as above):

(a)   issuing new shares in the company (CA 2006, ss 549, 551);

(b)   entering into contracts with individual directors by which the company will buy from or sell to that director something of significant value (CA 2006, ss 190–196); or

(c)   awarding long service contracts to individual directors (CA 2006, ss 188, 189).

Decisions of the shareholders will normally be made by a prescribed majority which depends on the decision in question. Some decisions (eg dismissing or appointing a director) require a simple majority of those voting and are described as 'ordinary resolutions'. Some (eg altering the company's name or its regulations) require a special majority, being 75% of those voting, and are described as 'special resolutions'.

Regrettably, it is not possible to give any rule for working out which decisions require which type of resolution – this has to be a matter of learning or checking, as necessary. The position in each instance will be governed by provisions in the CA 2006, by common law principles or by provisions in the company's constitution.

Decisions which are to be taken by the shareholders can be made only at a general meeting (or generally by a written resolution which is agreed in writing by all the shareholders).

2.7.3 Taxation

The company will pay corporation tax on the profits of the business. The directors and shareholders of the company cannot be made liable for payment of corporation tax. Typically, the directors and the shareholders will receive income from the company in the form of salaries and dividends respectively, both of which give rise to a charge to income tax at a rate dependent on the circumstances of the individual recipient.

2.8 EU companies legislation

European Union requirements have necessitated various changes to the companies legislation. This started as early as s 9 of the European Communities Act 1972.

The Third Company Law Directive (Directive 78/855/EEC ([1978] OJ L295/36)) regulates mergers between public companies where the assets of the acquired company are transferred to the acquiring company.

The Sixth Directive (Directive 82/891 ([1982] OJ L378/1)) concerned the division of an existing public company into separate corporate entities.

The Seventh and Eighth Directives (Directives 83/394 ([1983] OJ L193/1) and 84/253/EEC ([1984] OJ L126/20)) deal with accounts to be prepared by groups of companies.

The Prospectus Directive (2003/71/EC ([2003] OJ L345/64)) and the Market Abuse Directive (2003/6/EC ([2003] OJ L96/16)) deal with the offering to the public of shares and other securities.

The Transparency Obligations Directive (2004/109/EC ([2004] OJ L390/38)) deals with the preparation of financial reporting statements under international standards.

The Statutory Audit Directive (2006/43/EC ([2006] OJ L157/87)) revises the Eighth Company Law Directive and introduces new rules on the auditing of annual accounts of companies in the EU.

Part II

RUNNING A BUSINESS AS A COMPANY LIMITED BY SHARES

When a business is run by a company, it is owned by a person (the company) which is quite separate from the individuals involved, even though they are the directors and shareholders of the company. The company's separate legal personality leads to a number of complications in running the business. Decisions affecting the business must be made either by the directors or by the shareholders. Broadly, it depends on the Companies Acts or on the company's constitution (in particular its articles of association) whether a particular decision rests with the directors or with the shareholders.

This Part describes how to form a company, how to manage the company and its affairs in compliance with the Companies Acts and its constitution (the memorandum and articles of association), how to join and leave a company, and what liability may be incurred by the company and its directors in running the business.

Chapter 3

Why, and How to, Form a Company

3.1 Why form a company?

The effect of a company being 'limited' is that liability for debts and obligations rests with the company itself and does not pass to individuals involved in the company. This is important protection for entrepreneurs. However, there are circumstances in which the officers of the company do become personally liable either to the company itself or directly to third parties.

This is sometimes referred to as 'lifting the veil of incorporation', and happens only in exceptional circumstances (eg *Crown Prosecution Service v Compton* [2002] EWCA Civ 1720, where the company in question was a front for money laundering of the proceeds of drug trafficking, or *Ratiu v Conway* [2005] EWCA Civ 1302, where the Court of Appeal held that the veil could be lifted when examining a breach of fiduciary duty – see **Chapter 6**).

3.2 Liability of the company

Although a company is a separate legal entity, it does not have a physical existence and therefore it needs real people to act on its behalf (agents). When an agent acts for the company, he may be restricted in what he can do by the objects clause of the company and by his own authority. An act may be unauthorised because it is ultra vires the company or because it is outside the scope of the authority of the agent acting for the company.

3.2.1 Ultra vires acts

A particular course of action is ultra vires the company if it is not within the scope of the company's permitted activities as stated in the objects clause in the company's memorandum. At common law, an action which is ultra vires would be void. The doctrine had to be loosened when the UK entered the European Community in 1972, as it was incompatible with European law. The process of rolling back the doctrine has come to its ultimate conclusion with the CA 2006. So, under modern company law the doctrine has little effect, not least as ss 39 and 40 of the CA 2006 mean that being outside the objects clause cannot be pleaded against a company by a third party with which that company has contracted. Once an act is undertaken (ie some legal obligation has been incurred) that action cannot be challenged, even if it is outside the scope of the objects clause. Both the company and the other party to the transaction are bound by the act. The validity and enforceability of the contract is not affected by the fact that the action was outside that which is permitted by the company's constitution (CA 2006, s 39). However, any member can challenge a proposed ultra vires act on the basis that the company does not have the capacity to enter into the transaction concerned, and may ask the court to grant an injunction restraining the proposed action. This can be done only before any legal obligation is incurred by the company on the contract. After that, an aggrieved member's only remedy is to claim against the directors for breach of duty.

The outsider dealing with the company is not obliged to check the constitution of the company to see whether a particular transaction is authorised by the objects clause. The only relevance of the ultra vires rule to a third party dealing with the company is that an act which is not permitted by the objects clause could be restrained by injunction prior to it being undertaken, by which time both sides may have spent a great deal of time and money conducting protracted negotiations.

Where an objects clause is retained after 1 October 2009, it will operate as an article which restricts the directors, not the company. In effect, therefore, the ultra vires doctrine retains relevance only in so far as it means that the directors could be in breach of their duties to the company if they act outside the objects. Many existing companies will therefore wish to remove their objects clause after 1 October 2009. New companies formed after that date will not have such a clause.

3.2.2 Liability for acts of agents

The agents acting for the company are, principally, the directors and the secretary. This relationship is governed by the normal rules of agency. The officers of the company may have actual authority to act, thereby binding the company by their actions, or they may bind the company by acts within their apparent (ostensible) authority. Apparent authority is based on a representation to the third party by the company that the person in question is acting with the company's authority. The representation by the company could even just be a failure to correct a mistaken impression.

For example, the company secretary has, normally, actual authority to make contracts on behalf of the company relating to the administrative side of the company's business. If a person had never formally been appointed to the post of company secretary but had been held out by the directors as holding that position, the person in question would have the same apparent authority as if he was the company secretary. The third party has no duty to make enquiries unless there is some reason for him to doubt the authority of the agent with whom he is dealing (see **6.4.2**).

The Court of Appeal considered this area extensively in *Smith v Henniker-Major & Co (A Firm)* [2002] 2 BCLC 655. The interpretation was that it would protect a genuine third party from a defective decision of the board, and quite likely from where there had been no decision of the board. The judges seem to have been keen to interpret the relevant section as intended to protect the third party dealing with the company. To that end, they also considered the origin of the section, that is Article 9 of the First Directive on Company Law (68/151/EEC [1968(1)] OJ Special Edition 41.5).

An outsider dealing with the company is entitled to assume that the power of the directors to act on behalf of the company is unfettered. The third party is not required to consult the constitution (CA 2006, s 40(2)). A company cannot escape liability on a contract by denying the authority of the board to act on its behalf, provided the outsider is acting in good faith. He will be acting in good faith even if he knows that the directors are acting outside the scope of their actual authority. For these purposes, bad faith involves some element of fraud or deception, for example conspiracy with the directors to cheat the company and thereby the members.

If a member hears in advance that the directors are proposing to act beyond their authority, that member can apply to the court for an injunction to restrain the proposed misconduct. Once the unauthorised act has taken place, the aggrieved member's only remedy is to require the directors who are in breach of duty to indemnify the company for any loss it has suffered and account to the company for any profit they have made.

3.3 Forming a company

If a client wishes to run his business as a company, either a company must be created or an existing 'shelf' company will have to be bought. Once the client owns 'the company', it may then be necessary to adapt it to suit that client's needs and to consider what action to take in order for the business to begin trading as a company. The shelf company route will often be used for speed. It does involve more thought, as the shelf company has to be adapted to the commercial needs of the client (see **3.6**).

The formation of companies is not a skill to be neglected, as many law firms will incorporate their own shelf companies so that they have one 'oven ready' when the client walks through the door. Having formed the shelf company, the trainee solicitor may then subsequently have the job of adapting it for the client.

3.4 How to form a company

The CA 2006 has simplified the process of forming a new company. Under s 9, the requirements are to file:

(a) the memorandum, giving details of the subscribers and signed by them;

(b) an application for registration, specifying matters such as the proposed name of the company, registered office, whether the company is limited by shares or guarantee, and whether the company is private or public;

(c) a statement of capital and initial shareholdings, which replaces the authorised share capital;

(d) a statement of the proposed officers, including directors and secretary, if any;

(e) the address of the registered office;

(f) a copy of the articles of association; and

(g) a statement of compliance, the form of which has yet to be decided (s 1068).

One person is able to form either a private or public company. However, a public company needs two directors.

3.4.1 The company name

The application for registration must contain the intended name of the company. A client may already have in mind the name by which he wishes the company to be known, but he does not have complete freedom of choice. A company cannot be registered with a name which is the same as that of an existing company. Therefore it is important to search the index of names at Companies House at an early stage to ensure that the desired name is not already in use. It would also be wise to search the Trade Mark Index to make sure that the proposed name is not already registered as a trade mark. The Registrar will not accept a company name if it is offensive, or suggests criminal activity, and the use of certain words requires written approval of the Secretary of State (see **4.2.1**). If the chosen name is not already in use by another company, there is no procedure for reserving that name. Consequently, there is no means of preventing the formation of a new company which bears the name the client has chosen between the date of the search and the date on which the application for incorporation is received by the Registrar.

There is a new adjudication procedure to deal with disputes over a company's name, under which a company may be told to change its name if an objection is made within 12 months of the company having been registered (CA 2006, ss 66–74).

3.4.2 The memorandum

Under the CA 2006, the memorandum has become a more basic document. Much of the information which used to be required in the memorandum is now to be found in the application for registration. The memorandum therefore ceases to have its former central role.

The memorandum must be printed and then signed by at least one subscriber (unless it is submitted electronically, see **9.1**). Any subscriber automatically becomes a member of the company as soon as the company is registered. The following must be written in the memorandum:

(a)   the name, address and occupation of each subscriber;

(b)   the number of shares he intends to take in the company when it is formed.

Usually there are two subscribers. It is common for them to agree to take one share each at this stage, the true number of shares they require being allotted to them after incorporation. Alternatively, the subscribers may agree to take the full number of shares they ultimately require. The main purpose of signing as subscriber at this stage is to ensure that there will be at least one member of the company when it comes into existence. The subscribers' signatures to the memorandum should be witnessed and the document dated. One person can witness both the subscribers' signatures where there are two subscribers.

3.4.3 The articles of association

The Companies Act 2006 provides a precedent for a set of articles of association for a private company limited by shares (see **4.7.2**). The articles of a company can comprise this precedent in its entirety without amendment. Alternatively, it could be totally rejected in favour of a different set of articles specifically drafted for a particular company. Neither of these options is usually chosen. A common way of providing articles for a company is to utilise the precedent but to make specific amendments to it in order to make it more appropriate to the particular company.

The articles must be printed and signed by the subscribers to the memorandum. The date must be included and the signatures must be witnessed in the same way as for the memorandum.

3.4.4 Registered office

The company is obliged to keep most of its 'statutory books' (see **3.7.1**) at the registered office, for example internal registers and minutes of meetings. However, the registered office does not have to be, and frequently will not be, a place where the company carries on business. As the company has no physical existence, it has a registered office so that those who need to do so can 'find' it, for example to serve official notices or legal documents. It is not unusual for the registered office of a company to be its auditor's office or its solicitor's office. The registered office can be a place where the company carries on its business, provided that the statutory books are properly kept there.

3.4.5 The certificate of incorporation

If all the documents required are correctly prepared and sent to the Registrar, together with the fee, the Registrar will issue a certificate of incorporation (CA 2006, s 15(1)). It is this which brings the company into existence. Once the certificate is issued, it is conclusive evidence that the company has been properly formed and came into being on the date stated. When a company is formed, it will be allocated a company number by the Registrar. From then on every document sent to the registry must bear that number, as that is the way in which the company is identified at Companies House.

A public company must also be issued with a trading certificate before it can do business or use its borrowing powers. This certificate confirms that the company has met the requirement for authorised minimum capital for a public company under CA 2006, s 761.

3.4.6 Separate legal identity of the company

Once the certificate of incorporation has been issued, the company then exists as a legal person. This means that the company can, for example, own property or have debts quite independently of the people who are involved in the running of that company, ie the directors and shareholders. So, for example, employees are employed by the company, and the company will be named as the employer in any contract of employment. Even though it will be the directors who allocate employment duties and arrange for wages to be paid, they do so on behalf of the company and not in a personal capacity. Therefore, any employment claims, such as claims for breach of contract or redundancy, should be made by employees against the company and not against the directors (or shareholders). Only the company's money is available to pay any such claims.

3.4.7 Pre-incorporation contracts

Prior to incorporation the company does not exist, and there is no guarantee that it will ever exist. Any attempt to act on behalf of the company prior to the date stated on the certificate of incorporation is ineffective. The company, when it is incorporated, has no obligation under any contract purportedly made on its behalf before its registration. Any person who tries to act on behalf of the company before incorporation does so at his own risk, as he is personally liable on any contract made. If, when the company is formed, the directors wish the company to be party to the pre-incorporation contract, they cannot adopt the existing contract but must enter into a contract of novation (an entirely new contract) with the other party, replacing the earlier contract.

3.4.8 Miscellaneous matters

On forming a company, the secretary will receive a form from HM Revenue and Customs requiring that details of the company and its directors be provided to it. This is to keep HM Revenue and Customs up to date with potential taxpayers, both the company and the individuals behind it.

If the new company does not trade and had no significant accounting transactions, it can file dormant company accounts under ss 480 and 481 of the CA 2006. That is, it will usually be able to file Form DCA declaring that it is indeed dormant and has been since formation. Only a balance sheet is needed; a profit and loss account is not required. The accounts do not need to be audited (see **8.1**).

One person can form a private company.

3.5 Tailoring the company to the client's needs

When considering the best methods by which to form a company for a client, perhaps the most obvious way is to prepare all the documents personally after discussion with the client. A company formed in this way is often called a 'tailor-made' company. This would involve preparing the memorandum; searching the index of names; drafting the articles, using CA 2006 or other precedents (many firms will have their own in-house precedents for the more complex documents); completing the forms; and sending all these to the Registrar of Companies with the necessary fee.

It is also possible to take all the required documents to the Companies Registry, where the new company can be incorporated on the same day, provided that all the necessary documentation is in order and the name does not require approval (see **4.3**). The documents must be submitted before 3 o'clock in the afternoon. The main Companies Registry is at Companies House in Cardiff, but there are branches of the Registry located in London, Birmingham, Manchester, Leeds and Edinburgh which also provide this speedier service.

Alternatively, a company could be formed with the assistance of law stationers (ie a company whose business includes the provision of services in connection with company formation and administration). This is sometimes known as a semi-tailored company. The law stationers would arrange a search in the index of names, and would normally supply a standard memorandum, articles with standard amendments (and possibly some optional amendments as well) and the forms. The solicitor would complete the forms, discuss the other documents with his client, obtain the client's signature where necessary, and return all documentation to the law stationers, which would then lodge the papers and the fee with the Registrar for registration.

Note that electronic submission of documents is valid, see **9.2**.

3.6   Fast track route – a shelf company

Where a client wants to run a business through the medium of a company, it is possible to buy a company which has been incorporated already and therefore already exists, ie a shelf company. The shelf company will not have been trading, but will have been formed in anticipation of somebody wanting to buy it and use it as a method of running a business. As the company is already in existence, this can be a much quicker way of getting a client 'in business' in the form of a company than creating a company from scratch, which may be time-consuming because of the need to apply for registration. This method of obtaining a company is therefore used frequently.

Shelf companies are generally formed with standard articles, making them suitable for most purposes (see further **4.5**). If a shelf company is purchased, the supplier will send the buyer the certificate of incorporation, the memorandum and articles (and possibly other documentation, eg internal registers).

Nominees (usually employees of the supplier of the shelf company) will have been named as directors, will have signed as subscribers to the memorandum and thus will have become the first two members and directors of the company on incorporation. Before sending 'the company' to the buyers, they will have to hold a board meeting at which they appoint the buyers as directors (having received their signed consents to act as such). The buyers become directors of the company from that time. The original two directors will send with the other documentation their resignations, which may take effect immediately or from the next board meeting (which will be held by the buyers). In this way the original directors are replaced by those who have bought the shelf company.

The subscribers' shares must also be transferred into the names of the buyers. The correct way to do this is to ensure that the original subscribers' names are entered on the register of members. They then transfer their shares in the usual way by stock transfer form. A common practice has grown up whereby the original subscribers are not entered on the register of members but simply renounce their right to take up their shares in favour of the buyers without completing a stock transfer form. Although not strictly correct, this method does not seem to cause any problems in practice.

Further directors may be appointed either by the board or by the members.

The share capital will need to be increased as the shelf company will often have been formed with only two shares. The shares will be allotted to the new members.

If the shareholders are also directors, then ensure that they are complying with ss 182–189 and 190–196 of the CA 2006 (concerning directors' dealings with the company).

The company name will be changed, or possibly kept and a trading name used.

The registered office will be changed.

A new company secretary will need to be appointed, if it is decided to have a company secretary at all.

The articles may need to be amended. Those supplied will usually be the CA 2006 precedents.

The accounting reference date may be changed, if required by the buyers.

3.7 Immediate obligations and practicalities

Once a company has been formed or a shelf company acquired, certain matters will have to be dealt with as a matter of priority.

3.7.1 Statutory books

The statutory books comprise the register of members, register of directors, register of directors' residential addresses, register of company secretaries, register of charges, minutes of board meetings and of general meetings, accounting records, and copies of directors' service contracts. These must be written up on incorporation, and amended from time to time to reflect any changes so that they are always up to date. If this requirement is not satisfied, any director or other officer of the company in default may be liable to a fine.

Under the CA 2006, company records are defined in s 1134. They include registers, minutes, agreements and other documents required to be kept by company legislation. As before, they can be kept in hard copy form or as an electronic version.

Companies no longer need to keep records for as long as they once did. Thus, minutes of directors and general meetings need be kept for only 10 years from the date of the meeting (CA 2006, ss 248 and 355). Records of former members must be kept for 10 years (s 121).

Public access to the register of members' names is retained. However, the party requesting access must provide information about himself and the use to which the information will be put (CA 2006, ss 116–118). The purpose of these provisions is to counteract the problem of copies of the register being used for direct mail shots, or to intimidate members (as happened with animal rights activists and GlaxoSmithKline plc).

Companies House will have greater powers to specify the manner in which company information is submitted. At the time of writing, further provisions on electronic communication are to be brought into effect. There is a new offence of filing misleading information (s 1112).

There is a power for the Secretary of State to make regulations concerning correction of the Companies House records (CA 2006, ss 1075, 1076, 1093, 1095).

3.7.2 Registration for VAT

Most businesses, except those with a very small turnover, must register for VAT with HM Revenue and Customs. The company will be allocated a VAT number and must make returns every three months.

3.7.3 Stationery

All stationery used by the company must bear the company name, its place of registration, its registered number, the address of the registered office, and either the names of all the directors or the names of none of them (s 82). If the company trades under a business name, the company name must appear on all stationery, as must an address within Great Britain where documents can be served on the company (usually the address of the registered office).

3.7.4   Employees: PAYE and national insurance

If the company is to have employees working for it (in many cases the directors themselves will be employees) then the directors should contact the local tax inspector (HM Revenue and Customs) to arrange for the deduction of income tax from wages under the PAYE scheme and for the payment of national insurance contributions by them and on their behalf.

3.7.5   Insurance

Insurance should be taken out in the company's name, for example for any motor vehicles, for injury to employees or for occupier's liability.

3.7.6   Bank account

Although not legally necessary, it is essential from a practical point of view that the company has a bank account. The bank will require the directors to sign a mandate form, giving specimen signatures and specifying who can sign cheques on the company's behalf and whether there is any limit. For example the directors might decide that one director's signature is sufficient for cheques up to, say, £500, but that for any amount in excess of that sum two directors must sign the cheque. Thus the directors can tell the bank when it is authorised to pay out company money. They will probably make this decision at the first board meeting of the company.

3.7.7   The first board meeting

The directors will need to hold the first board meeting soon after incorporation because they will need to make decisions on a variety of matters.

At the start of the meeting a chairman may be elected from among the directors and the person so elected will then take charge of the meeting.

A list of some of the things which might be done at the first board meeting of a company is given below. It is not necessary for the directors to deal with all the items listed. Many other matters may be dealt with and almost certainly trading matters will be discussed. There is no particular format for board meetings, and exactly what happens in individual cases will depend on the circumstances pertaining and the people involved.

3.7.7.1   Opening a bank account

See **3.7.6**.

3.7.7.2   Appointing an auditor

The first auditor of the company is appointed by the directors. Theoretically, there is no urgency about this appointment, because the only requirement is that an auditor is appointed before the first AGM, but it is common for the directors to appoint an auditor much earlier than this, often at the first board meeting.

3.7.7.3   Awarding directors' service contracts

Directors often deal with the terms of their own service contracts (including terms as to remuneration, working hours, holidays and duration) at this meeting. If they attempt to award themselves fixed-term service contracts for more than two years, the fixed-term element can be valid only if approved in advance by the members in general meeting by ordinary resolution. (See further **6.8.3**.)

3.7.7.4   Adopting a company seal

The company seal is one way in which the company can sign documents, although the counter-signatures of either two directors or one director and the secretary are necessary in addition. A company does not have to have a company seal. It can rely instead on the signatures of directors or the secretary, but most companies do have one, and it makes company documents look more official. If the company is to have a seal then it must be formally adopted by the board of directors and needs a resolution of the board to authorise its use each time it is required.

3.7.7.5 Fixing an accounting reference date

The accounting reference date is the date to which the company must make up its accounts each year, ie it is the final day of the company's accounting year. When a company is formed, the Registrar will allocate a date, which will be the last day of the month in which the company was incorporated. For example, if the date given on the certificate of incorporation is any date in June, the company will be given 30 June as an accounting reference date. At the first board meeting, the directors may wish to consider choosing a different date. If they select a different date, they must file a change of accounting reference date with the Registrar of Companies (CA 2006, ss 394 and 395). The accounting reference date can be changed at any time during the company's existence by a resolution of the board and the filing of Form 225.

3.7.7.6 Using a business name

For practical reasons, if a business name different from the company's name is to be used, it should be used immediately in order to build up the goodwill of the business. This decision lies with the directors, so if they want to trade under a business name they should decide to do so at the first board meeting. (See further **4.2.1**.)

3.7.7.7 Allotting shares to the shareholders

The directors are likely to issue some or all of the available capital at the first board meeting, as this will raise money for the company and give it some working capital. (The details of issuing shares are given in **Chapter 10**.) The directors must ensure that they have authority to allot shares (it must either be included in the articles, or be given by ordinary resolution of the members at a general meeting: CA 2006, s 549) and that they are not bound by the statutory pre-emption rights in s 561 of the CA 2006. These can be removed either by the articles or by special resolution of the members. (For a private company with only one class of share, the directors can allot shares and grant other rights over the shares, provided there is nothing to the contrary in the articles: CA 2006, s 550.) If the directors do issue shares, they must also resolve to stamp the company seal (if the company has one) on the share certificates issued to members.

3.7.7.8 Approving the cost of formation

As the company does not exist before its incorporation, the cost of forming the company cannot be incurred on behalf of the company, and those instructing the solicitor to act are personally liable for any costs. However, once the company is in existence, it is common for the directors to resolve that the expense of incorporating the company should properly come out of company funds.

3.8 The elective regime

The aim of the elective regime was to deregulate the company, that is, to lessen the formal requirements where they were not necessary. The overall effect of the CA 2006 is to deregulate private companies. In effect, the elective regime has become the norm under the CA 2006.

3.9 Shareholders' agreements

A shareholders' agreement is essentially a contract. It can be made by all members of a company, or just some of them. Even people who are not shareholders can be party to the agreement if this is appropriate.

A shareholders' agreement can be made at any time during the lifetime of a company, but is most commonly made when a new company is set up, thereby establishing areas of agreement between those involved.

3.9.1 Why use a shareholders' agreement?

Members are already bound by one contract: the articles. However, the articles only form a binding contract in respect of membership rights, and are ineffective so far as non-membership rights are concerned. Therefore, if members wish to agree between themselves some matter which is unrelated to their membership rights, they may enter into a shareholders' agreement to this effect (see **3.9.2**).

The articles are a public document, open to public inspection at the Companies Registry. Any agreement which members wish to keep secret can be dealt with in a shareholders' agreement, which is a private contract between the parties which the general public have no right to see.

Additionally, the articles can be altered at any time by special resolution of the members, ie 75% of the votes of those present at a general meeting. A shareholders' agreement, like any other contract, cannot be amended except with the unanimous consent of the parties to that contract. Therefore any attempted variation of a shareholders' agreement will provide a remedy for breach of contract where a variation of the articles would not.

3.9.2 Common provisions in a shareholders' agreement

A shareholders' agreement usually contains a series of mutual promises by the parties to the agreement, which provide the consideration for the contract. Examples include the following.

3.9.2.1 Typical clauses in a shareholders' agreement

(a)   An undertaking that the company will not alter or modify provisions of its memorandum or articles, or will not do so without the consent of all parties.

(b)   Similar undertakings regarding changes in capital or share capital structure.

(c)   Requirements on unanimity for major decisions (eg sale of the business).

(d)   Restrictions on borrowing, etc.

(e)   Agreements regarding further financing.

(f)   Agreement on dividend policy.

(g)   Any disputes are to be referred to arbitration.

(h)   The right for each party, or specific parties, to be a director and/or be employed or take part in management, or right to nominate a specified number of directors.

(i)   Agreements not to compete, etc.

(j)   Agreement on confidentiality.

(k)   Agreement on intellectual property.

(l)   Duration of the agreement and exit provisions: ie buy out rights for (or against) all or particular members; pre-emption rights; option agreements.

(m)   Provisions for the resolution of deadlock.

(n)   The denial of intention to create a partnership (in a joint venture company).

(o)   The power to require the other members to join in a resolution for the voluntary winding up of the company.

3.9.2.2 Further provisions that may apply, especially in the shareholder agreement of a joint venture (JV) company

(a)   Scope of the agreement, ie the purpose for which the JV company has been formed.

(b)   The representations and warranties between the shareholders themselves.

(c)   The provision of share capital for the JV company.

(d)   The shareholders' steering committee.

(e)   The frequency and conduct of shareholders' meetings.

(f)   The membership of the board of directors.

(g)   Business plan, share capital and loans.

(h)   The provision of executive directors and seconded personnel.

3.10   Holding companies and subsidiary companies

A business may be so structured that it is run by a 'group' of companies, consisting of a holding company (sometimes called the parent company) and one or more subsidiary companies. A company is a holding company if it owns a majority of shares in the subsidiary company, or if it has power to control the composition of the board of directors. In some ways, a group of companies can be seen as one big organisation (eg annual accounts must be produced for the group as a whole and not just for each individual company). However, the principle that each company is a separate legal entity still applies, so that, save in exceptional circumstances, the debts of the subsidiary company cannot be claimed from the funds of the holding company and vice versa.

Owners of a business may decide to set up a group of companies rather than just one company for a variety of reasons, for example there may be tax advantages, or each subsidiary company may be concerned with a different aspect of the group's business.

3.11   Summaries and checklists

3.11.1   Documents, etc needed for company formation

(1)   memorandum

(2)   articles

(3)   application for registration (including name, and whether limited by shares or guarantee)

(4)   statement of capital and initial shareholdings

(5)   statement of proposed officers

(6)   address of the registered office

(7)   statement of compliance

(8)   fee.

3.11.2   Matters to consider on company formation

(1)   practicalities, eg registration for VAT, ordering stationery

(2)   first board meeting

and, if appropriate:

(3)   shareholders' agreement

(4)   group structure.

3.11.3   Use of a shelf company

A shelf company:

(1)   is already incorporated

(2)   is not trading

(3)   is formed by company formation agents

(4)   needs to be adapted to suit the client's purposes.

Adaptation of the shelf company (before starting to trade):

(1)   choose a new name for the company

(2)   members:

    transfer the subscription share to new members

(3)   shares:

    allot shares to members

(4)   appoint new directors (and remove the old ones):

    every private company has at least one director (CA 2006, s 154)

    every other company must have at least two directors

(5)   if any director is also a shareholder, consider the following problems:

    ss 177–187 of the CA 2006 (declaration of interest in contract with the company)

    ss 190–196 of the CA 2006 (substantial property transactions involving director)

(6)   new secretary:

    every public company should have a secretary

(7)   change the registered office

(8)   adopt new articles of association

(9)   accounting reference date – change it?

Chapter 4
The Company's Constitution

4.1 Introduction

Every company is obliged to have a memorandum and a set of articles. The articles, special resolutions and relevant agreements comprise the company's constitution (CA 2006, ss 17, 29). They govern the internal workings of the company.

4.2 The memorandum

Every company must have a memorandum.

Under the CA 2006, the memorandum of association has ceased to have a central role in the company's constitution. It is the articles which are all-important. A new company formed under the CA 2006 has a memorandum which only shows details of the initial subscribers for the shares (s 8). The concept of authorised share capital has disappeared (see **4.6**).

For existing companies, the current memorandum will be treated as part of the company's articles. It may be advisable in the future for existing companies to redraft the objects clause which was in the memorandum, as in future it will operate as a restriction on the directors, though not as a restriction on the company.

Thus, much of the information which used to be in a memorandum will no longer be present for companies formed under the CA 2006.

4.3 The name

Every company must have a company name. Obviously a name has to be chosen when a company is first formed, but it is possible to change the name of a company if the members agree to this by special resolution. Those involved in forming a company may have definite views on the name they would choose for their business, but there are various restrictions on their choice of company name.

A name cannot be used if there is already a company with that name on the index of names at the Companies Registry. It is important to check the index at an early stage to ensure that the desired name is not already in use. It is also wise to check the Trade Mark Registry to ensure that the proposed name is not already registered as a trade mark. The Registrar of Companies may refuse the use of a proposed name if:

(a) its use would constitute an offence, eg Kill Joe Bloggs Ltd, or be offensive, eg Prostitutes Ltd (s 53);

(b)   it suggests a connection with government or public authority, eg Treasury Financial Services Ltd (s 54);

(c)   it contains other sensitive words or expressions, eg names including the word 'bank' (s 55);

(d)   it uses prohibited characters or symbols, eg the Olympic 5-ring symbol (s 57);

(e)   it is the same as a name already on the register (s 66); or

(f)   it is misleading as to the nature of the company's activities (s 76).

The name of a private limited company must end with 'Limited' or 'Ltd', or the Welsh equivalents. The name of a public limited company must end with 'public limited company' or 'plc', or the Welsh equivalents. (There are some exceptions for non-profit organisations, and different requirements for community interest companies.) This warns outsiders dealing with the company that liability of the shareholders is limited and that they can look only to company funds for payment of company debts.

The written approval of the Secretary of State is required if the proposed name contains any of the words specified in the Company and Business Names (Miscellaneous Provisions) Regulations 2009 (SI 2009/1085). For example, the word 'bank', or 'NHS', 'Wales' or 'English', or words that imply an association with government or the Royal Family can be used only with the approval of the Secretary of State or, in effect, the staff at Companies House.

Under the CA 2006, any person may object to the name of a new company, if the name is the same as or similar to that of an existing business. An objection is possible at any time after registration of the name. There is a new procedure for adjudicating disputes about company names, following which an order may be made to change the name of the company (ss 69–74).

Once a company is registered with a particular name, that does not guarantee that there will be no problems in the future from other sources. The company may face a passing-off action in tort if it has adopted a name which is so similar to that of any existing business (whether it is a company or an unincorporated business) that the general public is likely to believe that there is some connection between the two. Thus the company is appropriating some of the other business's goodwill. Infringement of a registered trade mark is even more serious as it is easier for the claimant to prove. If either action is successful, the company will be restrained by injunction from trading under its current name.

Although the company must always have a 'company name', it may decide to trade under, and thus be known to the general public by, a business name. The directors of a company have the power to decide on the use of a business name, so all that is needed to implement this is a resolution of the board. A business name need not contain the word 'Limited', but if a business name is used, the company name must also appear on all company stationery so that the warning to the general public about the limited liability of the members is still apparent.

The company's name must be displayed on the outside of every place or business where it conducts its business. It must also appear on all business letters, notices, receipts, invoices and other official publications of the company (ss 82–85).

Directors of a company which has gone into insolvent liquidation may not be involved in a company of the same, or a similar, name for a period of five years after the liquidation, though a court can give consent to such a step (IA 1986, s 216). The idea is to stop the use of so-called 'phoenix' companies, where the insolvency of the old company is hidden by the new company continuing to trade under the same, or a similar, name.

4.4   Certificate of incorporation

On registration the Registrar of Companies gives the company a certificate showing that the company has been incorporated. The certificate states (CA 2006, s 15(2)):

- the name and registered number of the company;
- the date of its incorporation;
- whether it is a company with limited or unlimited liability; and if limited, whether by shares or guarantee (usually it will be a limited company, limited by shares);
- whether it is a private or public company; and
- whether the registered office is located in England and Wales, Wales, Scotland or Northern Ireland.

The certificate is conclusive evidence that the company has been properly registered.

4.5 The objects clause

The objects clause used to be part of the memorandum. It should set out the purpose for which the company is in business and what it is empowered to do. This is now of little importance to third parties who deal with the company. However, it is still relevant to members, as directors will be in breach of duty if they do something which is not in accord with the articles (where any objects clause will now be located). It may thus be safest for companies formed under past legislation to remove any existing objects clauses from their constitution.

Now, under s 39, the validity of any act done by the company vis-à-vis outsiders cannot be called into question by anything in the company's constitution. Indeed, a company's objects are completely unrestricted unless the constitution provides otherwise (s 31). In most cases, therefore, it seems that for existing companies, the objects clause will have little (if any) relevance, and new companies are unlikely to be formed with any objects clause. If a company amends its articles so as to add, change or remove any part of an objects clause, it must inform Companies House (s 31). Even though the doctrine of ultra vires is in effect dead, directors are still obliged under the CA 2006 to act within their powers, which includes observing any restrictions in the constitution (s 171).

Nevertheless, it is still worthwhile for us to consider how objects clauses have evolved.

For many years, Parliament had intended that the objects clauses of companies should be stated succinctly. However, this did not happen, because the courts, when attempting to protect the investor from misuse of his investment, tried to limit the scope of what a company could do by a strict interpretation of the objects clause. The result of this was that objects clauses tended to be lengthy and cumbersome because the draftsman attempted to cover every activity in which the company might become involved.

There was usually a main objects clause, followed by a number of sub-clauses. The CA 1989 introduced the possibility of having a main objects clause stating simply that the company was a 'general commercial company'. If this wording was used as the main objects clause, the company could carry on any business it wished, thereby enabling it to diversify its business without encountering problems with limitation from the objects clause. This wording also enabled the company to do anything incidental or conducive to its business. However, many companies now trading were formed before this possibility was introduced in 1989. Their main objects clause would have had to set out comprehensively the business which the company was to carry on. These 'old' main objects clauses are frequently fairly lengthy, in order to give the company as much freedom as possible for future business activities.

The sub-clauses which followed the 'old' main objects clause attempted to list everything the company might possibly want to do during its existence, sometimes extending to several pages of print. The most important of these sub-clauses were:

(a)   a *Bell Houses* clause (so called after *Bell Houses Ltd v City Wall Properties Ltd* [1966] 2 QB 656), whereby the company was authorised to 'carry on any other trade or business whatsoever which can, in the opinion of the board of directors, be advantageously carried on by the company in connection with, or ancillary to, any of the above businesses or the general business of the company'; and

(b)   an independent main objects clause, which allowed the company to have more than one object, each of the objects existing independently of the others, rather than being subject to the interpretation that there was only one main object for the company, anything other than that being merely subsidiary to that one.

Many companies were formed with an objects clause which was a combination of the old and new styles. It would have as a main objects clause the new wording 'general commercial company', but additionally would contain many of the old sub-clauses. This combination was being used because there was some doubt as to whether, without the additional sub-clauses, the company would be entitled to do anything it might want. For example, it was not clear whether a company would be acting intra vires if it sold off the whole of its business, or made gifts to charities. Although the CA 1989 allowed the company to do anything 'incidental or conducive to its business' as a general commercial company (CA 1985, s 3A), it was not certain whether the examples given above would be covered by this. Therefore most of the old-style sub-clauses from a pre-1989 standard objects clause were still included.

4.6   Capital of the company

Under the CA 2006, there is no longer a requirement for a maximum amount of capital to be stated on the memorandum (ie authorised share capital). Instead, there is a statement of capital and initial shareholdings made when the company was incorporated. Often, a new company is formed with 100 shares of a nominal value (par value) of £1 each. The issue of new shares above the amount with which the company was formed still has to be approved by the members, or authority to allot has to be given to the directors in the articles (see **4.7.3.1** and **10.3.2**). However, if the company is a private company with only one class of shares, no approval is needed (ss 549–551).

A company does not have to have shares of par value of £1 – other sterling amounts are feasible, as are other currencies such as the euro or US dollar.

4.7   The articles of association

Every company must have a set of articles of association which give detailed instructions as to how the company is to work. This is where the internal management structure is set out, so the articles will often provide the answer to the question whether the members or the directors are permitted to do some proposed act. The articles of a company cannot, however, change the rights given to members and others under the CA 2006, and will be invalid if they are inconsistent with the CA 2006 or the general law.

4.7.1   Contractual status

The articles form a contract between the company and all its members, but it is a contract which is valid only in so far as it deals with membership rights (see **5.5**). These include such entitlements as the right to vote, the right to attend general meetings and the right to a dividend if one is declared. Anything in the articles which purports to bind the company and its members but which deals with rights other than those of a member in his capacity as member (such as the right to be a director or the right to be appointed the company's solicitor) will be unenforceable if included in the articles of the company. It should be dealt with in a separate contract, such as a shareholders' agreement (see **3.9**).

4.7.2   New model articles

New sets of model articles for companies have been published in the Companies (Model Articles) Regulations 2008 (SI 2008/3229). They will apply to companies formed on or after 1

October 2009. The model articles apply by default if no other articles are registered, or as far as the articles registered for a particular company omit parts of the relevant model articles (CA 2006, s 20). For existing companies, their current articles will continue to function as before. However, it may be advisable for existing companies to amend their articles in line with the new versions, though whether many will take the trouble to do so must be doubtful. There are model articles for a private company limited by shares, a private company limited by guarantee and for a public company. We focus primarily on a private company limited by shares in this book.

The new set of model articles comprises a simple set of minimal articles which provide a 'fall-back' if those forming a company do not wish to use anything more comprehensive. This is in contrast to the model articles under the CA 1985, eg Table A, which were intended to be an 'oven-ready' set of comprehensive articles (see **4.7.3** below). It follows that the model articles under the CA 2006, especially those for a private company, are considerably shorter than their predecessors under the CA 1985. Some of the provisions of the old Table A are now contained in the CA 2006 itself.

The Registrar of Companies is to be sent any amended articles, and the special resolution which amended them, within 15 days of the amendment, and has the power to order a company to comply (ss 26–27).

The new model articles for a *private company limited by shares* are laid out as follows:

Article numbers	Subject
1	defined terms
2	the limitation of the liability of members
3–6	directors' powers and responsibilities
7–16	decision-making by directors
17–20	appointment of directors
21–29	shares
30–35	dividends and other distributions
36	capitalisation of profits
37–41	organisation of general meetings
42–47	voting at general meetings
48–51	means of communication, company seals, no right to inspect accounts, and provisions for employees on cessation of business
52–53	indemnity and insurance for directors

The previous model articles for a private company limited by shares under the CA 1985 were known as Table A, and were appended to the CA 1985. The new model articles are simplified, not least as they are intended for use by small family companies which do not need a full 'bells and whistles' set of articles.

The key differences are that the new model articles for a private company limited by shares:

- include the limitation of the members' liability, which is no longer in the memorandum as it was under the CA 1985;
- refer only to 'general' meetings (art 37). There are no annual general meetings (AGMs) or extraordinary general meetings (EGMs), though these terms will doubtless continue to be used in everyday parlance;
- do not require the holding of an AGM;
- do not include notice provisions, as the notice for private company general meetings is always 14 days (s 304(2));

- do not allow the use of a chairman's casting vote in a general meeting (ss 281–282);
- do not deal with written resolutions expressly, as they are dealt with in ss 291–297;
- allow proxies to vote on a show of hands;
- do not make provision for the use of alternate directors;
- do not require the directors to retire by rotation;
- specify that directors' decisions are reached by majority decision or by unanimity;
- specify that a unanimous decision can be made in writing, whether or not there has been a formal meeting of any sort; and
- specifically provide for meetings to be held by phone, video link or other methods, as the articles specify that for a meeting of directors, each director can be located anywhere and it does not matter how they communicate.

The new model articles for a *public company* are more comprehensive than those for a private company and are laid out as follows:

Article numbers	Subject
1	defined terms
2	the limitation of the liability of members
3–6	directors' powers and responsibilities
7–19	decision-making by directors, including general rules for voting, and use of alternate directors
20–24	appointment of directors, including retirement by rotation
25–27	alternate directors
28–33	organisation of general meetings
34–40	voting at general meetings, including demanding a poll and procedure on a poll vote
41	restrictions on members' rights
42	class meetings (for the holders of different classes of shares)
43–45	shares, including – issuing different classes of shares, – payment of commission on subscription for shares, and – company not bound by less than absolute interests
46–49	share certificates
50–51	shares not held in certificated form, share warrants
52–62	partly-paid shares, including – call notices, and – forfeiture of shares
63–68	transfer and transmission of shares, both certificated and uncertificated
69	consolidation of shares
70–77	dividends and other distributions
78	capitalisation of profits
79–84	means of communication, company seals, no right to inspect accounts, and provisions for employees on cessation of business
85–86	indemnity and insurance for directors

Interim model articles were produced to deal with the period when parts of the CA 2006 had been implemented and no new model articles had been produced at that stage, ie before 1

October 2009. So, for private companies limited by shares, an interim set of model articles was produced by amending the existing Table A articles, and this is available on the BERR website at <http://www.berr.gov.uk/whatwedo/businesslaw/co-act-2006/made-or-before-parliament/page35232.html>.

4.7.3   Table A

New companies will no longer be formed with Table A articles, but many existing companies use them, either in standard form or, more usually, with amendments. Thus, it is appropriate to be aware of the format of Table A.

The main areas of operation dealt with in Table A are as follows:

Articles 1–35	shares
Articles 36–63	members and general meetings
Articles 64–98	directors and board meetings
Articles 99–101	administration
Articles 102–110	profits
Articles 111–116	notices.

Table A was amended by the Companies Act 1985 (Electronic Communication) Order 2000 (SI 2000/3373), enabling, inter alia, the electronic appointment of proxies and sending of notices to members.

4.7.4   Special articles

A company could always exclude entirely the use of model articles, be they Table A or the new model articles, and simply use a set of special articles devised for that particular company. In the past, it was rare for this to happen for a small private company, as Table A was a comprehensive set of provisions that was generally suitable for that purpose. However, it was very common to amend Table A articles by the addition of special articles to deal with various circumstances. With the model articles for a private company being a minimalist set of articles, it is reasonable to suppose that adding special articles will continue to be the norm.

Special articles may be inserted either when the company is first formed, or during the currency of its existence. Examples of special articles which are commonly required are as follows.

4.7.4.1   To give the directors the power to allot shares

Directors must usually be given the power to allot shares by the members (s 551; see **10.3.2**). When a company is first formed, it is useful if this power is already in the articles because the directors can then issue shares and raise capital needed for the company to start up in business without having to call a general meeting in order to obtain the members' authority to do so.

4.7.4.2   To give the directors freedom to allot shares to whomsoever they wish

This is a special article which gives the directors the freedom to allot the shares for cash to whomsoever they wish by removing the statutory pre-emption rights of existing members (s 568; see **10.3.3**). This enables the directors to get on with the business of issuing the shares and raising the necessary capital for the company without having to call a general meeting of the members to ask them to release these pre-emption rights. Alternatively, there may be a special article giving existing members a right of first refusal of new shares.

4.7.4.3   To enable the directors to vote on issues in which they have a personal interest

A special article may be included which allows directors to vote on any issue at board meetings, even where they have a personal interest in the matter in question. Where the company has very few directors, such an article can prove useful as it is common for directors to have such a personal interest (eg when discussing the forms of a proposed contract with a separate company in which one of the directors is a shareholder, or when deciding the amount of their own salaries). If an insufficient number of directors is entitled to vote (and count in the quorum) then no business can be conducted on this matter at the board meeting. (See further **6.5.3**.)

4.7.4.4 To restrict members' rights to transfer shares

An article which restricts members' rights to transfer (give away or sell) their shares is likely to be required in a small company where those involved in the business want to retain control over membership. Under the old Table A and the model articles for public companies, the directors only have a limited discretion to refuse to register the transfer, so members can generally transfer their shares to whomsoever they like. This means that if one of the members disposes of his shares, the others may be forced into running the business with someone they would not have chosen. A restriction is therefore usually imposed in a small company, either directing to whom members should offer their shares if they wish to dispose of them (eg members of the family or other members of the company) or simply giving the directors an absolute discretion to refuse to register a proposed new member. This gives the directors control over the composition of the membership as registration is crucial (see **5.2.2**). In the model articles for a private company limited by shares, the directors have an absolute discretion to refuse to register a transfer, so a special article is not needed there.

4.7.4.5 To prevent removal of directors

An article can be included which gives directors who are also members extra votes on a resolution to remove them as director at a general meeting (a *Bushell v Faith* clause, but see also **4.8** below).

In many small private companies, most of the people involved in the company will be both directors and shareholders. In this situation, the position of director is very important because most decisions which govern the running of the company will be taken at board meetings. It is an intrinsic part of company law that members have the right to remove a director by ordinary resolution (CA 2006, s 168; see **6.16.2**). One way in which a director can effectively be given job security is by the inclusion in the articles of a *Bushell v Faith* clause which will multiply by a given figure the number of votes to which the director-shareholder is entitled on a poll vote (see **5.4.10**). Provided this gives that director-shareholder at least 50% of the total votes exercisable on a motion to remove him at a general meeting, he cannot be removed from office. In order to give total job security, the special article must give the director-shareholder weighted voting rights not only on a resolution to remove him but also on a resolution to change the articles to take away or change his weighted voting rights. Provided this gives him sufficient votes on a poll vote to block the necessary special resolution (more than 25%), the director-shareholder cannot be removed from office without his own consent or failure to vote. Another way is to have a term in the shareholders' agreement (if indeed there is such an agreement) to the effect that the parties will not vote against each other in the event of a motion to dismiss one of them as a director.

4.8 Changing the constitution

As a company evolves, the directors and shareholders may find that elements of the constitution which were, or were thought to be, suitable are no longer so. Circumstances change and sometimes the company's constitution must be amended to reflect this. If a shelf company has been used to start up a new business then changes may be necessary immediately in order to structure the company in the way the buyers wish.

The CA 2006 introduces new measures to deal with provisions which are entrenched into a company's constitution (ss 22–24). The intention is to make it harder for companies to have such provisions in their articles.

Companies will be able to have entrenched rights in the articles only on the first formation of the company, or at a later date by agreement of all the members, or by order of a court.

This will affect companies where the articles contain rights such as a *Bushell v Faith* clause. This is used to give a director enhanced voting rights on a motion to dismiss him, at a general meeting. Existing provisions will be able to be altered or removed by special resolution, but new ones will require a unanimous vote by the members.

4.8.1   Change of name

The name of a company is changed by the members passing a special resolution to that effect (CA 2006, s 77). There are restrictions on the choice of name (see **4.3**) and therefore it is essential to search the index of names at the Companies Registry, and the Trade Marks Registry, prior to calling the necessary general meeting. A fee must be sent to the Registrar of Companies, together with the written notice and copy of the special resolution. The Registrar will send back a new certificate of incorporation and the company will have to have new stationery.

A business which has been trading for a while is unlikely to change its name, because of the possible loss of goodwill which this might cause. Where a shelf company is purchased, it is highly likely that the buyers will not want the existing name given to the shelf company and will wish to change it at the outset. (Shelf companies tend to have purely functional names, eg 'CoL 12345' or 'Jordans 56789'.) Alternatively, they could retain the company name as it is and trade under a business name (see **4.3**).

The CA 2006 provides that any new name can be decided by the company names adjudicator, or by the court on appeal from the adjudicator.

If the company passes a special resolution to change its name, and that change is conditional, then notice must be given to the Registrar of Companies stating whether the condition has been fulfilled (CA 2006, s 78). This could happen, for example, in the context of an acquisition.

The CA 2006 allows the Secretary of State to make regulations specifying the style and content of a company's registered name (CA 2006, s 57). This includes typefaces and stylised names.

4.8.2   Change of articles

A special resolution of the members in a general meeting is required to change the articles of a company (CA 2006, s 21) and the articles would have to be reprinted to reflect whatever change was made. Both must be sent to the Registrar of Companies. Members are restricted in the changes they can make to the articles. They must be bona fide in the best interests of the company as a whole (see **5.6.2**).

It is common for the articles of a company to be amended during its existence, for a variety of reasons, including the need to deal with new situations. When a shelf company is purchased, it is extremely likely that the articles supplied will not be exactly what the buyers would wish and so changes will frequently have to be made.

The court can rectify the articles, as seen in *Folkes Group plc v Alexander* [2002] 2 BCLC 254. In this case there was an amendment to the company's articles which was disputed. The court said that the literal interpretation of the amendment led to an absurd result. In order to give proper commercial effect to the articles, new words would be inserted in the articles by the court.

4.9 Summary and checklist

4.9.1 Resolutions to change the constitution

name   –   special resolution

objects   –   special resolution

capital   –   none needed

articles –   special resolution

Chapter 5
Members and Meetings

5.1 Introduction

The terms 'members' and 'shareholders' are synonymous in the companies we deal with here. The members of a company are its financial backers. The members finance the company by purchasing shares in it and so become shareholders. This gives them certain rights as members but very few liabilities as they are protected by the company being 'limited'. Members may or may not also be directors of the company.

5.2 Joining the company

5.2.1 The subscribers to the memorandum

Those people who signed the memorandum as 'subscribers' automatically become the first members of the company when the Registrar of Companies issues the certificate of incorporation. Their names should be entered on the register of members, but their status as members is not dependent upon this being done.

5.2.2 New members

If anyone other than one of the subscribers wishes to join the company by becoming a member, he must ensure that his name is entered on the register of members, as only then does he become a member of the company. This applies irrespective of the method by which he acquires his shares, whether by sale or gift, allotment by the company or transfer by an existing member.

The directors cannot refuse to enter the name of a person who has received shares by transfer on the register of members unless the articles of the company allow them this discretion. If the directors wrongly refuse to do so, the prospective new member can apply to the court for an order for rectification of the register.

Directors must ensure that the new name is entered within a reasonable time (which should not be longer than the two-month period within which a new share certificate must be issued). The prospective new member's status between the date on which he acquires the shares and the date on which his name is entered on the register of members is that he is beneficially entitled to the shares but he is not the registered legal owner of them. This means that, although the original member will receive notice of general meetings and be entitled to attend, he must vote in accordance with the instructions of the prospective member. Although the original member will receive any dividends which are declared in connection with the shares, he must account to the prospective member for such amounts.

5.2.3   The register of members

Every company must keep a register of the names of those who own shares in it (CA 2006, s 113). The register will show the names and addresses of every member, together with the number of shares held by each of them. This register must be updated whenever necessary to reflect any changes in the membership of the company.

If the company becomes a company with only one member because the membership has fallen to one, the register of members must contain not only the name and address of the sole member, but also a statement that the company has only one member and the date upon which the company became a company with only one member (s 124).

If a company's membership increases from one to more than one, then the register of members must contain the name and address of the person who was previously the sole member and a statement that the company has ceased to have just one member, together with the date on which the number of members was increased.

If these special requirements for one-person companies are not complied with then the company and every officer in default is liable to a fine. In addition, there is a daily default fine if the error is not rectified immediately.

5.3   Status of membership

The members of a company own the shares in that company and thereby own the company in proportion to their shareholdings. (In common parlance, 'member' is the same as 'shareholder'.) The directors (usually) will decide how many shares to issue and, initially, will sell the shares to those persons who wish to become members. This process is known as allotment or issue of shares and occurs when a company commences its business. Later in the company's life the directors may decide that the company should have more shares, which will entail them allotting or issuing these additional shares either to the current members or to new shareholders. Members may dispose of their shares to other people by sale or gift, subject to any restriction imposed by the company's articles.

Note: 'allotting' and 'issuing'. These two terms are often used interchangeably. It seems that the conventional view is that shares are allotted to someone (ie 'allocated') and are then issued by the company. It was suggested in the DTI report on the Blue Arrow affair that 'issued' should mean when an entry is made on the register of members.

Members thus provide the financial backing for the company. The money produced by the sale of the shares from the company to its members enables the company to commence and continue in business (although companies frequently also require assistance in the form of loans). In exchange for leaving his money with the company (ie having bought the shares), a member may receive an income payment from the company (called a 'dividend') and may benefit from the capital appreciation of the value of his shares. Equally, a member's shares may decrease in value if the company is not successful. Thus a member cannot recover for the loss in value of his shares on the basis that the value of the company as a whole has decreased, see the Court of Appeal case of *Prudential Assurance Co Ltd v Newman Industries (No 2)* [1982] Ch 204. The shareholder's right is to participate in the company, not a right to a guarantee that there will only be gains. The principle was explained as being essentially a reflection of the general rule, illustrated by *Foss v Harbottle* (1843) 2 Hare 461, that the company is the proper claimant in an action to recover any loss that it has suffered. The House of Lords agreed with this reasoning in *Johnson v Gore Wood & Co* [2002] 2 AC 1. There, Lord Bingham described the principles of shareholder recovery for loss, namely:

(a)   where a company suffers a loss caused by a breach of duty, only the company may sue in respect of that loss;

(b)   where a company suffers a loss, but has no cause of action to sue to recover it, a shareholder (assuming he has a personal cause of action) may sue in respect of that loss; and

(c)   where a company suffers a loss caused by a breach of duty to it, and a shareholder suffers a loss separate and distinct from that of the company caused by a breach of duty separately owed to the shareholder, each may sue to recover the loss it has respectively suffered.

For other examples of failure to recover for reflective loss, see *Perry v Cowlishaw* [2004] EWHC 1398 (Ch) and *Gardner v Parker* [2003] EWHC 1463.

The procedure for bringing a claim for breach of duty has been put into statute in CA 2006, ss 260–263. This simplifies matters but does not replace the common law procedure. So, in either case, shareholders have a general right to bring a claim for breach of duty, provided it has not been authorised or ratified by the company, but:

(a)   the claim is on behalf of the company with all the proceeds going to the company; and

(b)   the permission of the court is needed to bring a claim.

5.3.1   Limited liability

Any liability of a member of a limited company is generally 'limited' to the agreed price of his shares. Other than in exceptional circumstances, members have no personal liability for the company's debts, however great those debts may be. For example, if a member buys 100 £1 shares in a company and that company becomes insolvent, owing millions of pounds to its creditors, the worst that can happen to the member is that he loses the £100 he invested. This is because the company is a legal person in its own right (see **3.4.6**). Any debts owed by the company are the responsibility of that company and not of any individuals involved in it, save in particular circumstances (see **6.10**). This is why limited companies must have as part of their name the word 'Limited' or 'Ltd'. It warns members of the public that the only money available to pay the company's debts is that which belongs to the company and that generally creditors cannot look to members (or directors) for payment of the company's debts.

5.3.2   Functions of a member

The degree of involvement by members in their chosen company will vary enormously depending, for example, on the size of shareholding, the size of company and the wishes of the member. A member may also be a director of the company (or of any other company) but is not required to be so. There is not necessarily any link between the two roles within the one company. The directors generally make the day-to-day decisions. However, more major decisions which may have an effect on members' rights are usually required by the CA 2006 to be approved by the members in a general meeting. Thus, the CA 2006 states that only certain acts can be done by the members, for example removing a director from office (CA 2006, s 168), changing the name of the company (CA 2006, s 77) or authorising a service contract for a director which gives him job security for more than two years (CA 2006, ss 188 and 189). It can be seen that the members have only very limited powers over the directors, apart from dismissal.

5.4   General meetings

The CA 2006 enables private companies to conduct their business by written resolutions, so avoiding the need for any general meetings. However, the members can require a general meeting to be called (s 303). General meetings must be called to dismiss a director (s 168) or an auditor (s 510), but overall the intention is that general meetings will be rarities for private companies. Nevertheless, public companies are still bound by the more formal requirements, so that, for example, they must call an AGM (s 336). The material in this section is therefore, in general, frequently applicable to public companies but much less so to private companies.

Although general meetings are meetings of members, it is normally the directors who have the power to call these meetings. The board may resolve to call a meeting of the members at any time, for any reason. All members are entitled to attend a general meeting and to speak at the meeting. Directors are also permitted to attend and speak, but cannot vote unless they are also members. A general meeting will be an EGM (extraordinary general meeting), except for once a year when the company has its AGM (annual general meeting).

5.4.1 The AGM

There is no longer a statutory requirement for a private company to hold an annual general meeting. (However, the articles may specify that an AGM is held.) The directors may call a general meeting on their own initiative, or at the request of the members (CA 2006, ss 302–304). The members themselves can call a meeting (ss 305, 306).

Records of resolutions and meetings must be kept for a minimum of 10 years (s 355), as indeed must records of board meetings (s 248(2)).

Although, commonly, the date of the AGM will be fixed from year to year (eg it might always be the first Monday in March, or the last Thursday in October), this does not have to be the case. A public company must hold an AGM in the six months after its accounting reference date (CA 2006, s 336).

Notice for general meetings is 14 days (except for public company AGMs where the minimum notice period remains at 21 days). It is still possible to use the short notice provisions (see **5.4.6**). It is open to members to agree that a shorter period of notice is acceptable. Their decision, however, must be unanimous.

In small companies where the members are not all directors, a general meeting provides those shareholders who are not on the board with an opportunity to confront the directors. A key issue is the company's finances, as an AGM would afford an opportunity to see the annual accounts. Members are not limited to challenging the directors on financial matters and may, for example, be able to remove a director from office, subject to the provisions on special notice in s 312 of the 2006 Act. If a private company does not hold an AGM, it is nevertheless required to send a copy of its annual accounts and report to every member and debenture-holder (s 423). It may be able to send a summary financial statement instead of the full accounts (s 426).

5.4.2 EGMs

The abbreviation 'EGM' stands for 'extraordinary general meeting'. This is the name given to every meeting of members other than the AGM. The period of notice required for an EGM is 14 clear days.

Strictly speaking, the CA 2006 uses the term 'general meeting', but AGM and EGM will continue to be used in everyday parlance.

5.4.3 The power to call general meetings

The directors are entitled to call general meetings (CA 2006, s 302). When they do so, they can also prepare a statement setting out their views on the issues to be raised at the meeting and urging members to vote in support of their policy. They are entitled to use company funds to pay for any expense incurred in doing this. In this way, directors who are not shareholders, or who are minority shareholders, can exert considerable influence over general meetings.

Alternatively, the directors may try to retain power within the company by not calling general meetings, thus excluding the shareholders from involvement in the running of the company and keeping them in ignorance about company matters.

To redress the balance, members too have a right to call a general meeting and to circulate their views, but only in certain circumstances (see **5.5.9** and **5.5.13**).

It is still necessary to have a general meeting dismiss a director or an auditor (ss 168, 510).

5.4.4 Notice of general meetings

Notice of general meetings must be given in writing or electronically (CA 2006, ss 307, 1168). It must be sent to all members, to the personal representative of a deceased member, to the trustee in bankruptcy of a bankrupt member, to all directors and to the auditor. Notice can be served personally on all of these people, or be sent by post to the address which appears on the register of members, or by electronic means or by publication on the company's website (ss 308, 309).

Members (and those others entitled) must be given 14 'clear' days' notice of a meeting, depending on the type of meeting and the type of resolutions to be proposed at that meeting. 'Clear' days means that, when allowing for the amount of notice required, the day on which the notice is served and the day on which the meeting is held cannot be counted (s 360). For example, if notice of a private company's AGM is served on all those entitled to it on 4 July, 5 July then becomes the first of the 14 clear days' notice required for the meeting. By looking at a calendar, it is clear that the fourteenth of the 14 clear days is 18 July, and thus the AGM can validly be held on 19 July. Public companies must give 21 clear days' notice of an AGM.

The written notice, or electronic equivalent, can be in any form but must fulfil certain requirements. It must state the name of the company and the date, time and place of the meeting (s 311). It must say whether the meeting is an AGM or an EGM, and must give details of the resolutions which are to be proposed at the meeting. The exact wording of a special resolution must be set out. This requirement means that at the general meeting itself no amendment can be made to the wording of any such resolution. In the case of ordinary resolutions, the requirement is that sufficient detail must be given to enable members to decide whether or not it is an issue on which they have a view and would wish to attend. The exact wording of such resolutions need not be given (although it may be given). Thus it is possible for there to be an amendment to an ordinary resolution at the general meeting, provided the change is not so radical that it would make the notice of the meeting ineffective. Notice of a general meeting must also contain a 'proxy notice', which is a statement telling the recipient member that if he is unable to attend or does not wish to attend the meeting he can send someone else in his place, and that the person he sends need not be a member of the company (ss 325–327) (see **5.4.13**).

Under the CA 2006, it is possible for a company to make electronic communication with its members the normal position, though members would still be able to request hard-copy versions (see **9.1.2**).

5.4.5 Invalid notice

It is essential that notice be given in the proper form to all those entitled to it, because if this is not done then any resolutions purportedly passed at the meeting are invalid. However, to allow some leniency on this, provided the error is accidental, the resolutions passed at the meeting are still valid (s 313). The important word here is 'accidental'. This provision will not assist the company where there is any suggestion that the 'mistake' was deliberate; for example, if a dissenting member has not been given notice in a deliberate attempt to exclude him from the meeting.

5.4.6 Short notice

If there is agreement between the members, general meetings can be held on short notice, ie less than the 14 clear days required. If the meeting is an AGM of a public company, all members must agree to this (s 337). If the meeting is any other general meeting of a company then the meeting can be validly held on short notice, provided a majority in number of the members agree and those members hold at least 90% of the shares for a private company or 95% for a public company.

However, if a company had (say) six shareholders, one who owned 95% of the shares and five others who each owned 1%, then although the majority shareholder has the required percentage of the shares, he does not constitute a majority in number of the members. As there are six members of this company, short notice can be effective only if the majority shareholder and three of the others (four in total) agree.

Members can increase the 90% shareholding requirement for an EGM if they amend the articles, but the percentage cannot be more than 95%.

It should be noted that there are some circumstances where short notice cannot be used, for example the dismissal of a director (see **6.16.2**).

An alternative to short notice is written resolutions (see **5.4.15**).

5.4.7 Quorum

Resolutions are validly passed at a general meeting only if that meeting is quorate, ie a certain number of people must be present at the meeting. Section 318 of the CA 2006 fixes the quorum for general meetings at two, unless either the company in question is a company with only one member (in which case the quorum is one) or the company agrees otherwise. If the company is not a one-member company, the quorum cannot be reduced to one (save in exceptional circumstances by the court, see **5.5.10**) because generally one person cannot constitute a 'meeting'. It can, however, be increased to any figure thought appropriate for that company by the members amending the articles by special resolution. In a small company, the statutory quorum of two may be suitable. In a two-person company, it is essential to prevent one person having complete dominance. In a larger company, the members may feel that it is inappropriate to validate a meeting when only two shareholders are present and a larger number may be specified in the articles as the quorum.

If a member sends a proxy to the meeting in his place, the proxy can count as part of the quorum. However, generally, there must be at least two people physically present in the room for there to be a 'meeting'. So, one person who attends as a member himself and is also a proxy for another member cannot, on his own, fulfil the requirement of a quorum of two.

A general meeting must be quorate when it starts and must remain quorate throughout. If too few people are present at the start of the meeting, or if someone has to leave and the meeting ceases to be quorate, the chairman will adjourn the meeting, usually to the same time and place in the following week. A further attempt will then be made to hold a quorate meeting.

5.4.8 Types of resolution

Members of a company participate by passing resolutions at general meetings. As to voting methods and the meaning of majority, see also **5.4.10**. There are two types of resolutions.

5.4.8.1 Ordinary resolution

An ordinary resolution is passed if a simple majority of the members present and voting at the meeting are in favour of it. Thus, the resolution will be passed if, on a show of hands, a majority in number of the members present vote for the resolution. If it is a ~~written vote~~ poll vote, more than 50% of the votes cast must be in favour. The period of notice required for an ordinary resolution depends on the type of meeting at which it is proposed: 21 clear days for the AGM of a public company, but in all other cases it is 14 days. Section 282 of the CA 2006 defines in statute the requirements for an ordinary resolution.

5.4.8.2   Special resolution

A special resolution requires a 75% majority for it to be passed. This means that, on a vote on a show of hands, at least 75% of the number of members present and voting must vote in its favour (CA 2006, s 283). On a poll vote, 75% of the votes of those members or their proxies present and voting must be in favour of the resolution.

Example

If a company has issued 100 shares, 10 shares to each of 10 members, then if all 10 members are present at a general meeting, or send a proxy, any eight of them can pass a special resolution because between them they would have 80% of the votes. However, if only eight shareholders turn up to the meeting and the other two do not send proxies in their place, any six of those members present would between them hold 75% of the votes, and thus could pass a special resolution.

A special resolution is needed to change the company's name, for example, or to change the articles of the company. All special resolutions, and equivalent resolutions and agreements, must be sent to the Registrar of Companies within 15 days of being made (ss 29, 30).

5.4.9   Which resolution to use?

Members can act by ordinary resolution (simple majority), unless they are required to use some other sort of resolution either by statute or by the company's articles. The CA 2006 insists that for certain decisions only a certain type of resolution is adequate – for example, a special resolution is needed to change the company's name or articles. Therefore, for these amendments to be validly made, a special resolution must be used. Where, however, the Act or the articles specify that an ordinary resolution may be used, it is open to the members to change the articles to require that a special resolution is to be used.

The two exceptions to this are removal of a director and removal of an auditor. The right to remove a director or auditor by a simple majority of the members under the CA 2006 is a right which cannot be taken away (ss 168, 510).

5.4.10   Voting

Members can vote at general meetings in one of two ways: on a show of hands or on a poll vote (ss 301, 320). If a vote is taken on a show of hands, every member has one vote; ~~but if any person is there as a proxy for an absent member, that person cannot vote on a show of hands in that capacity.~~ If a poll vote is taken, each member has one vote for every share he owns. In this case a proxy can vote, exercising the same number of votes as the member he represents.

Example

A company has issued 100 shares: six members each hold 10 shares; eight members each hold five shares. If all members are present at a general meeting then on a vote on a show of hands the eight 5% shareholders would outvote the six 10% shareholders, but on a poll vote the 10% shareholders would between them have 60% of the votes and would therefore be able to pass an ordinary resolution.

Initially, all votes will be taken on a show of hands, but this method is clearly disadvantageous to a majority shareholder ~~and to a proxy.~~ If, therefore, the result of the show of hands is not unanimous, or not the desired result of a proxy in attendance, then a poll vote may be demanded.

The articles will specify who can ask for a poll vote, and a proxy has the same right as the member he represents in this regard. The only restriction on this is that the articles cannot be amended so that more than five members or holders of more than 10% of the company's shares must request a poll in order for one to be held (CA 2006, s 321). Subject to this, the members have complete freedom to decide who can demand a poll.

Under the model articles for private companies (art 44), a poll vote must be taken if requested by the chairman, the directors, any two members or any member(s) holding at least 10% of the shares. Therefore, under the model articles for private companies, the only member or proxy who has no right to a poll vote is a single member who owns less than 10% of the company's shares. If the members wanted to amend this to allow any single member to insist on a poll being held, they could do so by passing a special resolution to change the articles. Clearly, there would be little point in a shareholder with a very small percentage of the shares asking for a poll vote if he was the only member who wished to overturn the result of the vote on a show of hands. Such a member's right to demand a poll may be important, however, where he holds the few votes that could affect the outcome of the vote.

5.4.11   The chairman of the meeting

The chairman at general meetings of members will usually be the same person as is appointed to be the chairman for board meetings (model articles for private companies, art 39). His task is to preside at meetings and to keep order. For example, he will take items in turn from the agenda, and will decide whether proposed amendments to ordinary resolutions can be allowed, bearing in mind the detail which was given on the notice of the meeting. He will declare whether a particular resolution has been passed or defeated. His statement on this is conclusive unless the vote was on a show of hands and a poll is subsequently demanded, or unless his declaration is clearly bad on the face of it. For example, if there are 10 members present at the meeting, each of whom holds 10 shares in the company, and, on a show of hands, nine of them vote for the resolution and one votes against, but the chairman declares that the resolution is defeated, that is a ruling which is clearly bad on the face of it.

5.4.12   The chairman's casting vote

The chairman does not have a casting vote in addition to any other vote he may have unless a special article has been included. The casting vote only operates if, without it, the number of votes for and against the resolution is equal. In a two-member company, it is usually thought inappropriate for the chairman to retain a casting vote as this effectively gives him complete control. In other cases, the casting vote is often considered to be a useful way of reaching a decision where there is deadlock. Without the chairman's casting vote, the rule is that where the number of votes for and against a particular resolution is equal then the negative view prevails and the resolution is defeated. The legal validity of having a casting vote is doubtful (ss 281, 282), so it may be better not to have a special article to this effect in any event.

5.4.13   Proxies

A proxy is a person who attends a general meeting in place of a member of the company (see s 324). If a member wants to send a proxy to a meeting rather than attending personally, he must formally appoint a person as his proxy by depositing notice in writing at the registered office (s 327). The company cannot insist on more than 48 hours' notice prior to a general meeting of the appointment of a proxy (s 327).

A proxy may be appointed for one meeting or for several meetings. The appointee may be told whether to vote for or against particular resolutions by the member who appoints him, or he may be required to attend the meeting, hear the arguments put forward and vote in whatever manner he feels appropriate.

A member could ask another member of the company to attend the meeting as his proxy, or he could ask a complete outsider to stand in for him.

A proxy can vote on a show of hands and if there is a poll (s 284). He has the same right as his appointor to request that a poll be taken. A proxy can also speak at a general meeting. Therefore, a member may wish to appoint a proxy not only where the member is unable to attend general meetings, but also where he feels that a proxy may be more articulate or persuasive when speaking on a particular issue.

Section 324(2) also allows a member to appoint different proxies for different shares.

Every notice for a general meeting must inform members clearly of their right to appoint proxies under s 324 and under any wider rights in the articles (s 325). It is an offence for every officer of the company if the information is omitted (s 325(4)).

If the articles provide that the proxy has fewer votes than the member, the provision is void (s 285(1)).

A proxy can be chairman of a general meeting (s 328), subject to the articles.

A proxy can demand a poll vote (s 329).

The minimum notice to terminate a proxy's authority is that the company must have received it before the start of the relevant general meeting (s 330). If the articles specify more than 48 hours' notice then that provision is void (s 330(6)).

5.4.14   What must be done after the meeting?

Copies of every special resolution (or written resolution which takes their place) must be sent to the Registrar of Companies within 15 days of the resolution being passed. Usually, copies of ordinary resolutions are not sent to the Registrar. There are some exceptions, notably an ordinary resolution to give the directors the authority to allot shares.

Minutes must be kept of every meeting which has been held, ie they are a written record of what happened at the meeting, including any decisions made and follow-up action to be taken (CA 2006, ss 355–360). These are usually written up by the secretary and then signed by the chairman as being an authentic record of the meeting. They must be kept for 10 years (s 355(2)).

5.4.15   An alternative to a meeting: written resolutions (ss 288–300)

There are new provisions for written resolutions. Under CA 2006, ss 288–300, there is no longer a requirement for unanimity. The provisions have been brought into line with those for resolutions at a general meeting. So, the resolution is either an ordinary resolution requiring a majority of 50% plus one vote, or a special resolution requiring a 75% majority. However, it is not possible to use written resolutions to remove an auditor or a director, so there is no change in that respect from the 1985 Act (CA 2006, s 288).

The key points are as follows:

(a)   both the directors and the members have the right to propose a written resolution (ss 291, 292). The members have to have at least 5% of the shares;

(b)   the resolution can be sent out as hard copy, or as an e-version or by publication on the website, if the requirements relating to electronic communication with members have been complied with (ss 298, 299);

(c)   when voted upon, a written resolution does not have to be physically signed by the member (s 296);

(d)   a proposed resolution lapses if not passed after 28 days, or the period specified in the articles (s 297);

(e)   the company must tell members how they should inform the company of their agreement to the proposed resolution, and the date by which the resolution needs to be passed (s 296);

(f)   the auditor needs to be sent the notice too (s 502); and

(g)   there is a new procedure whereby members can require the circulation of a proposed written resolution along with a statement of up to 1,000 words (ss 292, 293).

5.4.16   Decisions taken by a sole member

The sole member must either pass the resolution by means of a written resolution, or must provide the company with a written record of his decision (CA 2006, ss 288 and 357). Failure to do so renders the sole member liable to a fine, but does not affect the validity of the decision.

5.4.17   Informal agreements – no meeting needed?

If all shareholders are present at a meeting and unanimously give their consent to a proposal, it does not matter that no formal resolution was put to the vote. For examples of this, see *In re Express Engineering Works* [1920] 1 Ch 446 and, more recently, *Wright v Atlas Wright (Europe) Ltd* [1999] BCC 163, which concerned approval of a director's service contract under CA 1985, s 319. Cases such as *Re Duomatic Ltd* [1969] 2 Ch 365 have taken this concept further and held that all that is required is the unanimous consent of the shareholders who have a right to vote. There is no need to convene a shareholders' meeting. An example of this is *Euro Brokers Holdings Ltd v Monecor (London) Ltd* [2003] BCC 573, where the Court of Appeal held that an informal meeting of the only two shareholders was valid. The principle was also followed in *Deakin v Faulding (No 2)* [2001] 98 (35) LSG 32.

5.5   Rights of members

Generally, the rights of members in any particular company will be governed by the articles of that company. Additional rights may be given by special articles, but a member in any company can expect to have the following rights.

5.5.1   The right to vote (CA 2006, s 321)

The right to vote is an extremely important right for members, as this is the way in which they exercise their powers. They can attend general meetings and vote in person, or they have the right to send a proxy to attend, speak, and vote in their place. They may also use the written resolution procedure (see **5.4.15**). All except (usually) members with a very small percentage of the company's shares have the right to demand a poll vote, as only then is the size of their shareholding taken into account. By exercising their votes, members have the right to appoint additional directors to the board, and can remove directors from office. Thus they can control the composition of the board.

5.5.2   The right to receive notice of general meetings (CA 2006, ss 307, 308)

All members must be given proper notice of a general meeting, and if this is not done any business transacted at the general meeting is invalid. Members must be given sufficient information in the notice of the general meeting to enable them to know what is to be proposed. The exact wording of special, extraordinary and elective resolutions must be set out, and enough information given on any ordinary resolutions for members to decide whether they feel strongly enough about the issue to make it crucial that they attend.

5.5.3   The right to a dividend, if one is declared (model articles for private companies, art 30)

Initially, the directors decide whether it is appropriate to pay a dividend to members. If they decide that the company has sufficient funds, they will recommend the amount of the dividend. The members in a general meeting will actually declare the dividend. The members cannot vote to pay themselves more than the directors have recommended, although they could decide that a smaller amount was more appropriate. If a dividend is paid unlawfully, there is no obligation on the member to repay it, unless the member knew or had reasonable grounds to believe that the payment had been made improperly (CA 2006, s 847) (*It's a Wrap (UK) Ltd (In liquidation) v Gula* [2006] BCC 626).

5.5.4   The right to a share certificate (CA 2006, ss 768, 769)

Every shareholder must receive from the company a share certificate, which must bear the company's seal (if it uses one). A member is entitled to receive the share certificate within two months of either allotment (if new shares are being issued) or lodging the transfer with the company (if existing shares are being transferred). The certificate will say how many shares the member owns, and acts as prima facie evidence of title. (Note that this provision does not usually apply to members of a public company which is quoted on the Stock Exchange or on AIM, as the CREST electronic dealing system is used and this is 'paperless'.)

5.5.5   The member's right to have his name entered on the register of members (CA 2006, s 113)

This right of a member to have his name entered on the register of members is subject to the articles of the company. In a private company, the directors are often given, by special article, the right to refuse to register a 'new member'. In the absence of a special article to this effect, the board must enter the name of any new shareholder within a reasonable time, which will not be longer than the two months within which they are required to issue the new share certificate.

5.5.6   The right to a copy of the annual accounts (CA 2006, s 423)

Accounts must still be sent to all members each year.

A listed public company can send its members a summary financial statement rather than full accounts (CA 2006, ss 426–428).

5.5.7   The right to an AGM for public companies (CA 2006, s 336)

The obligation to hold an AGM now applies only to a public company. The right to an AGM is very important. It gives members a chance at least once a year to confront the directors and to express their opinions. It is at the AGM that the annual accounts will usually be considered and discussed. On this occasion, members may also take the opportunity to refuse to re-elect a director whose turn it is to retire by rotation (see **6.16.1**).

5.5.8   The right to inspect minutes of general meetings (CA 2006, s 358)

Minutes of all general meetings must be kept at the registered office of the company, and members must be permitted to read those minutes if they so wish.

5.5.9   The right to call a general meeting (CA 2006, s 303)

Many of the rights of members mentioned above are subject to the provisions of the company's articles, but the right to call a general meeting cannot be excluded by any contrary provision in the articles. Members holding at least 10% of the company's shares have the right to requisition a meeting by depositing a written request at the company's registered office. (See the case of *Re Woven Rugs* [2002] 1 BCLC 324, where a 60% shareholder used an earlier provision.) The requisition must say why a meeting is requested, and must be signed by those making the request. The directors are then obliged to take action to convene a meeting within 21 days. The meeting must actually be held within 28 days of notice of the meeting being sent out, which means that the maximum permitted delay between receipt of the requisition and the day of the meeting is seven weeks. If the directors do not take the required action then the requisitionists themselves can call a meeting. Their meeting must take place within three months of the date of the original request. They can recover any cost incurred in doing this from the company. The company can deduct this amount from the fees of the directors. If members call a general meeting in this way, they, rather than the directors, fix the agenda for the meeting. The remedy if the directors fail to call a general meeting is to go to court under s 306 of the CA 2006 and ask the court to order one.

If more than 12 months have elapsed since the last general meeting, the percentage of shares to be held by the members requiring the new meeting is reduced from 10% to 5% (s 303(3)).

5.5.10 The right to ask the court to call a general meeting (CA 2006, s 306)

Any member or director can apply to the court for an order that a general meeting be held if for some reason it is impracticable for one to be held otherwise (eg where other members are refusing to attend general meetings and it has proved impossible to hold one which is quorate). The court has the power to make such ancillary directions as it might think appropriate. In the situation above, where a quorate meeting is impossible, the court might order that the quorum for one general meeting should be reduced to one, as happened in *Re El Sombrero Ltd* [1958] Ch 900, or, for a more charismatic example, see Bill Wyman's problem in *Re Sticky Fingers Restaurant Ltd* [1992] BCLC 84 (decided under s 371 of the CA 1985).

More recently, the Court of Appeal dealt with the topic of s 306 (then CA 1985, s 371) in some detail in *Union Music Ltd v Russell Watson* [2003] 1 BCLC 453, in overruling the first instance ruling and allowing the use of s 306 to appoint a new director and break the deadlock on the board of directors. In particular, Peter Gibson LJ said:

> I venture to make a few preliminary observations about section 371 [now CA 2006, s 306]. It is a procedural section plainly intended to enable company business which needs to be conducted at a general meeting of the company to be so conducted. No doubt the thinking behind it is that a company should be allowed to get on with managing its affairs, and that should not be frustrated by the impracticability of calling or conducting a general meeting in the manner prescribed by the articles and the Act.
>
> One situation Parliament envisaged where section 371 might be utilised can be seen from section 371(2), allowing the court to direct that a meeting attended by only one member should suffice. That suggests that Parliament had in mind a situation where there was a quorum provision requiring the attendance of more than one member, such as is contained in regulation 40 of Table A. Save for the condition of impracticability, no other express conditions are imposed on the ability of a director or member to call for a meeting, or on the ability of the court to exercise its power.

In this case, the Court of Appeal held that the use of s 306 was more appropriate than the use of ss 994 and 996, that is, the right of a shareholder not to be unfairly prejudiced. The usual remedy under s 994 is for the disgruntled party to be bought out by his fellow shareholders (see **5.5.14**).

5.5.11 The right to restrain an ultra vires act or breach of directors' duties

The right to restrain an ultra vires act exists only before the ultra vires act is done. Once the company has incurred some legal obligation in relation to an ultra vires transaction, it is too late for members to take any action. Prior to the ultra vires act, however, any member can apply to the court asking for an injunction to restrain the company from pursuing the course of action in question. With the effective final demise of the ultra vires doctrine under the CA

2006, it is likely that in future the cause of action for members would be to restrain a breach of directors' duties.

5.5.12 The right to have an item placed on the agenda for an AGM of a public company (CA 2006, ss 338–340)

The CA 2006 assumes that the running of private companies will proceed by way of written resolutions. Thus, the members of a private company can simply use the provisions regarding written resolutions (ss 292–295; see further **5.4.15** above). The mechanism for members to put a resolution to a general meeting is needed only for a public company. However, a private company can still hold a general meeting if it wishes, so there are provisions covering the right to circulate a written statement (see **5.5.13**).

The right to have a resolution considered at the AGM of a public company applies to any member or members holding 5% or more of the company's shares, or at least 100 members who hold at least an average of £100 worth of paid-up share capital (ss 338–340).

The request must be given to the company in writing six weeks prior to the AGM. The shareholder(s) must sign the requisition and leave it at the registered office of the company, together with a sum of money to cover the company's expenses (although the general meeting may later vote that this is returned). Where the date of the AGM is fixed from year to year (eg it is always held on the first Wednesday in November) then it is easy for any member wishing to avail himself of this right to determine the date by which he must give notice to the company. If, however, the date of the AGM has not been fixed, the members concerned should simply give notice to the company whenever they choose. The item must then be placed on the agenda at the next AGM to be called. If the directors attempt to frustrate the members by calling the AGM within six weeks, they will not succeed in this, because if that happens the member is deemed to have given the required amount of notice.

This right is extremely useful, as it is the only way in which members can have matters which they want discussed and voted on included in the agenda for a general meeting.

5.5.13 The right to circulate a written statement (CA 2006, ss 315–317)

Private companies will usually use written resolutions rather than call general meetings. If a general meeting is called, however, members of the company have the right to circulate a written statement of up to 1,000 words about a proposed resolution or other business of the meeting. The right is given to members holding more than 5% of the shares in the company, or 100 members who hold at least an average of £100 of paid-up share capital.

Any request from members that the directors should send out such a statement in writing must be made, by written requisition deposited at the registered office, at least one week before the relevant general meeting. It is an important right because it is the counterbalance to the directors' power to circulate their views in advance of the meeting (see **5.4.3**).

5.5.14 The right not to be unfairly prejudiced (CA 2006, ss 994, 996)

If any member feels that what is happening within the company is 'unfairly prejudicial' to him, he has a right to petition the court. The complaint may be based on past, present or even anticipated future events, and may be unfairly prejudicial to all of the members or only some or one of them. Whether what has happened, is happening or will happen amounts to 'unfair prejudice' is judged on an objective basis, from the perspective of an impartial outsider. For the petition to be successful, the member must prove that he has been affected in his capacity as member, although this has been given a very wide interpretation. For example, if it was one of the terms of a takeover that the previous owner of the business would receive shares in the acquiring company and become a director of that company, it may follow that the loss of the directorship constitutes 'unfair prejudice' to the member as the two positions are inextricably linked. In order to establish unfair prejudice, it is not necessary to prove that the value of the member's shares has been adversely affected, although frequently this will have happened. Examples of potential unfair prejudice are:

(a)   non-payment of dividends;

(b)   directors awarding themselves excessive remuneration;

(c)   directors exercising their powers for an improper purpose (eg to 'freeze out' a minority shareholder); and

(d)   exclusion from management in a quasi-partnership type of company (eg a small company formed on the understanding that all those involved will share the running of the business and the profits).

If the court finds that a member has suffered unfair prejudice, it can make any order it thinks appropriate. However, the most common remedy given is an order that the other shareholders or the company itself should purchase the shares of the petitioner at a fair value (CA 2006, s 996). An example of this was *Gerrard v Koby* [2004] EWHC 1763, where the order was granted as it was impractical for the parties to continue to work together. The House of Lords in *O'Neill v Philips* [1999] 1 WLR 1092, held that the court's powers were wide under s 994 but did not give an automatic right to withdrawal from a company where trust and confidence had broken down.

In *Re Phoenix Office Supplies Limited* [2003] 1 BCLC 76, the Court of Appeal confirmed that s 994 is not available to effect an automatic exit route from a company. In this case, the petitioner had voluntarily severed his links with the company and was using a s 994 petition as a way of trying to obtain the highest price possible for the sale of his shares. In *Exeter City AFC v Football Conference* [2004] EWHC 831, it was held that the statutory right of shareholders to petition for relief under s 994 was inalienable and could not be diminished by a contract for arbitration between the parties. The Court of Appeal has reaffirmed that the normal way of dealing with internal company disputes in small private companies where unfairly prejudicial conduct had been proved is an order for a share purchase under s 996 (*Grace v Biagioli* [2005] EWCA Civ 1022). In *Nagi v Nagi* [2006] Lawtel AC011 1971, it was held that one director removing another director without notifying him amounted to unfair prejudicial conduct. A buy-out under s 996 was therefore ordered by the court.

If a company is a 'quasi-partnership', ie a small group of participants who are directors and shareholders, then equitable considerations come into play. This makes it more likely that a court would grant an order under s 996 to buy out the disaffected party: see the Court of Appeal judgment in *Strahan v Wilcock* [2006] EWCA Civ 13.

(These cases were in fact decided under ss 459–461 of the CA 1985 but the references here are to the equivalent provisions under the CA 2006.)

5.5.15   The right to have the company wound up (Insolvency Act 1986, s 122(1)(g))

Any member can make an application to have the company wound up on the ground that it is just and equitable to do so, provided he can prove that he has a 'tangible interest', ie that the company is solvent and he will therefore get back some or all of the money originally invested. The court has granted such applications in a wide variety of situations, for example where the management is in deadlock, where the members have no confidence in the management, where the company can no longer carry on the business for which it was formed and, in the quasi-partnership situation, where one of those involved is being excluded from management. A petition for winding up is a remedy of last resort, because if it is successful the company will cease to exist. This means that the members will no longer have an investment and the directors will no longer have a job. See **Chapter 19** on corporate insolvency.

5.6   Restrictions on members' rights

Any restrictions on what members can do are found in the articles of association of the company.

5.6.1   Voting

Generally, there are no restrictions on the way in which members exercise their voting rights. When voting at general meetings they need only have regard to their own self-interest and need not consider whether they are acting in the best interests of the company as a whole. Even if a member is also a director, when exercising his votes as a member he can ignore the duty to the company which he is obliged to take into account when exercising his vote as a director.

However, where a director is also the majority shareholder (he owns more than 50% of the shares), there is a restraint. Arguably, such a person should not use his majority of the shares at a general meeting to sanction an abuse of power by him in his capacity as a director. The same applies where a number of directors together constitute a majority shareholding at general meetings. They cannot use this to sanction their own misdemeanours.

Although there is generally no restraint on majority shareholders voting in accordance with their own self-interests, if the effect of their doing so amounts to 'unfair prejudice' to other members then those other members may obtain a remedy by petitioning the court (see **5.5.14**). There was one case (*Clemens v Clemens Bros Ltd* [1976] 2 All ER 268) which stated that the voting of majority shareholders was subject to 'equitable considerations' which might make it unfair for them to vote in a particular way. The court's decision was that a particular resolution passed by the majority shareholder should be overturned, but it is uncertain to what extent this reasoning would be appropriate in any other given situation.

Members can enter into a shareholders' agreement and, by so doing, they will be bound contractually to act in accordance with the terms of that agreement (see **3.9**). It is perfectly in order for them to limit their freedom to act in this manner. However, directors could not enter into an equivalent agreement in their capacity as directors, because limiting their future discretion to act is generally not in keeping with their duties to the company (see **6.6**).

5.6.2   Changing the articles

Although members can change the articles by special resolution (CA 2006, s 21), there are restrictions on what changes they can make. Generally, they can make a change only if it is bona fide in the best interests of the company as a whole. The test for this is that of the hypothetical individual shareholder. If, from an objective perspective, the proposed change is for the benefit of the 'typical' shareholder, then it is also in the best interests of the company as a whole. This is so even though it may not be beneficial to all shareholders. However, a change to the articles will not be in the best interests of the company if it amounts to a fraud on the minority, ie something which benefits majority shareholders at the expense of those with a minority holding. For example, a proposed inclusion in the articles of a provision stating that any member who holds less than 10% of the shares cannot vote at general meetings would be a fraud on the minority, as would a proposed amendment providing that any member holding less than a certain percentage of the shares must offer them for sale to the other members.

5.6.3   Powers of the directors

Members are not empowered to do those things which have been delegated to the board of directors. The question of who has power to do what within a company will be governed by the articles, but usually the directors take all management decisions (unless otherwise directed by special resolution (model articles for private companies, art 4)). Only those matters required by statute to be decided by the members are left in the hands of the shareholders. The effect of this is that if the members do not like the way in which the board is running the company, they cannot simply overturn the decisions of the board. They have the right to remove directors from office (CA 2006, s 168) and the right to appoint new directors to office (model articles for private companies, art 17), both by ordinary resolution. Thus, members could remove all the existing directors and replace them, or they could appoint a sufficient number of new directors to outnumber those currently on the board. The disadvantage with either of these methods is that, although the members may effect a change in the running of the company in the future, these steps do not have retrospective effect.

5.6.4 Restrictions on minority shareholders

Minority shareholders are very restricted in what they can do. Generally within a company there is majority rule. Even where some wrong is done to the company, or there is some irregularity in internal management, it is for the directors to decide whether to take action in the company name (the rule in *Foss v Harbottle* (1843) 2 Hare 461). If they cannot or will not take action, the majority shareholders can do so in the name of the company. Clearly, there is little point in allowing minority shareholders the right to commence legal action in the company name when the wrong can easily be ratified by an ordinary resolution passed by the majority. Thus, in many cases, the rule preventing minority shareholders from taking legal action is justifiable as it means that the court's time is not wasted.

However, there are exceptional situations where a minority shareholder is permitted to bring a 'derivative action' in the company's name. A derivative action will comprise two stages: first, a preliminary hearing to decide whether the applicant is entitled to bring a derivative action, then the hearing itself.

Minority shareholders can bring a derivative action in two main types of situations:

(a)   where the majority cannot ratify what has been done (eg where the company acts illegally, where an ordinary resolution has been used when a special or extraordinary resolution was required or where the company acts on a resolution which was not validly passed because notice was not properly given); or

(b)   where it would be unfair not to allow a derivative action (eg where there is fraud on the minority or where there is 'unfair prejudice').

The rule in *Foss v Harbottle* is relevant only when members wish to bring an action on the company's behalf. If they wish to take action in respect of their personal rights against the company, then they do so in their personal capacity and a derivative action is unnecessary. This rule has been applied in many circumstances, even where the minority shareholder alleged that the directors were acting in breach of EU competition law with the intention of damaging the company (*O'Neill v Ryan Air Ltd* [1990] 2 IR 200).

The principles of *Foss v Harbottle* were restated by Lord Bingham in *Johnson v Gore Wood & Co* [2002] 2 AC 1 as follows:

> Where a company suffers loss caused by a breach of duty owed to it, only the company may sue in respect of that loss. No action lies at the suit of a shareholder suing in that capacity and no other to make good a diminution in the value of the shareholder's share holding where that merely reflects the loss suffered by the company. A claim will not lie by a shareholder to make good a loss which would be made good if the companies assets were replenished through action against the party responsible for the loss, even if the company, acting through its constitutional organs has declined or failed to make good that loss.
>
> Where a company suffers loss but has no cause of action to sue to recover that loss, the shareholder in the company may sue in respect of it (if the shareholder has a cause of action to do so), even though the loss is a diminution in the value of the shareholding.
>
> Where a company suffers loss caused by a breach of duty to it and a shareholder suffers a loss separate and distinct from that suffered by the company caused by breach of a duty independently

owed to the shareholder, each may sue to recover the loss caused to it by breach of the duty owed to it but neither may recover loss caused to the other by breach of the duty owed to that other.

In order to bring a derivative action, leave of the court is needed under CPR, r 19.9. In *Mumbray v Lapper* [2005] EWHC 1152, Ch, leave was refused as the aggrieved party was a 50% shareholder. He therefore had other courses of action open to him, eg liquidation of the company. In any event, a derivative action was held not to be in the best interests of the company.

Sections 260 to 264 of the CA 2006 introduced a new procedure for bringing a derivative action. Such actions are exceptions to the rule in *Foss v Harbottle* (1843) 2 Hare 461. Thus, a claim can be brought by any member, even in respect of a proposed act or omission involving negligence, default, breach of duty or breach of trust on the part of a director. There is no need to demonstrate any actual loss suffered by the company, or indeed any benefit gained by the directors. Section 261 deals with the need to obtain the permission of the court and states:

(1) A member of a company who brings a derivative claim under this Chapter must apply to the court for permission (in Northern Ireland, leave) to continue it.

(2) If it appears to the court that the application and the evidence filed by the applicant in support of it do not disclose a prima facie case for giving permission (or leave), the court—

    (a) must dismiss the application, and

    (b) may make any consequential order it considers appropriate.

(3) If the application is not dismissed under subsection (2), the court—

    (a) may give directions as to the evidence to be provided by the company, and

    (b) may adjourn the proceedings to enable the evidence to be obtained.

(4) On hearing the application, the court may—

    (a) give permission (or leave) to continue the claim on such terms as it thinks fit,

    (b) refuse permission (or leave) and dismiss the claim, or

    (c) adjourn the proceedings on the application and give such directions as it thinks fit.

Section 263 of the CA 2006 deals with the factors which a court is to take into consideration in deciding whether or not to grant permission. Section 263(2) states:

(2) Permission (or leave) must be refused if the court is satisfied—

    (a) that a person acting in accordance with section 172 (duty to promote the success of the company) would not seek to continue the claim, or

    (b) where the cause of action arises from an act or omission that is yet to occur, that the act or omission has been authorised by the company, or

    (c) where the cause of action arises from an act or omission that has already occurred, that the act or omission—

        (i) was authorised by the company before it occurred, or

        (ii) has been ratified by the company since it occurred.

Under s 263(3), other matters which the court must take into consideration include whether or not the member is acting in good faith in bringing the claim.

It seems that the common law cause of action still exists alongside the statutory one under the CA 2006.

5.7 Rights of minority shareholders

Those members holding 50% or less of the company's shares have little power within the company, as they cannot be certain of passing any resolutions at a general meeting without the backing of other shareholders. Thus minority shareholders may appear to be powerless in the hands of the directors and of the other members. To redress the balance, some rights of members are especially useful to protect the position of a minority shareholder within the company.

5.7.1 The right to have an item placed on the agenda for an AGM of a public company (CA 2006, ss 338–340)

This right is available to holders of at least 5% of the company's shares (see **5.5.12**).

5.7.2 The right to circulate a written statement (CA 2006, ss 315–317)

This right too can be exercised by a member or members holding at least 5% of the company's shares (see **5.5.13**).

5.7.3 The right not to be unfairly prejudiced (CA 2006, ss 994, 996)

Any member can petition (see **5.5.14**).

5.7.4 The right to have the company wound up (IA 1986, s 122(1)(g))

Any member can petition (see **5.5.15**).

5.7.5 The right to call a general meeting (CA 2006, s 303)

Holders of at least 10% of the company's shares can exercise this right (see **5.5.9**).

5.7.6 The right to block a special resolution

This can be done provided that the member holds more than 25% of the company's shares.

5.8 Summaries and checklists

5.8.1 Power of membership

Shareholding	What they can do	Restrictions
100%	anything	legality
75%	pass special resolution	fraud on minority *Clemens v Clemens* weighted voting rights unfair prejudice
50%+	pass ordinary resolution	
25%+	block special resolution	
10%	call a general meeting demand poll vote	
5%	have item on agenda for AGM of a public company circulate a written statement	
any shareholder	vote notice of GMs dividend share certificates name on register copy of accounts inspect minutes ask court for general meeting restrain breach of directors' duties unfair prejudice winding up block written resolutions	see above if declared subject to articles if company solvent

5.8.2   General meetings

(a)   Examples of reasons for calling:

  (i)   to change constitution (articles, name)

  (ii)   to give directors authority to issue shares, buy-back shares, etc

  (iii)   to approve directors service contracts over two years, substantial property transactions involving directors, etc

  (iv)   to suspend restriction on directors voting

  (v)   to suspend pre-emption rights on issue of new shares

  (vi)   to declare dividends (if recommended).

(b)   Who calls?

  (i)   AGM –the board of directors

  (ii)   GM   – the board of directors, whenever it thinks fit

        – members holding 10% shares can requisition a meeting

  (iii)   any member can apply to the court for a general meeting

  (iv)   written resolution can be signed by all members instead of holding a general meeting (unless proposed resolution to dismiss a director or the auditor).

(c)   Notice

  (i)   agenda   – normally decided by the directors

        AGM   – holders of 5% shares can have item included on the agenda

        GM   – members decide the agenda if they requisition a meeting

            – if meeting ordered by the court on member's application, member's proposed resolutions included

  (ii)   contents – date, time, place, type of meeting (AGM or GM)

            – proxy notice

            – exact wording of special resolutions

            – general notice of ordinary resolutions

(d)   Quorum

  (i)   Meeting must be quorate – look at the articles to see the number of members needed for a quorum.

5.8.3   After meeting

(a)   File with Registrar

  (i)   all special resolutions

  (ii)   altered articles

  (iii)   appropriate forms

  (iv)   some ordinary resolutions, eg authorise share issue

(b)   Update statutory books, eg   register of members

                register of directors

                register of directors' addresses

                minute book.

(c)   Keep records for 10 years.

Chapter 6
Directors

6.1 Introduction

The directors of a company are the people who manage the company. They take business decisions and make contracts on the company's behalf. The company exists as a legal person but needs agents to act on its behalf. The directors are the company's agents and they have a considerable amount of power within the company structure. As a result, various safeguards are usually built into the company structure, both by statute and by the articles, in order to protect members. These subject the directors to a large number of restrictions and controls. Generally, the directors, like the members, are protected from personal liability by the fact of the company being 'limited', but there are a number of exceptions to this. The duties of directors come from an amalgamation of several elements (see **6.6**).

6.2 Appointment of directors

The first directors of any company will be those persons named as directors in the statement of proposed officers (s 9). They will automatically become directors on incorporation of the company. Under s 250 of the CA 2006, 'director' includes any person occupying that position, by whatever name he is called.

Subsequently, directors can be appointed either by an ordinary resolution of the members in general meeting, or by a resolution of the board. Whichever method is adopted, the procedural requirements will be laid down by the articles of the company. If the appointment is at a general meeting to replace a director who is removed at the same general meeting, a 'special notice' of the resolution to remove a director must be given by the proposing shareholder(s) to the company, as required by s 168 of the CA 2006 (see **6.16.2**).

Where appointment is to be made by the members, there is no longer a detailed procedure set out in the model articles for either a public or a private company.

It is much simpler for a new director to be appointed by the existing board. Under the former Table A (art 79), such an appointee held office only until the next AGM, at which point his continued position was subject to reappointment by the members. Under the new model articles, there is no such requirement for either public or private companies.

Any person seeking appointment as a director must be prepared to sign a form indicating his consent to act as a director. Thus a person cannot be appointed to office against his will or without his knowledge.

6.2.1 Number of directors

Normally a company can have as many directors as are required. A private company must have at least one and a public company must have at least two (CA 2006, s 154). The model articles for both private companies and public companies assume that there are two directors, as that is the quorum specified for a directors' meeting. If a different minimum number is required (eg if there is to be only one director or it is felt that there should always be four directors) then either a special article to this effect should be included on formation of the company, or the existing articles should be changed by special resolution of the members.

6.2.2 Qualification shares

Although not required by statute or by the model articles, it is sometimes thought to be appropriate to require directors to hold qualification shares, ie they are required to own at least a certain number of the company's shares in order to qualify for the office of director in that company. Any such requirement will appear as a special article of the company. This is of more significance in a large company than in a small one, as in many small companies the tendency is for most, if not all, directors to be shareholders as well.

6.3 Types of directors

6.3.1 Chairman of the board

The directors usually have the power in the articles to elect one of themselves to be the chairman (model articles for private companies, art 12). Nominally the chairman is the head of the company, although he has no special powers other than his casting vote in the event of an equal vote for and against a resolution if the articles so permit. Article 13 of the model articles for private companies gives the chairman the casting vote at board meetings. Even this one privilege may not be preserved by the articles if it is thought to be inappropriate. The main task for the chairman is to take charge at board and general meetings and to preserve order. The chairman is appointed by the board and can be removed from his position by the board at any time.

6.3.2 Managing director

The directors also usually have the power to delegate their powers, including to appoint a managing director, to whom they usually give authority to run the company on a day-to-day basis (see **6.4.1**). The board will fix the terms of the managing director's service contract, including the level of remuneration he is to receive. The managing director must be a director of the company, so if he is removed from the position of director he automatically also loses the managing directorship. The power to remove the managing director from office also lies with the board of directors.

6.3.3 Executive and non-executive directors

Broadly speaking, an executive director is an employee and is involved in the day-to-day management of the company. A non-executive director is not an employee and merely attends board meetings.

In the past, non-executive directors were often well-known personalities in the business world or members of the nobility whose reputation, or fancy title, gave some additional status to the reputation of the company. Today, non-executive directors are expected to be more involved, for example by monitoring the management of the company's affairs by its executive directors. They will often be encountered in public companies but much less frequently in private (limited) companies. In early 2003, there was a report produced by Derek Higgs at the behest of the Department of Trade and Industry into the governance of listed companies, especially the role of non-executive directors. This was part of the response to the mismanagement which had led to the downfall of the Enron company in the USA. In essence, the Higgs Report proposed an enlarged role for non-executive directors in that they should, in effect, police the activities of the executive directors. There were other measures suggested, including separating the roles of chairman and chief executive. Following approval by the Trade and Industry Select Committee of the House of Commons, the proposals set out in the Higgs Report have been incorporated into the revised Combined Code. (The Combined Code is composed of the principles of good corporate governance and a code of best practice. It applies to companies listed on the London Stock Exchange.)

Even though a non-executive director might only attend at the company premises for monthly board meetings, he can still be liable to the company for breach of his director's duties (*Equitable Life v Bowley* [2003] EWHC 2263).

6.3.4   Shadow directors

A person is a shadow director if he gives directions or instructions to the directors of a company and those directors are accustomed to act in accordance with his directions or instructions (CA 2006, s 251). A person advising in a professional capacity does not become liable as a shadow director under this provision. In the case of *Secretary of State for Trade and Industry v Deverell* [2000] 2 All ER 365, the Court of Appeal held that a shadow director was anyone, other than a professional adviser, who exercised real influence in the corporate affairs of a company. Many of the provisions of the CA 2006 which apply to directors also apply to shadow directors, eg s 190–196 on approval by members of interests in contracts.

In *Ultraframe (UK) v Fielding* [2005] EWHC 2506, Ch, the Court of Appeal considered the issue of the duties owed to a company by a shadow director (see **6.6**). It was held that the mere fact that a person fell within the definition of a shadow director did not necessarily impose on him the same level of fiduciary duty as was imposed on a properly appointed director. In the case in question, the individual concerned was not even held to have been a shadow director.

6.3.5   De facto directors

The term 'director' can include persons who have never been appointed, either properly or improperly, but nevertheless perform the functions of a director. A de facto director is converted to a director for the purposes of the CA 2006 and the IA 1986 by cases such as *In re Lo-Line Electric Motors Ltd* [1988] Ch 477 and *Re Moorgate Metals Ltd* [1995] BCC 143.

A person appointed, but with some defect in his appointment, would have his acts validated as far as third parties are concerned by s 161 of the CA 2006.

6.3.6   Alternate directors

An alternate director is someone who attends board meetings in place of the real director, ie a stand-in director. The ability to send a substitute to board meetings is governed by the articles of the company. Directors are permitted to appoint alternate directors. They can appoint another director of the company as their alternate, in which case that other director would have his own vote plus the absentee director's vote (ie he would have two votes as opposed to the usual one for each director).

The model articles for private companies do not contain any provision for the appointment of alternate directors, so if this was desired, special articles to that effect would need to be added.

An alternate director should be given notice of all meetings, and can attend and vote in the same way as the real director (model articles for public companies, arts 25–27).

6.4   Powers of directors

Generally, directors are given most of the powers of management required to run the company, and they exercise these powers by passing resolutions at board meetings. Their powers will be given to them by the articles. The usual provision is that they can exercise all the powers of the company (model articles for private companies, art 3).

Once directors have been given a certain power, that power then belongs to the board and cannot generally be exercised by the members. This means that the members cannot overrule the board or retrospectively alter a decision of the board. All that members can do if they dislike the way in which the directors are running the company is to alter the composition of the board, or change the articles by special resolution to take certain powers from the board. Both of these affect the position only in the future and have no retrospective effect. However, if directors become unable to exercise their powers, for example if the board is deadlocked, then powers may revert to the members.

Some decisions of directors need confirmation by members in a general meeting before they can take effect. For example, under CA 2006, ss 190–196, a substantial property transaction between the company and its own director requires prior approval by the members (see **6.8.2**).

An important aspect of the directors' powers of management is the power to declare a dividend. If the directors breach the statutory restrictions on declaring a dividend (CA 2006, ss 830–840) they could be liable to repay the dividends to the company even if they had not benefited personally (*Bairstow v Queens Moat Houses plc* [2000] 1 BCLC 549, [2001] EWCA Civ 712).

6.4.1   Delegation of powers

Generally, directors are required to exercise their powers by acting as a board. However, it is usual to find in the articles of a company certain provisions which enable directors to delegate some, if not all, of their functions (model articles for private companies, art 5).

If the board decides to appoint a managing director (see **6.3.2**), the board will, at the same time, decide which powers are to be delegated to him. It is common to give the managing director the ability to make day-to-day decisions on behalf of the company, more radical and important issues being reserved to the board as a whole. The managing director can be given all or any of the powers of the board, but these can be varied or withdrawn at any time by the board.

Directors can also delegate their functions to employees of the company, and will not be personally liable for failure by those employees to carry out their tasks satisfactorily, unless circumstances existed whereby the director concerned should have been on warning that the relevant employee might prove incompetent.

If a director is unable to attend one or more board meetings, he could appoint an alternate director to be there in his place, so delegating his powers to the alternate director (see **6.3.6**).

6.4.2   Authority of directors

The ability of a director to bind a company in a contractual relationship with a third party is based on the director's position as agent of the company (see **6.6**). There are two categories of authority, which are actual authority and apparent (or ostensible) authority.

Directors will bind the company if they act with either actual or apparent authority. If they exceed this, they will not bind the company. They will be personally liable for breach of warranty of authority to any third party with whom they were dealing. They will also be personally liable on the contract to the third party, as they would have failed to pass the contractual obligation back to the company.

Actual authority is where the principal (the company) gives the agent (the director) prior consent to the agent's actions. Apparent authority is where the agent acts without the principal's prior consent but still binds the principal in the contract with the third party, that is the principal is estopped from denying the agent's authority. In *Freeman and Lockyer (A Firm) v Buckhurst Park Properties (Mangal) Ltd* [1964] 2 QB 480, Lord Diplock explained the difference between actual and apparent authority in the following terms:

> An actual authority is a legal relationship between principal and agent created by a consensual agreement to which they alone are the parties. To this agreement the third party is a stranger; he may be totally ignorant of the existence of any authority on the part of the agent. Nevertheless, if the agent does enter into a contract pursuant to the actual authority it does create contractual rights and liabilities between the principal and the third party.

> An 'apparent' authority on the other hand, is a legal relationship between the principal and the third party created by a representation made by the principal to the third party, intended to be and in fact acted on by the third party, that the agent has authority ... To the relationship so created the agent is a stranger.

Actual authority may be express or implied. For example, in *Hely-Hutchinson v Brayhead Ltd* [1968] 1 QB 549, there was a chairman whom the other directors let act as if he were the managing director. The Court of Appeal held that he had implied actual authority to act as managing director.

Apparent authority is based on a representation to the third party by the company that the person in question is acting with the company's authority. The representation by the company could even just be a failure to correct a mistaken impression. Apparent authority cannot arise by the agent's own actions, only by those of the company. In effect, the basis of apparent authority is that the company is estopped from denying the agent's authority to bind the company in a contract with the third party. Without this, an 'agent' who acted without authority would not bind the company but would only bind himself to the third party.

The Court of Appeal had the chance to consider the apparent authority in *Pharmed Medicare Private Ltd v Univar Ltd* [2003] 1 All ER (Comm) 321, albeit the case concerned a contract made by a non-director. The Court of Appeal held that the company was bound by the contract in question. When a company puts forward an employee as someone whom the seller can contract with and the company honours the contracts so made, then those employees have apparent authority to make further contracts. In *Bank of Baroda v Shah (Dilip)* [1999] WL 851947, the Court of Appeal held that a representative of the bank had apparent authority to release Mr Shah from his personal guarantee of a loan made to his company. In *Mahomed v Ravat Bombay House (Pty)* [1958] (4) SA 704, the claimant was held to be entitled to rely on the apparent authority of a single director. In *Racing UK Ltd v Doncaster Racecourse Ltd* [2004] EWHC 2813, Doncaster Council was held to be bound by a contract entered into by someone who had apparent authority to act on behalf of the council. In effect, the council was bound because it failed to correct the mistaken impression upon which the claimant had entered the contract. The theme through these cases is that the courts found that a plausible representative of a company had apparent authority to third parties, in the absence of information from the company to correct this impression. However, in *Criterion Properties v Stratford UK Properties LLC* [2004] UKHL 28, the House of Lords held that an improper agreement entered into without the knowledge of the other directors was unenforceable against the company, as the director in question had neither express nor apparent authority.

The expression 'usual' authority has been used in a range of situations including both implied actual authority and apparent authority. Perhaps it is best to regard 'usual' or 'customary' authority simply as ways of describing the range of the agent's actual or apparent authority, depending on the circumstances. For example, the point might be the width of the authority which a managing director might be expected to have, thus would buying a corporate jet be beyond the usual extent of a managing director's authority? The facts of the situation in question will then indicate whether the situation is one of implied actual authority or of apparent authority.

6.5   Board meetings: calling and conduct

6.5.1   Notice

Any director can call a board meeting at any time on reasonable notice (model articles for private companies, art 9; see also *Re Homer District Consolidated Gold Mines, ex p Smith* (1888) 39 Ch D 546). There is no need for notice of a board meeting to be in writing, but it must be given to every director who is not out of the country. What amounts to reasonable notice will depend upon how serious or controversial are the issues to be discussed, and upon the composition of the board. For example, if all directors work full time for the company and there is a mundane decision to be made, any one director could call a board meeting on, say, five minutes' notice. However, more notice would be needed if some of the directors were not present, or if a major or sensitive issue was to be the subject of discussion.

The notice must specify the means of communication if the directors are not all going to be in the same place, ie telephone meetings, video meetings or meetings conducted on the Internet are all possible.

6.5.2   Voting

At a board meeting, each director has one vote and all resolutions can be passed by majority vote. If there is an equal number of votes for and against a resolution there is a deadlock and the negative view prevails, which means that the resolution is defeated. The chairman may be able to ensure that the resolution is passed by using his casting vote, depending on whether he has been given this power in the articles (model articles for private companies, art 13).

Directors must be aware of any restrictions in the articles on their capacity to participate in voting on matters where they have a personal interest (direct or indirect) in the outcome of the vote. For example, if a director is a shareholder in another company with which the company of which he is a director is proposing to make a contract, then clearly he has a personal interest in that contract. Another example of a personal interest is where a director wants to acquire more shares in the company and the directors meet to decide whether or not to allot to him the number of shares he has requested at the price he has offered to pay. Whenever a director has a personal interest, he would usually declare that interest to his co-directors at the first board meeting at which the matter is discussed, but could do so instead by written notice (CA 2006, s 182). Even where the director concerned may think it obvious to his fellow directors that he has such a personal interest, it is still advisable for him to make the formal declaration. If he fails to do so, he commits a criminal offence (CA 2006, ss 183(1), (2)). Even a one-director board has to comply with s 182 (*Neptune (Vehicle Washing Equipment) Ltd v Fitzgerald* [1995] 3 WLR 108).

Having made the necessary declaration, the director concerned may then be unable to vote on this particular issue, depending on the articles. Article 14 of the model articles for private companies prevents a director with a personal interest from voting on most relevant matters but provides a limited number of narrow exceptions. The main one is that a director can participate in the voting where he is subscribing shares in the company or guaranteeing a loan to the company.

Failure to declare an interest could be a breach of the director's fiduciary duty to the company and could make the contract voidable (not void), but only if the parties can be returned to their original positions (*Guinness plc v Saunders* [1990] 2 AC 663).

6.5.3 Quorum

The quorum for a board meeting is two (model articles for private companies, art 11), unless the directors themselves decide otherwise or there is a special article varying the number required. Any director unable to vote on a matter because he has a personal interest (see **6.5.2**) is also prevented from counting in the quorum (model articles for private companies, art 14). It can be particularly frustrating in a small company, where the result of this rule may be that it is impossible to obtain a quorum on a number of issues. It should be noted that a director cannot be excluded from a board meeting (*Hayes v Bristol Plant Hire* [1957] 1 All ER 685).

Directors cannot circumvent these provisions by reducing the quorum (*Re North Eastern Insurance Co Ltd* [1919] 1 Ch 198).

6.5.4 Resolving the problems

If there is any dispute over the ability of a particular director to vote and count in the quorum on any issue, it is the chairman who must decide this and his decision is final (model articles for private companies, art 14(6)).

The restrictions on directors voting and counting in the quorum can be overcome in various ways. When the company is formed, a special article can be included allowing directors to vote and count in the quorum even where they have a personal interest in the matter under discussion. Alternatively, at a later stage, the articles can be changed by special resolution of the members to remove the restrictions and allow more freedom. Another possibility is that the rules can be relaxed or suspended by the members passing an ordinary resolution to this effect, if a special resolution is added to permit this. Even where one of these possible courses of action is adopted by the company and directors are allowed to participate at board meetings irrespective of their personal involvement, they must still remember to declare any personal interest to the other directors, as this requirement cannot be dispensed with. A special provision can be added to the articles to deal with directors' service contracts, which enables each director to vote and count in the quorum on all other service contracts except his own.

6.5.5 Minutes

Minutes must be written up for every board meeting (CA 2006, s 248) and kept at the registered office for 10 years. They are open to inspection there by the directors, but not by the members. The minutes for each meeting will usually be signed by the chairman as being an authentic record of the business transacted at that meeting.

6.5.6 Use of written resolutions

If there is a possibility that all directors will agree to a proposed resolution, that resolution could be passed as a written resolution without the need to hold a board meeting. A copy of the proposed resolution should be sent to every director; and if each director then signs his copy of the resolution, or gives other written consent, and returns it to the company the resolution is validly passed. Unanimous consent is necessary (model articles for private companies, art 8).

6.6 General duties (including 'fiduciary' duties)

Directors are in a position of trust within the company, and as such they owe certain duties to the company. Their duty, however, is to the company and not to the shareholders. They might owe a duty to shareholders where, for example, they agreed to act as agents for the members, or they assumed responsibility for giving administrative advice to members, but generally it is the best interests of the company that directors must have in mind (see *Platt v Platt* [1999] 2 BCLC 745). It is possible for directors validly to fetter the future exercise of their discretion, provided it is for the benefit of the company (*Fulham Football Club Ltd v Cabra Estates* [1994] 1 BCLC 363).

This discussion deals with a director's 'general duties', as distinct from those administrative duties and restrictions primarily under the CA 2006 which are dealt with later in this chapter. The general duties come originally from common law and equity. General duties include fiduciary duties in the true sense. Unfortunately the term 'fiduciary duties' has been somewhat bastardised. It has been applied to a wide variety of situations where a person who is in a position of trust, in the broadest meaning of that word, has been found wanting. In *Bristol and West Building Society v Mothew* [1998] Ch 1, a case that did not concern directors but rather an errant solicitor, Millett LJ gave perhaps a narrower view of the concept than some, and said the following about fiduciary duties:

> This leaves those duties which are special to fiduciaries and which attract those remedies which are peculiar to the equitable jurisdiction and are primarily restitutionary or restorative rather than compensatory. A fiduciary is someone who has undertaken to act for or on behalf of another in a particular matter in circumstances which give rise to a relationship of trust and confidence. The distinguishing obligation of a fiduciary is the obligation of loyalty. The principal is entitled to the single-minded loyalty of his fiduciary. This core liability has several facets. A fiduciary must act in good faith; he must not make a profit out of his trust; he must not place himself in a position where his duty and his interest may conflict; he may not act for his own benefit or the benefit of a third person without the informed consent of his principal. This is not intended to be an exhaustive list, but it is sufficient to indicate the nature of fiduciary obligations ...

The extent of the fiduciary duties of an agent will vary with the circumstances. Lord Browne-Wilkinson in *Henderson v Merrett Syndicates Ltd* [1995] 2 AC 145 at 206 said:

> The phrase 'fiduciary duties' is a dangerous one, giving rise to a mistaken assumption that all fiduciaries owe the same duties in all circumstances. That is not the case. Although, so far as I am aware, every fiduciary is under a duty not to make a profit from his position (unless such profit is authorised), the fiduciary duties owed, for example, by an express trustee are not the same as those owed by an agent. Moreover, and more relevantly, the extent and nature of the fiduciary duties owed in any particular case fall to be determined by reference to any underlying contractual relationship between the parties. Thus, in the case of an agent employed under a contract, the scope of his fiduciary duties is determined by the terms of the underlying contract. Although an agent is, in the absence of contractual provision, in breach of his fiduciary duties if he acts for another who is in competition with his principal, if the contract under which he is acting authorises him to do so, the normal fiduciary duties are modified accordingly: see *Kelly v Cooper* [1993] AC 205, and the cases there cited. The existence of a contract does not exclude the co-existence of concurrent fiduciary duties (indeed, the contract may well be their source); but the contract can and does modify the extent and nature of the general duty that would otherwise arise.

Fiduciary duties arise in equity, so they do not depend upon a contract between the principal and the agent. Consequently, fiduciary duties may be imposed on both agents acting for remuneration and those acting without it. A contractual clause which attempts to modify or exclude an agent's fiduciary duty may be subject to the Unfair Contract Terms Act 1977, or the Unfair Terms in Consumer Contracts Regulations 1999 (SI 1999/2083), or both.

An example of breach of general fiduciary duty in the company context is the case of *Colin Gwyer & Associates Ltd v London Wharf (Limehouse) Ltd; Eaton Bray Ltd v Palmer* [2002] All ER (D) 226. There, directors were held to be in breach of their general duty to act in the interests of the company. They had voted to make a decision which favoured one of them personally to the detriment of the company. This was held to be a breach, even though there was a special article allowing a director to vote on a motion in which he had a personal interest. In contrast, fiduciary duties are not imposed on shareholders, not least as they do not manage the company. In *Halton International Inc (Holdings) Sarl v Guernroy Ltd* [2005] EWHC 1968 a voting agreement was held not to impose fiduciary duties on the shareholder in question.

The duties of directors evolved through decisions of the courts. Although the CA 2006 regulates certain activities of directors, it does not impose any general duty of good faith. The duties of a director are an amalgamation of several elements:

(a)   *Agent*, in that the director acts not on his own behalf but that of the company.

(b)   *Trustee*, in that he controls the assets and exercises powers for the company's benefit, not his own. As such, he owes fiduciary duties to the company.

(c)   *Employee*, in that an executive director is an employee with the same rights and duties as those of any other employee.

(d)   *Professional adviser*, in that he renders services for reward (even as a non-executive fee earner) and must accept the burden of skill and care which falls upon independent contractors of that type.

Directors' duties have been codified and reformed in the CA 2006 (eg the new duty to promote the success of the company). The revised requirements include those on substantial property transactions between the company and a director, loans, payments for loss of office and service contracts. There is also a revised procedure for derivative claims which is intended to make it easier for a company to claim against directors who are at fault.

6.6.1   Statutory statement of directors' duties (CA 2006, ss 170–180)

The statutory statement of a director's general duties is stated to replace common law and equitable principles. However, s 170(4) provides that common law rules and equitable principles are to be used in interpreting the general duties. The seven duties laid down in the CA 2006 are discussed further below.

The duties have been held, in one of the first cases under the CA 2006, to apply equally to executive and non-executive directors (*Commonwealth Oil and Gas Co Ltd v Baxter* [2007] Scot CS CSOH 198).

6.6.2   Duty to act within his powers

Under s 171:

> A director of a company must—
> (a)   act in accordance with the company's constitution, and
> (b)   only exercise powers for the purposes for which they are conferred.

In effect, this is a restatement of the principle that a director must use his powers for a proper purpose.

6.6.3   Duty to promote the success of the company

Under s 172, the director must promote the 'success of the company for the benefit of its members'. This replaces the common law criterion of acting 'in the best interests of the company'. It seems that 'success' for a commercial company would normally mean a long-term increase in value.

The directors must pay attention to various factors. These include, under s 172:

> (a)   the likely consequences of any decision in the long term,
> (b)   the interests of the company's employees,
> (c)   the need to foster the company's business relationships with suppliers, customers and others,
> (d)   the impact of the company's operations on the community and the environment,

(e)   the desirability of the company maintaining a reputation for high standards of business conduct, and

(f)   the need to act fairly as between members of the company.

In the *Company Law Review*, the above factors were stated as being those factors which a director should have borne in mind in any event.

The importance of how a hypothetical director would behave under s 172 was used in *Franbar Holdings v Patel* [2008] EWHC 1534 (Ch). On the facts, it was likely that the outcome would be that a derivative claim would be less likely to be used, ie a claim against the directors brought by a shareholder in the company's name. The complaints were really about breach of contract, ie the shareholders' agreement (see **5.6.4**).

6.6.4 Duty to exercise independent judgment

Under s 173, a director must exercise independent judgment. There is no prohibition on directors taking advice. It states in this section that:

(1)   A director of a company must exercise independent judgment.

(2)   This duty is not infringed by his acting—

(a)   in accordance with an agreement duly entered into by the company that restricts the future exercise of discretion by its directors, or

(b)   in a way authorised by the company's constitution.

6.6.5 Duty to exercise reasonable care, skill and diligence

Under s 174 there is a minimum standard required of all directors. This standard is increased for those directors who possess a higher standard of general knowledge, skill or experience. Thus, s 174 states:

(1)   A director of a company must exercise reasonable care, skill and diligence.

(2)   This means the care, skill and diligence that would be exercised by a reasonably diligent person with—

(a)   the general knowledge, skill and experience that may reasonably be expected of a person carrying out the functions carried out by the director in relation to the company, and

(b)   the general knowledge, skill and experience that the director has.

This provision is closely modelled on s 214(4) of the IA 1986 and involves an objective and a subjective element. Let us look at the background.

The starting point is the judgment of Romer J in *In re City Equitable Fire Insurance Co Ltd* [1925] Ch 407. This considered the earlier cases and reduced them to three general propositions, which can be expressly or impliedly displaced. They are as follows.

First, 'a director need not exhibit in the performance of his duties a greater degree of skill than may reasonably be expected from a person of his knowledge and experience'.

Secondly, 'a director is not bound to give continuous attention to the affairs of his company. His duties are of an intermittent nature to be performed at periodical board meetings'.

Thirdly, 'in respect of all duties that, having regard to the exigencies of business, and the articles of association, may properly be left to some other official, a director is, in the absence of grounds for suspicion, justified in trusting that official to perform such duties honestly'.

In more recent authorities, the law moved away from a subjective approach towards a more objective one. The tendency became to impose a higher standard of care and skill for directors than the old cases might suggest.

If 'skill' and 'care' are looked at separately then the situation can perhaps be explained in the following terms.

The standard of skill required of directors is usually judged on a subjective basis. They are required to exercise the degree of competence which could reasonably be expected from someone with their degree of knowledge and experience. It therefore follows that, for example, a higher standard is imposed on a director who is professionally qualified or who has had years of experience than on a complete newcomer to the business world.

The standard of care required of directors is usually judged on an objective basis. They are required to exercise the degree of care which a reasonable person would exercise on his own behalf.

Section 214(4) of the IA 1986 lays down how a court should judge a director in the case of wrongful trading (see **6.10.8**). In effect, this became a statutory definition of the standard of a director's duty, and was used in the cases of *Norman v Theodore Goddard (A Firm)* [1992] BCC 14 and *Re D'Jan of London Ltd; Copp v D'Jan* [1993] BCC 646. The test is now contained in s 174 of the CA 2006.

In general, all that directors are obliged to do is to attend board meetings when they are reasonably able to do so and to vote on the proposed resolutions, bearing in mind the seven statutory duties outlined above. An executive director (see **6.3.3**) would normally have a written contract of employment. This may contain express terms requiring a duty of skill and care to the company. If not, then it is likely that one would be implied. The more debatable issue, therefore, is the standard for non-executive directors.

6.6.6   Duty to avoid conflicts of interest

The main principle applying to any person in a fiduciary position is avoiding conflicts of interest (see, for example, *Boardman v Phipps* [1967] 2 AC 46, *Bhullar v Bhullar* [2003] EWCA Civ 424). This principle gives rise to specific provisions such as those in the CA 2006 on director's conflicts of interest. There are three types of situation dealt with in the CA 2006. However, in each case the director and the company must both have an 'interest', direct or indirect or even just possible, in the same area for there to be the possibility of any 'conflict', and therefore to trigger the provisions below. 'Interest' does not just mean direct dealings between the director and the company, though those are included in the wide ambit of the provisions.

The widest provisions are contained in s 175. Under this section, a director must not have any conflicts of interest with the company. Merely having a possible indirect conflict is enough to trigger the prohibition (though s 175(4)(a) does require there to be a reasonable likelihood of a conflict). Section 175(1) states:

> (1)   A director of a company must avoid a situation in which he has, or can have, a direct or indirect interest that conflicts, or possibly may conflict, with the interests of the company.

The wide remit of s 175(1) is then restricted by s 175(3), which states that if the transaction is with the company then s 175(1) does not apply. The more specific provisions of s 177 (below) or s 182 (see below and **6.7.1**) will apply instead.

The CA 2006 further alters the law in this area, in that the *directors* may authorise a fellow director's acts when he has a conflict. Section 175(5) states:

> (5)   Authorisation may be given by the directors—
>
> > (a)   where the company is a private company and nothing in the company's constitution invalidates such authorisation, by the matter being proposed to and authorised by the directors; or
> >
> > (b)   where the company is a public company and its constitution includes provision enabling the directors to authorise the matter, by the matter being proposed to and authorised by them in accordance with the constitution.

Under the CA 1985, it was only the *members* who could authorise the director's acts.

A condition for the approval is that the director in question cannot vote or count in the quorum. Section 175(6) states:

> (6) The authorisation is effective only if—
>
> (a) any requirement as to the quorum at the meeting at which the matter is considered is met without counting the director in question or any other interested director, and
>
> (b) the matter was agreed to without their voting or would have been agreed to if their votes had not been counted.

Under s 177(1), even an interest in a *proposed* transaction with the company has to be declared:

> (1) If a director of a company is in any way, directly or indirectly, interested in a proposed transaction or arrangement with the company, he must declare the nature and extent of that interest to the other directors.

The problem of the director being counted or not counted in quorum is not addressed under s 177 but is dealt with in the model articles for private companies, art 14, and the model articles for public companies, art 16. For private companies, if the matter in question is the director's service contract then he may vote and count in the quorum (and there are other exceptions).

Under s 182, a director must declare any interest in an *existing* transaction or arrangement with the company. This is equivalent to the former requirement under CA 1985, s 317. The terms of a director's service contract are exempted from the general duty to declare an interest (s 182(6)).

Under s 182 the offence is broader than under the old CA 1985, s 317, in that:

(a) it applies to any arrangement whether or not it is legally binding;

(b) it requires the extent of the interests to be declared; and

(c) the declarations must be updated.

There are further details in ss 183–187 (including the penalty of fines). Under s 187, the requirements also apply to shadow directors.

6.6.7 Duty not to accept benefits from third parties

This is a codification of the 'no secret profits' rule in cases such as *Industrial Development Consultants v Cooley* [1972] 2 All ER 162.

Under s 176(1), this prohibition is stated as follows:

> (1) A director of a company must not accept a benefit from a third party conferred by reason of—
>
> (a) his being a director, or
>
> (b) his doing (or not doing) anything as director.

There is an important exception under s 176(4):

> (4) This duty is not infringed if the acceptance of the benefit cannot reasonably be regarded as likely to give rise to a conflict of interest.

The background to this provision is as follows.

In relation to company property, the directors' position can be said to be similar to that of trustees. Company property includes money, tangible assets and also confidential information such as trade secrets and details of business opportunities. If any company property is misapplied, the directors are answerable as trustees, ie as fiduciaries. Therefore, directors should not allow their personal interests and their duty to the company to conflict. For example, if a director is in possession of information about business opportunities such as contracts soon to be available, and he has gained this information solely because he holds the office of director in the company, then he should not use that information to his own advantage, ie he should not enter into the contract in his personal name and take the profit from it (see, for example, *Belmont Finance Corporation v Williams Furniture Ltd (No 2)* [1980] 1 All ER 393, *CMS Dolphin Ltd v Simonet* [2001] 2 BCLC 704). If he does so, he will be obliged to account to the company for any profit made unless he fully discloses all relevant facts to the members of the company and obtains their approval by ordinary resolution at a general meeting. Members can ratify directors' actions in this way only if doing so would not constitute a fraud on the minority, ie if the directors concerned are not themselves the majority shareholders (see **5.5.14** and **5.6.1**).

The leading case in the area is *Regal (Hastings) Ltd v Gulliver* [1967] AC 134. In this case, directors were successfully sued by the company for the profit they had made. They had subscribed for shares in a subsidiary in order to provide it with the necessary paid-up share capital for it to take a lease on two cinemas. (The landlord had stipulated a paid-up share capital.) The cinemas were subsequently sold for a profit as a going concern. The directors were found liable for the profit they had made on their shares, even though they had acted honestly. The House of Lords held that only approval by the members in a general meeting would have saved the directors from liability. Some outsiders who had similarly profited were allowed to keep their profit, as they did not owe a fiduciary duty to the company. Likewise, the company's solicitor also escaped as his actions had been approved by the board.

In *Industrial Development Consultants v Cooley* [1972] 2 All ER 162, a director had resigned from the company by feigning illness in order to take for himself a lucrative contract for consultancy services. He was found liable to his company and had to hand over to the company his profit on the contract. Contrast this with *Island Export Finance v Umunna* [1986] BCLC 460, where the director in question had resigned some time before the business opportunity arose. Also, in this case the company had already decided not to pursue further contracts of that type. The director was therefore not liable to his former company.

More recently, in *Gwembe Valley Development Corporation v Thomas Koshy* [2004] WTLR 97, the Court of Appeal considered this area of law in some detail. The managing director of a joint venture company, which had been set up to develop a farm in Zambia, dishonestly failed to disclose his personal interest in transactions he made with the company. He was ordered to account to the company for the profits he had made personally. He was held to have been in breach of his fiduciary duty to the company.

If a director ceases to hold that office and then sets up a new business in competition, that is not a breach of his duty as a director (eg *Balston Ltd v Headline Filters Ltd* [1990] FSR 385) subject to contrary contractual agreement between the parties. On the other hand, a director can be liable if there has been improper behaviour on his part. This was the case in *Hunter Kane Ltd v Alan Watkins* [2003] EWHC 186, where a director resigned in order to attempt to divert to himself business opportunities which would have been rightfully that of the company. In *CMS Dolphin v Simonet* [2001] 2 BCLC 704, the errant director was also liable, though there he had already set up a competing company and poached his former company's clients.

The articles of most companies often contain a relieving provision permitting a director to have personal interests separate from those of the company and to keep any profit resulting from those personal interests, provided he discloses to the board the full nature and extent of any such interests, and provided he is not cheating the company. For example, if a director is awarded a service contract at a realistic salary by the board, he can keep his 'profit' (his salary) by virtue of such a provision. However, if a director sells an asset to the company for a price substantially in excess of what the asset is worth, he does not gain the protection. This general approach of not allowing directors to make a secret profit has been extended in various ways.

Sections 215, 217 of the CA 2006 require that payments made to directors for loss of office are approved by a general meeting of the members (see **6.8.1**).

In *Gardner v Parker* [2004] EWCA Civ 781, the Court of Appeal rejected a shareholder's claim for loss due to the decrease in the value of his shares caused by a breach of duty of a director.

There is a prohibition on making a profit from 'insider dealing'. This is not limited to directors. The concept is that persons who have access to information about shares and other securities, by reason of their fiduciary position, cannot profit from that knowledge. Typically, the situation is that of quoted shares (ie quoted on a stock market). The market price of the shares will go up or down on the release of news about the company, eg that its annual profits are poor, or that it is the subject of a take-over bid. The provisions are contained in the Financial Services and Markets Act 2000 and the Criminal Justice Act 2003.

6.6.8   Consequences of a breach of a director's duty (ss 178, 239)

The CA 2006 does not specify the remedies available for breach of a director's duty. Nevertheless, there is a new procedure for making so-called 'derivative' claims, ie a claim made on behalf of the company.

Section 178 preserves the existing remedies and states:

> (1)   The consequences of breach (or threatened breach) of sections 171 to 177 are the same as would apply if the corresponding common law rule or equitable principle applied.
>
> (2)   The duties in those sections (with the exception of section 174 (duty to exercise reasonable care, skill and diligence)) are, accordingly, enforceable in the same way as any other fiduciary duty owed to a company by its directors.

Under s 239, breaches of a director's duty may be ratified by the members. The votes of the director, if he is in fact a member, and of any member 'connected' with him will be disregarded. The common law principle that all members can ratify a director's actions by voting unanimously seems to be unaffected.

If a director does act in breach of any of his general duties owed to the company, the company (ie either the other directors, if they constitute a majority of the board, or the members) can take action against him, requiring him to compensate the company for any loss it has suffered and/or to account to the company for any profit made. However, in *Bell v Lever Bros Ltd* [1932] AC 161 the House of Lords held that an employee is not under a general duty to disclose any past breaches of duty. The Court of Appeal, in the more recent case of *Item Software v Fassihi* [2004] EWCA Civ 1244, declined to follow *Bell* in the case of a director. It held that a director's duty to act in the best interests of the company was a broad and well-established principle that was not restricted in its application.

Whilst the usual breach of duty will involve a director doing something he should not, it is also possible to breach a duty by inaction, ie by failing to do something. In *Lexi Holdings plc v Luqman* [2009] EWCA Civ 117, the Court of Appeal held that two directors were in breach of their duty of skill and care to the company by allowing another director to commit a fraud on the company, involving the embezzlement of £60 million over a period of years. It was no defence that they would have been bamboozled or dominated by the miscreant director if they had tried to stop him.

6.6.9   Persons connected to a director (ss 252–256)

The definition of 'connected person' has been widened under ss 252–256 of the 2006 Act to include the following:

(a)   the director's parents;

(b)   children and stepchildren over 18 years old;

(c)   a person, other than a sibling or other close family member, with whom the director lives as partner in an 'enduring family relationship';

(d)   a civil partner; and

(e)   children or stepchildren of the director's unmarried partner if they are under 18 years old and live with the director.

Perhaps the most obvious omission from the new list of persons is the director's siblings, who are therefore not 'connected persons'.

6.7   Administrative duties of directors

Various administrative duties are also imposed upon directors of a company by statute. One of the ways in which the CA 2006 exercises control over directors is that it requires that certain information cannot be kept secret.

6.7.1   Declaration of personal interests (CA 2006, ss 177, 182–187)

If a director has a personal interest (direct or indirect) in any matter to be discussed at a board meeting, he must formally declare to his co-directors that he has such an interest (CA 2006, s 182). He may be prevented from voting on that matter and counting in the quorum (depending on the terms of the company's articles) (see **6.5.2**).

6.7.2   Disclosure of service contracts (CA 2006, ss 188, 228)

Members always have the right to inspect the terms of directors' service contracts at the registered office, even where approval of the contract by the members is not required because the service contract is not for a fixed term exceeding two years (CA 2006, s 188).

6.7.3   Annual accounts (CA 2006, ss 393–397; 442)

It is the directors' responsibility to ensure that full accounts are produced each year and that they are sent to all members within nine months of the accounting reference date (the final day of the company's accounting year to which the accounts are made up).

The accounts consist of:

(a)   a profit and loss account, which shows whether the company has made a profit or a loss over the last year;

(b)   a balance sheet, which sets out the company's financial position on a specified day, the accounting reference date;

(c)   the auditor's report, which should say whether these final accounts present a true and fair view of the company's finances;

(d)   details of any loans to directors in the last year (loans to directors are generally forbidden but there are exceptions (see **6.8.4**)), details of directors' salaries and directors' pensions and any situations in the last year when directors have had personal interests in proposed contracts; and

(e)   the directors' report, which deals with what has happened to the company over the last year and must include a business review (CA 2006, s 417).

The accounts must also be sent to the Registrar of Companies each year, whereupon they become a public document open to public inspection. The time limit within which they must be sent to Companies House is also nine months from the accounting reference date. 'Small' and 'medium-sized' companies are permitted to deliver abbreviated accounts to the Registrar giving less detailed information than companies which do not qualify for this concession, but they must still supply full accounts to their members. The auditor will certify that for this purpose a company can be categorised as 'small' or 'medium-sized'.

Auditing of accounts is not required in the case of small *private* companies – those with a turnover of less than £6.5 million and a balance sheet total of less than £3.26 million.

6.7.4 The annual return (CA 2006, ss 854–859)

It is the directors' responsibility to submit an annual return to the Registrar within 28 days after its 'return date' (the date to which the annual return is made up) (CA 2006, s 854). A company's first return date is the anniversary of its incorporation. Otherwise, it is the anniversary of the previous return date.

The annual return is designed to ensure that the information at Companies House is kept up to date. In practice, the Registrar of Companies will send the annual return form to the company partially completed, using the information already stored at Companies House. It is then for the company secretary to check the accuracy of the information, to complete the form as necessary and return it to the Registrar. The information required on the annual return is the address of the registered office, details of the company's main business activities, details of the directors and the company secretary, details of issued share capital, and the names of past and present members. All this information is kept at Companies House and is available to anyone who chooses to make a company search.

Under the Companies Act 1985 (Electronic Communications) Order 2000 (SI 2000/3373) it is possible for companies to communicate electronically with Companies House and also with their members (and see **Chapter 9**).

6.7.5 The register of directors (CA 2006, ss 162–167)

Details about each director (name, address, business occupation, date of birth, nationality and details of other directorships) must appear on the register. This register must be altered whenever there is a change in the composition of the board.

6.7.6 The register of directors' interests

This register has ceased to exist under the CA 2006.

6.7.7 Company stationery (CA 2006, s 82)

To prevent the public being misled, either the names of all the directors or the names of none of them must appear on the company stationery (CA 2006, s 82; Companies (Trading Disclosures) Regulations 2009 (SI 2009/388)).

6.7.8 Contracts with a director who is also the sole member (CA 2006, s 231)

Where a contract is to be made between the company and the only member of that company, and that sole member is also a director of the company, then either the contract itself must be in writing or the terms of the contract must be set out in a written memorandum or must be recorded in the minutes of the first board meeting following the making of the contract. If this is not done, the company and every officer in default is liable to a fine. This provision is also relevant to the situation where a contract is proposed between the company and a sole member who is also a shadow director (that is, there is one 'proper' director plus a shadow director).

6.8 Statutory restrictions on directors

The board is limited by statute in various ways. Certain actions are forbidden and some things can be done only with the consent of the members.

6.8.1 Gratuitous compensation to directors (CA 2006, ss 215, 217)

If a director is removed from office, he may be entitled to compensation for breach of contract or for unfair dismissal, or to a redundancy payment. These are payments to which the director is legally entitled, and such payments can be made by the directors without needing to consult the members. Section 220(1) provides that the prohibition on payments made to a director do not include pensions or damages for breach of contract. However, if the board wishes to pay a director who is leaving a 'golden handshake', eg as an expression of appreciation for years of loyal service, it is required to obtain the prior approval of members by ordinary resolution.

6.8.2 Substantial property transactions (CA 2006, ss 190–196)

If a director, in his personal capacity, is buying something from or selling something to the company, then the consent of the members by ordinary resolution is necessary if the asset being bought or sold is of 'requisite value', ie a substantial property transaction (CA 2006, s 190). If the asset in question is worth less than £5,000, it is not of requisite value and the transaction will not be a substantial property transaction. If the asset is worth more than £100,000, it will always be a substantial property transaction. If the asset being bought or sold is worth between £5,000 and £100,000 then it will qualify as being of requisite value if it is worth more than 10% of the company's net relevant assets (the net assets figure shown on the latest set of accounts or, if no accounts have been prepared, the amount of the company's called-up share capital). This provision also covers other dealings with non-cash assets, for example charging or leasing an asset of requisite value (see CA 2006, s 1163).

The key elements of s 190 are:

(a)   a transaction between a company;

(b)   and its director or a 'connected person', eg a close family member;

(c)   involving a 'non-cash' asset, ie anything that is not money;

(d)   of the 'requisite value' – either the asset is worth more than 10% of the company's assets and is over £5,000, or the asset is over £100,000; and

(e)   an ordinary resolution by the shareholders in a general meeting is needed.

If a substantial property transaction takes place without the members' authority being obtained, the contract is voidable by the company. The director who was party to the transaction and any other director who authorised the transaction become liable to indemnify the company for any loss it has suffered and to account to the company for any gain they have made.

This provision applies to all directors of a company, including any shadow directors.

On incorporation of a business, it is very likely that s 190 will be relevant, as the former partners or sole trader will become directors of the new company (which has a net asset value of virtually nil) and will sell their business to the company. The business will inevitably be worth more than 10% of the company's net relevant assets.

It should be noted that s 190 is also relevant to transactions between the company and persons 'connected' with a director, eg family members – spouses, civil partners and children under 18, companies with which the director is 'associated' (broadly, where the director owns 20% of the shares) and partners acting in their capacity as partners of the director (CA 2006, s 253).

The new provisions under CA 2006 also include:

(a)   a transaction can be entered into subject to *subsequent* member approval;

(b)   benefits which a director is entitled to under his service contract are excluded;

(c)   the value of a series of transactions is *aggregated* to see if the threshold of £100,000 or 10% of net assets has been met; and

(d)   transactions with a company which is in compulsory liquidation or in administration are exempt.

Examples of cases under the old legislation where there was a failure to obtain proper consent under s 320 of the CA 1985 are *British Racing Drivers' Club Ltd v Hextall Erskine & Co (A Firm)* [1996] 3 All ER 667, *Demite Ltd v Protec Health Ltd* [1998] BCC 638 and *Re Duckwari plc (No 3); Duckwari plc v Offerventure Ltd (No 3)* [1999] 1 BCLC 168. In *British Racing Drivers' Club Ltd*, the club was negligently advised by its solicitors. The matter in question was the purchase by the club from one of its own directors of a large quantity of shares in *another* company. The club lost money on the deal. The solicitors had said this was not a s 320 issue, but the court held that it most certainly was. In *Re Duckwari*, the Court of Appeal held that there was a breach of s 320 when a director had sold a building to his company and the transaction had never been ratified by the shareholders. The company had lost money when the property market crashed.

6.8.3   Service contracts in excess of two years (CA 2006, s 188)

If directors wish to award themselves service contracts for a fixed term in excess of two years, the prior approval of the members in general meeting by ordinary resolution is necessary.

If such approval is not obtained in advance, although the rest of the terms contained in the service contract are valid, the fixed term is ineffective and the contract is terminable on reasonable notice (see **6.13.2**).

6.8.4   Loans to directors (CA 2006, ss 197–214)

There is no longer any absolute prohibition on loans to directors. Thus, the CA 2006 removes the criminal penalties for granting a loan to a director. Members can now approve any loan, provided that they are informed of the nature of the transaction, the amount of the loan, its purpose and the extent of the company's liability.

Members' approval of quasi-loans is required only in the case of public companies or associated companies (s 198). Section 256 defines 'associated companies'. (A quasi-loan is defined in s 199 as reimbursable payment of a director's debts or expenses, but it may turn out to be an ex gratia payment in disguise.) In the case of a connected person to such a company, the members' approval is needed in the case of both loans and quasi-loans (s 200).

There were various minor exemptions under the 1985 Act to the approval requirement on directors' loans. These remain, with revisions. Thus, there is now no maximum in the case of a money-lending company, ie a bank, which lends money in the course of its business (s 209). The other limits have been increased as follows, so no approval is needed:

(a)   for loans and quasi-loans, from an aggregate value of £5,000 to £10,000; and

(b)   for credit transactions, from £10,000 to £15,000.

The current exemption for a loan to a director to meet expenses incurred for the purposes of the company has been relaxed (s 204). There is no longer a requirement for shareholder approval. The permitted amount is now a maximum of £50,000.

There is a new exemption for expenses incurred by a director in defending himself against an investigation by a regulatory authority (s 206), so again no shareholder approval is necessary.

6.8.5   Payments for loss of office (CA 2006, ss 215–222)

The new, comprehensive definition of payment for loss of office is contained in s 215 of the CA 2006. This covers payments for:

(a)   dismissal, redundancy or retirement;

(b)   loss of office on the sale of the company; and

(c)   loss of office on a transfer of shares as a result of a takeover.

The provisions include payments to connected persons and to past directors. A payment to an employee who is also a director is caught. Non-cash benefits are also caught.

Under ss 217–219, each type of payment referred to in s 215 can be made if the members approve it.

Some exceptions to the need to seek approval are listed in s 220. So, under s 220(1), the following payments do not need approval, ie those made:

(a)   in discharge of an existing legal obligation;

(b)   by way of damages for breach of such an obligation;

(c)   by way of settlement or compromise of any claim arising in connection with the termination of a person's office or employment; or

(d)   by way of pension in respect of past services.

Section 221 includes an exemption for small payments, ie having a total value of less than £200. Section 222 deals with the civil consequences of breach of the provisions. There are no longer any criminal sanctions.

6.8.6 Interests of employees (CA 2006, s 172(b))

There is a statutory obligation imposed on directors (and shadow directors) to have regard to the interests of the employees of the company (CA 2006, s 172(b)). It may sometimes be necessary, therefore, to balance the interest of members against those of employees where the two do not coincide. However, employees have no right to enforce this obligation.

6.9 Liability of directors to the company

The company is bound where an agent has made a contract which was outside his actual authority but within his apparent authority. However, since the action which has taken place was unauthorised, this is relevant to the question of the directors' (and other agents') liability to the company (see **6.6.2**).

6.9.1 Liability for exceeding actual authority

Where a director or other agent of the company (eg the company secretary) binds the company by acting within his apparent authority but exceeds his actual authority, that director or agent is acting in breach of duty. The person concerned is therefore liable to indemnify the company for any loss it has suffered and to account to the company for any profit he has made (see **6.4.2**).

Any action by an officer of the company which is in breach of his duty to the company can be sanctioned by the company if the members in a general meeting agree to ratify the breach of duty by passing an ordinary resolution to that effect, eg *Bamford v Bamford* [1968] 2 All ER 655. This absolves the director or agent only if such approval of the members does not amount to a fraud on the minority. The ratification may be ineffective if those holding the majority of the shares in the company and thereby passing the ordinary resolution are the same people as those who have acted in breach of duty.

Under s 1157, a court may relieve a director of liability where it has found him to be liable for negligence, default, breach of duty or breach of trust. The conditions are that he acted honestly, reasonably and 'ought fairly to be excused'.

Brocks Mount Ltd v Stephen Paul Beasant, Lawtel, 28 April 2003 was a case where an application under s 1157 was refused, on the basis that the director had not acted honestly and reasonably. He had made an unauthorised payment to another company in which he was involved and was held to have been reckless in doing so. (The case was decided under s 727 of the CA 1985.)

Companies may indemnify their directors against the legal and financial costs of proceedings brought by third parties (ss 232–234). This does not include criminal proceedings. The details of the indemnity need to be disclosed in the annual report and accounts.

6.9.2   Enforcement by the company (CA 2006, s 994)

If a wrong is done to the company (eg if the directors have acted in breach of duty in some way) then the proper claimant in any legal action for breach of duty is the company itself. This means that generally it is for the directors or (if they are the ones in breach of duty and therefore unable to take action) the members to institute legal proceedings in the name of the company. The rule in *Foss v Harbottle* ((1843) 2 Hare 461) generally prevents minority shareholders from taking legal action on the company's behalf, although there are certain limited exceptions (see **5.6.4**). However, an action under s 994 of the CA 2006 on unfair prejudice may be more realistic.

6.9.3   Declaration of dividends

Directors can be liable to the company for a dividend which was wrongly declared, even though they did not benefit from it personally (*Bairstow v Queens Moat Houses plc* [2000] 1 BCLC 549).

6.10   Liability of the directors to outsiders

Generally, in the absence of misconduct, directors have no liability whatsoever for any debts they incur on the company's behalf. If a director is also a shareholder in a company which goes into insolvent liquidation, then the worst that can happen to that director is that he loses his job as director, together with the salary that goes with it. He also loses whatever money he invested in the company when he bought his shares.

Although this is the general rule, there are situations where a director can incur personal liability (see **6.10.1–6.10.8**).

Also, a director may be liable in tort if he:

(a)   commits a tort separate from that of the company (eg *Standard Chartered Bank v Pakistan National Shipping Corporation (No 2)* [2002] 1 All ER 173, where the director in question committed the tort of deceit);

(b)   voluntarily assumes personal responsibility for the tort (eg creates a special relationship between himself and the third party – *Williams v Natural Life Health Foods Ltd* [1998] 1 WLR 830); or

(c)   procures or induces another (ie the company) to commit a tort (eg a director acting beyond his constitutional role in the company – *MCA Records Inc v Charly Records Ltd* [2003] 1 BCLC 93).

A director may be liable for debts under the general law if he engages in misconduct. For example, a director was found liable for his company's debts because of his fraudulent misrepresentation in entering a contract with a supplier when he knew that his company would be unable to pay for the goods (*Contex Drouzbha v Wiseman and another* [2007] EWCA Civ 1201).

6.10.1   Criminal penalties

Criminal sanctions usually apply not just to the directors of the company, but also to any 'officer' of the company. The term 'officer' applies to the directors, any manager and the company secretary (CA 2006, s 1173). For example, the company secretary is liable, along with the directors, for failure to file the necessary returns with the Registrar of Companies. Directors can have liability imposed on them by statute. For example, under s 37 of the Health and Safety at Work, etc Act 1974, directors and officers can have personal criminal liability for breaches of health and safety requirements.

6.10.2 Breach of warranty of authority

Where a director purports to act on behalf of the company, but is acting outside the scope of his actual and apparent authority, he may not bind the company by his actions (see **6.4.2**). This liability is based on the assumption that the director has impliedly warranted to an outsider that he has the authority to enter into the contract. If he has exceeded the powers of himself, or of the board of directors, or of the company, then he has broken that warranty and he is liable accordingly to the third party. The director will also be personally liable to the third party on the contract, as he will have failed to pass the contractual liability back to the company if he is acting in good faith.

Section 40(2) of the CA 2006 provides that an outsider dealing with a company is not bound to check on the powers of the directors or of the company. Section 40(1) provides that, as regards an outsider, the power of the directors to bind the company shall not be limited by the company's constitution, ie the outsider is not affected by any such restraints inside the company if he is acting in good faith.

In addition, the company could also be liable (as well as the director) under the common law principle of 'holding out' where the director is allowed to deal with third parties in a way which would normally imply authority to enter into such contracts.

6.10.3 Personal guarantees

If directors have personally guaranteed a loan to the company and the company defaults under the terms of that loan, the lender (the debenture holder; see **11.1**) may choose to enforce the guarantees against the personal assets of the directors. In extreme cases, directors could be required to sell their homes to repay the company's debt, or even be declared bankrupt.

6.10.4 Acting as director while disqualified

Any director who is guilty of acting while disqualified causes himself to be personally liable for the company's debts incurred during the period when he did so act (CDDA 1986, s 15). He is also liable to a fine or imprisonment (CDDA 1986, s 13).

6.10.5 Misfeasance (IA 1986, s 212)

A liquidator can bring an action against directors of the company after liquidation if misfeasance has occurred. Basically, misfeasance under s 212 of the IA 1986 is any breach of any fiduciary or other duty of directors. If misfeasance is established then, under s 212(3), directors can be ordered to repay any money or personally contribute to the assets of the company to compensate for their misfeasance. In *Whalley (Liquidator of MDA Investment Management Ltd) v Doney* [2003] EWHC 227, the sole director of an insolvent company was found liable for misfeasance under s 212. He had sold the business just prior to liquidation and part of the proceeds were channelled to another of his companies. In *Swan v Sandhu* [2005] EWHC 2743, the liquidator failed in her claim of misfeasance against the directors. The allegation was that they had given preference to debts owed to a company controlled by a family member. These debts were therefore paid before debts owed to third parties when the company went into liquidation.

6.10.6 Failure to maintain company records (CA 2006, ss 1134–1138)

All directors and officers of the company are required to maintain proper up-to-date records both at Companies House and internally (the statutory books). Under ss 1134–1138 of the CA

2006, the relevant information to be kept in 'books' or other registers may in fact instead be kept as computer records, and printed out whenever required. Failure to keep proper records renders those in default liable to a fine (CA 2006, s 1121) and, in the case of accounting records, to imprisonment (see *R v Nigel Garvey* in **6.10.7**).

6.10.7 Fraudulent trading (IA 1986, s 213)

Fraudulent trading is not limited to directors but applies to any persons knowingly party to such action (see IA 1986, s 213(2)). It does not require the company to be insolvent.

In order for fraudulent trading to be established it must be shown that the business of the company was carried on with an intent to defraud creditors. Basically, the directors must have known full well that creditors would not be paid. The case of *In re Patrick and Lyon Ltd* [1933] Ch 786 suggests that 'real moral blame' must be established before fraudulent trading can be successfully proceeded with.

In practice, fraudulent trading actions are rare due to the difficulty of establishing intent and are only used against persons engaged in criminal conduct (see *R v Nigel Garvey* [2001] EWCA Crim 1365, where the accused was sentenced to four years' imprisonment). Liquidators tend to rely on wrongful trading which achieves substantially the same recovery of assets for the creditors.

If fraudulent trading is established, the directors can be made liable to make such personal contribution to the company's assets as a court thinks proper.

In *Morphitis v Bernasconi* [2003] BCC 540, the Court of Appeal held that it was not enough that a creditor had been defrauded for a director to run foul of s 213. Rather, the company had to have been actually run with the intent to defraud creditors, which is a higher standard of proof. Here, it was held that the intention was in fact to protect the directors from liability under s 216, which provides for penalties for directors of a 'phoenix' company. This is a company which succeeds to the business of a predecessor company and has the same or very similar name. The object of such a manoeuvre is to leave behind unwanted liabilities. Here, it was a lease on commercial premises that were no longer needed for the reorganised business. The defendants were thus held not to be liable for fraudulent trading. Rather unhelpfully, the Court of Appeal then held, per curiam, that under s 213(2) it would only have had the power to award a contribution from the directors on the basis of the loss suffered by the creditors due to the running of the business with intent to defraud. It would not have interpreted s 213 as including a power to impose a punitive award which was totally unrelated to the losses suffered.

In *Bank of India v Christopher Morris* [2005] EWCA Civ 693, the Court of Appeal again looked at s 213. It held that s 213 attracted only civil liability and was not a penal provision, unlike the legislation it replaced. Thus, there was a liability under s 213 to pay 'compensation' in cases where the company which traded fraudulently was being wound up. However, a 'collective' action could be brought by the liquidator of the fraudulent company for contribution to be made to the assets of that company for the benefit of its creditors. The Court pointed out that criminal punishment for fraudulent trading was dealt with separately, in s 458 of the CA 1985 (now CA 2006, s 993).

6.10.8 Wrongful trading (IA 1986, s 214)

Section 214 requires some level of financial understanding and diligence of every director. Wrongful trading actions can only be brought by a liquidator and can only be brought against directors, in contrast to fraudulent trading (IA 1986, s 214(1), (2)(c)). At some time before the winding up the director must have known, or ought to have known, that there was no reasonable prospect that the company would avoid insolvent liquidation.

When looking at whether a director knew, or ought to have known, whether the company could not avoid insolvent liquidation, both subjective and objective tests are applied. That is: what did this particular director know, and what would a reasonable director have known in the circumstances (see s 214(4))? Matters such as the size of the business, the directors' function (for example, a finance director is expected to have a greater degree of competence on accountancy matters than other directors), are looked at. In practice, the liquidator seeks overwhelming evidence of insolvency that any director should have known about. This could be:

(a)   insolvent on a balance sheet basis;

(b)   creditor pressure;

(c)   late filing of accounts;

(d)   qualification on the accounts by the auditors;

(e)   the practice of only paying the creditors when creditors issue proceedings or statutory demands; or

(f)   numerous judgments against the company.

Section 214(3) provides a defence. This is that the director took every step with a view to minimising a potential loss to the company's creditors after he became aware that the company had no prospects of avoiding insolvent liquidation. It would certainly include taking professional advice, both legal and accountancy, minimising further goods taken upon credit, rigorous collection of debts, and management accounts (possibly daily) to establish the financial position of the company. It does not usually include resigning.

If wrongful trading is established then a director can be ordered to make a personal contribution for the loss that he has caused by his actions. In this case, the personal contribution is compensatory rather than punitive.

Precautions that a director may wish to take to protect himself from an accusation of wrongful trading include:

(a)   keeping an accurate record of his own activities, including board meetings;

(b)   being satisfied that the financial records kept are sufficient;

(c)   seeking professional advice at the earliest sign of financial problems in the company;

(d)   raising with the board financial concerns when these start to become evident; and

(e)   possibly resigning but he could be liable whether or not he remained on the board.

For an example of a case of wrongful trading, see *Official Receiver v Doshi* [2001] 2 BCLC 235 where, amongst many other matters, the director was found to have submitted false invoices, ie unwarranted demands for payment, for goods which had not in fact been delivered. In *Rubin v Gunner* [2004] EWHC 316, the directors had continued to pay themselves salaries after a date when there was no reasonable prospect of the company avoiding insolvent liquidation. They could therefore not use the s 214(3) defence. They were held liable to make a contribution to the assets of the company, and thereby in effect to the creditors of the company.

6.11 Notification to the Registrar

Except for the first directors of the company named on the statement of proposed officers, whenever a director is appointed to or removed from office, the Registrar of Companies must be informed by sending either a form for appointment or a form for resignation to Companies House. Where a new director is being appointed, his signed consent to act must appear on the form. Any change in the particulars of a director or secretary (eg change of address) should also be notified.

Normally, a director notifies his home address to Companies House for inclusion on the records. Under ss 240–246, a director can use a service address. Directors have to provide their usual residential addresses to the company. The company maintains a record of directors' usual residential addresses, which will not be open to public inspection (s 165).

Provisions were previously inserted into the CA 1985 whereby a director could withhold his residential address from the public register, if he could establish a serious risk of violence or intimidation. The provisions were needed because of the activities of animal rights activists. Police certification of the risk was required under the CA 1985. This is not needed under the provisions of the CA 2006.

6.12   Fees for non-executive directors

A director is not necessarily someone who also works in the company (an executive director). Instead, he could be someone who only attends board meetings to give the company the benefit of his experience of the commercial world (a non-executive director). A non-executive director would not have a contract of employment, not least as he is not of course employed by the company. He would be paid directors' fees, the amount of which is usually decided by the members in general meeting.

6.13   Miscellaneous provisions on directors

Details of a director's other directorships will not need to be recorded on the Companies House register.

There is a new minimum age for directors of 16 years (CA 2006, s 157). There is no maximum age.

At least one director of the company must be a 'natural person', that is a human being rather than another corporate entity (CA 2006, s 155).

Under ss 205 and 206, a company may provide a director with funds to defend legal proceedings without the need for approval of the members. The scope of the proceedings in question is narrower than under the 1985 Act.

There is a power under s 1182 of the 2006 Act for the Secretary of State to prevent someone from being a director of a UK company if that person is subject to restrictions under foreign law. The idea is that if a person is disqualified under foreign law from being a director, he should not be able to be one in the UK.

6.14   Business review in the annual report

There is a duty on directors to include a business review in the annual report and accounts as specified in s 417.

6.14.1   Directors' liability to the company for directors' reports

Section 463 of the CA 2006 deals with this area and provides that:

> (2)   A director of a company is liable to compensate the company for any loss suffered by it as a result of—
>
> (a)   any untrue or misleading statement in a report to which this section applies, or
>
> (b)   the omission from a report to which this section applies of anything required to be included in it.
>
> (3)   He is so liable only if—
>
> (a)   he knew the statement to be untrue or misleading or was reckless as to whether it was untrue or misleading, or
>
> (b)   he knew the omission to be dishonest concealment of a material fact.

(4) No person shall be subject to any liability to a person other than the company resulting from reliance, by that person or another, on information in a report to which this section applies.

It is important to note that the liability is only to the company.

See **8.1.1**.

6.15　Directors' service contracts

Where directors are to work for the company not just as directors but in some other, often full-time capacity, they are likely to want written service contracts (contracts of employment). Such directors are known as executive directors.

6.15.1　Contracts awarded by the board

Directors are empowered to award service contracts to themselves under the articles (model articles for private companies, art 19). The board will decide the terms of each service contract, including the amount of salary to be paid to each such director and any authority the director is to have to act on behalf of the board (see **6.4.1**).

When service contracts are being discussed and voted upon at a board meeting, the directors who are to be awarded the service contracts must declare formally to the board that they have a personal interest in this matter (CA 2006, ss 182–187). There are restrictions on these directors concerning voting and counting in the quorum for that meeting. Each service contract will usually be taken as a separate issue, and a director can vote and count in the quorum on every other director's service contract, but not on his own. This will create a problem where there are only two directors and the quorum for board meetings is two. The problem can be overcome by changing the articles (by special resolution of the members) to allow directors to vote whenever interested in the matter (including in relation to their own service contracts). This would perhaps be seen as undesirable in the interests of fairness. The alternative is to relax temporarily the rules on voting and counting in the quorum on this particular resolution by ordinary resolution of the members, if the articles allow this.

6.15.2　Fixed-term contracts

Sometimes directors will think it appropriate to award themselves fixed-term contracts, under which they are contractually guaranteed to be employed for a certain period of time. For example, one of the directors may, by his service contract, be appointed for a period of 10 years. The advantage of this type of contract is that if the company breaches the contract by removing him from this job within the 10-year period, the now ex-director can claim damages. The amount would be calculated on the basis of the salary he would have received over the whole 10-year period had he not been dismissed.

Where directors are proposing to award themselves service contracts for a fixed term greater than two years, they are required to obtain the prior consent of the members in a general meeting by ordinary resolution (CA 2006, s 188). Where they call a general meeting for this purpose, all the proposed terms of the service contracts in question must be available for inspection by members at the meeting and for 15 days prior to the meeting at the registered office. If a written resolution of the members is to be used instead of calling a meeting, the terms of the proposed service contracts must be sent out to members with the written resolution itself (CA 2006, s 188(5)).

If the approval of the members is not sought and obtained, the service contract will still be effective, save for the clause stating that the director is to be employed for a fixed term. Instead of that director's job being guaranteed for a specified period of time, the contract will be capable of termination on reasonable notice. All the rest of the terms of the contract decided upon by the directors will be valid and enforceable against the company, but the fixed-term element will not. Therefore, if the director concerned were to be dismissed in breach of contract, his damages would be based not on the fixed period of time stated, but on the period of time deemed by the court to be 'reasonable notice'.

The term 'service contract' has been expanded under the CA 2006. It now includes letters of appointment and contracts for services, eg consultancy. The sanctions for breach of the provisions are the same as before, ie that the fixed term is not valid and that the contract is terminable by the company on reasonable notice.

Section 188 provides, inter alia, as follows:

> (1) This section applies to provision under which the guaranteed term of a director's employment—
>
>   (a) with the company of which he is a director, or
>   (b) where he is the director of a holding company, within the group consisting of that company and its subsidiaries,
>
>   is, or may be, longer than two years.
>
> (2) A company may not agree to such provision unless it has been approved—
>
>   (a) by resolution of the members of the company, and
>   (b) in the case of a director of a holding company, by resolution of the members of that company.

6.15.3 Inspection of service contracts

Copies of all directors' service contracts must be kept at the registered office where they are open to inspection by members (CA 2006, ss 228–229). The copies must be kept for one year after the contracts expire. Members may wish to check the service contract of any director they are proposing to dismiss to ascertain the likely cost of removing him in breach of contract.

6.16 Disqualification of directors by the court

The most far-reaching provisions on disqualification are those under the Company Directors Disqualification Act 1986 ('CDDA 1986'). The period of disqualification ranges from two years up to 15 years in some cases. The director's previous behaviour and seriousness of the current offence will be relevant in determining the length of disqualification.

The grounds for disqualification under the CDDA 1986 are:

(a) conviction of an indictable offence (s 2);

(b) persistent breaches of companies legislation (s 3);

(c) fraud in a winding up (s 4);

(d) on summary conviction for a filing or notice default (s 5);

(e) unfit director of insolvent companies (s 6) (see **6.14.1** for further details);

(f) disqualification after investigation (s 8);

(g) fraudulent or wrongful trading (s 10); and

(h) a breach of competition law (s 9A).

The factors to be taken into account in deciding unfitness under s 6 are in Sch 1 to the CDDA 1986. These include:

(a) any misfeasance on the part of the director;

(b) the extent of the director's responsibility for voidable transactions;

(c) the extent of the director's responsibility for failure to comply with Companies Act regulations;

(d) the extent of the director's responsibility for insolvency;

(e) the extent of the director's responsibility for failure to supply goods which have been paid for (in full or in part); and

(f)   the extent of responsibility for preferences, transactions at under values.

A director is expected to have a prudent businessman's sense of reality (*In the matter of Queens Moat Houses plc; sub nom Secretary of State for Trade and Industry v Bairstow* [2005] 1 BCLC 136). In *Bairstow*, the director was held not to have been dishonest but had failed to guard against the publication of seriously misleading financial information, and could not rely on his ignorance of accountancy. He was thus disqualified as a director by the court.

The primary aim is to protect the public from the future activities of such persons. In *Re Sevenoaks Stationers Ltd* [1990] 3 WLR 1165, the tariff for disqualification was suggested to be:

(a)   2–5 years for not particularly serious offences;

(b)   6–10 years for serious offences not meriting the top bracket; or

(c)   11–15 years for particularly serious cases.

In *Vintage Hallmark plc* [2006] EWHC 2761, two directors were disqualified for 15 years each. They had sought money from investors, even though the directors knew that the business had liabilities of £52 million but assets of £5 million.

In *Official Receiver v Stern (No 2)* [2002] 1 BCLC 119, Mr Stern was found to have made unauthorised drawings from the companies concerned, traded at risk of the creditors and paid off his own guarantee when the company was insolvent. The Court of Appeal confirmed his disqualification for 12 years.

A director was disqualified for 10 years where he had failed to keep accounting records, pay customers and had made false statements to the company's liquidator (*Secretary of State for Trade and Industry v Vandevivere* [2005] Lawtel AC0108520).

At the other end of the scale, a director who was held to have breached his fiduciary duties to the company and ignored statutory obligations concerning the filing of accounts and returns was disqualified for two years (*Secretary of State for Trade and Industry v Goldberg* [2003] EWHC 2843).

6.16.1   Unfit director of insolvent companies

Disqualifications under s 6 are the most common.

The basic question is whether there has been a breach of the 'common standard of commercial morality'. This could include:

(a)   failure to keep books and records;

(b)   failure to file returns;

(c)   paying excessive amounts of directors' remuneration;

(d)   recklessly trading whilst insolvent; or

(e)   purchasing stock before liquidation in the knowledge that it would be of no use to anyone but the present trade. The company then goes into liquidation and the directors repurchase the stock from the liquidator at a knock-down price.

Other negative points which may arise:

(a)   trading on 'Crown monies' is serious, that is not paying the VAT, PAYE, NIC to the Government and using the money as working capital; and

(b)   'reckless trading whilst insolvent', which does not mean that a wrongful trading action has to be established.

Positive points that would count in a director's favour are:

(a)   employing qualified financial staff;

(b)   taking professional advice;

(c)   regular budgets; and

(d)   a large personal financial commitment to the company.

In *In the matter of Uno plc & World of Leather plc; sub nom Secretary of State for Trade and Industry v Gill* [2004] EWHC 933, the directors had continued to trade and take customer deposits for the furniture which the company sold. However, the directors had tried to find a buyer for some of their shops. They had also taken legal and accountancy advice. They were not found to be unfit under s 6.

6.16.2 Effects of disqualification

When a disqualification order has been made against an individual, he may not without leave of the court:

(a)   be a director; or

(b)   be concerned in any way in the promotion, formation or management of a company.

Under s 13 of the CDDA 1986, contravention of a disqualification order is a criminal offence and is punishable by up to two years' imprisonment. By s 15, if someone is involved in management of a company in breach of a disqualification order, he also becomes personally liable for the relevant debts of the company.

It is possible for a disqualified director to apply for leave to act as a director during his period of disqualification (CDDA 1986, s 17).

In *In re Gibson Davies Ltd* [1995] BCC 11, Sir Mervyn Davies said:

> On an application under section 17 . . . the court must be satisfied that there is a need to make the order and, more importantly, that if the order is made the public will remain adequately protected.

In the case, *In the matter of China Worldwide Jazz,* Lawtel, 6 June 2003, the court granted leave to act. The basis was that the director had not been dishonest and that the business was a profitable one (and was therefore unlikely to go insolvent). Such permission is often qualified by requiring the presence on the board of someone professionally qualified, eg an accountant, to keep an eye on the errant director. There could also be a requirement to accept personal liability for debts of the company.

In *Re Amaron Ltd* [1997] 2 BCLC 115, Neuberger J did not allow the application. This was a case in which the applicant had allowed the company to trade while insolvent and to retain money owed to creditors in order to fund continued trading.

6.17 Disqualification under the articles

It is usual for the articles of a company to provide that in certain circumstances a person is disqualified from acting as a director. Article 18 of the model articles for private companies provides that a director shall automatically cease to hold office in a variety of situations, for example if he becomes bankrupt or if he is mentally ill.

It is an offence for an undischarged bankrupt to act as a director except with leave of the court (CDDA 1986, s 11).

6.18 Removal from office by members

6.18.1 Retirement by rotation

Only the model articles for public companies require directors to retire by rotation (art 21). At the first AGM of the company, all the directors are required to retire from office but will automatically be reappointed unless a resolution to the contrary is passed by the members. At each subsequent AGM, one-third of the total number of directors must retire from office and be subject to re-election (or a number as near to one-third as can be achieved). It is thus open to the members to remove a director from the board when his position as director is subject to confirmation in this way.

Executive directors, including the managing director, are not exempt from the requirement to retire by rotation.

The requirement that directors retire by rotation is an important safeguard to members, as it enables them periodically to consider removal of a director from office without the need to ensure that the matter is put on the agenda for a general meeting. However, in a company where the composition of the members and the directors is largely the same, this device is unnecessary, in which case the articles can be amended by a special article excluding the relevant provisions of the model articles.

6.18.2 Removal by ordinary resolution

Members always have the right to remove a director from office at any time, and this right cannot be taken from them by anything contained in the director's service contract or in the articles (CA 2006, s 168(1)).

Any member wanting to propose a resolution to remove a director must give the company 'special notice' (CA 2006, ss 168(2) and 312). He must leave a formal notice at the registered office at least 28 days before a general meeting, setting out his request. (If a director is to be appointed at the same meeting, special notice must be given of this appointment as well.)

If a general meeting has already been called for a fixed date, a member will know whether he has time before the meeting to give the required notice. However, if no date has been fixed for a general meeting, the member should give the notice to the company. Then, if the directors attempt to call a general meeting within the next 28 days, the member will be deemed to have given proper notice (CA 2006, s 312(4)). This provision prevents the directors from being able to defeat the members by calling a meeting within the 28-day period.

If the directors are unwilling to convene a general meeting themselves, the shareholders can do so if they have the requisite shareholding under ss 303–305 to call a general meeting. For a public company, the shareholders have a right to have a resolution put on to the agenda of the AGM (ss 338–340). See the case of *Pedley v Inland Waterways Association Ltd* [1977] 1 All ER 209, where the shareholder had only one share and so had no rights under ss 303–305 or 338–340 (though the case was decided under ss 368, 376 of the CA 1985).

Alternatively, the directors may try to frustrate the member's intentions by not calling a general meeting at all. Faced with this situation, a member could request a general meeting if he owns at least 10% of the shares in the company (see **5.5.9**). For a public company, provided he owns at least 5% of the shares in the company, he can use his right to have an item included on the agenda for an AGM to ensure that the resolution was put to the meeting (see **5.5.12**).

Whenever the company receives 'special notice' of a resolution to remove a director, the board must ensure that the director concerned is informed immediately. That director then has the right to make written representations to the members and can circulate a statement in writing to them. He can also speak at the meeting, whether or not he is also a member.

An ordinary resolution is required to remove a director from office in this way, so if a general meeting is called purely for this purpose, only 14 clear days' notice of the meeting is required from the company to the members. Only a majority of the votes cast at the meeting is needed to pass the resolution.

Before giving special notice to the company for the removal of a director, a member should check the articles to see whether or not they contain a *Bushell v Faith* clause, giving directors who are also members weighted voting rights on a resolution for their removal. Provided the director is also a member of the company, this could prevent the members from being able to remove the director from his position as director as long as his shareholding is sufficient to defeat an ordinary resolution when multiplied by the figure stated in the special article. A member wishing to remove a director should check whether it would be possible to remove the special article by passing a special resolution at a general meeting or whether directors have also been given weighted voting rights in this respect.

Even if there is no such special article, or if the multiplier is not sufficient to protect the director concerned, the member proposing the ordinary resolution should also check the director's service contract (open to inspection at the registered office) to check the amount of compensation which might be payable for breach of contract (wrongful dismissal). It could be extremely expensive for the company to get rid of him, particularly where the director concerned has been given a long fixed-term contract.

If a director is removed from the board, then he automatically loses any job he might hold within the company, because the two are inter-dependent. This may entitle the ex-director to make a claim against the company for wrongful dismissal, unfair dismissal, or even possibly redundancy. In *Cobley v Forward Technology Industries plc* [2003] EWCA Civ 646, the director in question had been removed from the board of directors and had his service contract terminated in accord with its terms. The Court of Appeal held that the termination of the service contract was for 'some other substantial reason' under s 98(1)(b) of the Employment Rights Act 1996, and therefore his dismissal was not an 'unfair dismissal' under the 1996 Act (see **33.2.10**).

The issue of employment rights only applies to a director who is employed by the company, ie an executive director. If the ex-director were a non-executive director, his duties would have been confined to attending the board meetings. He would have had no job within the company. Therefore, he could not have a claim for breach of any employment rights.

If a director is removed from the board, the officers of the company are under an obligation to notify the Registrar of Companies, and must delete that person's name from the register of directors.

6.18.3   Removal by power in the articles

Sometimes, there is a power given to directors in the articles to dismiss a fellow director by majority vote at a board meeting. The caveat to this is that they are acting bona fide in the best interests of the company.

6.18.4   Protecting a director from dismissal

There are various ways of protecting a director before things get to the stage of a motion to dismiss him. The possibilities include:

(a)   a *Bushell v Faith* clause (from *Bushell v Faith* [1970] AC 1099) to give him multiplied voting rights if a motion to dismiss him is put forward at a general meeting (plus a secondary clause giving multiplied rights on a motion to remove the *Bushell v Faith* clause itself), but note that it will now be harder to 'imbed' such rights under the CA 2006 than was the case previously (CA 2006, ss 22–24);

(b)   a fixed-term service contract of long duration and without a break clause, so that he would have to be paid the balance of his salary, more or less, if he were to be dismissed as a director;

(c)   a shareholders' agreement (see **3.9**) under which the parties to the agreement, who could include the director, agree not to vote against specified directors on a motion to dismiss any of those directors; or

(d)   a loan from the director to the company which is expressed to be repayable if the director loses his position, as this would act as a financial disincentive to dismiss him.

6.19 Corporate governance

This has been a popular 'sound bite' in the financial world for the last few years. In fact, it is used to mean good corporate governance. The issues arose because of the perception that directors in large listed public companies, especially the privatised utilities, were awarding themselves exorbitant salaries. Part of the problem has been the demise of the direct private investor in companies and in their place institutional shareholders, typically pension funds and insurance companies. The feeling was that there was no one interested in keeping an eye on the directors.

Various reports were produced on improving the situation, culminating in the Hampel Report. This suggested broad principles for good corporate governance, including that non-executive directors in public companies should play a monitoring role over the actions, and salaries, of the executive directors. These principles were incorporated in the Combined Code on corporate governance. This is available on the site of the Financial Reporting Council at http://www.frc.org.uk/corporate/combinedcode.cfm. The Code was updated in June 2006. Listed companies have to state in their annual accounts whether they abide by the terms of the Combined Code and to explain any discrepancies. See the reference to the Higgs Report at **6.3.3**.

The National Association of Pension Funds, which represents major investors in quoted companies, publishes a corporate guidance policy which is available at www.napf.co.uk/Policy/governance.cfm.

6.20 Summaries and checklists

6.20.1 Appointment

First directors	statement of proposed officers
Subsequently	by board, or
	by members – ordinary resolution
	– 14 clear days' notice (or consent to short notice)
	inform Registrar
	register of directors and register of directors' addresses
Alternate directors	notify company (restrictions on choice).

6.20.2 Board meetings

(a)   Called on reasonable notice by any director.

(b)   Must be quorate.

(c)   Check whether any director has a personal interest – must declare it and may be prevented from voting and counting in the quorum.

(d)   Resolutions passed by simple majority.

(e)   Can use written resolutions instead.

6.20.3 Service contracts

(a)   Board decision but granting a contract over two years' duration needs prior consent of members by ordinary resolution.

(b)   Contract kept at registered office if more than 12 months left to run.

6.20.4 Disqualification

(a)   Under Company Directors Disqualification Act 1986.

(b)   Under the articles.

6.20.5 Dismissal – procedure

(a)   Special notice to the company 28 days prior to general meeting (if already called).

(b)   Board informs director forthwith.

(c)   Director entitled to circulate written representations to members.

(d)   (If not already called, board calls general meeting to pass ordinary resolution. Special notice not invalidated if called within 28 days.)

(e)   Director entitled to speak at general meeting.

(f)   File form with Registrar and complete register of directors.

(g)   *Note*: Written resolution cannot be used.

6.20.6 Possible claims available to dismissed director

(a)   Statutory employment claims – unfair dismissal, redundancy payment.

(b)   Wrongful dismissal (for breach of contract).

(c)   Unfairly prejudicial conduct if also a member (s 994).

Chapter 7

The Company Secretary

7.1 Introduction

Although every public company must have a company secretary, it is for the directors of that company to decide exactly what the secretary of their company should be required to do. The functions of a company secretary are not prescribed and can vary enormously, but will generally centre around the administration of the company. A private company is not obliged to have a company secretary, but in practice many will do so (CA 2006, s 270).

7.2 Appointment

A public company must have a company secretary (CA 2006, s 271). He is an officer of the company (CA 2006, s 1121). The first secretary of any company will be named on the statement of directors and officers with the first directors, but need not be a director as well. Like them, he automatically takes office when the certificate of incorporation is issued. Subsequently, if any change occurs, the new company secretary is appointed by the board of directors.

7.3 Terms and remuneration

The directors decide the contractual terms on which the company secretary is to hold office and they fix the amount of his remuneration.

7.4 Functions

The company secretary is in charge of the administrative side of running the company. His exact duties will depend upon the requirements of the directors. The duties are likely to be influenced by the size of the company and whether or not he works for the company full time. The full-time company secretary of a large company may be the head of an administration department. In a small company, he may well hold this post as an 'extra' on top of other full-time duties, such as a director. Alternatively, a professionally qualified person, such as a solicitor or accountant, may be the company secretary.

The duties commonly assigned to a company secretary are to write up the minutes of board meetings and general meetings, to keep up to date the company's internal registers and to send the necessary returns to the Registrar of Companies.

The company secretary also has apparent authority on behalf of the company to make contracts connected with the administrative side of the company's business, for example to order routine office supplies. He will usually also have actual authority to enter into contracts of this type and so bind the company. He has no apparent authority to enter into trading contracts on the company's behalf, for example to borrow money in the company's name.

7.5 Removal from office

The directors have power to remove the company secretary from office at any time. The consequences of such removal (eg whether any compensation is due for breach of contract) will depend upon the terms of the contract fixed by the directors at the time of his appointment.

7.6 Public companies

The company secretary of a public company has to be qualified as specified in CA 2006, s 273. This includes persons qualified as a solicitor, and certain other professions such as chartered accountants and chartered secretaries.

Chapter 8
The Auditor

8.1 Introduction

A company has a duty to keep records of its accounts under s 386 of the CA 2006. These accounts must give a 'true and fair view of the state of affairs of the company as at the end of the financial year' (CA 2006, s 395). A company must file with the Registrar of Companies its year-end accounts or, in the case of 'small' or 'medium-sized' companies, an abbreviated version of the year-end accounts (CA 2006, ss 444, 445). The time limit for filing accounts is nine months from the end of the accounting reference period for a private company, and six months therefrom for a public company (CA 2006, s 442). The form and content of company accounts is prescribed by ss 396–413, and is also governed by standards set by the accountancy profession and contained in Financial Reporting Standards (FRSs). There is a general duty to appoint auditors to review those accounts independently every year (CA 2006, ss 485, 489). These duties are to ensure that those who have put up the money for the business (the shareholders) are not defrauded or misled by those in charge of the company's finances, that is the directors.

The audit requirement is, however, relaxed for small private companies with a balance sheet of not more than £3.26 million and a turnover of not more than £6.5 million. Such a company is exempt from the statutory audit requirements (CA 2006, s 477).

To comply with the exemption the directors have to declare on the balance sheet, under s 475(3), that the directors acknowledge their responsibility to keep accounting records that comply with the CA 2006, and the shareholders have not exercised their right under s 476 to call for an audit.

However, shareholders holding not less than 10% of the issued share capital can require the company to have its accounts audited by lodging a written notice at the registered office during the financial year in question, but not more than one month before the end of the financial year (CA 2006, s 476).

8.1.1 Business review in the annual report

Section 417 of the CA 2006 preserves the need for companies to prepare a business review as part of their directors' report, equivalent to s 234 of the 1985 Act. However, the new provisions do clarify the situation somewhat. (See also **6.14.1**.)

Section 417(2) states:

> (2) The purpose of the business review is to inform members of the company and help them assess how the directors have performed their duty under section 172 (duty to promote the success of the company).

Section 417(5) states:

(5)   In the case of a quoted company the business review must, to the extent necessary for an understanding of the development, performance or position of the company's business, include—

(a)   the main trends and factors likely to affect the future development, performance and position of the company's business; and

(b)   information about—

(i)   environmental matters (including the impact of the company's business on the environment),

(ii)   the company's employees, and

(iii)   social and community issues,

including information about any policies of the company in relation to those matters and the effectiveness of those policies; and

(c)   subject to subsection (11), information about persons with whom the company has contractual or other arrangements which are essential to the business of the company.

If the review does not contain information of each kind mentioned in paragraphs (b)(i), (ii) and (iii) and (c), it must state which of those kinds of information it does not contain.

8.2   Appointment

If a company must have an auditor, it must appoint someone who is qualified (a certified or chartered accountant) and independent (not connected with anyone involved in the company) (ss 1212–1215). Usually a firm of accountants is appointed to be the company's auditor, which means that any qualified member of that firm at the date of the appointment can undertake the audit (see **8.4**).

The directors will appoint the first auditor. As private companies are no longer required to hold an AGM, there is no natural point at which to decide whether or not to reappoint the auditors. So, under s 485 of the CA 2006, an auditor's term of office will usually run from the end of a 28-day period after circulation of the accounts until the equivalent period in the following year. Under s 487, an auditor is deemed to be reappointed. A reappointment could be prevented by 5% of the members (s 488). A general meeting would still be required to dismiss an auditor before the end of his term of office (s 510).

8.3   Terms and remuneration

The terms on which the auditor holds office and his fee for doing so will be a matter for negotiation between him and the company. The directors approve the contract with the first auditor; in subsequent years the approval of members is necessary.

8.4   Functions

The main duty of the auditor is to report to the members on the annual company accounts. The auditor must check that proper accounting records have been kept and that the final accounts (profit and loss account and the balance sheet) accord with those records. The auditor is required to certify that the accounts give a true and fair view of the company's financial position (CA 2006, ss 394, 395). If the auditor qualifies his report in any way, he is warning the members that there may have been some unethical business dealings or even fraud.

Notice of all general meetings must be sent to the auditor, and he then has a right to attend and speak at any such meeting, although he does not have a right to vote (CA 2006, s 502).

8.5   Liability of auditors

The leading case on the liability of auditors is *Caparo v Dickman* [1990] 2 AC 605. The House of Lords held that auditors conducting an annual audit did not owe a duty of care either to the shareholders or to potential investors, ie potential shareholders. Foreseeability alone was not enough to impose such a duty; there would also have to be a proximity between the relevant parties. Otherwise, the auditors would have an unlimited duty of care. There can be liability in other circumstances, for example where auditors make a statement about the reliability of the accounts to purchasers of a company, eg *Peach Publishing Ltd v Slater & Co* [1996] BCC 751 and *Electra Private Equity Partners v KPMG Peat Marwick* [2001] 1 BCLC 589. In *Equitable Life v Ernst & Young* [2003] EWCA Civ 1114, the insurance company failed in its attempt to sue its auditors for their alleged failure to point out problems in the company's allocation of resources to deal with future liabilities.

Auditors can be sued if they fail to spot a fraud against the company. However, in *Moore Stephens v Rolls Ltd* [2008] EWCA Civ 644, it was the company itself, through its owner and director Mr S, which had been used to defraud several banks. The liquidator of the company claimed for these losses, for which the company had successfully been sued by the banks. It was held that the company was in effect a party to the fraud and could not claim against the auditors.

The whole issue of auditor liability was thrown up by the *Enron* financial scandal in the United States, which resulted in immense liability for the auditors in question, to the extent that that firm of auditors no longer exists. The Companies (Audit, Investigations and Community Enterprise) Act 2004 introduced into the CA 1985 stricter controls on audits and auditors, in order to lessen the chance of some of the abuses in the US *Enron* scandal occurring in the UK (see CA 2006, ss 1212–1215). There is also a proposal for an EC Directive on audit standards but this is at an early stage.

As a result of concern by auditors that their liability was unlimited, there are provisions in the CA 2006 to deal with this situation. Essentially, members of a company can agree to limit the liability of their auditors by passing an ordinary resolution (ss 532–538). However, no limitation could reduce the auditors' liability to less than an amount which would be fair and reasonable in all the circumstances. The agreement would also have to be disclosed in the annual accounts or directors' report. The agreement can only relate to acts or omissions in the course of the audit for one financial year.

There is a power in s 535 for the Government to make regulations about agreements limiting an auditor's liability.

There are two new criminal offences for auditors under s 507. These are knowingly or recklessly either including misleading material, or omitting required statements under the CA 2006.

8.6 Removal from office and resignation

The auditor can be removed from office at any time by the members (CA 2006, s 510). The procedure is exactly the same as that required for the removal of a director, ie an ordinary resolution of which special notice has been given by the proposing shareholder to the company is required under s 511 of the CA 2006 (see **6.16.2**). Members must hold a general meeting. A written resolution cannot be used to achieve this. The consequences of removal (eg whether compensation is payable) are dependent upon the terms of the contract between the company and the auditor (CA 2006, s 510(3)).

An auditor may resign from office by notice in writing sent to the registered office (CA 2006, s 516).

Under s 519 of the CA 2006, an auditor who ceases to hold office for any reason must deliver a statement to the company of the circumstances connected with the cessation. The statement must be filed with the Registrar of Companies. In certain circumstances, either the auditor or the company or both have an obligation to inform the appropriate audit authority, which is the Professional Oversight Board of the Financial Reporting Council (CA 2006, ss 522, 523).

Chapter 9

Electronic Communication by Companies

9.1 Electronic communication between the company and its members

Under the CA 1985, it was possible to communicate with the members by electronic means only if there was prior consent from the members in question. The CA 2006 has extended these provisions, in keeping with the increased use of such means of communication in the modern business world. For example, under ss 308 and 333, a company can now electronically both send to and receive from its members notices and other documents concerning general meetings.

9.1.1 Websites

The members may pass a resolution authorising the use of a company website for communication, or the articles may so provide. If either is the case, the individual members are required to opt out of using the website rather than to opt in (Sch 5, Pt 4, para 10).

Companies need to tell members when they post new members' documents on the website. There would therefore also need to be consent from the members for email communication, if that is to be used (s 309).

9.1.2 Email

Individual members need to give their consent to be contacted by email or other electronic means, rather than by post (Sch 5, Pt 3, para 6).

A member is still entitled to receive documents in hard copy, if he so requests within 21 days of receiving the electronic form (s 1145). This has to be provided free of charge.

Electronic communication from the member to the company is also allowed, subject to the company's consent (s 333, Sch 4).

9.2 Communication with Companies House

Much of the paperwork to form a company, or to inform Companies House of changes to the company, can be submitted electronically. For further information, see the Companies House website at http://www.companieshouse.gov.uk/toolsToHelp/fileInformation.shtml.

Chapter 10
Financing a Company I – Shares

10.1 Introduction

In this book, we only consider companies limited by shares, as this is the form of company used for a business. Thus, members of a company own shares in that company and will be given a share certificate as evidence of title. The value of shares is not constant. Depending on the company's performance, the capital value of shares may appreciate or depreciate, and they may or may not produce income in the form of a dividend.

10.2 Maintenance of share capital

The maintenance of share capital is one of the principles of company law. In *Aveling Barford v Perion Ltd* [1989] BCLC 626, Hoffman J said that:

> a company cannot, without the leave of the court or the adoption of a special procedure, return its capital to its shareholders. It follows that a transaction which amounts to an unauthorised return of capital is ultra vires and cannot be validated by shareholder ratification or approval.

Capital must generally be maintained, as it is the fund which the creditors look to for payment of their debts. In other words, paid up share capital must not be returned to its members, and their liability in respect of capital not paid up on shares must not be reduced.

The principle has the following consequences:

(a)   a company must not generally purchase its own shares (CA 2006, s 658);

(b)   a public company may not generally give financial assistance to anyone for the purposes of buying the company's shares;

(c)   dividends must not be paid out of capital (but only out of distributable profits);

(d)   if a public company suffers a serious loss of capital, a general meeting must be called to discuss the problem; and

(e)   a subsidiary may not be a member of its own holding company, and any allotment or transfer of shares in a holding company to its subsidiary is void.

After members have paid for their shares, the money produced constitutes the company's capital. Creditors will expect this fund to be available to meet the company's debts and, because the liability of the members of the company is limited, this capital sum should not be diminished. The impact of this on the members of the company is that, having bought their shares in the company, they cannot normally hand back their share certificate to the company in exchange for the consideration they originally provided. If they want to realise their investment, they must sell their shares to another investor. The company cannot generally reduce its share capital by exchanging members' shares for valuable consideration.

Like all principles, there are exceptions to it, so that a company can:

(a)   reduce its share capital with the consent of the court, or if a private company by passing a special resolution, under ss 641–648 of the CA 2006;

(b)   buy back (s 690) or redeem (ss 684–689) its own shares;

(c)   purchase its own shares under a court order made under s 994 to buy out an unfairly prejudiced minority, or under ss 98–99 to buy out a minority on the conversion of a public company to a private company; or

(d)   return capital to members, after payment of the company's debts, in a winding up.

For the record, the principle of maintenance of capital also applies to the sums received when:

(a)   redeemable shares are redeemed by the company (the money being paid in to the capital redemption reserve); or

(b)   shares are issued at a premium (the money being paid in to the share premium account).

10.3   Issuing shares

Shares can be issued by the directors provided the company has sufficient unissued nominal capital and the directors have authority to do so.

It should be noted that the two words 'allotting' and 'issuing' are often used interchangeably. It seems that the conventional view is that shares are allotted to someone (ie 'allocated') and are then issued by the company. It was suggested in the DTI report on the Blue Arrow affair that 'issued' should mean when an entry is made on the register of members. For an account of the Blue Arrow affair, see *re Blue Arrow* [1987] BCLC 585.

10.3.1   Share capital

Under the CA 2006, the concept of authorised (nominal) share capital was abolished from 1 October 2009. So, there is no 'ceiling' which needs to be raised before new shares can be created. The issue of shares would still have to be approved though (see **10.3.2**).

For many private companies, the initial capital is £100. Once all the initial capital has been issued, the company can only raise additional finance by issuing more shares.

For a public company, the minimum share capital is £50,000, of which 25% must be paid up (CA 2006, s 763). However, subject to those requirements, the remaining capital could be in a variety of currencies (*Re Scandinavian Bank Group* [1987] 2 WLR 752).

10.3.2   Directors' power to issue shares

The board will usually want to allot shares in the company at the first board meeting of a new company, and may subsequently wish to issue more shares to raise additional finance. The directors can issue shares in the company only if they have authority to do so. This authority must be given specifically, either in the articles (by a special article) or by ordinary resolution of the members in a general meeting (ss 549–551). Where a new company is formed, it is useful if the authority is contained in a special article so that the matter does not have to be considered at a general meeting or by written resolutions. If an ordinary resolution is required, this is one of the exceptional ordinary resolutions which must be filed with the Registrar (s 551(9)).

However the necessary authority is given, it must state the number of shares which the directors are authorised to allot. Authority can be given for the directors to allot just one batch of shares, or it can be given generally, allowing them to issue any number of shares up to the amount of the nominal capital. It must also give the period of time for which the authority is to last, which cannot normally be longer than five years, although it can be renewed at any time for a period not greater than five years (s 551(3)). In order to ensure that the authority does not expire by oversight, a company should have renewal of the authority as a standing item on the agenda for the AGM, if indeed it holds AGMs. The directors' power to allot shares can be revoked by the members at any time by the passing of an ordinary resolution.

Unusually, an ordinary resolution is even sufficient to remove this authority if the authority was originally given by the articles (which normally require a special resolution for any amendment). Any such ordinary resolution is one of the exceptional ordinary resolutions which must be filed with the Registrar (s 551(9)).

Under the CA 2006, a private company does not need to have authority to allot its shares, provided the company has only one class of shares (s 550).

Under s 555, a return of allotments must be filed with Companies House within one month, as must a modified statement of capital (s 555(3)). This ensures that the public record always gives an up-to-date view of the company's capital. The requirement to file a new statement of capital applies following all alterations of capital.

10.3.3 Statutory pre-emption rights

Even where directors have the authority to issue shares, they cannot necessarily allot them to whomsoever they may choose. Sections 561 and 565 provide that where shares are being issued in exchange for cash (and only for cash, not for anything else), those shares must first be offered to the existing members of the company. The number that each current member is offered is dependent upon the percentage of the shares he currently holds. The offer to the existing members must remain open for at least 21 days, and only if the present members decline to take up the shares can they be offered elsewhere. Where shares are issued wholly or partly for non-cash consideration, s 561 has no application. It is relevant only where the shares are to be paid for in cash.

Pre-emption rights apply to both private and public companies, but private companies can exclude them in various ways. A private company can remove the statutory pre-emption rights either by a special article (CA 2006, s 567), or by a special resolution of the members (s 571). With notice of the general meeting called to pass such a special resolution, directors must send to all members a written statement setting out their reasons for proposing the special resolution, the consideration which the company is to receive and their justification of this amount. The pre-emption rights can be dispensed with either generally or for just one particular issue of shares.

If the directors do not wish to allot new shares to the existing members in accordance with their current shareholdings, they should first check the articles to see whether the statutory pre-emption rights have been removed. If not removed by the articles, a special resolution is necessary to dispense formally with the need to offer the shares to the present members. However, it is possible for all the members to decline to take up the shares they are offered, if this is thought to be quicker and simpler than holding a general meeting. The danger in relying on this procedure is that there is no guarantee that all members will refuse the offer. The directors may feel that a more formal removal of the right to be offered the shares is preferable. An issue of shares in accordance with the pre-emption rights is known as a 'rights issue'.

A private company with only one class of shares can give the directors power either in the articles or by special resolution to ignore the pre-emption provisions in s 561, or to modify them as they think appropriate (s 569).

Under the CA 2006, s 565, an exception to the existence of pre-emption rights is if the shares in question are to be wholly or partly paid for by *non-cash* consideration. In such a case, there would be no need to have a resolution to disapply, as there would not be any pre-emption rights in the first place.

Under ss 570–573, the directors are given powers to allot new shares according to the pre-emption provisions in the articles, or by special resolution, as if the statutory pre-emption rights under s 561 did not apply or applied in modified form. The condition is that the directors have already been given a general power to allot shares under s 551 (otherwise they would not have power to allot any shares to anyone).

10.3.4 Procedure

The procedure which must be followed in order to allot shares in the company is as follows:

(a)   A board meeting must be called by any director on reasonable notice.

(b)   Directors must check:

   (i)   whether they have authority to allot the shares; and

   (ii)   whether they are obliged to offer the shares to current members first.

   If there is any problem with either of these issues, the directors will need to call a general meeting or propose written resolutions for the members to agree. Fourteen clear days' notice is sufficient. Notice in writing must be sent to all members. The general meeting will then be held and the resolutions passed. Copies of all resolutions will be sent to the Registrar of Companies, along with a new statement of capital.

(c)   If there is no problem with either of the above matters, or if any problem has been resolved by the passing of a members' resolution, then the directors can issue the shares at a board meeting. They will resolve to issue the shares to those persons who have made written application for them. Private companies are not in general permitted to offer their shares to members of the public (see **10.7**). Therefore, it is necessary that the offer to buy comes from the prospective member and that that offer is accepted by the company.

(d)   If the company has a seal, the directors will resolve to seal the share certificate, which will be sent to the new member, and will instruct the secretary to enter the name of the new member on the register of members. They will also instruct the secretary to notify the Registrar that new shares have been issued.

10.3.5 Payment for shares

A prospective member must normally pay for his shares in cash. He can provide non-cash consideration only if the company, ie the board, agrees. If consideration in kind is acceptable to the directors, they must send a return to the Registrar, and must also send a statement of capital (ss 555–557).

10.3.6 Partly paid shares

When the directors of a company decide to issue shares, they will expect the prospective new shareholder to pay for those shares. For example, if a prospective new member offers to buy 100 £1 shares at £1 each, the directors will expect him to pay the company £100 (or they may agree to accept assets worth £100 in payment for the shares). Throughout this book, it has been assumed that company shares are fully paid shares. However, the directors may agree to issue shares partly paid, which means that although the full price of the shares must be paid eventually, it does not have to be paid immediately. For example, the directors could issue 100 £1 shares on the basis that 50p per share was payable on issue and the remaining 50p per share was payable six months later.

10.3.7 Issue at a premium

The nominal value of each share, as stated in the memorandum of the company, is also known as the par value. Depending on their market value, the shares may be issued for a price greater than their nominal value. If this happens the excess amount of consideration paid above the nominal value of the shares must be recorded in a separate share premium account (s 610). It is treated as share capital, and thus subject to the requirement that this fund must be maintained.

Section 610 of the CA 2006 specifies the permitted uses for the share premium account. For example, paying up bonus shares will still be permitted. However, some existing uses will not be allowed in future (eg to pay off expenses incurred in the company's formation).

10.3.8 Issue at a discount

Shares may not be issued for less than their nominal value (s 580). If this happens the shareholder is obliged to pay the amount of discount to the company with interest (s 588).

10.3.9 Redenomination of share capital (CA 2006, ss 622–628)

A company is able to redenominate its shares into a different currency by passing an ordinary resolution. If the exchange rate between the currencies produces an unacceptable value per share then the company's share capital can be reduced by up to 10% by the passing of a special resolution. The amount of the reduction is transferred to a 'redenomination reserve', to be used for paying bonus shares. Alternatively, it will be possible to increase the new value of the shares by using distributable reserves for that purpose.

10.4 Financial assistance by a public company for the purchase of shares

If someone wants to buy shares in the company but cannot afford to do so without a loan, that person may ask the company itself to lend him the necessary money. Alternatively, he may ask a financial institution such as a bank to do so and the bank may then ask the company to guarantee the loan. The general rule is that a public company cannot give a prospective or an actual member any financial assistance to enable him to purchase shares in the company (s 678). Section 678(1) deals with financial assistance given before, or at the time of, the acquisition, whereas s 678(3) deals with financial assistance given after the event.

Financial assistance means a gift, loan, indemnity, guarantee, assignment or other transaction by which the acquirer is directly or indirectly put in funds (s 677). Any other transaction may amount to assistance if it materially reduces the company's assets, for example the payment by the target company of the legal fees of a bidder company on a takeover. In *Chaston v SWP Group plc* [2003] All ER (D) 179, the Court of Appeal held that payment by a target company of the fees of accountants retained by the purchaser to produce a report amounted to unlawful financial assistance. In *Harlow v Loveday* [2004] EWHC 1261, a loan given to purchase shares was held to be financial assistance. In *Dyment v Boyden and Others* [2004] EWCA Civ 1586, the Court of Appeal was asked to consider both s 151(1) and s 151(2) of the 1985 Act (now CA 2006, s 678(1) and (3)). It held that the claimant failed to show that any financial assistance was given by the company before or at the same time as the acquisition of B's shares, as required under s 151(1) (now s 678(1)). The judge at first instance had therefore not erred in dismissing that claim. On the second aspect of the case, the company's entry into the lease in question was 'in connection with' the acquisition by the claimant of B's shares. However, it was not 'for the purpose of' that acquisition, so did not fall within s 151(2) (now s 678(3)).

Section 678(2) exempts from s 678(1) two categories of transactions, that is those where the principal purpose was not the giving of financial assistance, or where it was incidental to some larger purpose. However, these provisions are vague and difficult to rely on (see *Brady v Brady* [1989] AC 755). In that case, a bona fide arrangement to split a family company into two new businesses was held by the House of Lords not to be saved by what is now s 678(2). The deal in question was to split a family company's assets between two new companies, so that the brothers who ran the family businesses could go their separate ways. Although the arrangement involved the existing company giving financial assistance, it was held at first instance to be incidental to the larger purpose of the rearrangement and to fall within (now) s 678(2)(b). The House of Lords disagreed and thus severely restricted the use of this provision. There are also specific common-sense exceptions to s 678 in ss 681 and 682, such as the payment of a dividend to shareholders.

The most important exception is for private companies, which are expressly excepted from the provisions on giving financial assistance (s 682(1)).

The provision of financial assistance by the company can be useful where a new member wishes to join the company and the current members and directors are keen that he should do so. It is also useful where one member wishes to leave the company and the other members want to buy him out rather than have someone new involved in the business. However, if the person seeking financial help from the company is also a director of the company, an additional restriction applies as loans to directors are generally prohibited (see **6.8.4**).

More recent cases on financial assistance tend to consider in detail the commercial context of the transaction in order to decide whether or not it is financial assistance 'for the purposes of acquiring shares'. This is not very helpful to the lawyer trying to advise a client, as general lessons often cannot be drawn from a particular decision. In *MT Realisations Ltd (in liquidation) v Digital Equipment Co Ltd* [2003] EWCA Civ 494, the comment was made that:

> the authorities provide useful illustrations of the variety of fact situations in which the issue can arise, but it is rare to find an authority on s 151 [on financial assistance] which requires a particular result to be reached on different facts.

In *MT Realisations* the Court of Appeal held that the matters in question did not amount to financial assistance. The facts concerned inter-company loans which were payable on demand and secured by fixed and floating charges. There was therefore no option but to repay the loans, or allow the creditor to enforce their security. This meant that there was no 'assistance', as the company had no choice.

Some examples of the problems of the pervasive nature of financial assistance are as follows. In these scenarios, P plc is proposing to buy the shares of S plc from V plc, the parent company of S plc. Will s 678(1) and (3) prohibit the following?

Examples

(a)   S agrees to lend P £3m so that the deal can go ahead. When P has taken over, P can repay the money to V from the profits it makes from S's business.

  This is direct financial assistance and therefore caught. Section 677(1)(c)(i) covers loans.

(b)   P borrows the £3 million from Global Bank. It plans to repay the money to Global Bank from the profits it expects to make from S's business after the takeover.

  This is legal and general.

(c)   P wants to borrow £3m from Global Bank. S guarantees the loan so that the deal can proceed. The deal goes ahead, P makes money from the deal, the loan to Global Bank is paid off, and the guarantee is not called upon. It has not cost S anything.

  This is caught. Section 677(1)(b)(i) includes security for a loan. The purpose of the loan is to provide financial assistance.

(d)   In order to get the deal done, S agrees with P not to charge P for the warehouse which S owns. This brings the price down to a level that P can afford without borrowing money from Global Bank.

  This is financial assistance. It is a gift under s 677(1)(a), or a loan under s 677(1)(c)(i), or 'any other financial assistance which results in a reduction of net assets'.

> (e) P owes S £1m. S waives the debt, and P can go ahead with the purchase of S.
> Waiving the debt would seem to be a gift under s 677(1)(a), hence it is financial assistance.
>
> (f) P wants to borrow £3m from Global Bank. S lets Global Bank look at its up-to-date accounts, not just the published ones. Global Bank is happy with the accounts and agrees to lend £3m to P.
> This is assistance, but it is not financial assistance and therefore not caught by ss 677 and 678.

10.5 Buy-back of shares by the company

Generally, a company is forbidden to take back its shares because the share capital, once raised, must be maintained in the interests of fairness to creditors. However, a company can buy back its own shares from its members (CA 2006, s 690) provided various conditions are satisfied. The main requirement is that the articles of the company must not forbid this. The members must authorise the purchase by special resolution (s 694).

The ability of the company to buy back its own shares can be useful in a variety of situations. Examples are when:

(a) the majority of shareholders want to buy out a dissenting member;

(b) a member wants to leave;

(c) a shareholder dies and the other members do not want to increase their own shareholdings or to take in a new member;

(d) redeeming redeemable shares (see **10.6.4**);

(e) a company which is quoted on the Stock Exchange believes that its share price is too low and if it reduces the number of shares then the quoted share price will improve; and

(f) a company has accumulated more capital than it needs and would like to return some of it to its shareholders.

An example of share buy-back was provided by BP plc, which announced on 29 March 2004 that it would buy back £2.76 billion of its own shares in 2004. This was part of a buy-back programme that was set to take three years.

Note that there is a distinction between a buy-back of shares on a stock market, and one done outside that framework – so-called 'market' and 'off market' purchases, as defined in s 693(2). Here, we deal only with 'off market' purchases. Section 701 deals with 'market' purchases.

With either route, the contract, or a summary of it, must be available for inspection for 10 years after purchase of the shares, at the company's registered office or another notified location (s 1136). If the company is a private company, any member of the company may inspect the contract; if it is a public company, any person may inspect it.

The company can buy its own shares only if it has the funds available to do so. It can use money produced by profits, in which case reserves of profit are allocated to a capital redemption reserve to replace shares bought back; or the company can use the proceeds of a fresh issue of shares, the fresh issue being used to replace the shares bought back.

As a last resort, a *private* company can use some of its capital (s 709), but various additional conditions must be satisfied in order for the company to be able to use its capital in this way (s 713). Under the CA 1985, a company which wished to reduce its capital needed to seek the approval of the court. Under the CA 2006, this is deregulated for private companies. The main requirements are that the articles of the company must not prohibit the use of capital. Various people, including creditors of the company, must be officially notified that this is happening (s 719). The auditor must report to the directors that the permissible capital payment is in order and that he does not know of anything that would make the statutory declaration unreasonable (s 714(6)). The directors must make a statutory declaration of solvency, stating that the company is solvent and will remain so for the next 12 months (s 714). The directors should not make such a declaration without careful thought, because if the company is wound up within one year of their declaration and proves to be insolvent, then both the seller of the shares and the directors of the company may be required to contribute to the financial deficiency of the company (IA 1986, s 76). In addition, directors face criminal sanctions for making such a declaration without having reasonable grounds (s 715). If shares are to be bought back from capital, a second special resolution must be passed, specifically authorising the use of capital in this way, in addition to the one simply authorising the buy-back of shares (s 717). The statutory declaration by the directors must be made no sooner than one week before the general meeting. The payment out of capital must be made between five and seven weeks after the general meeting (s 723).

Any member of the company who did not vote in favour of the special resolution to fund the purchase out of capital can apply to the court within five weeks of the general meeting (or written resolution) to cancel the resolution (s 721). The court has wide powers. However, it does not seem to be the appropriate route for an 'unfair prejudice' action, which should instead be brought under s 994.

If shares are bought back by the company, a return must be sent to the Registrar of Companies stating the number of shares involved and their nominal value (s 707). The register of members must be altered to reflect the change. If the shares are cancelled, the company must send a notice of cancellation to the Registrar along with a statement of capital (s 708). In the case of a listed company, the shares could be kept as treasury shares rather than being cancelled (see **10.5.1**).

The effects of a buy-back are, after the shares are cancelled:

(a)   the company does not become the holder of its own shares;

(b)   the issued share capital of the company is decreased;

(c)   voting control between the members may have been altered;

(d)   a capital redemption reserve will need to be created, or increased if one already exists; and

(e)   the share premium account is reduced, if a premium paid on buy-back or redemption has been financed out of a fresh issue of shares.

Under the CA 2006, companies can alter their share capital in various other ways. There is a comprehensive list of the permitted methods under s 617 of the Act.

Share capital can be redenominated from one currency to another without a court order (CA 2006, s 542(3)).

If the reduction is made to create a distribution to members, this can only be in those instances which are to be laid down in regulations made under s 654 of the 2006 Act.

10.5.1 Treasury shares

Normally when a company buys back its shares, it has to cancel them. However, listed companies (and some others) which buy back shares out of distributable profits can now hold them 'in treasury' (ss 724–732). This means that a company can resell such shares without the complications of issuing new shares. A company can hold up to 10% of any relevant shares in treasury. These shares are shown on the register as being owned by the company. The shares are still part of the share capital of the company.

10.5.2   Reduction of share capital

There is a statutory procedure by which a company limited by shares can reduce its capital (CA 2006, ss 641–657). This is a much rarer procedure than a buy-back of shares (see **10.5**). A reduction of capital may be undertaken if the company wishes to:

(a)   cancel further liability on partly paid shares;

(b)   actually pay back to members capital which is not needed (eg preference shares which are often seen as being equivalent to a loan to the company); or

(c)   reduce the value of the company's share capital to reflect capital losses.

The first two methods reduce the amount of capital available to pay creditors. The third simply recognises a capital loss which has already been made and therefore does not prejudice creditors.

The procedure under the CA 1985 largely restated by the CA 2006. It involves the shareholders passing a special resolution, an application to the court and the approval by the court of the scheme, including the protection given to creditors. It can be used by both public and private companies. As part of the deregulatory aspects of the CA 2006, there is a simple procedure where a *private* company limited by shares can reduce its capital by an out-of-court route (CA 2006, ss 642–644). This involves all the directors swearing a statement of the company's solvency at the time and for the next 12 months, and the shareholders then passing a special resolution on the matter. The resolution, solvency statement and some other documents must then be filed at Companies House (CA 2006, s 644).

10.6   Classes of shares

A company may decide to create different classes of shares. Usually some shares will be described as ordinary shares, but there may be more than one class of ordinary shares within the company. For example, two different classes of ordinary shares may carry different voting rights.

In any one company, the rights attached to a share are dependent on the articles of that company. If no separate rights attach to a particular class of shares, the common law rule is that all shares are to rank equally (*Birch v Cropper* [1889] 14 App Cas 525, HL, *Scottish Insurance Corp Ltd v Wilsons & Clyde Coal Co Ltd* [1949] AC 462).

Types of shares can include those discussed in **10.6.1** to **10.6.4** below.

10.6.1   Ordinary shares

These carry the primary voting rights of the company, right to a dividend if declared, and rights to participate in a surplus in a winding up.

If no differences between shares are expressed, it is assumed that all shares have the same rights. If, for example, the statement of capital states that the capital of the company is to be £100 divided into 100 shares of £1 each, the shares all have the same, unrestricted rights. It is unnecessary to classify them as *ordinary shares* since there are no others. But there is no objection to doing so.

A company may, at its option, attach special rights to different shares, for example as regards dividends, return of capital, voting (or less often the right to appoint a director).

A not uncommon example of classes of shares is ordinary shares with voting rights and ordinary shares without voting rights (often distinguished as 'A' ordinary shares).

10.6.2 Preference shares

A preference share is any share having priority over the ordinary shares. The priority could be in relation to capital or dividends or, usually, both. There are no other *implied* differences between preference and ordinary shares, though there are often express differences between them.

The preferential dividend may be cumulative, or it may be payable only out of the profits of each year. The dividend will generally be a fixed one, ie it is expressed as a fixed percentage of the par value of the share. It is not a right to compel the company to pay the dividend if it declines to do so. This issue is likely to arise if the company decides to transfer available profits or reserves or makes a provision in its accounts for a liability or loss instead of using the profits to pay the preference dividend.

Preference shares often exist in a company's structure for historical reasons. For example, they are often created in the financing of a management buy-out of a company, so that the institutions which provided the finance can have first bite at the profits of the company. In due course, those shares will be sold on to new investors. However, preference shares do not usually carry a vote.

In many ways, preference shares are an alternative to lending money to the company, ie debentures. Their attraction is that they have first bite at any profits of the company at a fixed rate, and that the dividend is usually paid quarterly. Preference shares are usually redeemable, so the investor can exchange the shares for cash at some stage in the future (see **10.6.4**).

There are four kinds of preference shares:

(a)   cumulative;

(b)   non-cumulative;

(c)   participating; and

(d)   convertible.

Cumulative means that the preference shareholder has to be paid any missed dividends as well as the current dividend, if the preference share dividend has not been paid on a preceding occasion. This ranks before payment of dividends to the ordinary shareholders.

Participating shareholders have a further right to participate in profits or assets, in addition to the fixed preference rights. For example, if the ordinary shareholders are paid a dividend above a specified amount, this could trigger a right to an additional payment to the preference shareholders.

Convertible preference shares can be exchanged for ordinary shares at a specified price and after a specified date.

The rights of a preference shareholder will turn on the articles of the company (or possibly on the terms of the issue, depending on the facts).

10.6.3 Non-voting shares

These are not common in private companies but can occur in public companies, eg to enable existing shareholders to retain control of the company by only allowing new investors to buy non-voting shares.

10.6.4 Redeemable shares

Section 684 allows a private company to issue redeemable shares, provided it is not forbidden to do so by its articles. If the company is a public company, it must be so authorised by its articles. In order to prevent a company being left with no share capital as a result of redemptions, s 684(4) forbids the issue of redeemable shares when the company has no issued non-redeemable shares. The articles must provide for the terms and manner of the redemption. Redeemable shares have to be redeemed from distributable profits. *Private* companies can redeem out of capital if so permitted by their articles (s 687) upon the passing of a special resolution and the directors making a declaration of solvency.

If the directors decided to issue redeemable shares they would need to ensure that a special article was included in the company's articles setting out details of the terms and conditions of issue. For example, shares may be redeemable at the option of the member, or the company, or either. If shares are redeemed, they are effectively cancelled (s 688). This reduces the issued share capital of the company. If the company redeems shares, it can repay the member concerned using money which has come from profits, from the proceeds of a fresh issue of shares or, if neither of those is possible, from capital, subject to certain safeguards being observed (which are the same requirements as those which are necessary when the company buys back its own shares (s 687) (see **10.5**)).

Redeemed shares are treated as being cancelled. A notice must be sent to the Registrar of Companies within one month of the shares being redeemed, along with an amended statement of capital (ss 688, 689).

Redeemable shares are sometimes used by venture capital investors to ensure a straightforward exit route from the company when they invest in it. They will want an easy exit route after three to five years, when they can extract their investment and gains, and go on to their next project.

The remainder of this book assumes only one class of shares within a company.

10.7 Offering shares

Offering shares for sale in a company has the potential for fraud. Thus, private companies are in general prohibited from offering their shares to the investing public (Financial Services Act 1986, s 143(3) and CA 2006, ss 755–760). A private company may not be listed on the Stock Exchange (Listing Rule 2, FSA Handbook).

Although the prohibition against offering shares to the public is maintained in the CA 2006, it is no longer a criminal offence (s 755). The court can order re-registration as a public company, or can make a remedial order which could include repurchase of the shares by the company.

However, ss 755–760 of the CA 2006 allow a private company to offer securities to the public as part of the process of re-registering as a public company.

Public companies are controlled in their share-offering activities.

The most common way for companies to raise finance from the public is to issue shares to the public (or debentures but that is debt finance). A company which wishes to do this has to issue a document giving details about itself – a prospectus.

In practice, a company which wishes to have its shares listed on the Stock Exchange has to comply with the Listing Rules, controlled by the Financial Services Authority which is the UK Listing Authority ('UKLA'). The Listing Rules were extensively overhauled in 2006 to comply with the Market Abuse Directive 2003/6/EC ([2003] OJ L96/16) and the Prospectus Directive 2003/71/EC ([2003] OJ L345/64). The revised Rules also set out when a prospectus is required, and specify its content. The Rules now include six overarching Listing Principles which are designed to ensure adherence to the principles as well as to the letter of the Listing Rules.

10.8 Dividends

Initially, it is the directors who must decide whether or not to pay a dividend to members. They are only permitted to recommend the payment of a dividend (an income payment on shares) if there are 'profits available' (CA 2006, s 830). To ascertain whether there are profits available, the directors must deduct from all the realised profits of the company to date all the realised losses to date. If there is any profit left after doing this, that money is available to pay a dividend. The directors can find this information by looking at the latest set of audited accounts. This means that even if the company has not made a profit this year, it may still be able to pay a dividend if the profits from previous years are sufficient.

If a dividend is paid when there are insufficient profits available for the purpose, the directors who authorised the payment are jointly and severally liable to the company for the full amount. Any member who has received the dividend must refund it to the company if he knows or has reasonable grounds for believing that the payment is unauthorised.

Directors of a public company who authorise the payment of dividends otherwise than out of distributable profits may be personally liable to repay those dividends to the company whether or not they themselves were members (*Bairstow v Queens Moat Houses plc* [2000] 1 BCLC 549).

If funds are available and the directors decide that a dividend should be paid, they suggest the amount of dividend which they think appropriate and propose this to the members in a general meeting. It is the members who actually declare the dividend. They can vote to pay themselves the same amount as the directors have recommended or less, but they cannot decide to declare a larger dividend than the directors have suggested (model articles for private companies, art 30(2)). The form of the dividend is usually that shareholders receive, for example, 5p in the £, which means that for every £1 share they hold they receive 5p.

10.9   Transfer of shares

Shares are transferred if the member who owns them, sells them or gives them to another person.

10.9.1   Procedure for transfer

The seller or donor of the shares ('the transferor') should complete and sign a stock transfer form, which he should then give to the buyer or recipient ('the transferee') (CA 2006, s 770–772). There is no need for the transferee to sign the stock transfer form (unless the shares are partly paid). There is no need for the signature of the transferor to be witnessed. The transferor should also hand the share certificate to the transferee.

If the shares are being sold, the buyer must pay stamp duty (currently charged at 0.5% rounded up to the nearest £5) on the stock transfer form. If the shares are a gift, no stamp duty is payable. The minimum stamp duty is £5.

The transferee should then send the share certificate and stock transfer form to the company.

The company should send the new member a new share certificate in his name within two months, and should also ensure that his name is entered on the register of members (CA 2006, s 771).

The change in the composition of the membership of the company is notified to the Registrar of Companies on the annual return.

10.9.2   Restrictions on transfer

The ability of the members of a company to transfer their shares to whomsoever they choose will be governed by the articles of the company. Under the model articles for private companies, art 26, directors have an absolute discretion in this matter and may refuse to place a name on the register of members. Alternatively, members may be permitted to transfer their shares without restriction only to other members of the company or to members of their own family. A further alternative is that members may be allowed to consider transferring their shares to people who are not already members of the company only if they first offer those shares to the other shareholders at a fair value, and those shareholders reject this offer. The directors should have an absolute discretion to refuse registration of such a transfer even so.

Unless they are given power under the articles, the directors cannot refuse to place a new member's name on the register of members. If they wrongly refuse to do so, their decision can be challenged by an application to the court for an order for rectification of the register (s 125). If directors are given some discretion in this matter, they must make a decision within a reasonable time, which will be not more than the two-month period within which they are obliged to deliver the new share certificate. If directors exercise their discretion and refuse to register a new member, the court generally will not interfere with that decision unless the transferee can show that the directors did not act in good faith. If the directors properly exercise their power to refuse to register the name of the transferee, the transferee has no claim for damages or for rescission of the contract. The transferor remains the legal owner of the shares, his name continues to appear on the register of members, and he holds the shares on trust for the transferee (see **5.2.2**). In any event, there is a longstop time limit of 10 years, after which claims cannot be made (s 128).

10.10 Transmission of shares

Transmission is the automatic process whereby, when a shareholder dies, his shares immediately pass to his personal representatives (PRs) or, if a member is declared bankrupt, his shares automatically vest in his trustee in bankruptcy.

When this happens, the PRs or trustee are entitled to any dividend declared on the shares, but they cannot exercise the votes which attach to the shares as they are not members of the company (model articles for private companies, art 27).

The PRs of a deceased shareholder must produce to the company the grant of representation to establish their right to deal with the shares as PRs of the estate, but they then have a choice:

(a)   They can elect to be registered as members themselves. In such a case, the entry on the register of members does not show that they hold the shares in a representative capacity. This choice is subject to the articles of the company which may give the directors a discretion to refuse to place any name on the register of members. The directors cannot prevent the PRs from acquiring the shares by transmission in their capacity as PRs, but they can prevent their being registered as members if the articles give them the power to refuse registration. If the PRs are registered as members of the company, they can then transfer the shares in the usual way (see **10.9.1**), either passing them to the beneficiary under the deceased member's will or selling them to a third party for the benefit of the deceased member's estate.

(b)   They can transfer the shares directly to the ultimate beneficiary or to a third party in their representative capacity. There is no need for them to be registered as shareholders in order to do this. This choice is also subject to the articles of the company.

A trustee in bankruptcy has the same choice, ie he can elect to be registered as a member and then sell the shares, or he can sell them directly in his representative capacity. He must produce the court order concerning his appointment in order to establish his right to deal with the shares.

10.11 Serious loss of capital

Under s 656 of the CA 2006, the directors of a *public* company are obliged to call an EGM within 28 days from the earliest date on which any director knew that the company had suffered a serious loss of capital. The EGM date must be fixed for not more than 56 days ahead. A serious loss of capital is where the net assets are worth less than half the called-up share capital.

10.12   Other ways of selling shares

The following methods will apply to substantial companies, including those that are quoted on the Stock Exchange. They are unlikely to apply to small family companies.

10.12.1   A placing

Here, new shares are created. The company's broker will sell them direct to a range of investors, usually at a slight discount on the market price.

10.12.2   Placing and open offer

This mechanism preserves the basic principle of pre-emption rights, but does so indirectly. Thus, the new shares are created and sold to financial institutions, usually at a small discount. However, the existing shareholders have the right to take up the new shares at the same price, referred to as a 'claw back' feature. So, only those new shares that the existing shareholders do not want will end up with the financial institutions.

10.12.3   The bought deal

The company invites bids for all the new shares from a number of financial institutions. The successful bidder is the one offering the highest price for the shares. It pays cash for the shares and then sells them on at a profit to investors. These deals are potentially high profit ones for the institution but they are also high risk, as the value of the shares could fall after they have bought them but before they have sold on the shares. An example of these problems occurred in 1999 when the merchant bank Kleinwort Benson paid £138 million to Burmah Castrol for its 29% stake in Premier Consolidated Oilfields. The price fell sharply immediately after the bank had bought the shares and it lost £34 million on the deal.

10.12.4   A vendor placing

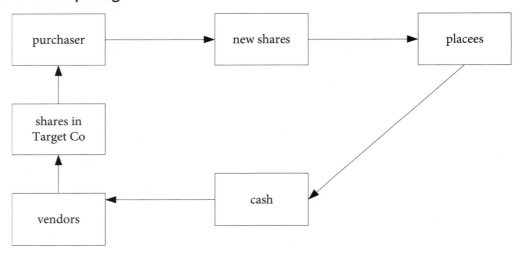

This is where a purchaser is able to buy 'Target Co' (ie buy the share capital of Target Co) without paying cash. The mechanism is that the purchaser issues new shares in itself and uses these to raise money to fund the acquisition.

The results are:

(a)   the vendor receives cash and gives Target Co shares to the purchaser;

(b)   the purchaser receives the Target Co shares and gives its own newly issued shares to the placees; and

(c)   the placees have bought shares in the purchaser for cash.

10.13 Summaries and checklists

10.13.1 Procedure for transfer of shares

(a)   Give share certificate and transfer form to transferee.

(b)   Buyer pays stamp duty (no stamp duty on a gift).

(c)   Apply to company for registration.

(d)   Board considers whether to refuse registration (if the articles give them this power).

(e)   Board resolves to seal new share certificate (if company has seal).

(f)   Update register of members.

10.13.2 Procedure on death/bankruptcy of shareholder

(a)   Shares pass automatically by transmission to PR/trustee.

(b)   PR/trustee in bankruptcy can either:

    (i)   have himself entered on the register; or

    (ii)   transfer shares to some other person.

Note: Both of these are subject to any restrictions on transfer which may be contained in the articles.

Chapter 11

Financing a Company II – Debt

11.1 Types of debt finance

A company can *borrow* from the banks or other lenders (*indirect* debt financing), or it can issue debt securities to investors (*direct* debt financing). The terminology is commercial rather than legal. In both cases it is a loan to the company, either from a bank or from an investor. All loans have to be repaid sooner or later.

With direct debt financing, short-term debt securities are referred to as 'commercial paper'. This offers an alternative to short-term borrowing from a bank. It is really just a type of unsecured short-term IOU with a life, usually, of three months. Long-term securities are called 'bonds'. In the case of both commercial paper and bonds, if they are secured they are usually called 'debentures', and if unsecured they are 'loan stock'. Debt securities (that is direct debt financing) can be issued at a discount, or a premium can be added on redemption, which in both cases can be paid for out of the share premium account (CA 2006, s 610). This is in total contrast with the issuing of shares, see **Chapter 10**.

A large company may raise money by issuing bonds and selling them in the specialised market for bonds. These are known as 'corporate bonds' to distinguish them from government bonds which are also sometimes referred to as 'gilts' or 'gilt-edged stocks'. These corporate bonds are 'bearer' securities of a given nominal value. In other words, they belong to whoever has possession of them at any one time, and they have a face value. The company promises to redeem the bond at a specified date in the future. In effect, the bonds can be thought of as a type of currency. It is really only large companies which are quoted on the Stock Exchange that have a market for direct debt financing. We will not consider debt securities further here.

'Debenture' is also used in the context of secured lending from a bank or other institution (ie indirect financing). A debenture can be thought of as an 'IOU' used in the context of secured lending, for either direct or indirect debt financing. The aim in any event is that the lender can still get his money back even if the borrower defaults on the loan. See **Chapter 12** for an account of security.

A debenture holder is therefore a creditor of the company, ie someone to whom the company owes money. He is a lender who has taken a charge over some or all of the company's property, thereby becoming a secured creditor. This increases his chances of being repaid, especially on insolvency of the company as, in general, secured creditors must be repaid in full before any ordinary unsecured creditors receive anything (but see **Chapter 19** for details). There is no requirement in law that a debenture must be secured by a charge over some or all of the company's property. However, the word 'debenture' is in practice used to indicate a loan document where there is some form of security, ie a charge. See **Chapter 12** for more details of fixed and floating charges. (In fact, the definition of 'debenture' in CA 2006, s 738 is narrow. The term is used more widely than that in practice, as indicated above.)

Another type of debt finance is where a company utilises *short-term trade credit*. This is where it will only be required to pay its suppliers 30 days after the invoice has been received, not on delivery of the goods.

A company could also use *debt factoring*, where a company 'sells' its trade debts to a collection agency. The agency pays the company a proportion of the debts assigned to it. The agency then collects the debts at full value and hopes to make a profit.

In this book, we are primarily concerned with lending by banks and other institutions, and we do not consider further other forms of loan finance.

11.2 Equity or debt finance for the company?

The major difference between equity finance (shares) and debt (loans) is that equity is tightly controlled by statute, mainly the CA 2006. There is little company legislation directed toward debt. Instead, the law of contract is used. Debt can therefore be a more fluid medium than equity. It can also be argued that over-reliance on debt would result in profits going to the lender, not the shareholders. See **11.8** for more detail on the advantages and disadvantages of equity versus debt finance.

11.3 The legal nature of debt finance: terms of the contract

Here we will consider only indirect finance, ie borrowing from a bank or other lending institution. As noted above, debt finance is a matter of contract law between the lender and borrower. There is little control apart from the law of contract. There is no requirement for a borrower to give the lender security. However, if the lender has security then the loan can be more easily recovered if the borrower defaults on the loan. A company could in theory borrow from its banks or other lenders on a secured or unsecured basis. It will pay a higher interest rate for an unsecured loan, if indeed the bank will lend on that basis at all, eg the rates payable on an overdraft are higher than for secured loans.

A company could have loan facilities on which it can draw from time to time, such as an overdraft. It could borrow the principal in instalments, and pay interest only on the amounts actually borrowed. Interest would be payable on amounts borrowed. The company may also have to pay 'commitment' fees, or negotiation fees, in respect of lending facilities that have been made available to it.

The principal sum borrowed could be payable on demand, or lent for a fixed term. It all depends on the terms of the contract. The borrower will prefer to have a fixed term as then the borrower knows that repayment does not have to be made until the specified date.

11.4 Overdrafts

This is *current account* financing, ie the company draws on its current account to the extent that it goes into a negative balance. The company is then the debtor of the bank for the amount of the overdraft. The maximum amount of the overdraft will be agreed with the bank beforehand and the company will have to pay a commitment fee for this facility. Most medium and small businesses which require outside finance rely heavily on overdraft facilities.

In the absence of agreement, the bank is not bound to meet any withdrawal not covered by funds in the account. A company attempting to withdraw money in excess of the funds in its account can be regarded as making an offer, which the bank accepts by meeting the drawing. There then exists a contract in regard to the overdraft.

An overdraft is usually payable on demand, in much the same way as credit amounts in a bank account are. In other words, a bank is expected to pay money out immediately at the cash machine or over the counter, and not to tell a customer to come back in two months. However, in commercial reality, a bank is unlikely to demand that an overdraft be payable immediately, as this would be detrimental to its reputation if it risked making a customer insolvent on a whim. However, this is always a risk for the borrower.

'On demand' means that the borrower has enough time to effect the mechanics of payment, not enough time to go and raise the money: see *Bank of Baroda v Panessar* [1986] 3 All ER 751.

Interest is charged on a compound basis, ie the previous interest amounts are added to the capital and interest is charged on them as well. Unpaid interest would be added to the outstanding capital. Such general banking practice will be implied in overdraft contracts unless the parties have agreed otherwise, see *Kitchen v HSBC Bank plc* [2000] 1 All ER (Comm) 787.

Money paid in to an overdraft account is treated as discharging the earlier debit unless the parties have agreed otherwise – the rule in *Clayton's case* (1816) 35 ER 781. This is especially relevant where a bank takes security over an existing overdraft account, and the company continues to draw on, and make payments into, the account. Under the Insolvency Act 1986, a security can be held to be invalid if it is in respect of monies advanced to the borrower *before* the security was put in place (IA 1986, ss 239, 245). So, the rule in *Clayton's case* determines whether the outstanding balance on the account is new money advanced after the security was granted, in which case the security is valid: see *Re Thomas Mortimer Ltd* [1964] 3 WLR 427 (Note) and *Re Yeovil Glove Company Ltd* [1965] Ch 148.

11.5 Term loans

A term loan is simply a loan that is made for a specified period, ie a 'term'. Short-term loans are usually up to one year. Medium-term loans are one to five years. Long-term loans are five to ten years or longer.

11.5.1 Payment of principal to the borrower

The primary clauses of the loan agreement determine:

(a)   the amount of the loan;

(b)   the currency (eg dollars or euros);

(c)   if it is to be paid out by the bank as a lump sum or in instalments; and

(d)   the availability period of the loan facility.

Thus, the borrower may be able to draw down (ie withdraw) the loan in instalments at, or by, specified times. The loan may be available to the borrower only for a specified period and, if so, will not be available thereafter even if the borrower has not drawn it all.

11.5.2 Repayment

The agreement may provide for repayment of the whole loan at one time (a 'bullet' payment) or the repayment may be made in instalments (sometimes referred to as 'amortised' repayment). Amortised repayment gives the lender early notice of the borrower's difficulty in making repayments, if the borrower defaults on a payment.

The borrower may be granted an option to repay early. The lender can demand repayment of the loan if the borrower does something unacceptable (see 'events of default' in **11.5.7**). Some of the events of default will be outside the borrower's control. The most obvious event of default is going insolvent.

It is not clear whether a borrower has a basic right to repay early, but there are usually express provisions to that effect. They will include that the borrower gives notice of an intended early repayment, and will specify the acceptable dates, eg the last day of an interest period. Part of the reason for this is that banks will themselves borrow at least some of the money which they lend. If they accept early repayment from their borrower, they could find that they have to pay interest to another bank without having the income from the borrower. The practice is often referred to as 'borrowing long and lending short'. In other words, the bank makes its profit by borrowing money long-term, and lending it at the higher interest rates which apply to shorter-term loans. The bank's profit is the margin between the borrowing and the lending interest rates.

It is usual to require that any early repayments are applied in reverse order to their maturity, ie they are applied to the last scheduled repayment first, and then the next to last. This has the effect of shortening the period of the loan.

An ability to require repayment of the loan on demand is incompatible with the concept of a term loan. It is one factor that differentiates a term loan from an overdraft. In practice, the situation is taken care of by negotiation of the detail of the events of default.

11.5.3   Breach of the loan agreement – 'events of default'

If the lender refuses to lend in breach of the loan agreement, the borrower would be entitled to damages. If the borrower can obtain the same loan elsewhere, then the damages would be nominal. However, if the loan was to have been at a low rate of interest that is not obtainable elsewhere, the damages could be substantial. This can be regarded as damages for loss of expectation, to compensate the borrower for the position that he should have been in, see *Robinson v Harman* (1848) 1 Exch 850. There is also a reasonableness factor to be taken into account in deciding the damages, see *Ruxley Electronics & Construction v Forsyth* [1996] 1 AC 344. Specific performance is usually refused where damages are an adequate remedy.

(Section 740 of the CA 2006 provides that a contract with a company to take up and pay for debentures may be enforced by an order for specific performance. It seems more likely that s 740 is aimed at debt securities issued directly to investors, ie direct debt financing.)

If the borrower declines to take up the opportunity to borrow the money (an unlikely scenario), the lender's remedy would be damages.

The loan agreement will contain 'events of default'. If the borrower breaches any of these terms, then the lender may terminate the agreement if it so wishes (see **11.5.7**).

11.5.4   Interest rates

This is basic contract law. If there is a course of dealing or trade custom, then a requirement to pay interest can be implied but it would in any event be an express term of the contract in normal banking transactions. There is no statutory control of the interest rate applicable to companies. (The Consumer Credit Act 1974 only applies to individuals and so is not applicable here.) Non-payment of an interest payment is a key 'event of default', not surprisingly.

The interest rate may be fixed for the period of the loan or could be variable, ie 'floating'. Floating rate loan agreements commonly provide for the interest rate to be altered at specified intervals, eg three or six months, by reference to a formula which is intended to maintain the lender's return on the loan. The reason for this is that the base interest rate for sterling is reviewed every month by a committee of the Bank of England and can be altered up or down. At the time of writing, March 2009, the UK has been through a period of very low interest rates which are falling even lower.

The money which the bank lends may be its own, or may be borrowed from depositors or from other lenders. There needs to be a mechanism in the agreement for the borrower to pay to the lender an interest rate which allows the lender to repay the interest on its own borrowings and to make a profit. The mechanism also needs to take into account the variability of the rate at which the *lender* is borrowing the capital from the market.

Lenders will often want to impose default interest, ie an increased interest rate. However, the law on penalty clauses could cause problems. Contract law allows the courts to strike down a provision which constitutes a penalty clause, as opposed to a clause for liquidated damages. One indicator of a penalty clause is where the breach is failure to pay a sum, and the sum stipulated to be paid under the contract is greater than the sum actually owed, see *Bridge v Campbell Discount Co Ltd* [1962] 1 All ER 385. In *Jeancharm Ltd (t/a Beaver International) v Barnet Football Club Ltd* [2003] EWCA Civ 58, it was held that default interest may not constitute a penalty. The condition to this was that the rate had to be such as only to compensate the lender for its additional funding costs and the increased credit risk of lending to a defaulting borrower. In that case, however, a 5% a week rate represented a yearly interest rate of 260%. The Court of Appeal held that such a sum did not amount to a genuine pre-estimate but was a penalty clause in the sense of *Dunlop Pneumatic Tyre Co v New Garage* [1915] AC 79.

11.5.5 Express covenants

A covenant is a promise given by the borrower to the bank. The function of covenants is to give the lender some control over the manner in which the borrower conducts his business. There are parallels with the powers given to shareholders under the Companies Act 2006, but here the matters are contractual, not statutory. The areas covered by covenants tend to be the borrower's liquidity (ie 'ready cash'), general risk and management of the borrower. The restrictions on the financial structure of the borrower are to ensure that the borrower stays solvent, and is not too dependent on debt. So, for example, the borrower will be required by the lender to pay all debts as they fall due (cash flow solvency). The borrower will also usually be obliged to seek equity finance for new ventures, as opposed to further debt finance.

Covenants on the following matters are also commonly included.

(a) *Limitation of dividends* The borrower must ensure that dividends and other distributions to shareholders do not exceed a specified percentage of the net profits.

(b) *Minimum capital requirements* The borrower must ensure that current assets exceed current liabilities by a specified amount of money or a specified percentage.

(c) *No disposal of assets, or change of business* The borrower must not dispose of assets without the lender's consent, or change the scope or nature of the business. (This may help to prevent asset strippers.)

(d) *No further security over the assets* The borrower must not create any further security over the whole, or any part, of the undertaking without the lender's consent (a 'negative pledge' clause, see **Chapter 12**).

(e) *Information on the borrower's business* This would include annual accounts, interim financial statements, communications sent to shareholders and such other information as the lender may require.

The final form of the covenants will depend on negotiations between the parties but remember that the lender has the money, and the borrower needs the money so the commercial strength is on the lender's side. However, the lender does not wish to run the borrower's business by remote control, so the lender will leave the borrower reasonable commercial latitude.

If a corporate borrower goes insolvent, the lender will be looking to the share capital, share premium account and other undistributable reserves to pay off the debt.

11.5.6   Implied covenants

As with any contract, terms can be implied, eg by trade usage such as the bank's right to charge compound interest. The court's power to imply terms is limited. A contractual term would be implied only if it were necessary to give efficacy to the contract, see *Thames Cruises Ltd v George Wheeler Launches Ltd* [2003] EWHC 3093. In any event, the court could not imply a term that was inconsistent with an express term of the contract.

11.5.7   Events of default

There are various events of default that will entitle the lender to terminate the contract if the lender wishes to do so. These include failure to pay any sum due, and breach of an obligation under the loan agreement. A somewhat unusual event is cross-default, where the borrower fails to meet some other indebtedness or financial payment due, ie has defaulted on a loan to another lender. The rationale is that this is the first sign of financial trouble.

11.5.8   The lender's role in management

In *re a Company (No 005009 of 1987)* [1989] BCLC 13, it was held that there was a triable issue as to whether a bank had become a shadow director of an insolvent company in the context of s 214 of the IA 1986 on wrongful trading. It seems unlikely that the lender could be so liable unless it stepped outside the normal lender-customer relationship. In that case, the borrower had reached its overdraft limit. The lender commissioned a report on the financial affairs of the company which included steps that should be taken by the borrower's management. The company then implemented these steps. Advisers are protected under s 251 of the IA 1986 from liability as a shadow director but there is a difference between advising and instructing. In *Secretary of State for Trade and Industry v Deverell* [2000] 2 All ER 365, the Court of Appeal held that a shadow director was anyone, other than a professional adviser, who exercised real influence in the corporate affairs of a company.

One way round this problem is for the lender to make continuation of the loan conditional on certain steps being taken by the borrower. The borrower then has the choice of taking a new loan on those conditions or looking elsewhere. Another route is for the lender to appoint a director to the board to act on the lender's behalf. There is considerable scope for such a director to have a conflict of interest as he will owe a duty to both the lender and the borrower.

As a matter of general commercial common sense, a lender will monitor very closely the borrower's current account. This will provide good information on how the borrower is progressing financially. It will also give early warning of any problems.

11.5.9   The lender as monitor of corporate governance

The lender can be in a strong commercial position vis-à-vis its corporate borrower, and can influence how the borrower is managed. The lender in effect controls the flow of money into the company. Small or medium-sized companies will be more vulnerable than large ones, especially those large ones which are in a position to borrow from other sources.

It may well be in the lender's interest to ensure that the principles of good corporate governance are observed, eg those contained in the Combined Code for companies quoted on the Stock Exchange.

Problems that can occur include acquiring information about a borrower which could give the lender inside knowledge of one particular area. This would preclude it from dealing in securities in the affected area on its own behalf, or for other customers. It could also create problems of conflict of interest.

11.6 Secured debt

A lender with security can claim the secured assets if the borrower fails to meet its obligations. Secured creditors are therefore in a much stronger position if the company becomes insolvent than are unsecured creditors.

Unsecured debts are governed by the equality (*pari passu*) principle, which means that the unsecured debts are all reduced pro rata if there are insufficient funds to pay all the company's debts. Security allows the lender to avoid this principle. Security may also allow the lender to follow secured assets into the hands of a third party, subject to certain constraints.

A secured creditor can appoint an administrator, or alternatively may be able to block the appointment of an administrator as there is a general suspension of claims whilst a company is in administration. See **Chapter 12** on debentures and charges, and **Chapter 19** on corporate insolvency.

11.6.1 Economics of security

As security puts the lender in a favourable position, it may allow the borrower to borrow money at a rate that is lower than would otherwise be the case. The downside is that unsecured creditors may demand higher interest rates because their interests rank behind those of the secured creditor.

Secured debt may reduce the costs to the lender in monitoring the borrower's business. However, it may make the unsecured creditors more nervous, and induce them to increase their monitoring, and therefore monitoring costs. (If there were an insolvency, the existence of the secured debt reduces the pool of money available to pay unsecured debtors.)

11.6.2 Influence of legislation

The creation of security is a matter of contract law between the parties and so the law will not interfere, in general. The exceptions are the provisions of the IA 1986, especially s 239 (avoidance of voidable preferences) and s 245 (invalidity of certain floating charges); see **Chapter 19**.

11.6.3 Nature of security

With a secured debt, the borrower receives money (or other credit) and gives the lender rights over the borrower's property. These rights will not come into play unless the borrower defaults. At that point, the secured property will be sold to repay the debt. This is an interest granted by the borrower. Security interests are registrable (s 860), and indeed must be registered for the lender to maintain its position in the queue of creditors (see **Chapter 12**). There are ways around s 860, eg a sale and leaseback to the vendor.

An obvious point about the nature of a security interest is that it is extinguished on payment of the debt which is the subject of the security. Equity renders void any attempt to hinder a borrower's right to redeem a charge, as this is a type of penalty (see *Kreglinger v New Patagonia Meat and Cold Storage* [1914] AC 25 which concerned redemption of a floating charge).

Section 739 provides an exception, in that it states that a condition in a debenture rendering redemption improbable (because the period is long or it is conditional on the happening of a remote contingency) is valid notwithstanding any rule of equity.

A secured debt should be distinguished from a retention of title in a sale of goods where the buyer does not get title to the goods until he pays the full price to the seller. If the buyer defaults then the goods are repossessed by the seller. This is an interest retained by the creditor. Such a clause is not registrable (see **32.8.7**).

11.6.4   Forms of property that can be charged

(a)   Land, freehold or leasehold, fixtures and fittings.

(b)   Tangible property – eg stock in trade.

(c)   Intangible property – eg debts, intellectual property.

11.7   Subordination of debt

Secured and unsecured creditors can enter into contractual arrangements whereby they vary the priority ascribed to their debts by the law. The basic order of priority is that fixed charges rank ahead of floating charges which in turn rank ahead of unsecured creditors. Within each category of secured charge, the charges rank in order of creation, assuming they have been properly registered under s 860. The order of priority becomes important when the borrower becomes insolvent as, by definition, the borrower cannot pay all its debts. Usually, unsecured creditors will receive very little, if anything, on an insolvency.

Secured debt may be subordinated where a secured creditor gives up its priority possibly because a new lender to the company insists on its debt ranking ahead of the other debts. Subordination of secured debt is achieved by a deed of priority which is executed by the creditors. The company may, or may not, be a party.

Unsecured debt subordination is where one of the unsecured debts is made to rank after the others. For example, perhaps the directors or shareholders lend the company money to help it out. The existing creditors insist that their debts should rank ahead of the one from the insiders.

A company which is able to raise capital by issuing securities to investors may offer subordinated debt securities to the markets. Usually, subordinated debt pays a higher interest rate to compensate for the decrease in the ranking of the debt. Unsecured debt would usually be subordinated by contract between the creditors. There could be an event which triggers subordination, often the liquidation of the company.

11.8   Advantages and disadvantages of debt: comparison with shares

11.8.1   For the investor

11.8.1.1   The relative risk of the investment

It is generally perceived that shares are a more risky investment than loans. If the company is in financial difficulties, then it will not declare a dividend. The shareholder may also lose the capital value of his shares if the company goes insolvent. However, with loans, the interest payments are a contractual liability of the company which must be met. Also, a loan will often be secured over the company's property and there may be personal guarantees from the directors. In short, a lender is much more likely to be repaid than a shareholder.

11.8.1.2   Involvement in the company

A shareholder is a member of the company, which gives him certain rights within the company (see **5.5**), including the right to attend general meetings and to vote. A lender is merely a creditor of the company and has no say whatever in the way the company is run.

11.8.1.3   Income

A shareholder has no guaranteed income from the investment in shares. A dividend will be paid only if the directors decide to recommend one, and they can do so only if the company is sufficiently profitable. A lender must be paid the agreed rate of interest at the times specified in the debenture itself. The payment of such interest is a debt owed by the company and is not dependent upon the company making a profit.

11.8.1.4 Repayment of capital

Generally, a shareholder's capital is not repaid by the company. In contrast, a lender will agree with the company a date for repayment of the capital sum loaned, and this date will be stated in the debenture. On that date the company must repay the loan.

11.8.1.5 Restrictions on sale

If a member wishes to sell his shares in order to realise his capital investment in the company, the transfer of his shares is governed by the articles, which may restrict his choice. If a lender wishes to realise his capital earlier than the repayment date agreed, he can sell his debenture to whomsoever he chooses. No restriction in the articles will affect his right to sell.

11.8.1.6 Capital value of the investment

The value of a company's shares may increase or decrease. Many shareholders make such an investment hoping for capital appreciation rather than income.

The capital value of a debenture generally remains constant, being the value of the loan. There is usually no possibility of capital appreciation or depreciation with this type of investment. The purpose of an investment in this form is the receipt of income.

11.8.2 For the company

As we have seen, the major difference between equity finance (shares) and debt is that equity is tightly controlled by statute, mainly the CA 2006. There is little company legislation directed toward debt, instead the law of contract is used. Debt can therefore be a more fluid medium than equity.

11.8.2.1 Payment of income

The company can pay a dividend to its members only if there are profits available (see **10.8**). Even if the company is sufficiently profitable, the directors have a complete discretion as to whether a dividend should be paid.

Debt interest must be paid in accordance with the terms of the loan agreement whether or not the company has profits available. If there are no profits which can be used, the company must use capital to make the interest payment. If the company fails to make a payment of interest, the lender is entitled to enforce the terms of the debenture by the appointment of a receiver or administrator (see **19.6**).

11.8.2.2 Tax treatment of income payments

The payment of a dividend is not a deductible expense for the company. It is simply a distribution of profit, after it has suffered corporation tax.

Payment of debenture interest, as it is incurred for the purposes of the trade, is a normal trading expense and so deductible in computing trading profit, before corporation tax is assessed.

11.8.2.3 Involvement of investor

If a person buys shares in the company and has his name entered on the register of members, he is then a member of the company and has certain rights as a member. He could thus have a degree of influence over the way in which the company is run. Even a minority shareholder may be a nuisance (at the very least) to those persons running the company, if that member's views are not in accordance with those of the directors and other members.

A lender generally cannot interfere in the way the company is run. If the company complies with the terms of the debenture, the lender can take no action to influence company policy.

11.8.2.4   Repayment of capital

The company generally does not have to repay to members the capital which they have invested until the company ceases in business and is wound up. Therefore, this is not a matter which the directors need to consider.

Loan capital must be repaid at some date in the future (possibly on demand), therefore the directors must make provision for this and ensure that funds are available to repay the loan whenever it falls due.

11.8.2.5   Cost – debt

The cost of debt is easy to establish. Basically, it is the interest rate charged by the lender to the borrower. The rate will depend on commercial factors such as the security offered by the borrower, how much is borrowed, how long it is borrowed for, and the borrower's creditworthiness.

The tax system favours debt financing because interest, unlike dividends, is tax deductible. In assessing the cost of borrowing, the tax savings have to be taken into account.

Debt financing may increase earnings per share, but it may depress the share price. If investors believe that the company has too much borrowing, then they may want to sell their shares in case a downturn in trading conditions causes the company to have greater liabilities than assets (ie to be insolvent).

11.8.2.6   Cost – equity

The cost of equity is the likely returns to the new shareholder, including dividends, capital appreciation and share buybacks. These returns are the cost to the existing shareholders, as their share of future dividends or capital growth is decreased. Dividends are not deductible for corporation tax purposes.

In the economic climate where interest rates are comparatively low, debt is cheaper than equity, so most acquisitions of companies would be financed by debt under these conditions.

11.8.2.7   Existing capital structure

If the company already has a lot of debt (its 'gearing' is high), it may only be able to obtain more finance in the form of equity (eg by an issue of shares).

Gearing is the ratio of borrowings to shareholder funds (in effect, share capital and retained profits). High gearing means a greater burden of borrowings and the greater possibility of insolvency if trading conditions worsen.

11.8.2.8   Existing restrictions

The articles may restrict the company's ability to borrow.

The terms of existing loan agreements may restrict the taking of new loans or debt, at least without the existing lender's consent.

11.8.2.9   Availability and cost of debt

Are banks prepared to lend money to the would-be borrower, and, if so, at what cost?

11.8.2.10   How is the company rated in the market-place?

What is the company's reputation? If it is good, then investors may be keen to buy its shares, so an issue of new shares may be the way to raise finance.

11.8.2.11 Impact on earnings

This will depend on the cost of borrowing as against the market value of the company's shares. A low interest rate favours debt finance. A highly-rated company would be more likely to use equity finance.

11.9 Share and loan capital – from whom?

11.9.1 Directors and shareholders

Initially, a significant amount of the company's capital will have to be provided by the individuals who will run the company (the directors and shareholders). In terms of value, their own investment may be expected to match any 'outside' investment in the company although, depending on circumstances, outside investors may be willing to provide three or four times as much capital as the 'inside' investors. It may also be possible for the persons setting up or running the company to encourage family or friends to provide some finance.

11.9.2 Clearing banks

For many small businesses, their primary source of outside finance is their 'High Street' bank, ie a clearing bank such as Barclays or HSBC. The banks can provide overdraft facilities, or term loans, or finance for specific items such as new machinery.

11.9.3 Venture capital

Where major 'outside' finance is required (say £1m or more), this may be sought from a venture capital organisation. These are generally organisations looking for investment in business which have the potential for fairly rapid growth so that after a few years the company may apply to the Stock Exchange for its shares to be listed there, or on the Alternative Investment Market. In this way, the venture capitalist will have the opportunity of selling its investment and realising a substantial gain. Typical features of venture capital include the following.

(a)   The investment will be in ordinary shares in the company. The shareholding taken will be a substantial stake in the company but not normally a majority stake since such a surrender of control would usually be unacceptable to the individuals already running the company.

(b)   Part of the investment may be in the form of loan finance.

(c)   The venture capitalist may require that there are management changes in the company, including a seat on the board for its own representatives.

(d)   Before investing, the venture capitalist will carry out a thorough investigation into the company's finances and future prospects by an examination of management accounts.

In 2006, British venture capital firms invested £11.7 billion in 1,500 companies across the UK and the rest of Europe. The people behind the venture capital funds are the insurance companies, pension funds, banks and ordinary investors. In general, venture capital firms prefer to provide money to buy an existing business, or development finance for companies that are past the initial stage and need finance to develop further. However, they will sometimes provide 'seed corn' capital to finance a start-up venture, but such ventures are the most risky.

The biggest venture capital organisation in the UK is 3i. It typically invests £1.5 million to £35 million in start-up or young companies, rising to £7 million to £100 million for investments in medium-sized companies. See the websites of the British Venture Capital Association at www.bvca.co.uk and 3i at www.3i.com.

11.10 Summaries and checklists

11.10.1 Preliminary considerations for the lender

(a) Is the company financially sound?

    (i) check published accounts and, if possible, more recent accounts.

(b) Is satisfactory security offered?

    (i) take fixed and/or floating charge(s)

    (ii) check for existing charges

    (iii) get personal guarantees from directors

    (iv) take charge(s) over directors' assets (eg their homes).

11.10.2 Procedure on borrowing

(a) Check

    (i) that the company has the power to borrow

    (ii) that the directors have the authority to borrow.

(b) Prepare debenture

    (i) what property is charged?

    (ii) rate of interest and repayment date

    (iii) fixed and/or floating charge?

    (iv) define default

    (v) methods of enforcement

    (vi) prohibition on later charges taking priority etc.

(c) Board meeting to enter into contract and execute debenture.

(d) If directors are lending money to the company, they must declare their personal interest (CA 2006, ss 182–187) but can vote and count in the quorum in some cases (model articles for private companies, art 14).

(e) Registration

    (i) at Companies Registry within 21 days

    (ii) at HM Land Registry/Land Charges Department.

(f) Write up statutory books: register of charges (if relevant).

(g) Charge may be invalid/ineffective security if:

    (i) not registered

    (ii) insolvent liquidation in near future

    (iii) assets are supplied under *Romalpa* clause.

Chapter 12

Security for Loans: Debentures and Charges

12.1 Introduction

We looked in **Chapter 11** at financing a company by borrowing money, that is debt finance, as opposed to selling shares in the company. In this chapter we look at how the loan is secured. In other words, if the borrower defaults on the loan, how can the lender be sure to get his money back? There are two classes of charges, fixed and floating. They each have their own merits. We also need to consider the matter of registering charges, and the problems that result from failure to do so.

As part of the process of looking at security for lending, we also need to look at the general nature of secured loan agreements, that is debentures, and some typical contract terms.

12.2 Pre-contract considerations

12.2.1 For the directors of the company

The directors should ensure that they have been given the power to borrow on behalf of the company by the articles and thus will not be acting outside their authority and in breach of duty. The model articles for private companies do not address this issue.

The lender may require the directors of the company to guarantee personally a loan to the company, particularly, but not exclusively, where the company is a small company or where it is a new company. If the directors are guaranteeing the loan in this way, they have a personal interest in the matter and must declare that interest formally at the first board meeting at which the question of the loan is discussed (CA 2006, ss 182–187). The articles will then determine whether they can vote and count in the quorum (model articles for private companies, art 14) (see **6.5.2** and **6.5.3**).

12.2.2 For the lender

The lender should make sure that the directors have the authority to act on behalf of the company in the transaction and that the people he is dealing with have actually been properly appointed as directors of the company. He can do this by inspecting the articles of the company and searching the records at Companies House.

If, as is usually the case, the loan is to be secured by a charge contained in the debenture, it would again be sensible to search at Companies House. This will unearth details of any charges currently registered against the company's property and so ensure that there is sufficient equity in that property to provide adequate security for the proposed loan. Even if the loan is to be unsecured, the lender should search at Companies House to determine the extent of the company's current secured borrowing. From the charges register, the lender can discover:

(a) the date of creation of any existing charge;

(b) the amount secured;

(c) which property is the subject of the charge; and

(d) who holds that charge.

If the charges register reveals any floating charges already in existence, the lender should obtain from the charge holder a letter of non-crystallisation (a letter in which the charge holder confirms that his floating charge has not yet crystallised). This is necessary as it will not be apparent from the company search whether the floating charge has crystallised or not (see **12.3.3**).

If the lender is proposing to take a charge over land held by the company, he should also search at HM Land Registry.

On ultra vires, see **3.2.1**.

12.3 Security for the loan

There are fixed charges and floating charges. They have certain features in common:

(a) most charges need to be registered with the Companies Registry (CA 2006, s 860) and are void against a liquidator, an administrator or a creditor with an interest in the secured assets if not so registered (s 874), though the contract between the lender and the company is still valid;

(b) the charge holder's rights prevail over other creditors on insolvency; and

(c) the charge holder can take possession and sell the assets which are the subject of the charge.

A creditor who holds a charge is referred to as being 'secured', whereas other creditors are 'unsecured'.

12.3.1 Priority of charges

A fixed charge will take priority over a floating charge on the same assets. It is possible for creditors to enter an agreement between themselves to alter the order of priority of their charges. This could happen, for example, if the holder of a fixed charge allowed a bank to have priority for its floating charge, without which priority the bank would not advance new funds to allow the borrower to continue to trade (see **19.5.4** and **19.5.5**).

12.3.2 Fixed charges

The most attractive security for a lender is land, including buildings and major items of machinery. A company can create a number of fixed charges over such assets. The company cannot deal with the asset, for example sell it, without the charge holders' consent. The purchaser from the company of the charged property can only take it subject to the charge, as long as the charge has been registered.

If the company goes into receivership or liquidation, then the fixed charge holders are paid out of the proceeds of the sale of the relevant asset before any other claimants. This makes a fixed charge a strong security.

As a general rule, a fixed charge will take priority over a floating charge over the same assets.

The holder of a fixed charge is in a good position. The charge is often over business premises, which are assets that are highly marketable.

An unusual subject for security, at first glance, is book debts, that is taking security over money which is owed *to* the company. It is established that such charges constitute a floating charge, not a fixed one; see the House of Lords decision in *National Westminster Bank plc v Spectrum Plus Limited and Others* [2005] UKHL 41.

12.3.3 Floating charges

If a company has no scope for granting any new fixed charges, how can a lender be offered security (and without which they are unlikely to lend to the company)? The answer came from the Court of Chancery in *In re Panama, New Zealand and Australian Royal Mail Company* (1870) LR 5 Ch App 318. The court allowed the creation of an equitable charge over the company's undertaking and stock in trade. It is therefore possible to have a charge over assets such as stock which is constantly changing (and therefore where a fixed charge would be impracticable).

The three basic features of a floating charge were analysed in *Re Yorkshire Woolcombers Association Ltd; Houldsworth v Yorkshire Woolcombers Association Ltd* [1903] 2 Ch 284, and are:

(a) it is an equitable charge over the whole or a class of the company's assets, for example over the book debts;

(b) the assets subject to the charge are constantly changing; and

(c) the company retains the freedom to deal with the assets in the ordinary course of business until the charge 'crystallises'.

It is the company's freedom to deal with the assets which is the primary characteristic of a floating charge.

A floating charge will crystallise on the company:

(a) going into receivership;

(b) going into liquidation;

(c) ceasing to trade; or

(d) any other event specified in the charge document.

The terms of the loan agreement will determine the power of the lender to appoint an administrator. This will arise on the occurrence of specified events, for example failure to pay principal or interest.

12.3.4 Advantages of floating charges

The advantage of a floating charge from the company's viewpoint is that it allows it to use another source of finance even though its scope for granting fixed charges (for example over its premises) has been exhausted.

Under the revised regime introduced by the Enterprise Act 2002 (EA 2002), the holder of a floating charge is not able to appoint an administrative receiver (IA 1986, s 72A). Instead, he is only able to appoint an administrator (see **19.4**). The role of administrative receiver will thus become much less important as it is restricted to floating charges created before 15 September 2003. There are also some very specialised exceptions that need not concern us here. It should be emphasised that floating charges themselves are unaffected by the revised regime.

12.3.5 Disadvantages of floating charges

The disadvantage of a floating charge from the viewpoint of the holder (the lender) is that the company is allowed to deal with the assets. Thus, they could sell their existing stock and not purchase new stock to replace it. So, a floating charge over stock would be of little value in those circumstances. This freedom also allows the company to create further charges.

The solution to this last problem is to include in the charge documentation for the floating charge a negative pledge clause. This prohibits the company from creating later charges with priority to the floating charge. However, this only works if the subsequent charge holder has actual knowledge of the earlier charge. Constructive knowledge, due to filing the charge at Companies House, is not enough. In practice, the form which is sent to Companies House to register the earlier charge under s 869 should carry notice of the negative pledge clause, if it has been competently completed. A search of the records at Companies House will reveal the form with this notice on its face. Also, a properly drafted agreement for the subsequent charge should contain a covenant by the company to the effect that there are no earlier charges which are subject to a negative pledge clause. If this is not true, then the company is in breach of that agreement and it can be terminated immediately.

In the negative pledge covenant, it is arguable that the pledge could bind a third party, ie a subsequent lender, under the equitable principle in *de Mattos v Gibson* (1858), see eg *Den Norske Bank ASA v Acemex Management Company Ltd* [2003] 2 All ER (Comm) 318. However, this would require actual knowledge of the earlier rights, and also that the third party seeks to deal with the property in a manner inconsistent with the earlier contract, in effect ignoring those rights. It is also possible for the lender to sue the third party for inducing breach of contract, see eg *Swiss Bank Corp v Lloyds Bank Ltd* [1979] 2 All ER 853.

Preferential creditors take priority over the holder of a floating charge (but not over the holder of a fixed charge). These were bodies such as the Inland Revenue and Customs and Excise, as they then were, who were required to be paid before the other creditors. This was a major problem before the EA 2002. However, the EA 2002 amends the IA 1986 and abolishes preferential status for the Crown. The two main categories which remain are contributions to occupational pension schemes and the wages of employees. The amount which would have gone to the Crown will now be paid to the unsecured creditors, as a so-called 'top slice' or 'ring-fenced' sum.

Another problem is goods subject to a retention of title clause (a '*Romalpa*' clause) (see **32.8.7**). If the clause is effective, it deprives the holder of a floating charge of rights they might otherwise have over those goods, because the supplier of the goods still owns them. The charge holder therefore has no rights to sell those goods to pay the debt owed to them.

Under s 245 of the IA 1986, a liquidator or administrator can apply to have a floating charge set aside. If the person benefiting from the floating charge is connected to the company and it has been created within two years preceding the administration or winding-up order, then the charge can be set aside. On the other hand, if the person is not connected with the company, the time limit is 12 months and the company has to have been insolvent at the time the floating charge was created (see **19.7.4**).

12.3.6   Personal guarantees

Directors are sometimes required by a lender to guarantee personally a loan to their company. Usually only company money can be used to pay company debts because of the principle of limited liability. However, if the directors give personal guarantees for a loan they will have to pay the lender whatever amount is outstanding if, for some reason, the lender is unable to recover the loan in full from the company, for example because the company is insolvent. Directors who do give personal guarantees in this way risk the loss of their personal assets if the company fails, possibly even loss of their home. A director who cannot pay the sum he guaranteed from his own resources may even face bankruptcy.

12.4   Typical terms of a debenture

12.4.1   Repayment date

The amount the company borrows under the debenture will have to be repaid at some future date. Sometimes a loan will be for a fixed period of time (eg 12 months) and there will be a specified date when repayment is due. Sometimes, for example in the case of a bank overdraft, the loan will be repayable on demand.

12.4.2 Interest

The debenture must specify when interest is payable and how much is agreed. There may be a fixed rate of interest, or the interest rate may be linked to bank rates and may therefore fluctuate (ie, be a floating rate).

12.4.3 Security

Although there is no need for a loan to be secured, the lender's position is improved if he does take a charge over the company's property and therefore secured loans are very common. The security could be in the form of a fixed charge or a floating charge, or could be a combination of the two, for example a fixed charge on anything owned by the company over which it is possible to take a fixed charge and a floating charge over the whole of the company's undertaking.

12.4.4 Power to appoint an administrator

If the company defaults under the terms of the debenture, because it does not pay either the interest or the capital when due, the debenture holder's right to recover the money owed to him is achieved by the appointment of an administrator. Therefore power to make such an appointment should be contained in the debenture.

Under the revised insolvency regime, qualifying floating charge holders (QFCHs), the company or directors are empowered to appoint an administrator without petitioning the court. A QFCH is a creditor who has the benefit of a floating charge created after the commencement of the EA 2002 (see **19.4**).

12.4.5 Power of sale

The administrator appointed by the debenture holder will need power to sell the assets which are the subject of the charge in order to recover the sum due to his appointor, and therefore a power of sale should be included in the debenture.

12.5 Procedure for issue of debenture

It is the directors' decision whether to borrow money in the company name and it is they who will negotiate with the lender the terms on which the loan is to be made. A resolution of the board of directors is sufficient to authorise borrowing by the company.

However, there may be problems over the ability of the directors to vote and count in the quorum on the resolution to borrow, particularly where the directors have been asked personally to guarantee the loan. The articles may prevent any director who has a personal interest (possibly all directors) from being involved in the decision to borrow (see **6.5.2** and **6.5.3**). It may therefore be necessary to call a general meeting, either to suspend any prohibition in the articles by ordinary resolution or to change the articles by special resolution.

Once the directors have resolved to enter into the loan, the debenture will be signed by either two directors or a director and the secretary. The directors will also resolve to affix the company seal (if the company has one) to the debenture.

12.6 Registration

Section 860(7) lists those types of charges which are registrable.

Once the company has formally entered into the loan, it is the company's responsibility to register prescribed particulars of any charge contained in the debenture at Companies House, together with the original charging document, within 21 days of creation of that charge (s 870). If the debenture contains a floating charge and a negative pledge clause, then that clause should be noted on the form. Although it is primarily the responsibility of the company to register prescribed particulars of any charge, it is the debenture holder who suffers if the charge is not registered or is registered late (see **12.6.1**). The debenture holder would usually undertake the registration of the charge himself. The Registrar of Companies will return the original charging document with a stamp signifying registration, as well as a certificate which is conclusive evidence that the charge is properly registered.

If a fixed charge is taken over land (for practical reasons, floating charges are generally not used where land is concerned) then this must also be registered at HM Land Registry. In other words, a charge involving land must be registered twice – at Companies House and at HM Land Registry.

If such a charge is not registered at HM Land Registry, then a buyer of the land in question can take free of the fixed charge, even if he actually knew of its existence. The position of a buyer is governed solely by what is apparent from the Land Registry documents, even if the fixed charge over land has been registered at Companies House.

Details of any charge created by the company should also be kept in the company's own register of charges at its registered office, but failure to do this does not affect the validity of the charge in any way.

12.6.1   Failure to register at Companies House

Registration of a registrable charge at Companies House gives constructive notice of that charge to those persons who could reasonably be expected to search the register (*Re Standard Rotary Machine Company Co Ltd* (1906) 95 LT 829), including, of course, subsequent chargees. It seems unlikely that it would constitute notice to purchasers of the company's property.

Failure to register renders the charge void against the company's liquidator or administrator, and also against the company's other secured creditors (s 874). It is not void as such against purchasers of the company's property, but they may take free of it under the rule on a bona fide purchaser without notice for value. The security remains valid against the company itself, although the money secured by the charge becomes payable immediately (s 874(3)).

12.6.2   Late or inaccurate registration

If the 21-day registration period is missed or the details supplied on the form are inaccurate, the court has the power under ss 873 and 874 to order an extension of time or allow rectification of the register. The court will usually allow this, subject to not prejudicing a person who has acquired a subsequent interest in the charged property before the application. The priority date granted will be the date of the application, not the date of creation of the charge. In *In re Joplin Brewery Co Ltd* [1902] 1 Ch 79, there were registered charges and a complex form of order was used. In *Watson v Duff Morgan & Vermont (Holdings) Ltd* [1974] 1 WLR 450, the modern form of order was devised. Thus, the order was expressed to be given 'without prejudice to the rights of any parties acquired prior to the time when the said debenture is to be actually registered'.

An example of registration being granted out of time is *Re Chantry House Developments plc* [1990] BCC 646. There, a building society was given permission to register a mortgage out of time. There were no other secured lenders. It was held that 'the failure to register was accidental and it was just and equitable to allow late registration to give the building society security that it had contracted for'.

12.6.3   Memorandum of satisfaction

When a debt, or other obligation, secured by a registered charge is repaid then the fact may be made public by filing a memorandum of satisfaction with Companies House in the prescribed form (s 872).

12.7   Remedies of the debenture holder

See **19.4** on administration.

12.8   Redemption of the loan

When the loan is repaid to the lender, a director or the company secretary will make a statutory declaration that the debt has been paid and will send this form to the Registrar of Companies. The lender will endorse his receipt of the money on the debenture (s 872).

If any entries were made against land at HM Land Registry, these should now be removed.

Part II Summary – Running a Business as a Company Limited by Shares

Topic	Summary
Key concepts	The two key concepts of a company are that: (a) it has its own legal personality, separate from that of its members; and (b) it permits limited liability. Separate legal personality means that a company can, in its own name, enter contracts, own property, employ people and take legal actions. Limited liability means that the liability of the company's shareholders for the company's debts is limited to the agreed price of their shares.
Principal legislation	The principal legislation regulating companies in the UK is in the Companies Act 2006.
Ownership and control	Companies are owned by shareholders, who are the members of the company. Ultimately, they control the business of the company and certain decisions are reserved to them by law. They make these decisions by resolutions at general shareholder meetings or by way of signed written resolutions.
Management	The day-to-day business of a company is delegated by shareholders to directors, who manage the company.
Formation	A company is formed by sending relevant documents and a fee to Companies House. The documents include the memorandum and articles of association. The Registrar of Companies issues a certificate of incorporation which records the date on which the company is formed, its name and unique registration number.
Shelf companies	Shelf companies are companies incorporated for the purpose of being transferred to clients, saving the time of formation.
Constitution	A company's constitution is set out in its articles of association. The memorandum sets out the name, registered office and capital of the company. The articles are a set of regulations which govern the internal workings of the company and its directors. A company may adopt a standard set of articles or draft its own regulations. The Companies Act 2006 reduced the importance and content of the memorandum, with the articles becoming the predominant document.
Shareholders	Shareholders can join as initial subscribers to the company's memorandum or by buying shares at a later date, once the company has been formed. They effectively own the company in proportion to their shareholding and will have limited liability for the company's debts. Their shares will generally entitle them to vote on company resolutions and receive dividends. They will also, subject to any restrictions in the articles, be able to realise the capital value of their shares by selling them.

Topic	Summary
Shareholder meetings	These are usually referred to as general meetings. An Annual General Meeting (AGM) must be held each calendar year, although private companies are not, under the Companies Act 2006, required to have an AGM at all.
	Shareholder meetings are usually called by the company's directors, but there is a process by which shareholders may do so. Notice must be given to all shareholders, the length of which notice will depend on the notice period required for the type of resolutions being proposed. For business to be validly transacted, the meeting must be quorate, that is, a required number of shareholders must attend.
Shareholder resolutions	The Companies Act determines the form of resolution required for differing decisions or changes to be made to the company. Ordinary resolutions require a simple majority of the shareholders to vote in favour, and special resolutions require 75% to be in favour. Shareholders' voting power is normally in proportion to the number of shares held. Where there is a stalemate, the meeting chairman may, if the articles provide, have a casting vote. In terms of notice to be given of resolutions, it is 14 days for all resolutions but 21 days for resolutions at the AGM of a public company. However, meetings can be held and resolutions passed on shorter notice if specified percentages of members agree.
Written resolutions	Shareholder resolutions can also be passed without general meetings, by using the written resolution procedure.
Minority shareholders	The basic principle is that of majority rule: unless shareholders have 50% or more of the company's shares, their power is limited. However, in limited situations, minority shareholders may be permitted to bring a derivative action in the company's name.
Company directors	The day-to-day business of a company is normally delegated by shareholders to the company's directors. The latter are appointed either by being noted as such on incorporation or, subsequently, by the board or by ordinary resolution.
Board meetings	Directors make decisions by passing resolutions at board meetings, which can be called on reasonable notice by any director. Like shareholder meetings, they must be quorate. Directors with a personal interest in the business being transacted must declare such interest and may not be allowed to vote on related resolutions. Resolutions are passed by a simple majority with the possibility of a casting vote for the chairman in the event of a stalemate. Alternatively, resolutions can be passed by way of written resolution.
Office and service contracts	Directors are appointed to the office of director; however, directors holding executive positions will often be given a separate service contract. This needs shareholder approval if it is for a period exceeding two years, and cannot be terminated on reasonable notice.
Disqualification of directors	Directors can be disqualified for specific breaches of the Company Directors Disqualification Act 1986, or under specific regulations in a company's articles.

Topic	Summary
Dismissal of directors	Directors can be dismissed by an ordinary resolution of the shareholders. There is a specific procedure to be followed in attempting to pass such a resolution. If dismissed, the director may have rights of redress under employment law for unfair dismissal or redundancy, or under contract law for wrongful dismissal
Statutory control of directors	The Companies Act 2006 provides a statutory statement of seven duties owed by a director to a company. These are to be interpreted in the light of existing common law rules and equitable principles.
	There are also specific provisions regulating transactions between directors and their companies. These include substantial property transactions and loans to directors.
Company secretary	Every public company must appoint a company secretary to deal with the administrative side of running the company. This may involve writing up minutes of meetings and maintaining the company's statutory registers. Under the Companies Act 2006, private companies are not required to have a secretary, although they may still choose to have one.
Financing a company	The two principal means by which companies are financed are by way of shares or debt. Each form creates various obligations for the company and rights for the financing party. Share capital is often referred to as equity finance. Debt finance can range from overdrafts to loans to bonds.
Shares	Share capital is contributed by shareholders when they purchase shares in the company. In return for their finance, shareholders have shares issued (or allotted) to them by the company. The decision to issue shares is taken by the directors of the company, who must first be authorised to do so by an ordinary resolution of the existing shareholders. Where shares are to be allotted to new shareholders, it is normally necessary also to pass a special resolution to disapply statutory pre-emption rights. These rights entitle existing shareholders to be offered first any new shares in proportion to their shareholding.
Payment for shares	Payment is normally required in cash unless otherwise agreed by the board. Shares may be issued partly-paid, although the shareholder remains liable to pay the remainder when called upon to do so. The nominal (or par) value of each share is effectively its face value, for example, £1 or 50 pence. Shares may be issued at a premium to the nominal value, that is, above that value. Any such premium must be recorded in a separate share premium account and the use of such premium is restricted. Shares cannot be issued at a discount to the par value.
Financial assistance for the purchase of shares	The general prohibition on the provision by a company of assistance for the purchase of its shares has been removed for a private company by the CA 2006. The prohibition still remains for public companies. Financial assistance could be by way of gift, loan or security.

Topic	Summary
Buyback of shares	Generally, the principle of capital maintenance prohibits a company from buying back its shares from shareholders. However, a procedure exists whereby this can take place provided it is approved by special resolution and only certain funds are used for the purchase.
Classes of shares	Shares of different classes may be issued, with differing rights as to voting, dividends, redemption and treatment on a winding-up.
Transfer of shares	Shareholders may, subject to any restrictions in the company's articles, transfer their shares. A stock transfer form is used, on which stamp duty at 0.5% on the price of the shares transferred must be paid. Private companies may often restrict transfers of shares to ensure that they are held by approved or specified parties.
Transmission of shares	Transmission is the automatic process by which a deceased shareholder's shares pass to his personal representative.
Debt finance	Debt finance can be thought of in two main categories: borrowing by way of overdraft or loan; and raising finance through the issue of debt securities.
Overdraft	This is where a company draws on its current account such as to create a negative balance. It will agree an overdraft limit with its bank and pay a fee for this facility. Interest will be payable and the overdraft is, potentially, repayable on demand, that is, immediately.
Loans	Term loans are loans of specific amounts made for specific periods of time. The capital will be required to be repaid either in instalments ('amortised' repayment) during the period of the loan or in a single, 'bullet' repayment. Interest will be payable at either a fixed or floating (variable) rate. There will normally be specified events of default which, when breached, will trigger repayment of the outstanding capital and interest.
Security	A lender will often require a loan to be secured to provide an alternative source of funds should the borrower be unable to repay a loan. In addition, security will usually put the lender in a better position then many other creditors if the borrower becomes insolvent. Security will often be taken by a charge over assets of the borrower.
Charges	Charges may be fixed or floating. Both forms must be registered at Companies House in order to be effective against liquidators, administrators and other creditors. Fixed charges take priority over floating charges and are taken over specified assets, such as land, major items of machinery or book debts. A company cannot freely deal with assets the subject of a fixed charge. Floating charges are equitable charges over the whole or a class of assets, which assets change from time to time. Unlike a fixed charge, a floating charge allows a company to deal freely with the charged assets in the ordinary course of its business. The floating charge will crystallise on specified events, at which time the assets the subject of the charge will be caught.

Topic	Summary
Guarantees	A director of a company may be asked to provide personal guarantees by way of security for loans made to the company of which he is a director. This puts at risk the director's personal assets should the company be unable to repay the loan.

Part III

RUNNING A BUSINESS IN PARTNERSHIP

When a business is run by a partnership, the relationships between the key players are less formalised than within companies.

This Part considers how and on what terms a partnership may be established, the ongoing implications of being in partnership, both as regards fellow partners and as regards debts of the business, and how a partner may retire from or break up the partnership.

This Part is also applicable to a partnership formed by two or more companies to undertake a joint venture.

Chapter 13

The Start of a Partnership

13.1 Introduction

Where two or more persons wish to establish a business relationship between themselves without becoming a company, partnership is only one of a number of possibilities. Other possibilities include the relationships of employer and employee, principal and agent, franchisor and franchisee.

The chapters which follow deal with the law of partnerships. The principal Act is the Partnership Act 1890 ('PA 1890'), though partnership as such existed long before this Act. The Act was drafted to deal with a collection of human beings who were in business together, in effect regulated by a contract, written or oral. One of the main advantages of partnership is a lack of formality which was an even more important advantage in the past, as formation of a new company in the nineteenth century used to be very difficult.

Where there are documents governing relations within a partnership (and there is no obligation to have such documents), that documentation can be kept away from the public gaze as there are no disclosure requirements for partnerships, but there are such requirements for companies.

The Law Commission issued a Consultation Paper in the autumn of 2000 on revision of the law of partnerships.

13.2 What is a partnership?

13.2.1 Definition

A partnership arises where two or more persons agree that they will run a business together and actually do so. The term 'partnership' therefore describes no more than a business relationship based on an agreement (ie contract). The agreement can be oral or in writing or may even be implied by conduct. A partnership need not necessarily be recognised as such by the parties since the existence of a partnership depends on whether or not the definition contained in s 1 of the PA 1890 applies. By this section, 'partnership is the relation which subsists between persons carrying on a business in common with a view of profit'. An example of s 1 is the case of *Khan v Miah* [2000] 1 WLR 2123, where the House of Lords held that the partnership in that case had commenced, even though the restaurant in question had not opened before the partnership between the parties had broken down. In *Young v Zahid* [2006] EWCA Civ 613, a partner in a law firm who was only paid a fixed salary, and not a share of the profits, was held to be a 'partner' under s 1. In other words, in both cases, the s 1 definition decided when the partnership commenced, not any agreement to the contrary between the parties.

'Carrying on a business in common' means that two or more persons share responsibility for the business and for decisions which affect the business; in effect, that there are two or more proprietors. In contrast, an employer and his employee may be running a business together, but this will not mean that they are partners. The employee must accept the decisions and instructions of his employer, and he has no right to interfere.

It is important to realise at the outset that the partnership does **not** have a separate legal existence. In contrast, a company does have such a separate legal existence.

A partnership can be created:

(a)   for a specific purpose or for a pre-determined period of time; or

(b)   so as to continue for as long as the parties want – a partnership 'at will'.

The 'persons' in partnership would usually be people but they could be two or more companies. This could be the case where companies form a joint venture, often specifically to take on a new project.

In order to be able to identify a particular relationship as being a partnership, it is necessary to appreciate the fundamental characteristics of a partnership.

13.2.2   Fundamental characteristics

Typical rights and responsibilities of partners which are fundamental to the relationship include:

(a)   the right to be involved in making decisions which affect the business;

(b)   the right to share in the profits of the business;

(c)   the right to examine the accounts of the business;

(d)   the right to insist on openness and honesty from fellow partners;

(e)   the right to veto the introduction of a new partner; and

(f)   the responsibility for sharing any losses made by the business.

Theoretically, any or all of these fundamental characteristics can be varied or excluded by the agreement governing the relationship, although at some point variations or exclusions could go as far as to deny the existence of the partnership.

13.3   Setting up a partnership

Since the existence of a partnership is established by applying the definition to the relationship (which may be based on an oral agreement), it follows that there is no necessary formality. However, a written agreement is invaluable as evidence of the relationship and of its terms. It is also useful for the partners to have a written 'constitution' to which they may refer. It may, amongst other things, provide solutions to possible disagreements or disputes and thus perhaps avoid future litigation. It also helps in ensuring that the undesired aspects of the PA 1890 have been in fact avoided. Typical terms of a partnership agreement are considered in **Chapter 14**.

13.4   Formalities required by statute

13.4.1   Business names

Where ss 1192–1206 of the CA 2006 apply, there are controls over the choice of partnership name (ss 1193, 1194) and requirements as to revealing the names and business address of the partners (s 1201). These controls and requirements will not apply, however, if the name of the partnership business consists simply of the names of the partners, because the Act itself will not then apply. For example, if Paula Jones and Alan Burns commence business in partnership, the following business names will not be subject to the Act: 'Jones and Burns', 'P Jones and A Burns', 'Paula Jones and Alan Burns'. Conversely, if they choose one of the following business names, they will be subject to the Act: 'P Jones', 'Jones, Burns & Co', 'JB Services'.

If the Act applies, certain words or expressions forming part of the business name will require the written approval of the Secretary of State for Trade and Industry (and possibly the prior approval of another relevant body). These include words or expressions contained in the Company and Business Names (Miscellaneous Provisions) Regulations 2009 (SI 2009/1085). In addition, prescribed information must appear on all stationery (s 1202) and on a notice at any place of business to which customers or suppliers have access (s 1204). This information consists of the names of the partners and (for each partner) an address in Great Britain for service of documents. Non-compliance with the obligations is an offence punishable by a fine and the partners will be unable to enforce contracts if the other party can show that he was prejudiced by the non-compliance (ss 1205, 1206).

In some partnerships, it would be unrealistic to comply with the legislation requirements for stating partners' names on stationery. There is no limitation on the size of a partnership. It is provided, therefore, that the partnership can instead include on its stationery a statement that a full list of partners is available at the principal place of business (s 1203).

13.4.2   Other statutory obligations

Other statutory obligations which may arise at the start of a partnership are not peculiar to partnerships and may arise at the start of any business. These include obligations concerning income tax (or corporation tax, where the partners in a joint venture are companies), VAT and national insurance. A partnership will have the additional obligation, in this context, of notifying HM Revenue and Customs of the identity of the partners.

13.5   The law of partnership and its use in joint ventures

Partnership can be a suitable vehicle for a group of individuals to engage in a business venture together because of the informal nature of partnerships, the commercial secrecy that is possible, and the ability for the partners to claim tax relief for start-up losses. However, these attributes can also serve to make partnership a suitable vehicle for two or more companies which wish to combine forces to start a new venture together, perhaps in a new country or in a new field of technology. Although the partners are companies, not human beings, the law is still the same, primarily the PA 1890, even though the Act was not drafted with that situation in mind. This situation of 'old' law being used for a 'new' factual situation is a recurring theme in English law. You will come across this type of situation throughout your legal career.

Chapter 14
The Partnership Agreement

14.1 Introduction

Section 24 of the PA 1890 contains a number of provisions concerning the running of the partnership that will be implied into a partnership agreement in the absence of express provision. However, the Act is rather limited in scope and inevitably cannot do more than treat all partners equally. The length of a partnership agreement will depend on the imagination and thoroughness of the partners and their advisers. The following range of topics gives some idea of the possible provisions of a comprehensive agreement, although there will always be scope for additional provisions. Do not forget that the Partnership Act is over 110 years old and cannot be expected to meet modern business practices, so many of its terms will need to be varied by the agreement between the parties.

14.2 Commencement date

The existence of a partnership is established when the statutory definition in s 1 of the PA 1890 is satisfied. The date specified in the agreement will not necessarily be correct therefore, but it is desirable to specify a date from which the parties regard their mutual rights and responsibilities as taking effect.

14.3 Name

The name of the partnership should be stated since this means that it is fixed and any partner can insist as a matter of contract on there being no change to it. The firm name may be different from the business (or trading) name, in which case both names should be stated in the agreement.

14.4 Financial input

Each partner is likely to be putting capital into the business, whether this is the result of borrowing or from his own resources. This is one of the ways in which the partnership will finance the purchase of assets needed to run the business. The agreement should state how much capital each partner is contributing and, possibly, deal with the question of future increases in contributions, if such increases are anticipated.

14.5   Shares in income profits/losses

Partners may be content to share income profits of the business equally. Indeed, if there is no evidence of contrary agreement, this will be the effect of the PA 1890 which will imply such a term. Any losses may also be shared equally. Again, this will be implied by the PA 1890 if there is no evidence of contrary agreement. In practice, the circumstances will often suggest that a different, more detailed, basis for division of profits is appropriate. The partnership agreement may provide for various possibilities in dividing profits, including the following.

14.5.1   Salary

Salaries of differing fixed amounts might be appropriate before any surplus profit is divided between the partners. Their purpose is to ensure that certain factors are reflected in the partners' incomes. These factors might include different amounts of time devoted to the business (eg allowing for a part-time or even a sleeping partner) and the different degrees of skill and experience of the partners.

14.5.2   Interest

Interest (at a specified rate) might be allowed on partners' capital contributions, again before any surplus profit is divided between the partners. This is simply to reward partners in proportion to their contribution to the financing of the partnership.

14.5.3   Profit-sharing

A suitable ratio in which the profits remaining after salaries and interest on capital are to be shared should be stated. If salaries and interest on capital have achieved sufficient 'fine tuning', then equal shares may be appropriate. On the other hand, the longer-serving partner or partners may negotiate for a higher share to reflect, for example, seniority in the business.

Any provisions of this kind in the agreement should also state what is to happen in the event of a loss. In particular, are salaries and interest on capital still to be awarded, thus exacerbating a loss?

14.6   Drawings

One source of future ill-feeling and possible dispute between partners is the amount of money that they each withdraw from the business from time to time in respect of their shares of the profits. One partner may be conservative, wishing to maintain a healthy bank balance for the partnership, while another is more cavalier in his attitude. Often a partnership agreement will state a monthly limit on how much each partner can withdraw, perhaps with provision for periodic review. The clause may also stipulate the consequences of exceeding the stated limit.

In a joint venture agreement between companies, the way in which losses or profits are dealt with will be a key consideration.

14.7   Shares in increases/decreases in asset values

If a fixed asset of the partnership (such as premises) is sold, realising an increase or a decrease in its value, how is this to be shared between the partners? If the assets are revalued, without the disposal, to show their current value in the accounts (eg in anticipation of a new person joining the partnership), how is this increase/decrease to be reflected in the value of each existing partner's share in the business, as shown in the accounts? Partners may be content to share these increases/decreases equally and, as with income, this will be the effect of PA 1890 which will imply such a term if there is no agreement to the contrary. However, as with income, there may be circumstances where the partners would agree a different basis for division. In particular, if there is disparity in capital contributions, the partner who contributes the greater share of the capital may feel that he should receive the greater share of any gain. The basis for division of increases (or decreases) in asset values is sometimes known as the 'asset-surplus sharing ratio'. As with all aspects of any agreement, this provision will be a matter for negotiation and the other partners may feel that, if interest on capital is to be allowed (as in **14.5.2**), this provides sufficient recognition of the disparity in contributions.

14.8   Place and nature of business

The agreement may contain clauses which describe the premises at which the business will be carried on, the geographical area of its operations and the nature of the business which will be carried on. Once agreed, any change would need the unanimous consent of the partners.

14.9   Ownership of assets

A partnership asset is an asset where beneficial ownership rests with all the partners, although not necessarily in equal shares. Many disputes have arisen over the factual question of what is a partnership asset and what belongs to a partner individually. This may arise as a result of the partnership being formed where certain assets which are to be used by the business (eg freehold premises or a lease of premises) already belong to one of the persons who is becoming a partner and there is no clear agreement as to what was intended as to ownership. That partner could have continued to own the asset personally (allowing the firm the use of the asset) or the asset could have become partnership property, either by its value representing a capital contribution from that partner or by that partner receiving payment from the others. Equally, a dispute may arise over an asset which has been acquired during the partnership where there was no clear agreement (either express or implied) as to the partners' intentions as to ownership.

In many instances no dispute will arise because there will be evidence of what was intended. Title deeds may indicate who was the owner, but these need not be conclusive since one partner may have legal title in his sole name whilst holding as trustee for all the partners beneficially so that the asset is in fact a partnership asset. The accounts of the partnership should reveal what capital contributions have been made and should correspondingly record what are the assets of the partnership, but these may not be conclusive evidence. To avoid the possibility of there being a dispute over the available evidence or no clear evidence, the agreement should stipulate what are the assets of the partnership (eg by referring to a list contained in a schedule to the agreement).

If there is a dispute, what circumstances are likely to trigger it? The dispute may arise on dissolution when it becomes necessary to establish how much each partner is entitled to receive. The value of an asset owned by just one partner will not be shared. It may be that a profit is made out of a particular asset. A profit on an asset owned by just one partner will not be shared. Any or all of the partners may incur liability to capital gains tax or inheritance tax by reference to a particular asset and wish to claim certain reliefs. Liability to tax and the availability or amount of certain reliefs will depend on whether the asset is or is not a partnership asset.

For an unusual problem on partnership property, see *Don King Productions Inc v Warren (No 1)* [2000] Ch 291, where the property was contracts relating to boxing.

14.10   Work input

The PA 1890 will imply a term into a partnership agreement, in the absence of contrary agreement, that all partners are entitled to take part in the management of the business, albeit without any obligation to do so. There is no implication that a partner must devote his full time and attention to the business. Wilful neglect of the business (as opposed to a degree of laziness) may mean that the other partners are entitled to be compensated for the extra work undertaken by them.

The agreement should set out the degree of commitment expected of each partner. The term might require the partner to work in the business full-time or part-time or even not work at all (being a dormant or sleeping partner). To express these degrees of work with precision in terms of fixed hours of work may well be inappropriate, particularly for full-time working partners. Often the agreement will be expressed in more general terms so that, for example, a full-time working partner 'must devote his whole time and attention to the business'. In order to reinforce this rather widely expressed obligation, often there is further provision to the effect that such partners must not be involved in any other business whatsoever during the partnership. This absolute bar is enforceable and does not fall foul of the public policy issues which may make such covenants in restraint of trade void after termination of the relationship of the partners (see **14.17**).

Inevitably, there must be qualifications to the main statement as to the amount of work required of a partner. There must be provisions dealing with holiday entitlement, with sickness and with any other reasons for being absent from work, such as maternity (or even paternity). The 1890 Act offers no guidance as to what would be implied here in the absence of express provision.

14.11   Roles

Partners may have differing functions within the partnership so that not only must the agreement describe the amount of work input but also each partner's function. For example, a sleeping partner's role might be defined as being limited to attending meetings of the partners and the agreement would state that he has no authority to enter into contracts on behalf of the partnership. The agreement might state that a particular partner (with limited experience) only has authority to make contracts within specified limits, thereby partly defining his role.

Whatever is agreed along these lines is binding between the partners. Any partner who ignored any such restriction would be acting in breach of contract. The question of whether any contract made by him in breach of the partnership agreement would be enforceable against the firm by the third party depends on the application of s 5 of the PA 1890 which is considered in **Chapter 16**.

14.12   Decision-making

Unless the agreement provides to the contrary, all partnership decisions will be made on the basis of a simple majority (where each partner has one vote), except that decisions on changing the nature of the business or on introduction of a new partner require unanimity. However, it may be that the agreement should be more detailed, perhaps describing certain decisions which may be made by any partner on his own (such as routine sales and purchases of stock). Other decisions may require a simple majority (such as hiring staff) and certain decisions may require unanimity (such as borrowing money). In this context, it is important to appreciate that anything contained in the agreement (eg type of business) is a term of the contract between the partners and therefore cannot be altered without the consent of all parties to the contract (ie all partners would have to consent). That consent might be built into the contract itself, in that the agreement might contain provision for altering its terms (eg that a change in the type of business is to be effective if agreed by a majority of the partners).

In a joint venture between companies, a decision-making mechanism will need to be included in the agreement.

14.13   Duration

14.13.1   Dissolution by notice

How long is the partnership to last before it may be dissolved either by just one partner who wishes to leave or by all the partners wishing to go their separate ways? If there is no provision in the agreement, the partnership can be dissolved at any time by any partner giving notice to the others. This is a partnership at will. A partnership cannot be a 'partnership at will' under s 26 if there is any limitation placed on a partner's right to terminate the agreement by him alone giving notice (see *Moss v Elphick* [1910] 1 KB 846). The notice of dissolution can have immediate effect and need not even be in writing unless the agreement itself was by deed. Although having the advantage of allowing each partner freedom to dissolve the whole partnership at any time and for any reason, a partnership at will has the corresponding disadvantages for the firm as a whole of insecurity and instability. Frequently, therefore, a partnership agreement will restrict the right of partners to dissolve the partnership.

A somewhat unusual example of a partnership at will occurred in *Byford v Oliver* [2003] All ER (D) 345. This case concerned the heavy metal band, 'Saxon'. Over the 20 years of its existence, the line-up of the band had changed but the claimant had been there throughout that time. It was held that he owned the name and goodwill of the band, not the defendants. The claimant would therefore have been entitled to register the name 'Saxon' as a trade mark, but the defendants were not.

Section 32 of the PA 1890 defines the basis on which partnerships of any type are to be dissolved, subject to alternative agreement between the partners.

14.13.2   Other solutions

One possible provision is that any notice of dissolution must allow a minimum period (of, say, six months) before taking effect. This at least gives time to settle what should happen on the dissolution (eg, some partners might negotiate the purchase of the interest of another in order to continue the business).

Another possibility is to agree a duration of a fixed term of a number of years. This provides certainty but is inflexible in committing each partner to the partnership for a certain duration. A fixed-term agreement can also be criticised if it fails to provide for what should happen if partners wish to continue after the expiry of their fixed term. However, this can be dealt with by providing that the partnership will continue automatically on the same terms after the fixed term except that thenceforth it will be terminable by, say, three months' notice.

Yet another possible provision is that the partnership is to continue for as long as there are at least two remaining partners, despite the departure of any partner by reason of retirement (see **14.14**), expulsion (see **14.15**), death or bankruptcy. This provision has the merit of providing some degree of security and stability whilst allowing individuals the flexibility of being able to leave. In case the departure of a partner might present financial problems for the others in purchasing his share from him, ancillary provisions can be included delaying payment to the outgoing partner so that he is, in effect, forced to lend money to the partnership.

14.13.3   Death and bankruptcy

Under s 33 of the PA 1890 unless there is contrary agreement, the death or bankruptcy of a partner will automatically cause dissolution of the entire partnership. Therefore, it is appropriate to add a further provision that on the death or bankruptcy of a partner the remaining partners will automatically continue in partnership with one another on buying out the deceased or bankrupt partner's share in the business.

Again, with a joint venture between companies, the agreement will need to provide a mechanism for unwinding the joint venture if one party goes insolvent.

14.13.4   Court order

Situations may arise where a partner is 'locked into' a partnership by an agreement which contains no provision allowing him to dissolve the partnership or even to retire. To deal with this, s 35 of the PA 1890 provides that, on certain grounds, the court can make an order for dissolution. This effectively enables the partner to break his agreement with his partners without being liable for breach of contract. If none of the grounds in the Act are satisfied, the partner has no escape without being liable for breach of contract.

14.14   Retirement

In the context of partnership law, the word 'retirement' does not mean being eligible to collect the old age pension. It means leaving the partnership, perhaps to follow other business opportunities. The PA 1890 does not provide for retirement.

It is easy to assume that a partner must have the right to retire from the partnership when he pleases. Yet the agreement may contain provisions on duration which will have the effect of preventing retirement other than by the partner acting in breach of contract (such as a fixed term with no get-out provisions). Even if there is no provision on duration, strictly a partner's exit route is by dissolving the entire partnership by giving notice. It would then be for the others to re-form the partnership if they could reach agreement with the outgoing partner for the purchase of his share.

It is usually desirable therefore to have express provision governing the question of when a partner can retire (without dissolving the partnership so far as the others are concerned) and of payment for his share by the others (see **14.16**).

14.15   Expulsion

Expulsion of a partner is analogous to retirement, save that expulsion happens at the instigation of the other partners while retirement is a voluntary act of the outgoing partner. It amounts to terminating the contract (the partnership agreement) with the outgoing partner without his consent. It is an important sanction for breach of the agreement or for other stipulated forms of misconduct. As with retirement, the PA 1890 does not provide for the possibility of a partner being expelled by the others without his consent. There should therefore be provision in a partnership agreement for the possibility of expulsion. The agreement should state on what grounds the right to expel is to be exercisable and how it will be exercised (eg by a unanimous decision of the other partners with immediate effect). As with a retirement clause, the expulsion clause should also deal with the question of payment for the outgoing partner's share.

14.16   Payment for outgoing partner's share

Where a person ceases to be a partner by reason of retirement, expulsion, death or bankruptcy and others continue in partnership together, the remaining partners will need to pay for the outgoing partner's share in the business. To avoid any need to negotiate the terms of the purchase at the time, the agreement should contain the appropriate terms. If the agreement is silent on this and a settlement cannot be agreed at the time, s 42 of the PA 1890 becomes relevant. Under this section, if a person ceases to be a partner and others continue in partnership but there is delay in final payment of the former partner's share, then the former partner or his estate is entitled to receive either interest at 5% on the amount of his share or such share of the profits as is attributable to the use of his share.

The terms that may be appropriate for inclusion in the partnership agreement will depend on the circumstances but they should deal with the following.

(a) Whether there is to be a binding obligation on the partners to purchase the outgoing partner's share, or whether they are merely to have an option to purchase. Apart from the question of certainty as to what will happen, these alternatives have differing tax implications. In order to obtain business property relief for inheritance tax, an option to purchase is preferable.

(b) The basis on which the outgoing partner's share will be valued.

(c) Provision for a professional valuation if the partners cannot reach agreement between themselves.

(d) The date on which payment will be due (or dates, if payment by instalments is agreed).

(e) An indemnity for liabilities of the firm if these were taken into account in the valuation.

14.17 Restraint of trade following departure

14.17.1 Competition

There will be no implied term preventing an outgoing partner from setting up in competition with the partnership or joining a rival business or even poaching the employees of the partnership to work in a rival business. There should always be a provision limiting an outgoing partner's freedom to compete with the firm to protect the business connections of the continuing firm (broadly to preserve its customers and its employees) and to protect its confidential information. The drafting of such clauses is critically important because a restraint of trade clause which is held to be unreasonable will be void as a matter of public policy. However, courts are more likely to uphold a restraint of trade clause when it is to protect the purchaser of a business, rather than to restrict the activities of an individual partner departing from a continuing business.

14.17.2 Drafting a non-competition clause

One type of clause commonly used to restrain an ex-partner's activities is a clause which seeks to prevent the person from being involved in any way in a competing business. The key issues to address in drafting such a clause (a non-competition clause) are:

(a) What is the clause aiming to protect? There must be a legitimate interest; this will usually be the firm's business connections, its employees and/or its confidential information.

(b) Is the clause reasonable, as drafted, for the protection of that interest? It must be limited as to its geographical area and as to its duration, and both the area and the duration must not be greater than is reasonable for the protection of the legitimate interest in question.

Suppose, for example, that the partnership of X, Y and Z carries on business as double glazing installers throughout Cheshire and North Wales, where all three partners are fully involved throughout the area. Their agreement contains a clause stipulating that, on leaving the partnership, a partner will not work in any way in the building trade for 10 years in England or Wales. This clause will be void because it is unreasonably wide on all three aspects. If the clause had stipulated that, on leaving the partnership, a partner would not work in the business of double glazing installation for 12 months throughout Cheshire and North Wales, this might be valid and enforceable.

14.17.3 Other forms of restraint of trade

Other forms of restraint of trade clauses may also be considered. A 'non-dealing clause' seeks to prevent the former partner from entering into contracts with customers or former customers or employees of the partnership which he has left. A 'non-solicitation clause' merely seeks to prevent him from soliciting contracts from such customers or employees. Both types of clauses are less restrictive of the former partner's freedom to continue his trade and therefore more likely to be held enforceable, provided that the effect of the clause is limited to what is reasonable for the protection of the firm's legitimate interest.

14.18 Arbitration

To avoid the expense, delay and adverse publicity arising out of litigation between partners, the agreement may provide that certain disputes should be referred to arbitration. Usually the disputes in question will be described as those arising out of the interpretation or application of the agreement itself rather than disputes over the running of the business.

Chapter 15
Partners' Responsibilities

15.1 Introduction

Although a partner has no definable role other than under the terms of the partnership agreement (which may be express or implied), he does have certain responsibilities towards his fellow partners and correspondingly certain rights against his fellow partners which arise as a result of the existence of the partnership relationship.

15.2 Utmost good faith

By common law, partnership is a relationship onto which is imposed a duty of the utmost fairness and good faith from one partner to another. Particular applications of this principle, contained in ss 28–30 of the PA 1890 are that:

(a) partners must divulge to one another all relevant information connected with the business and their relationship;

(b) they must be prepared to share with their fellow partners any profit or benefit they receive that is connected with or derived from the partnership, the business or its property without the consent of the other partners; and

(c) they must be prepared to share with their fellow partners any profits they make from carrying on a competing business without the consent of the other partners.

Examples

In negotiating to sell to the partnership business premises owned by him, a partner must not suppress information which will affect the valuation. The doctrine of caveat emptor does not apply to partners' dealings with one another.

If a customer of the firm asks a partner to do some work for cash in his spare time, the cash belongs to the partnership unless the other partners choose to allow him to keep it.

If a partner sets up a competing business in his spare time, the profits of that business belong to the partnership unless otherwise agreed.

If the partnership owns a lease of its business premises which contains an option to purchase the freehold, a partner who exercises the option in his own name must allow his fellow partners to share in the profit that he makes.

In *Broadhurst v Broadhurst* [2006] EWHC 2727, a partner was held to be in breach of his duties of utmost good faith under ss 28 and 29 of the PA 1890. The errant partner in a car dealing business had not remitted all the sale proceeds for a consignment of cars into the accounts of the business. He had also caused cars to be impounded abroad and therefore not to be imported into the UK in good time.

15.3 Further responsibilities implied by the Act

Further responsibilities that can be enforced by the partners against one another are:

(a)   the responsibility for bearing a share of any loss made by the business (the particular share depending upon the terms of their agreement) (PA 1890, s 24(1));

(b)   the obligation as a firm to indemnify fellow partners against bearing more than their share (as above) of any liability or expense connected with the business (PA 1890, s 24(2)).

15.4   Contractual responsibilities

Most of the responsibilities of a partner to his fellow partners derive from the terms of their partnership agreement and may be express or implied.

Chapter 16
Liability for the Firm's Debts

16.1 Introduction

Transactions which may affect a partnership generally involve contracts. Contracts may be made by all of the partners acting collectively (eg they all sign a lease of business premises) or by just one of the partners. Some or all of the partners may seek to deny that they are liable on the contract (or for breach of it). In such cases, it is necessary first to identify whether the firm itself is liable and then, if the firm is liable, to identify which individuals are liable. These matters are governed by the following sections of the PA 1890. They are based on agency principles and are explained in the text which follows.

5 Power of partner to bind the firm

Every partner is an agent of the firm and his other partners for the purpose of the business of the partnership; and the acts of every partner who does any act for carrying on in the usual way business of the kind carried on by the firm of which he is a member bind the firm and his partners, unless the partner so acting has in fact no authority to act for the firm in the particular matter, and the person with whom he is dealing either knows that he has no authority, or does not know or believe him to be a partner.

6 Partners bound by acts on behalf of firm

An act or instrument relating to the business of the firm and done or executed in the firm-name, or in any other manner showing an intention to bind the firm, by any person thereto authorised whether a partner or not, is binding on the firm and all the partners.

Provided that this section shall not affect any general rule of law relating to the execution of deeds or negotiable instruments.

7 Partner using credit of firm for private purposes

Where one partner pledges the credit of the firm for a purpose apparently not connected with the firm's ordinary course of business, the firm is not bound, unless he is in fact specially authorised by the other partners; but this section does not affect any personal liability incurred by an individual partner.

8 Effect of notice that firm will not be bound by acts of partner

If it has been agreed between the partners that any restriction shall be placed on the power of any one or more of them to bind the firm, no act done in contravention of the agreement is binding on the firm with respect to persons having notice of the agreement.

Remember that a partnership has no legal existence separate from that of the partners (unlike a company). So, when the PA 1890 refers to the 'firm', it means the partners.

Under s 5, the act has to be in the usual course of the firm's business. In *Hirst v Etherington* [1999] Lloyd's Rep PN 938, the debt incurred by one partner in a solicitors' firm was held not to have been entered into in the usual course of the firm's business. His partner was therefore not also liable on the debt.

16.2   When will the firm be liable?

It should be noted that s 5 deals with a partner's authority. There is no equivalent provision for companies in the CA 2006.

16.2.1   Actual authority

The firm will always be liable for actions which were actually authorised. An action may be actually authorised in various ways.

(a)   The partners may have acted jointly in making the contract; clearly they are not then at liberty to change their minds.

(b)   Express actual authority: the partners may have *expressly* instructed one of the partners to represent the firm in a particular transaction or type of transaction. For example, one of the partners may have the function, under their agreement, of purchasing stock for the business. That partner is then acting with actual authority and the firm is bound by any contract that he makes within the scope of that authority.

(c)   Implied actual authority: the partners may have *impliedly* accepted that one or more partners have the authority to represent the firm in a particular type of transaction. If all the partners are actively involved in running the business without any limitations being agreed between them, it will be implied that each partner has authority, for example, to sell the firm's products in the ordinary course of business. Alternatively, authority may be implied by a regular course of dealing by one of the partners in which the others have acquiesced.

16.2.2   Apparent (ostensible) authority

The firm may be liable for actions which were not actually authorised but which may have appeared to an outsider to be authorised. This liability derives from application of the principles of agency law, based on the fact that each partner is an agent of the firm and of his fellow partners for the purposes of the partnership business. Thus, even though as between the partners there is some express or implied limitation on the partner's authority, the firm will be liable by application of s 5 where:

(a)   the transaction is one which relates to the type of business in which the firm is apparently engaged (ie 'business of the kind carried on by the firm' per s 5);

(b)   the transaction is one for which a partner in such a firm would usually be expected to have the authority to act (ie 'in the usual way' per s 5);

(c)   the other party to the transaction did not know that the partner did not actually have authority to act; and

(d)   the other party deals with a person whom he knows or believes to be a partner.

It can be seen that points (c) and (d) relate to the knowledge or belief of the third party who has dealt with the partner. It will be a subjective test as to whether these conditions are satisfied. On the other hand, points (a) and (b) call for an objective test of what would appear to an outsider to be the nature of the firm's business and what authority one would expect a partner in such a firm to have.

Example 1

At a partner's meeting of the firm of A B & Co, it is decided that the firm should enter into a contract for the purchase of new premises at 21 High Street and a contract for the sale of their present business premises at 13 Side Street. Both written contracts are duly signed by all of the partners. The firm is bound by these contracts because they were actually authorised by means of the partners acting together. Note that the result would be the same if one partner had been instructed to sign the contract on behalf of the firm.

Example 2

Without consulting his fellow partners, C, the senior partner of C, D & Co seizes an unexpected opportunity to purchase new business premises at 12 High Street and to sell the firm's present business premises at 31 Side Street by signing a written contract for each on behalf of the firm. Although undoubtedly connected with the firm's business, the firm is not bound by the contract because C was not actually authorised and, because a third party would not normally expect that one partner would have authority to make such a major contract on his own, there is no apparent authority. However, C is personally liable to the third party under the contract.

Example 3

E, a partner in E F Plumbers, has placed several unconnected orders on credit in the name of the firm without consulting his partner F. In each case, the supplier has assumed that E was authorised to make the contract on behalf of his firm. The orders were:

(a)   a quantity of copper piping;

(b)   a jacuzzi and luxury bathroom suite;

(c)   a brand-new van with 'E F Plumbers' printed on the side;

(d)   a quantity of roofing felt and heavy timber.

In the first three instances, each contract is apparently connected with the business and so it would only be necessary to resolve whether a single partner would usually be expected to have the authority to make the contract. The order for the van may be too major for there to be apparent authority, but the other two contracts would seem to be binding on the firm. The contract for the roofing felt and timber has no apparent connection with the firm's business and therefore it is likely that the firm would not be bound unless there were special facts (eg some representation by the firm and not just by E) which led the supplier to believe that E had the authority to make this contract.

Example 4

J K Hairstylists are visited by Morris, a salesman for a manufacturer of a new range of shampoos for salon use. After an inspection of his products, Morris hears J and K discussing their merits and J being adamant that the firm should stick with its present supplier and order nothing from Morris.

Ignoring this deadlock with his partner, K orders a supply from Morris. Although K would have had apparent authority to make such a contract if Morris had not been aware of their discussion, in fact Morris has reason to believe that K had no authority to make the contract and so the firm is not liable.

See the case of *JJ Coughlan v Ruparelia* [2003] EWCA Civ 1057 for an example of when the other partners will not be liable in contract (see **16.2.4** for the facts of this case).

In *Bourne v Brandon Davis* [2006] EWHC 1567 (Ch), it was held that musicians in a pop group could not have their performing rights assigned *en bloc* by another member of the group without their consent. The rights were personal to each of them and not 'the business of the partnership', so s 5 did not apply.

16.2.3 Personal liability

In any of the above instances the partner who has acted will be personally liable to the other party under the contract. Also, if the partner who has acted has done so without actual authority but has made the firm liable by virtue of his apparent authority, then he is liable to indemnify his fellow partners for any liability or loss which they incur. This is on the basis that he has broken his agreement with his fellow partners by acting without actual authority. See also **16.3**.

16.2.4 Tortious liability

Only liability in contract has been considered so far. Occasionally the firm (as well as the partner in question) is liable for some act of a partner which is tortious by nature, for example, negligence. The position here is governed by s 10, which makes the firm liable for any wrongful act or omission of a partner who acts in the ordinary course of the firm's business or with the authority of his partners.

The text of ss 10 and 12 of the PA 1890 is as follows.

> **10   Liability of the firm for wrongs**
>
> Where, by any wrongful act or omission of any partner acting in the ordinary course of the business of the firm, or with the authority of his co-partners, loss or injury is caused to any person not being a partner in the firm, or any penalty is incurred, the firm is liable therefor to the same extent as the partner so acting or omitting to act.
>
> **12   Liability for wrongs joint and several**
>
> Every partner is liable jointly with his co-partners and also severally for everything for which the firm while he is a partner therein becomes liable under either of the two last preceding sections.

The House of Lords held in *Dubai Aluminium Co Ltd v Salaam* [2002] 3 WLR 1913 that s 10 covers all types of wrongdoing, including a dishonest breach of trust or fiduciary duty, and is not limited to common law torts. However, in *JJ Coughlan v Ruparelia* [2003] EWCA Civ 1057 the Court of Appeal held that ss 5 and 10 did not make the other partners liable for breach of contract and deceit arising out of a fraudulent investment scheme. The solicitor in question was found liable but his partners were not. The making of the agreement in question by the partner was not 'an act for carrying on in the usual way business of the kind carried on by the firm' under s 5, as would have been needed to make the other partners liable in contract. They were also not liable in the tort of deceit under s 10 as the scheme was not 'in the ordinary course of the business of the firm'.

16.3   Against whom can the firm's liabilities be enforced?

16.3.1   Potential defendants

The person who is seeking to enforce a liability of the firm under the principles considered in **16.2**, or who is seeking to claim damages for breach of such a contract, will want to know who can be sued. The range of potential defendants may be quite extensive:

(a)   The partner with whom the person made the contract can be sued individually because there will be privity of contract between them on which the potential claimant can rely. This will only be a real problem for that partner if he has acted without authority in entering the contract.

(b)   The firm can be sued. In fact, any claim should be commenced against the partnership as such, if it has a name and if it is 'appropriate' to do so: CPR Pt 7, PD 7, 5A.1 and 5A.3. All those who were partners at the time when the debt or obligation was incurred are jointly liable to satisfy the judgment (PA 1890, ss 9 and 17, Civil Liability (Contribution) Act 1978, s 3).

(c)   Any person who was a partner at the time when the debt or obligation was incurred can be sued individually. However, it is unlikely that a creditor would sue only one partner in this way, but any partner who is so sued is entitled to claim an indemnity from his partners so that the liability is shared between them.

(d)   Although generally someone who left the firm before the debt or obligation was incurred or who has joined the firm since that time is not liable (PA 1890, s 17), such a person may be sued or made liable for a judgment against the firm as a result of:

    (i)   'holding out' (see **16.3.3**); or

    (ii)   failure to give appropriate notice of retirement (see **16.3.4**); or

(iii) a novation agreement (see **16.3.5**).

In the case of *Dubai Aluminium Co Ltd v Salaam* [2002] 3 WLR 1913, partners in a partnership were held liable for the fraudulent act of their partner who acted dishonestly but in the ordinary course of business of that partnership, a law firm. Section 1(1) of the Civil Liability (Contribution) Act 1978 states that:

(1) ... any person liable in respect of any damage suffered by another person may recover a contribution from any other person liable in respect of the same damage (whether jointly with him or otherwise).

Section 2 states:

(1) Subject to subsection (3) below, in any proceedings for contribution under section 1 above the amount of the contribution recoverable from any person shall be such as may be found by the court to be just and equitable having regard to the extent of that person's responsibility for the damage in question.

16.3.2 Suing in the firm's name

In practice, the most appropriate way of proceeding if court action is necessary is to sue the partners as a group of persons in the firm's name (see **16.3.1(b)**). This has the merit that if judgment is obtained against the partners in the firm's name, this can be enforced against the partnership assets and also potentially against assets owned personally by any of the persons who were partners at the time that the debt or obligation was incurred (or who were liable as if they were partners (see **16.3.1**)).

Example

'Hot Pots' are distributors of potatoes for the catering industry. Originally, the firm consisted of A, B and C as partners. In December, two weeks after A had retired from the firm, Hot Pots agree to purchase the entire crop of Farmer Giles's potatoes in the coming year at a price which is fixed. As a result of ideal growing conditions, there is a glut of potatoes and the contract price turns out to be much higher than the market price at the time of delivery. Hot Pots cancel the order and Farmer Giles sues for breach of contract. Before judgment is obtained against the firm, B retires and D joins the firm. Once judgment is obtained against Hot Pots it can be enforced against the assets of the partnership and/or the assets of B personally and/or the assets of C personally. It could not be enforced against the assets of A, unless there was a 'holding out' (see 16.3.3) or a failure to give appropriate notice of retirement (see 16.3.4), or against the assets of D unless there was a novation agreement (see **16.3.5**).

16.3.3 Persons liable by 'holding out' (PA 1890, s 14)

Where a creditor of a partnership has relied on a representation (or 'holding out') that a particular person was a partner in that firm, he may be able to hold that person liable for the firm's debt. This would be so even though it transpires that the person has never been a partner or, perhaps, had been a partner but had retired before the contract was made. The representation in question may be oral (eg where the person is described as a partner in conversation), in writing (eg on headed notepaper) or even by conduct (eg in a previous course of dealing). The representation may be made by the person himself or, provided it is made with the person's knowledge, by another person.

In *Sangster v Biddulphs* [2005] EWHC 658 (Ch), the test relied on for liability under s 14 was that from *Nationwide Building Society v Lewis* [1998] Ch 482. This was that for liability there had to be (a) holding out, (b) reliance thereon, and (c) the consequent giving of credit to the firm.

Example 1

A has retired from the firm of 'Hot Pots', leaving B and C to carry on the business. After A's retirement B and C wrote to Farmer Giles on some of the firm's old headed notepaper offering to purchase his entire crop of potatoes at a fixed price. On the notepaper, A's name still appears as a partner and Farmer Giles has observed this and relied upon it. If A knows that the firm is using up the old stock of notepaper without removing his name, this may operate as a representation with his knowledge that he is a partner. Conversely, if he stipulated that the old notepaper should be destroyed on his retirement, but B and C have failed to do this, then any such representation is not made with his knowledge and he is not liable.

Example 2

Varying the facts of Example 1, the contract between 'Hot Pots' and Farmer Giles for the purchase and sale of potatoes was made orally when B and C met Farmer Giles on his farm and the contract was subsequently confirmed on the old notepaper. Since the contract was already made before Farmer Giles saw the notepaper, he cannot have relied on the notepaper as containing any representation and therefore cannot hold A liable.

Example 3

Again varying the facts of Example 1, Farmer Giles in fact knew that A had retired when goods were ordered on the old notepaper; because of his knowledge of the retirement, he cannot have relied on the notepaper as containing any representation and therefore cannot hold A liable.

16.3.4 Persons liable by failure to notify leaving (PA 1890, s 36)

The firm's debts can be enforced against all those who were partners at the time when the debt or obligation was incurred (see **16.3.1**). Although a person may retire from a partnership, he remains liable on those contracts already made. The terms for the purchase of his share in the business should include a provision whereby the purchasing partner(s) indemnify him against liability for any such debts which were taken into account in valuing his share (see **14.16**).

A separate point arises under s 36. Where a partner leaves the partnership (eg on retirement or expulsion), he must give notice of his leaving since otherwise he may become liable under s 36 for the acts of his former partner or partners done after he leaves the firm, if the creditor is unaware of the fact that he has left. The notices which he should give are prescribed by s 36 and consist of:

(a) actual notice (eg by sending out standard letters announcing his leaving) to all those who have dealt with the firm prior to his leaving (s 36(1)); and

(b) an advertisement in the *London Gazette* (or, for Scotland, the *Edinburgh Gazette*) as notice to any person who did not deal with the firm prior to the date of that partner's retirement or expulsion (s 36(2)).

A creditor who was unaware of the partner's leaving and who can establish that the type of notice appropriate to him (as above) was not given, will be able to sue the former partner for the firm's debt, in spite of the fact that he has ceased to be a partner. The principle on which s 36 is based, unlike that on which s 14 is based, does not depend on the creditor having relied on some representation at the time of the transaction. Rather the creditor is given the right to assume that the membership of the firm continues unchanged until notice of the prescribed type (as above) is given. It follows that, if the creditor was never aware that the person had been a partner, no notice of any sort will be required since that creditor cannot be assuming the continuance of that person in the partnership.

If the reason for ceasing to be a partner is death or bankruptcy (rather than retirement or expulsion), no notice of the event is required. The estate of the deceased or bankrupt partner is not liable for events occurring after the death or bankruptcy.

> **Example 1**
>
> If, in the 'Hot Pots' examples (see **16.3.2** and **16.3.3**) Farmer Giles had dealt with 'Hot Pots' previously, he is entitled to assume that A remains a partner until he receives actual notice of his retirement. If Farmer Giles has not heard that A has retired, he will be able to sue A, as well as the others, on the contract for the potatoes.

> **Example 2**
>
> If Farmer Giles has never dealt with 'Hot Pots' previously, but was aware that A was a member of the firm, he will be able to assume that A remains a partner unless the fact of A's leaving is advertised in the *London Gazette*. Therefore, if A's retirement has not been so advertised and Farmer Giles has not heard that A has retired, he will be able to sue A, as well as the others, on the contract for the potatoes. Where the retirement has been so advertised there is no requirement that Farmer Giles was aware of the advertisement or even that he had heard of the London Gazette! The advertisement operates as deemed notice to Farmer Giles.

> **Example 3**
>
> If Farmer Giles has never dealt with 'Hot Pots' previously and was not aware that A was a member of the firm, he cannot hold A liable to him on the basis of s 36 even if A fails to give any notice of his retirement.

16.3.5 Liability under a novation agreement

A novation agreement in this context is a tripartite contract involving the creditor of the firm, the partners at the time the contract with the creditor was made and the newly constituted partnership. The partnership may change because one partner leaves and/or a new partner joins. Under this contract of novation, it may be agreed that the creditor will release the original partners from their liability under the contract and instead the firm as newly constituted will take over this liability.

It may be that a retiring partner will be released from an existing debt whilst substituting an incoming partner. This is clearly advantageous to the retiring partner whilst disadvantageous to the incoming partner, and the latter will usually agree to this only as part of the broader package of terms on which he is taken into partnership. It may be that a partner retires and no new partner joins. In this case, in order to ensure that the novation is contractually binding, either there must be consideration for the creditor's promise to release the retiring partner from the liability or the contract must be executed as a deed.

A novation agreement, which, as described, is a tripartite agreement releasing a retiring partner from an existing debt, should not be confused with an indemnity in relation to existing debts. Such an indemnity is a bipartite agreement between the retiring partner and the other partners. Since the firm's creditors will not be party to this agreement they are not bound by it and can still sue the retired partner. It would then be for the indemnifying partners to meet the liability and thus protect the retired partner from it.

> **Example**
>
> In the example in **16.3.2**, the incoming partner D was not liable to Farmer Giles. If Farmer Giles, the partners in 'Hot Pots' and D had entered into a novation agreement as described above, then in fact D would be liable to Farmer Giles.

16.4   What if a partner cannot pay?

16.4.1   Non-payment generally

A creditor can sue the firm as a group of persons or can sue individually any of the persons who are liable as partners. If the creditor has obtained judgment against a partner individually and that partner cannot pay, the creditor is then at liberty to commence fresh proceedings in order to obtain judgment against the firm. Even if the firm cannot pay out of its assets, either because it cannot raise the cash to do so or because its assets in total are insufficient to meet its liabilities in total, judgment against the firm can be enforced against the private assets of any person liable as a partner. If the claim of the creditor cannot be satisfied in any of these ways, it follows that the firm is insolvent and all of the individuals liable as partners are also insolvent, so that insolvency proceedings are likely to follow.

16.4.2   Insolvency

Insolvency is considered in **Chapters 19** and **20**. The law on insolvency of a partnership and of its partners individually is governed by the Insolvent Partnerships Order 1994 (SI 1994/2421) (as amended by SI 2002/1308) and the Insolvency Act 1986. The provisions are complex, but the main point is that, although a partnership is not a person in its own right, nevertheless an insolvent partnership may be wound up as an unregistered company or may avail itself of the rescue procedures available to companies, such as a 'voluntary arrangement' with creditors or an 'administration order' of the court (see **19.3** and **19.4**). A partnership is not governed by the laws on bankruptcy which relate to individuals. Thus, the partnership may be subject to a winding-up order and the individual partners may be subject to bankruptcy orders.

With a partnership joint venture involving companies, the agreement will need to provide a mechanism to unwind the joint venture in the event that one party may be heading for insolvency.

16.5   Summary

The key question is:

Where a contract has been made by a partner (X), is the firm (and therefore all the partners and possibly other persons) liable in relation to that contract?

The path to the answer is:

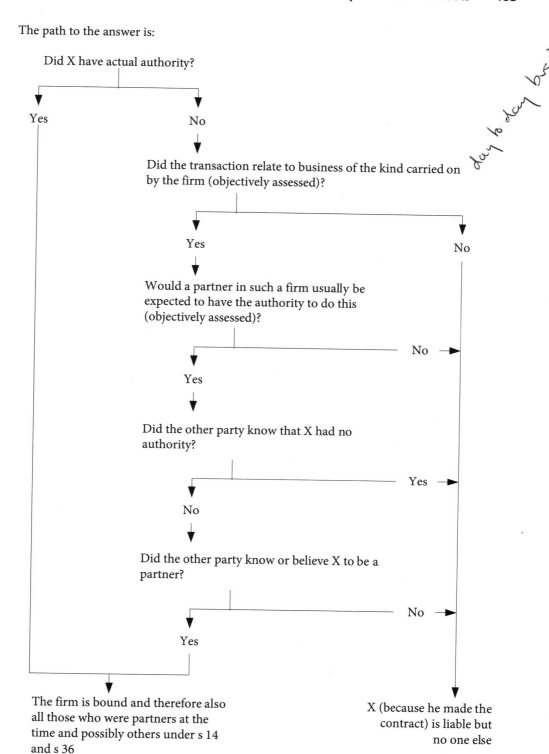

day to day business?

Chapter 17

Dissolution

17.1 Introduction

Dissolution is when a partnership ends. It may be by agreement between the partners, it may be where one partner is in a position to insist (contrary to the wishes of the other(s)) or it may be by circumstances which had not been anticipated. One of the main implications of dissolution is the question of what happens to the business and its assets. Should one or more of the partners take over the business by paying off the other(s)? The circumstances for, and the consequences of, dissolution should be dealt with in a partnership agreement but, failing that, the Partnership Act 1890 (PA 1890) provides the details.

17.2 When does dissolution occur?

Dissolution of a partnership means that the contractual relationship joining all of the current partners comes to an end. It may be that some of the partners in fact succeed to the business and continue in a new partnership with one another. For example, if one of the partners retires and the others continue in partnership, strictly one partnership is dissolved and a new one formed.

Under ss 32–35 of the PA 1890, a partnership is expressed to be dissolved on the occurrence of any one of several events, although most of these provisions can be excluded by agreement (see **17.3**).

17.2.1 Notice (PA 1890, ss 26, 32)

A notice of dissolution can be given by any partner to the other or others (PA 1890, ss 26 and 32). This notice need not state any reason for the dissolution and can have immediate effect. It need not even be in writing unless the partnership agreement was by deed. A partnership which is terminable under s 26 is known as a partnership at will.

17.2.2 Expiry of fixed term (PA 1890, ss 27, 32)

A partnership dissolves on the expiry of a fixed term for which the partners have agreed to continue in partnership, unless their agreement provides for continuance after the fixed term has expired (PA 1890, s 32). This must be taken to give effect to what the partners intended in agreeing a fixed duration. If the partners in fact continue their relationship after the fixed term has expired (and hence after the original partnership has dissolved), they will be presumed to be partners on the same terms as before except that their new partnership is a partnership at will and its terms must be consistent with that type of partnership (s 27).

17.2.3   Charging order over partner's assets (PA 1890, s 33)

A notice of dissolution may be given by the other partners to a partner whose share in the partnership assets has been charged under s 23 by order of the court as security for the payment of that partner's private debt (PA 1890, s 33).

A judgment creditor of a partner in his private capacity may use s 23 as a means of enforcing the judgment. He is not permitted to make any direct claim on the partnership assets even though the partner will be joint owner of those assets. The effect of a charging order under s 23 is that the creditor of that partner has an indirect claim by becoming the chargee of the partner's share in those assets. The creditor's charge may also entitle him to receive the partner's share of the profits of the partnership. At this stage, the other partners have the right to pay off the creditor and then look to their partner for recompense. If this does not happen, then, in order to enforce the charge (and hence the indirect claim on the partnership assets), the creditor may obtain an order of the court for the sale of the partner's share in the assets. If such a sale is ordered the most likely buyers are the other partners, but if they do not wish to purchase the share an outsider may do so. This will not make the outsider a partner in the firm since he is merely the owner of a share in the assets. Since this situation is likely to be unsatisfactory from the other partners' point of view, they have the right just mentioned to give notice of dissolution of the partnership.

17.2.4   Death or bankruptcy (PA 1890, s 33)

Death or bankruptcy will automatically terminate the partnership (PA 1890, s 33) so that the personal representatives of the deceased or the trustee in bankruptcy of the bankrupt can collect for his estate the amount to which the former partner was entitled for his share.

With a joint venture between companies, the agreement will need to provide a mechanism for unwinding the joint venture if one party goes insolvent.

17.2.5   Illegality (PA 1890, s 34)

Where it is illegal to carry on the business of the partnership, the partnership will dissolve (PA 1890, s 34). This situation might arise where the partnership business consists of the sale of alcohol and the partnership loses its licence to sell alcohol or where the partnership business is that of a solicitors' practice and one of the partners is struck off the Roll of Solicitors. The provisions of s 34 cannot be excluded even by a written partnership agreement, in contrast to ss 32–33, 35 which can be excluded by agreement.

17.2.6   Court order for dissolution (PA 1890, s 35)

The court has power (PA 1890, s 35) to order dissolution on various grounds, one of which (the 'just and equitable' ground) provides the court with such a wide discretion that it effectively makes the other, more specific, grounds unnecessary. Broadly, the other grounds are designed to cover circumstances where one partner ought to leave (eg on account of his conduct) but he is unwilling to do so and the others cannot expel him because their agreement failed to provide for this. Cases under s 35 are unusual because most partnerships, whether governed by an express or an implied agreement, can be dissolved without court intervention. This may be because there is nothing in their agreement to prevent a partner from giving notice to dissolve the partnership. Even if this is prevented by their agreement, the partners may be able to negotiate dissolution, for example where one partner will leave and be paid for his share, allowing the others to re-form in partnership.

On occasions, however, there will be a partnership agreement which would prevent dissolution unless all of the partners agreed. For example, the agreement may state that the partnership will continue for a long fixed term, or even for the joint lives of the partners. In such cases, unless the agreement provides for an unhappy partner to retire or for a troublesome partner to be expelled, it may be necessary to apply to the court for an order for dissolution. The order effectively breaks the partnership agreement without any partner being liable to the others for breach of contract.

17.3 Express terms on dissolution

17.3.1 Restrictions on dissolution

Generally, it will be inappropriate to leave the question of duration and dissolution to be governed by the PA 1890. The partners will not want the insecurity of a partnership at will, nor will they want the death or bankruptcy of one partner to cause a dissolution of the partnership between the survivors. Usually, therefore, it will be appropriate for the partnership agreement to exclude at least these possibilities and to make express provision as to the duration of the partnership (see **14.13**).

17.3.2 Purchase of outgoing partner's share (PA 1890, s 42)

If dissolution occurs where one partner leaves (by retirement, expulsion, death or bankruptcy) and the others are to continue as partners, the agreement should contain provisions allowing for the remaining partners to purchase the share of the former partner and fixing the terms of the purchase. If the agreement does not contain such provisions, it may be possible for the parties involved to negotiate terms for the outgoing partner's share to be purchased by the continuing partners. Inevitably, it may be some time after the partner has left that a price is settled and the others agree to purchase. If the agreement does not deal with the question of payment for the use of the former partner's share in the assets since he left, he will be entitled to receive, at his option, either interest at 5% per annum on the value of his share, or such sum as the court may order as representing the share of profits made which is attributable to the use of his share (PA 1890, s 42). The purchase agreement can exclude this entitlement (see **14.16**).

17.4 The business, its goodwill and other assets following dissolution without continuing partners

17.4.1 Disposal of the business

Sometimes dissolution occurs where the partners cannot reach agreement as to some of the partners carrying on with the business and purchasing an outgoing partner's share. Then it will be necessary for there to be a disposal of the business and for the proceeds of sale to be used to pay off creditors and then to pay to the partners the amount to which they are entitled. This disposal of a business may be by sale as a going concern or, if a buyer cannot be found, by breaking up the business and selling its assets separately. This position is reinforced by s 39 of the PA 1890 which gives every partner the right to insist on a disposal and payment as above, if necessary by application to court for the business and affairs of the firm to be wound up.

17.4.2 Goodwill

There is a serious financial disadvantage to the partners if the business is not purchased as a going concern but is broken up with the assets being sold separately. A valuable asset of any successful business is its goodwill. Goodwill can be described as the benefit of the business's reputation and connections and the benefit of having its own momentum so that profits will continue to be earned because the business is established.

A common basis for valuing goodwill is to take a number (perhaps two) of years' profit. For example, if the business generated £25,000 and £30,000 profit in the previous two years, the goodwill of the business might be valued at £55,000. Another approach to understanding the meaning of goodwill is to consider a person who is contemplating either purchasing an established business as a going concern or setting up a new business. In either instance, the cost would include the purchase of the necessary tangible assets like premises, equipment, stock, etc, but if purchasing an established business the buyer will have to pay for the benefit of its being established and already making a profit. This payment (of whatever amount is negotiated) is for goodwill. It can be seen therefore that, in the context of dissolution of partnership, the question of someone (whether it be continuing partners or an outsider) taking over the business as a going concern (and therefore paying for goodwill) is of considerable financial significance to a partner who is leaving.

Financial considerations apart, one other aspect of selling goodwill is worth considering at this point. The buyer of goodwill is likely to insist on the seller(s) entering into a covenant in restraint of trade for the protection of the goodwill which he is purchasing. If the seller was free to become involved immediately in a competing business, the benefit of having purchased (effectively) an established set of customers might be seriously undermined. Therefore, in return for the financial benefit of selling his share in the goodwill, an outgoing partner will have to accept the limitations imposed on his future activities by a covenant in restraint of trade. It should be remembered that a covenant in restraint of trade will be valid only if it is reasonable in the circumstances (see **14.17**).

However, courts are more likely to uphold a restraint of trade clause when it is to protect the purchaser of a business, rather than to restrict the activities of an individual partner departing from a continuing business.

17.5   Distribution of proceeds following sale of the business or its assets

Unless there is agreement to the contrary, the proceeds of sale of the business or its assets will be used in the following sequence (PA 1890, s 44). First, creditors of the firm (ie anyone with a claim against the firm except for the partners themselves) must be paid in full. If there is a shortfall so that the firm is insolvent, the partners must pay the balance from their private assets, sharing the loss in accordance with their partnership agreement. Secondly, partners who have lent money to the firm must be repaid, together with any interest to which they are entitled. Thirdly, partners must be paid their capital entitlement. Finally, if there is a surplus, this will be shared between the partners in accordance with their partnership agreement. For an example of the problems of dissolution, see *Hurst v Bryk* [2000] 2 All ER 193, where the partner who did not want the partnership to be disolved was still liable for his share of the partnership debts under s 44.

17.6   Following dissolution, who winds up the firm's affairs?

Each partner (except a bankrupt partner) has continuing authority to act for the purposes of winding up the firm's affairs (PA 1890, s 38). It may be that there is no need for any person outside the partnership to become involved in the dissolution. On the other hand, if there is a dispute between the partners, or if the assets are in jeopardy, any partner (or the trustee in bankruptcy of a bankrupt partner or the personal representatives of a deceased partner) may apply to the court for the appointment of a person (even one of the partners) as receiver to deal with the assets or as receiver and manager to conduct the business in addition to the above, perhaps with a view to selling the business as a going concern. The receiver or receiver and manager is an officer of the court and will be entitled to receive remuneration for his services from the partnership assets, although not from the partners' personal money.

Chapter 18
Limited Liability Partnerships

18.1 Introduction

Limited liability partnerships (LLPs) were created by the Limited Liability Partnerships Act 2000 ('LLPA 2000') in response to pressure from professional firms for more protection from liability than was possible with existing partnership law. An LLP is, in effect, a hybrid between a partnership under the PA 1890 and a limited company under the CA 2006. The main users of the LLP structure are professional firms. There is a set of draft regulations on applying the CA 2006 to LLPs, the Limited Liability Partnerships (Application of the Companies Act 2006) Regulations 2009.

Partners in an LLP ('members') have full limited liability. The LLP is a corporate body with a separate identity from the members. The provisions under the IA 1986 and CDDA 1986 are applied to LLPs.

An LLP is required by s 8 of the LLPA 2000 to have at least two 'designated members' who are responsible for sending documents to Companies House.

An LLP is registered by sending two forms to Companies House, but there is no need to send a copy of any partnership agreement or other constitutional document. The main form is generally equivalent to that used for a company and is called the 'incorporation document', which must contain (LLPA 2000, s 2(2)):

(a) name of the LLP;

(b) country where the registered office is situated;

(c) address of the registered office;

(d) name and address of each member of the LLP; and

(e) identities of the designated members.

An incorporation form equivalent to that used for companies is also lodged, that is containing a statement that the requirements of s 2(1)(a) have been complied with, including that two or more of the partners must have subscribed their names to the incorporation form. A statutory declaration is not required.

Companies House will issue a certificate of registration. The name of an LLP has to end with the words 'limited liability partnership' or 'LLP', or their Welsh equivalents. The rules on registration of names are similar to those for companies.

There is no management structure imposed on an LLP, that is, there is no equivalent of the model articles for a company. Implied terms which would apply in the absence of contrary agreement are provided by regulations (see **18.7**).

Members will owe a duty to the LLP as a body corporate in common law, but it seems unclear whether they owe a duty of good faith to each other.

Members are agents of the LLP, under s 6 of the LLPA 2000 (see **16.1** above) which is equivalent to s 5 of the PA 1890 .

The relationship between the members is set out in s 5 of the LLPA 2000, which is equivalent to s 24 of the PA 1890 (see **14.1** above).

An LLP has no share capital and therefore there are no requirements to maintain share capital. There are no directors and shareholders. There are just 'members'. The members are free to decide upon management and decision processes.

There is no restriction on membership numbers, though there have to be at least two members to constitute an LLP. The LLP structure is open to any type of business (LPPA 2000, s 2(1)(a)).

The LLP itself can be liable for, eg, torts and debts, but the members have limited liability.

An LLP has to file annual accounts, which are then a public document.

The provisions relating to wrongful and fraudulent trading also apply to the members of an LLP (Limited Liability Partnerships Regulations 2001, SI 2001/1090 ('LLP Regulations 2001'), reg 5).

An LLP cannot convert into a limited company.

For tax purposes, an LLP is to be treated as an ordinary partnership, that is, the partners will be liable to income tax under the ITTOIA 2005 for their share of profits, and to capital gains tax on gains made on the disposal of partnership assets.

Overall, LLPs are a curious mix of the law of partnership and the law of companies. For example, in *Feetum v Levy* [2005] EWCA Civ 1601, the Court of Appeal looked at the rule in *Foss v Harbottle* (1843) 2 Hare 461, which is a case that deals with the rights of shareholders (see **5.3**). The Court held that, on the facts in question, the rule did not stop members of an LLP from challenging the appointment of an administrative receiver to the partnership (see **18.6**).

In July 2001, the accountancy firm of Ernst and Young became an LLP. Pricewaterhouse Coopers became an LLP on 1 January 2003. Most LLPs are professional firms, for example solicitors, accountants and surveyors.

The limited liability partnership has a legal personality separate from that of its members. Thus, it is the limited liability partnership that carries the duties and liabilities of the business which are owed to outsiders. Unlike the position with a partnership, the existence of the LLP is separate from that of its members. So, a partnership will cease to exist if there are not two or more members, ie partners. This is not the case with an LLP. It continues to exist as a separate legal entity until it is dissolved.

18.2 Formalities

The LLP must have its name on the outside of its place of business. Similarly, its business stationery must mention its name, its place of registration and its registration number, and the address of the registered office (CA 2006, s 82(1), (2)). It must always have a registered office, as it is an address for service of official documents (LLPA 2000, Sch, para 6).

Entering into contracts and executing other documents is much the same for LLPs as for companies. Thus, a contract may be made on behalf of an LLP by anyone acting with express or implied authority. So, a document is executed on behalf of an LLP by that document being signed by two members of the LLP, or by applying the common seal of the LLP, if it has one.

An LLP can change its name at any time. There is no procedure prescribed in legislation for doing so. This should be a matter addressed in the LLP partnership agreement. If it is not then the default rules apply (see **18.7**), and the consent of all the members is needed (LLP Regulations 2001, regs 7 and 8).

Every LLP must send to the Registrar an annual return (CA 2006, ss 854, 855). This covers the following items:

(a)   the address of the registered office;

(b)   the names and addresses of the members of the LLP;

(c)   the identity of the designated members, if not all members are designated; and

(d)   the address where the register of debenture holders is kept, if it is not the registered office.

The appropriate form is a variation of the standard form for companies. It must be signed by a designated member (see **18.8**) who certifies that the return is accurate.

Changes to the membership of an LLP must be notified to the Registrar of Companies as they occur (LLPA 2000, s 9(1)(a)).

18.3   Authority of a member to bind the LLP

Every member of an LLP is the agent of the LLP (LLPA 2000, s 6(1)). Section 6(2) provides for limitations to be placed on a member's actual authority. So, an LLP is not bound if the member has no authority to act for the LLP in that matter and the third party in question knows that fact. The LLP agreement, if there is one, should provide for limits on the authority of members. However, this still leaves open the question of apparent authority. The extent of the apparent authority will be determined by the nature of the business concerned, and therefore what constitutes the 'normal course' of that business. Apparent authority is dependent upon the representations which the LLP makes to the third party or, more likely, the mistaken impressions which the LLP fails to correct (see **6.4.2**).

The member will cease to be the agent of the LLP whenever he ceases to be a member of that LLP.

18.4   Owning property and the granting of charges

An LLP can issue debentures and grant fixed or floating charges. Every LLP must keep a register of charges and a copy of every charge requiring registration at its registered office (CA 2006, ss 869–873). The register must include all charges affecting property of the LLP and all floating charges. The register must be open for inspection by any creditor or member of the LLP without payment of a fee.

The LLP is required to register charges with the Registrar in the same way that a company is so required. An amended version of the form for companies is used for registration of charges for an LLP. As with companies, there is a power of the court to rectify omission of registration of a charge (CA 2006, s 873).

18.5 New members

The LLP is incorporated with its first members. Thereafter, any person may become a member with the agreement of the existing members. As with a traditional partnership, being a member of an LLP is a matter of contract. Any LLP agreement therefore needs to make provision for new members joining the LLP.

18.6 Effect of limited liability

If the LLP becomes insolvent, both the LLP and the members will be subject to the IA 1986 regime with regard to the liquidation of companies. Thus, there is the possibility of the member being found liable for misfeasance, fraudulent trading or wrongful trading (see **6.10.5**, **6.10.7** and **6.10.8** respectively). The member may therefore be required to contribute to the assets of the insolvent LLP in the same way that a company director can be, under the equivalent provisions for companies (but see **18.10** re protection of members' personal assets). The Company Directors Disqualification Act 1986 also applies to members of an LLP.

It seems that members of an LLP do not have as great a problem with restrictions on their right of action as do members of a company (see **5.6.4**). Thus, the Court of Appeal held in *Feetum v Levy* [2005] EWCA Civ 1601 that the rule in *Foss v Harbottle* did not prevent members of an LLP from challenging the appointment of administrative receivers.

18.7 The LLP agreement

Section 5(1) of the LLPA 2000 provides that the mutual rights and duties of an LLP and its members are governed by an agreement between the members, or in the absence of an agreement by the provisions of the LLP Regulations 2001. The Regulations provide a set of 'default rules'. These rules adopt some of the provisions contained in ss 24–30 of the PA 1890, with appropriate modifications. The matters covered by the default rules are as follows, with references to the PA 1890 for comparison:

(a)   sharing in capital and profits (PA 1890, s 24(1));

(b)   indemnity to members (s 24(2));

(c)   right to take part in management (s 24(5));

(d)   no entitlement to remuneration (s 24(6));

(e)   introduction of a new member and voluntary assignment of a member's interest (s 24(7));

(f)   ordinary matters connected with the business to be decided by majority (s 24(8));

(g)   books and records to be available for inspection by any member (s 24(9));

(h)   each member to render true accounts and full information to any member (s 28);

(i)   obligation to account to the LLP for any profits made from a competing business without consent (s 30);

(j)   obligation to account to the LLP for any private benefit derived without consent from use of LLP property (s 29(1)); and

(k)   no majority power to expel without express agreement as to such power (s 25).

18.8 Designated members

At least two of the members of the LLP must be 'designated members' (LLPA 2000, ss 2(1)(a), 8(2)). The original two designated members will be the subscribers to the incorporation document. One possibility is that all members of the LLP will be designated members. Alternatively, the LLP may specify named members as the designated members in addition to, or in place of, the original subscribers (LLPA 2000, s 8(4)(b)).

The responsibilities of the designated members are contained in the LLPA 2000, the CA 2006 and the IA 1986. Broadly, designated members have powers equivalent to directors in a company. However, they also have the duties and responsibilities of being a member of the LLP.

Designated members must:

(a)   sign and file the annual accounts with the Registrar (CA 2006, s 444(6));

(b)   appoint, remove and remunerate auditors (CA 2006, s 485(4));

(c)   file the annual return (CA 2006, s 854);

(d)   send notices to the Registrar, for example concerning a member leaving or joining the LLP (LLPA 2000, s 9(1));

(e)   send a statement of release of a charge to the Registrar (CA 2006, s 872);

(f)   apply for a change of name of the LLP (LLPA 2000, Sch, para 5(2)(b));

(g)   apply to strike off the LLP from the register (CA 2006, s 1003); or

(h)   wind up the LLP or apply for a voluntary arrangement (IA 1986, s 89(1)).

All the functions of a designated member must be carried out consistent with the core fiduciary obligation owed by every member to the LLP itself, ie an obligation of loyalty and promoting the best interests of the LLP (see **18.9**). The designated members will also owe a duty to the LLP of reasonable care and skill.

18.9   The duties and responsibilities of members

Many LLPs will have a written agreement. However, this will not be the only source of the duties and responsibilities of the members. As a member is in the position of agent with the LLP as principal, the member will owe a fiduciary duty to the LLP. There are also the default rules to be considered.

The member's duties to the LLP will include:

(a)   a duty to account for any money received on behalf of the LLP;

(b)   a duty not to apply LLP monies improperly;

(c)   fiduciary duties, for example a duty of good faith towards the LLP;

(d)   duties on members as a whole, for example to prepare financial accounts which give a true and fair view of the LLP's financial position;

(e)   duties on individual members, for example to give the auditors such information as they require from him; and

(f)   duties to his co-members, for example a duty to render true accounts and full information on matters concerning the LLP.

18.10   Capital and profits

Funding for a business comes either from debt or equity, ie borrowing or shares. With an LLP, the equity is the members' capital which they have contributed to the business. Default rule 1 provides that members are entitled to share equally in the capital and profits of the LLP, in the absence of contrary agreement. The default rules do not deal with losses, as it is the LLP itself which bears any losses, just as a company does. In other words, this is where limited liability applies and benefits the members of the LLP. The only thing that the member has at risk is the contributions he has made to the LLP's finances, ie his capital and any profits due to him, and loans from him which the LLP cannot repay.

18.11   Management and decision-making

Default rules 3 and 4 provide that every member may take part in the management of the LLP, and that no member is entitled to remuneration for doing so. These rules are adapted from s

24(5) and (6) of the PA 1890. The LLP agreement can depart from these rules and the members can create any management structure that is desired.

Default rule 6 is adapted from s 24(8) of the PA 1890 and provides that ordinary matters of the LLP are to be decided by a majority of the members. No change in the nature of the business of the LLP can be made without the consent of all members.

18.12 Cessation of membership and its consequences

A person may cease to be a member of an LLP by giving reasonable notice to the other members (LLPA 2000, s 4(3)). There is no equivalent provision to this in a traditional partnership. The bankruptcy of a member does not automatically cause a termination of membership of the LLP, unless the LLP agreement so provides. Also, a member cannot be expelled or be required to retire, unless the LLP agreement deals with this (default rule 8, which adopts s 25 of the PA 1890).

If a person ceases to be a member, the LLP must notify the Registrar within 14 days.

It seems that under the default rules, there is no automatic right for a lending member to be repaid his capital. This is therefore a matter that should be addressed in the LLP agreement.

18.13 Advantages and disadvantages of an LLP

Advantages

(a)   limited liability and separate legal personality (like a company);

(b)   a flexible organisational structure: the members can decide what they want;

(c)   the ability to grant fixed and floating charges over its assets; security needs to be registered with the Registrar of Companies;

(d)   the ability to appoint an administrator.

Disadvantages

(a)   the requirement to file accounts with the Registrar of Companies, which will then be public documents;

(b)   the potential 'clawback' provisions in the event of an insolvency;

(c)   the transfer of a personal interest in an LLP is more complex than transferring shares (but a transfer can be less problematic with an LLP that with an ordinary partnership structure as LLP membership can be assigned);

(d)   an LLP cannot convert into a limited company.

18.14 Applications of an LLP

The LLP structure has been primarily of interest to professional partnerships, eg solicitors, accountants and engineers. An LLP could also be used in the context of joint ventures or in project finance.

Under the Limited Partnerships Act 1907, a form of limited partnership was, and still is, available. However, under the 1907 Act the size of the partnership was limited to 20 partners, the limited partners could not take part in the management of the business, and the liability of at least one partner had to be unlimited. Hence, it was not widely utilised.

The Government has been consulting on proposals to repeal the 1907 Act and insert new provisions into the PA 1890 to deal with limited partnerships. The consultation period closed in November 2008 and updated proposals are awaited at the time of writing.

Part III Summary – Running a Business in Partnership

Topic	Summary
Definition	A partnership is 'the relation which subsists between persons carrying on a business in common with a view of profit'. There must be two or more persons for a partnership, and whether a partnership exists is a question of fact. A written agreement is *not* required, although most partnerships have one.
Liability	Partners have unlimited liability for a partnership's debts. A partnership is not a separate legal entity from its partners and one partner can be liable for all of a partnership's debts.
Registration	There is no registration process to form a partnership and no obligation to make accounts public. A partnership is usually referred to as a 'firm' to distinguish it from a company.
Duration	Most partnerships are 'at will': a partnership has no set duration and will continue until dissolved, unless otherwise agreed.
Regulation	The main regulation is the Partnership Act 1890 (PA 1890). Partners can regulate their affairs as they wish so long as this is not inconsistent with the PA 1890. The PA 1890 has, in s 24, rules which will regulate the partners and their business, unless varied by agreement.
Management and decisions	The PA 1890 allows all partners to take part in managing the business and for decisions to be taken by a majority. However, in certain situations, unanimity is required. These are: a change in business; introducing a new partner; altering the partnership agreement; and expelling a partner.
Duty of good faith	Partners must act in good faith towards each other. They must disclose information about the business to each other (s 28); account for any benefits gained from using partnership property or its name (s 29); and account for any profits made from a competing business (s 30).
Finance	Partnerships can be financed by the partners, bank borrowing and retention of profits. Partners can invest by way of capital or lending. Capital investment can be in the form of assets or cash. This capital is a debt owed to the partner, usually repaid only on dissolution or the departure of the partner. There is no entitlement to any interest on capital unless agreed. A loan made by a partner is like a bank loan, save that the PA 1890 stipulates a 5% interest rate unless otherwise agreed.
Sharing capital and profits	Partners share equally in capital and profits unless otherwise agreed. Where capital is provided in varying amounts, it is implied that this will be repaid in proportion to these amounts. There is no such implication for profits and losses: partners share them equally unless otherwise agreed.

Topic	Summary
Drawing and salary	Profits are calculated annually but partners may take out money periodically against expected profits: these are called drawings. Some partners receive a salary, which is seen as an appropriation of profit, so is not a deductible expense of the business for tax purposes.
Actual authority	A partnership is bound by the acts of a partner acting within his authority. Express actual authority is where authority has been given by the partnership. Implied actual authority can arise from a course of dealing or where the authority arises naturally from an express authority.
Apparent authority	A firm is also bound where a third party can rely on apparent authority, defined in s 5. Here, a partner must act in the usual way for carrying on the business of the kind carried on by the firm. The third party can rely on this *unless* the partner has no authority to act on the particular matter and the third party either (a) knows he has no authority; or (b) does not know or believe him to be a partner. Where a firm is bound by a partner acting beyond authority, it can require the partner to indemnify the firm for any liabilities incurred.
New and retiring partners: liability	A new partner is not liable to creditors for anything done before joining. However, he can agree with his partners to pay a share of existing debts. A retiring partner remains liable for debts incurred whilst he was a partner but not those incurred after his departure. This may not, however, be the case if it appears to a third party that the retiree is still a partner or the retiree holds himself out to still be a partner. To avoid this, retiring partners should give formal notice of their departure to existing customers and suppliers. A notice in the *London Gazette* provides similar notice to any new customers of the firm. The partner should also ensure removal of his name from the firm's stationery.
Dissolving a partnership	A partnership can be dissolved at any time by notice from one or more partners, unless its agreement states otherwise. Similarly, the death or bankruptcy of a partner will dissolve the partnership unless otherwise agreed. Partners may also agree that the partnership will expire at the end of an agreed period or venture.
Court dissolution	A court can dissolve a partnership on a number of grounds: where a partner becomes permanently incapable of performing his role; where a partner's conduct prejudicially affects the business or makes it unreasonable for the other partners to carry on working with him; where the business can only be carried on at a loss; or where it is felt just and equitable to dissolve the firm.
Winding-up a partnership's affairs	Where a firm is dissolved, its affairs are wound up. Its assets and liabilities are calculated, and debts owed to creditors are paid first. Then, advances made by partners are repaid, followed by capital and, finally, a division of any remaining amounts according to the profit-sharing ratio. If the partnership has made losses, these have to be met in the following order: from profits; from capital; and then from contributions from partners according to the profit-sharing ratio.

Part IV
INSOLVENCY

This Part first considers the insolvency of a company. An insolvent company may be put into liquidation, whereby all assets are taken and shared between the creditors. This is broadly equivalent to the bankruptcy of an individual. However, liquidation differs fundamentally from bankruptcy, in that at the end of the liquidation the company ceases to exist. Consideration is also given to alternative processes applicable to companies which may enable the company to survive the insolvency, ie CVA and administration.

Lastly, we consider the implications of the insolvency of an individual (a 'debtor'). The debtor who is unable to pay his debts is faced with the possibility of bankruptcy, whereby virtually all his assets are taken and shared between his creditors. At the end of the bankruptcy, the debtor is largely freed from outstanding claims and able to start afresh. As an alternative to bankruptcy, a debtor may succeed in making a 'voluntary arrangement' with creditors, whereby they will accept payment which is delayed or which is less than their entitlement.

Part IV

INSOLVENCY

Chapter 19
Corporate Insolvency

19.1 Aims of the insolvency regimes

The basic aims of corporate insolvency law are to:

(a) protect creditors of the company;

(b) balance the interests of competing groups of creditors;

(c) control or punish the directors; and

(d) promote rescues.

19.2 Corporate insolvency procedures

The statistics from the Insolvency Service for the different insolvency procedures for England and Wales for 2008 are as follows.

Compulsory liquidation	5,494
Creditors' voluntary liquidation	10,041
Receivership (both LPA and administrative)	867
Administration (pre-2003 procedure)	2
Administration (post-2003 procedure)	4,820
Voluntary agreement	587

Liquidation is in effect the death of the company. The process is also known as 'winding up', as the first legislation on corporate insolvency was the Winding Up Act 1844. In this process, the company's assets are distributed to its creditors, in so far as the assets can discharge even part of the debts. Liquidation procedures are compulsory or voluntary. Voluntary liquidation can be either members' or creditors' liquidation. 'Voluntary' is perhaps a slight misnomer, certainly for a creditors' voluntary liquidation. The situation can be likened to an employee who resigns rather than be dismissed.

The Insolvency Act 1986 (IA 1986) introduced procedures which were designed to promote rescues of ailing companies. These are administration orders and company voluntary arrangements ('CVAs').

An administration order places the company under the management of a person appointed by the court. The aim could be to rescue the company or to ensure a better realisation of assets than in a liquidation or to obtain agreement to a CVA.

Company voluntary arrangements are agreements where the company's creditors will formally agree either to forgo or wait for part of their debt. The aim is to ensure either that the company continues to trade, or that they obtain a better realisation of their debts than on a liquidation (as a CVA is cheaper).

There are two common types of receivership. The first is receivership under the Law of Property Act 1925. This is where a lender with a fixed charge appoints someone under the terms of a loan agreement to take control of the fixed assets which are subject to the fixed charge. He will sell those assets in order to pay the debt to the lender. The second type is administrative receivership. This is where a lender with a floating charge appoints someone to take charge of a company's affairs under the terms of the loan agreement. The receiver will sell the business after keeping it trading for a short period, or sell the assets of the company in order to pay the debt to the lender. Administrative receivers could only be appointed by a lender holding a floating charge over the whole of the company's property (IA 1986, s 29). Both types of receivership can often lead to liquidation, either because the most important fixed asset, the premises or machinery, have been sold or because a buyer for the business as a going concern cannot be found. As we will see, receivership is now much less important than it once was.

Under the amendments introduced by the Enterprise Act 2002 (EA 2002), administrative receivership is no longer possible for charges created after 15 September 2003. Instead, a lender is only able to appoint an administrator. In many ways, this development removes an anomaly, as receivership was not a 'rescue' procedure at all but rather a special right for lenders to get their money back, no matter what.

19.3 Company voluntary arrangements

A CVA is a potential rescue mechanism and is therefore an alternative to liquidation. In reality, it is also an alternative to receivership as a CVA will require the support of anyone entitled to appoint a receiver. A CVA is an easy and comparatively low-cost procedure.

A CVA is available for solvent companies (unlike administration) as well as insolvent ones (IA 1986, s 1A). Only the directors can apply for a CVA. In the past the big disadvantage of a CVA was the lack of a moratorium (a 'freeze' on debts), but this is now available for small companies, as defined in s 382 of the CA 2006.

Third parties are not subject to the CVA, so a creditor could pursue a director under a personal guarantee.

Perhaps the downside of a CVA for creditors is that it may simply be postponing the inevitable – the liquidation of the company.

19.3.1 Procedure for a CVA

(a)   The directors make a written proposal to the creditors. It will identify an insolvency practitioner, known as the nominee at this point. The nominee has 28 days to look at the proposal and to report to the court on its viability. If it is, then he decides whether to call meetings of members and creditors. This almost always happens. It is possible to have a moratorium on actions by the creditors in the case of small companies. It will last for 28 days after filing the proposal at the court. It can be extended for up to a further two months, that is giving a total period of almost three months (IA 1986, Sch A1, paras 8, 32). Floating charges cannot crystallise during the moratorium.

(b)   At the creditors meeting, a majority of more than 75% in value of the creditors present and voting is required to approve the proposal. The chairman of the meeting must report its outcome to the court. All unsecured creditors who had notice of the meeting are bound by the proposal as regards past debts but not as regards future debts. Secured creditors and preferential creditors are not bound by the CVA. They could find that assets which are subject to their charge are dealt with in a way they disapprove of, or are even impressed with a quasi trust in favour of the unsecured creditors (*Re Leisure Study Group Ltd* [1994] 2 BCLC 65).

(c)   The nominee (now the 'supervisor') must be handed control of the assets that are subject to the CVA.

(d)   On completion of the CVA, the supervisor must make a final report to the creditors and members within 28 days.

A recent example of a successful CVA was the rescue of JJB Sports.

19.4 Administration

Administration is one of the alternatives to liquidation of a company. It is only available for insolvent companies (IA 1986, Sch B1, para 11). Administration is intended as a rescue mechanism. The purpose of an administration is for the company to carry on running its business. One example was Railtrack plc, which was in administration but continued to function (though strictly speaking the Railtrack administration was under the Railways Act 1993, not the IA 1986). Another example was ITV Digital, which has since gone into liquidation (owing the writer of this chapter £144). In late 2005, Leyland Daf Vehicles went into administration, received substantial new finance from a new investor, left administration, and has now returned to normal functioning. However, administration need not always be the preferred route. In *Dollarland (Manhattan) Ltd* [2005] Lawtel AC9 601056, it was held that the company would be wound up rather than put into administration, as in this case there were no significant economic advantages to the creditors in an administration. Any small advantage did not warrant the creditors being deprived of the complete independence and objectivity of the Official Receiver.

The revised regime for administration was implemented on 15 September 2003. The revised regime replaces administrative receivership (see **19.6**) for charges coming into existence on or after that date, and radically remodels the old form of administration. The reasons for the reform are twofold:

(a)   Administrative receivership was seen to be too slanted toward the interests of the secured creditor who appointed the administrative receiver. This was at the expense of other creditors, and hampered the 'rescue' of a company in financial difficulty.

(b)   The old model of administration was unwieldy, expensive and often of indeterminate duration.

Administrative receivership still exists for charges created before 15 September 2003 but will become less important as time passes.

Key features of the new administration regime include the following.

(a)   Qualifying floating charge holders (QFCHs), the company or directors are empowered to appoint an administrator without petitioning the court, though the court route still exists. A QFCH is a creditor who has the benefit of a floating charge created after 15 September 2003 (see **19.4.3**). (As a matter of fact, the company will be unable to pay its debts before this step is considered, ie it will be insolvent.)

(b)   Creditors other than QFCHs can petition the court for an administration order.

(c)   A QFCH can apply to court for an order that its own administrator replace the one proposed or appointed by the creditor or directors. This would apply when the QFCH receives notice that creditors have applied to court for the appointment of an administrator, or that directors have appointed an administrator.

(d)   The administrator is under a duty to act in the interests of all creditors, unlike the situation under administrative receivership. This applies even where a QFCH has appointed the administrator.

(e)   Administrators have powers to make payments to creditors.

The upshot of the reforms should be that administration as a process is capable of dealing with all creditors, rather than merely being a precursor to CVA or liquidation.

19.4.1 Nature of an administration

The advantage of administration is that there is a moratorium ('freeze') on creditor actions. This is a major factor as it gives the administrator the time to try to rescue the company, if that is in fact possible.

An administrator can be appointed by the court, the creditors, the directors or the company. The administrator has to perform his duties with the object of (IA 1986, Sch B1, para 3(1)):

(a)   rescuing the company as a going concern; or

(b)   achieving a better result for the company's creditors as a whole than would be likely if the company were wound up (without first being in administration); or

(c)   realising property in order to make a distribution to one or more secured or preferential creditors.

He has to perform his duties in the interests of the company's creditors as a whole (para 3(2)).

An administrator is an officer of the court, no matter which route is used to appoint him (IA 1986, Sch B1, para 5). He has to be such in order to comply with EC Regulation 1346/2000 (OJ L160/1) on insolvency proceedings. He has to be an insolvency practitioner (IA 1986, Sch B1, para 6), and will almost always be an accountant.

19.4.2 Appointment by the court

The court may make an administration order only if it is satisfied that:

(a)   the company is or is likely to become unable to pay its debts (as defined in IA 1986, s 123); and

(b)   the administration order is reasonably likely to achieve the purpose of administration, typically that administration would achieve a better result for the company's creditors than would liquidation (see, eg, *In the Matter of Redman Construction Ltd* [2004] Lawtel AC9400298, and *In the Matter of AA Mutual International Insurance Co Ltd* [2004] EWHC 2430).

As soon as reasonably practicable after making the application, the applicant must notify:

(a)   any person who has appointed (or is entitled to appoint) an administrative receiver of the company;

(b)   any qualifying charge holder who may be entitled to appoint an administrator; and

(c)   such other persons as may be prescribed by the new insolvency rules.

The application cannot be withdrawn, except with the consent of the court. The court may do the following:

(a)   grant the administration order;

(b)   dismiss the application;

(c)   adjourn the hearing;

(d)   make an interim order;

(e)   treat the application as a petition for winding up (ie a liquidation petition); or

(f)   make any order it thinks appropriate.

19.4.3 Appointment out of court by a QFCH

The out of court routes are procedures brought into the IA 1986 by the EA 2002. This is a key aspect of the amendments to the IA 1986, namely that administration is the available route for lenders, not administrative receivership. The rationale is that administration is likely to promote a rescue of all or part of the business, if at all possible.

The procedure is to be found in para 14(1) of Sch B1 to the IA 1986. The lender must have a floating charge created on or after 15 September 2003:

(a)   which qualifies under para 14(2), eg by purporting to have the power to appoint an administrator or administrative receiver; and

(b)   which extends over substantially the whole of the company's business (para 14(3)).

If there is another QFCH whose charge would have priority, then the lender cannot appoint until he has given two business days' written notice of his intention to appoint an administrator. This allows the holder of the prior charge to consider whether to appoint an administrator himself. However, any administrator appointed by any route has to act in the interests of all creditors, not just the one who appointed him. An interim moratorium exists whilst the other QFCH deliberates on his options.

The floating charge in question must have crystallised, that is the floating charge holder is entitled under the loan agreement to enforce his security, eg because of failure of the borrower to meet a repayment date.

If an administrator, liquidator or administrative receiver has already been appointed, then an administrator cannot be appointed by the para 14 route.

Notice of appointment has to be filed at court by the lender together with various documents. The notice must include a statutory declaration by the lender to the effect that:

(a)   the lender is the holder of a qualifying floating charge in respect of the company's property;

(b)   the floating charge has become enforceable; and

(c)   the appointment is in accordance with Sch B1 to the IA 1986.

Once these documents have been filed at court (and the other parts of para 18 are complied with) the administration begins.

19.4.4   Appointment out of court by the company or directors

This procedure is intended to make corporate rescue easier.

The directors, or the company, will need to give notice to any QFCHs. The QFCH will agree or will appoint an alternative administrator. The moratorium comes into effect immediately the notice of intention to appoint is filed at court. However, the first step will be that, if it is the company which appoints, a general meeting will be needed for the members to approve such a step. If it is the directors, then they will need to pass a board resolution.

The first stage of appointment is that a notice of intention is served on (IA 1986, Sch B1, para 26):

(a)   the court;

(b)   any QFCH; and

(c)   any lender entitled to appoint an administrative receiver.

The directors must also file a statutory declaration that (IA 1986, Sch B1, para 27(2)):

(a)   the company is unable to pay its debts;

(b)   the company is not in liquidation; and

(c)   the restrictions in paras 23 to 25 do not apply (eg there has been no administration within the previous 12 months).

There is an interim moratorium before the next stage. This gap is five business days.

In the second stage, the company or its directors have to file at court a notice of appointment and another statutory declaration, amongst other matters. The appointment takes effect from the date of filing at court. The statutory declaration is to convince the court that the appointment has been properly made, ie is in accordance with Sch B1 of the IA 1986, and that the facts in the first statutory declaration are still correct.

19.4.5   Administration process

The main moratorium then comes into effect and protects the company whilst the administrator tries to rescue it.

The administrator will put forward his proposals to a creditors' meeting. They can seek further details or can amend the proposals (IA 1986, Sch B1, para 53(1)(b)). It is important to remember that the administrator could have been appointed by the directors and the creditors may regard him as the directors' stooge.

The initial creditors' meeting can be dispensed with under para 52 of Sch B1 to the IA 1986, if:

(a)   the creditors are likely to be paid in full;

(b)   the unsecured creditors are unlikely to be paid at all; or

(c)   only the third purpose applies (realising property in order to make a distribution to one or more secured or preferential creditors).

The administrator is required to convene further meetings of the creditors if the court orders him to do so, or creditors holding 10% of the debts request it. The creditors may establish a creditors' committee (para 57).

The effects of the administration order are that:

(a)   the company is managed by the administrator;

(b)   the directors' powers cease, though they are still in office;

(c)   the moratorium continues;

(d)   the administrator controls the company's assets (but does not own them); and

(e)   the administrator carries out his proposals, which have been approved by the creditors.

19.4.6   Powers and duties of an administrator

The administrator has statutory powers under Sch 1 to the IA 1986. He is, however, an officer of the court and obstruction of him could constitute contempt of court (*Re Exchange Travel Holdings Ltd (No 1)* [1991] BCLC 728). An administrator acts as an agent for the company (IA 1986, s 14(4)). He is not personally liable on contracts made by him. He has 14 days to reject the existing contracts of employment.

He could be sued for misfeasance under s 212 of the IA 1986, although he can seek judicial pardon under s 1157 of the CA 2006. An example of s 1157 is *In the matter of MDA Investment Management Ltd v Doney* [2004] EWHC 42, where the director in question was held not to be relieved of liability by s 1157, as although he had acted honestly, he had not acted reasonably. (The case was decided under s 727 of the CA 1985.)

In addition to these powers, he has the power to do anything necessary or expedient for the management of the affairs, business and property of the company. He is required to exercise his powers for the purpose of the administration (IA 1986, Sch B1, para 3; see **19.4.1**).

An administrator also has the power (under IA 1986, Sch B1) to:

(a)   remove and appoint directors (para 61);

(b)   call a meeting of creditors or members (para 62);

(c)   apply to the court for directions (para 63);

(d)   pay money to a creditor (para 65), but only with the court's permission if it is to an unsecured creditor;

(e)   pay money to any party if it is likely to assist the administration (para 66);

(f)   deal with property that is subject to a floating charge (para 70);

(g)   deal with property subject to a fixed charge, subject to the permission of the court (para 71); and

(h)   deal with property that is the subject of a hire purchase agreement (para 72).

19.4.7 End of the administration

One of the problems of the old administration procedure was the difficulty of exiting. The revisions brought in by the EA 2002 have greatly simplified the procedures.

The procedures for ending administration (under IA 1986, Sch B1 (as revised by the EA 2002)) are:

(a)   automatic end of the administration after one year from the date the administration took effect (para 76);

(b)   on application by the administrator to the court, under para 79, if:

    (i)   he thinks the purpose of administration cannot be achieved in relation to the company;

    (ii)   he thinks the company should not have entered administration;

    (iii)   a creditors' meeting requires him to make an application; or

    (iv)   he thinks that the purpose of administration has been sufficiently achieved in relation to the company;

(c)   termination where the object has been achieved (for administrator appointed by the out of court route) (para 80);

(d)   the court ending the administration on the application of a creditor (para 81);

(e)   the court converting the administration into liquidation, in the public interest (para 82);

(f)   the administrator converting the administration into a creditors' voluntary liquidation (para 83);

(g)   the administrator dissolving the company where he believes there is no property which might permit a distribution to creditors (para 84); and

(h)   the administrator resigns (para 87), is removed (para 88), ceases to be qualified (para 89) or is replaced by those who appointed him in the first place (paras 92, 93, 94).

19.4.8 'Pre-pack' administration

Pre-packaged administration occurs when a company is placed into administration and almost immediately its assets and business are sold by the administrator, often to the management of the insolvent company. The unsecured creditors are not consulted and are unlikely to be paid much, if any, of their debts. The name of the new business is often close to that of the insolvent company. The perception is that the jobs of the employees are more likely to be saved by using this 'pre-pack' route.

As from 1 January 2009, administrators are bound by an additional statement of insolvency practice, SIP 16, issued by the Joint Insolvency Committee. This strives to satisfy the unsecured creditors that their interests have been considered, by requiring the administrator to disclose to them various information, including:

(a)   the source of the administrator's introduction;

(b)   the extent of the administrator's involvement prior to his appointment;

(c)   any valuations of the business or the underlying assets;

(d)   the alternative courses of action which were considered;

(e)   why it was not appropriate to keep the business trading and sell it as a going concern;

(f)   whether efforts were made to consult major creditors; and

(g)   the identity of the purchasers and any connections they have to the former management.

19.5 Liquidation

Liquidation, also known as a 'winding up', is the most common form of insolvency procedure. Liquidation is the end of the road for a company; it ceases to exist thereafter.

The basic steps are:

(a)   commence liquidation proceedings;

(b)   appoint liquidator;

(c)   liquidator collects company's assets and can review past transactions;

(d)   liquidator distributes assets in the statutory order to the creditors; and

(e)   the company is dissolved.

These steps apply to both voluntary and compulsory liquidations. 'Voluntary' simply means that the parties concerned are bowing to the inevitable and are going down this route rather than have someone force a compulsory liquidation. Liquidation can be used for either solvent or insolvent companies.

19.5.1 Members' voluntary liquidation

This is only available to a solvent company. If it is not solvent then the creditors' voluntary liquidation should be used.

19.5.1.1 Procedure for a members' voluntary liquidation

(a)   The directors have to make a statutory declaration of solvency. In this they state that they have made full inquiry into the company's affairs and have concluded that the company will be able to pay its debts in full within 12 months (IA 1986, s 89). There must also be a statement of the company's assets and liabilities.

(b)   Within five weeks after the declaration, a meeting of the members must take place at which two resolutions are considered:

(i)   a special resolution to wind up the company, and

(ii)   an ordinary resolution to appoint a liquidator (ss 89(2) and 91).

(c)   The declaration and the special resolution must be lodged at Companies House within 15 days of the date of the special resolution (ss 84(3) and 89(3)).

(d)   Once the liquidator has been appointed he must provide the chairman of the meeting at which he was appointed with a 'consent to act'. The chairman at the meeting will certify the liquidator's appointment.

(e)   Upon his appointment the directors' powers cease (s 91(2)). Note that the directors are not automatically removed from office.

(f)   Within 28 days, the liquidator must send notice of his appointment to all creditors of whom he is aware.

(g)   Within 14 days, he must place notice of his appointment in the *London Gazette* and send notice of his appointment to the Registrar of Companies (s 109).

(h)   Once the company has been wound up the liquidator must call a general meeting at which he lays his accounts of the liquidation before the members (s 94(1)). In practice, although this meeting is always called, no one ever attends it. Again, the reason is that the creditors have been paid in full and there is therefore little interest in the liquidator's accounts (see **19.5.1.3**).

19.5.1.2 Powers and duties of the liquidator in a members' voluntary liquidation

Once a liquidator has been appointed, his duties are basically the same as in any other liquidation. He must gather in the assets and distribute them in accordance with the statutory order. He is still under a duty to investigate past transactions (for example preferences – see **19.7.2**) and to look at the directors' behaviour prior to liquidation (except wrongful trading which only applies to insolvent companies). However, it is rare in practice that any detailed investigation is undertaken. Quite simply, the reason for this is that the whole nature of the members' voluntary liquidation is that all the creditors will be paid in full. If creditors are paid in full there is usually very little to complain about.

The liquidator is agent of the company during his appointment and is therefore not personally liable on any contracts made.

In order to carry out his duties, the liquidator is given extensive powers under Sch 4 to the IA 1986. These include power to:

(a)   sell assets;

(b)   use the company bank account;

(c)   appoint agents;

(d)   litigate on the company's behalf and defend litigation on the company's behalf;

(e)   carry on the company business; and

(f)   do all of the things necessary to facilitate winding up.

If it appears to the liquidator during the course of the members' voluntary liquidation that the company is insolvent, the liquidator must convert the liquidation to a creditor's voluntary liquidation (s 95).

19.5.1.3 End of the members' voluntary liquidation

The members' voluntary liquidation concludes when:

(a)   the liquidator sells the available assets;

(b)   he distributes the money to the creditors;

(c)   he holds a final meeting of members (s 94);

(d)   the liquidator is released by the meeting or by the court;

(e)   the accounts are forwarded to Companies House; and

(f)   three months later the company is dissolved by the Registrar of Companies.

19.5.2 Creditors' voluntary liquidation

A creditors' voluntary liquidation is initiated by the directors of the company and is then taken on by the creditors of the company. However, whilst the creditors' voluntary liquidation procedure is voluntary (in that the directors are not being forced to recommend liquidation), it is usually the result of either outside creditor pressure or professional advice to the directors that the company is insolvent. Directors are usually unwilling to put the company into liquidation as they always think that better times are around the corner. However, the threat of potential actions against them for fraudulent and wrongful trading usually concentrates their minds (see **6.10.7** and **6.10.8**).

19.5.2.1 Procedure for a creditors' voluntary liquidation

(a)   The starting point for a creditors' voluntary liquidation is the directors calling a meeting of directors. At this, they resolve to call a meeting of members and resolve to recommend to members that they pass a special resolution to the effect that the company cannot, by reason of its liabilities, continue its business and that it be wound up.

(b) At the meeting of members two resolutions will then be passed:

    (i) the special resolution to wind up the company; and

    (ii) an ordinary resolution to appoint a liquidator.

(c) A liquidator appointed by the members will usually be one that has been recommended by the directors. It will usually be an insolvency practitioner who has advised the directors as to insolvency and advised them that a creditors' voluntary liquidation is the most appropriate route.

(d) Within 14 days of the members' meeting there must be a creditors' meeting. This is known as a s 98 meeting because s 98 of the IA 1986 is the statutory provision under which creditors' meetings are governed. Although the creditors' meeting must be within 14 days of the members' meeting, in most cases the creditors' meeting takes place around one hour after the members' meeting on the same day.

(e) The directors must send notice of the meeting to all known creditors at least seven days before the creditors' meeting. Notice should also be placed in the *London Gazette* and in two local newspapers.

(f) At the creditors' meeting under s 98, the directors must lay a sworn statement of affairs before the meeting. This is in essence a statement of the company's assets and liabilities (and the shortfall as regards funds to pay creditors). The statement of affairs is often used by creditors at the meeting to ask directors questions about the conduct of the company. Also, it is used to compare with the last audited accounts filed by the company to look at how quickly the company has deteriorated and to see if there is any evidence of wrongdoing.

(g) The purpose of the s 98 meeting is that it is a forum for the creditors to:

    (i) ask directors questions as to why the company is in its present state and what the directors did to prevent it; and

    (ii) choose a liquidator.

(h) Creditors can vote for a different liquidator to that nominated by the members. If the creditors vote for a different liquidator then the creditors' choice prevails. This is why it is called 'creditors' voluntary liquidation'. Many creditors do not trust the person nominated by the shareholders. They fear that the company will not be investigated properly and that the shareholders may have chosen the liquidator because he will take a 'softly softly' approach. The way in which the creditors appoint a liquidator is by a majority value of their debts.

(i) Once an appointment is made at the creditors' meeting the liquidator files a consent to act and the chairman of the meeting certifies his appointment.

(j) Within 14 days he must place notice of his appointment in the *London Gazette* and send notice of his appointment to the Registrar of Companies (s 109).

(k) After he has completed his work, the liquidator holds a final meeting of members and creditors (s 106) and explains to that meeting how the assets have been realised and distributed (see **19.5.2.3**).

19.5.2.2 Powers and duties of the liquidator in a creditors' voluntary liquidation

The duties of the liquidator in a creditors' voluntary liquidation are essentially the same as those in a members' voluntary liquidation. Again he is the agent of the company and the directors' powers cease (but the directors are not removed).

The liquidator's duty is to collect the assets in and distribute them in accordance with the statutory order and to investigate past transactions and the conduct of the directors. It is this latter point which will usually take up much more time in a creditors' voluntary liquidation. The liquidator will be concerned to attack any past transactions and to investigate the directors in order to swell the fund of assets available to creditors. This is a liquidation where a company is insolvent. Therefore the assets are certainly not going to be enough to pay off the creditors in full. The liquidator is concerned to increase the pool of assets to get as big a return as possible for the creditors.

19.5.2.3 End of the creditors' voluntary liquidation

The creditors' voluntary liquidation concludes when:

(a)   the liquidator sells the available assets;

(b)   he distributes the money to the creditors;

(c)   he holds a final meeting of members and creditors (s 106);

(d)   the liquidator is released by the meeting or by the court;

(e)   accounts are forwarded to Companies House; and

(f)   three months later the company is dissolved by the Registrar of Companies.

19.5.3 Compulsory liquidation

Compulsory liquidation is normally a result of a hostile process initiated against the company's wishes. This can lead to much litigation. In any event, the court is more intimately involved in compulsory liquidation than in voluntary. In a compulsory liquidation, the company is insolvent.

Compulsory liquidation also differs from voluntary liquidation in that the Official Receiver (a civil servant) is always involved. This and the fact that the liquidation is brought about by court order makes it slower than voluntary liquidation, generally more expensive, more formal and more rigorous in terms of examination of the directors and reasons for failure of the company.

19.5.3.1 Grounds for compulsory liquidation

The most common ground on which a petition for liquidation can be founded is that the company is unable to pay its debts (IA 1986, s 122). Section 123 sets out the four circumstances in which a company is unable to pay its debts. These are:

Neglecting to comply with a statutory demand made by the creditor for a sum of over £750

If a creditor is owed more than £750 he can serve a statutory demand upon the company. A statutory demand is a prescribed form which details who the creditor and debtor is, what the debt is and the circumstances upon which the debt occurred. If the company does not comply with the statutory demand within 21 days then the creditor can issue a petition for winding up. The debt must not be one which is disputed (see *Re Cooling Equipment Wholesale Ltd* [2002] 2 BCLC 745 and *Celltech International Ltd v Dalkia Utilities Services plc* [2004] EWHC 193).

An unsatisfied judgment

If a creditor has a judgment against the company he can file a petition based on that judgment.

The company's assets are exceeded by its liabilities, including contingent and prospective liabilities

This is the 'balance sheet' test, and is not often used in practice.

The company is unable to pay its debts as and when they fall due

This is the cash-flow insolvency test. There are a number of indicators that a court may take into account as to whether a company may be unable to pay its debts as and when they fall due. These include:

(a)   the creditor having demanded money and the company (without reasonable excuse) having failed to comply with that demand; and

(b)   the company admitting it cannot pay the debt (for example in open correspondence).

19.5.3.2 The procedure for compulsory liquidation

(a)   Compulsory liquidation is begun by petition. The possible petitioners under s 124(1) include creditors, directors, the Secretary of State and the company itself. The facts in the petition are verified by affidavit.

(b)   The petition is advertised in the *London Gazette* not less than seven days after service of the petition on the company and not less than seven days before the hearing of the petition. In reality, advertisement of the petition is the key date. Usually, the bank will freeze the company's bank account. There are a number of reasons for doing this, for example it may be that presentation of the petition against the company triggers crystallisation or constitutes default by the company in relation to a loan. Advertisement usually leads to other creditors 'jumping on the bandwagon' and demanding any sums due. It is rare, once advertisement occurs, for a company to survive a petition for compulsory winding up.

(c)   Section 127 provides that any disposal of the company's property is void without consent of the court, after presentation of the petition (s 129(2)).

(d)   The petitioner files a certificate of compliance on all statutory matters with the court at least five days before the hearing.

(e)   At the hearing itself, the court has the discretion to dismiss, adjourn or make the winding-up order. Generally speaking, if one of the grounds in s 122 is established, a petitioning creditor is entitled as of right to a winding-up order.

(f)   Once the order has been made, the court notifies the Official Receiver of the order. Three copies of the winding-up order are sent to the Official Receiver, who then serves the company with a copy of the order and also serves Companies House.

(g)   The Official Receiver must then place notice of the winding-up order in the *London Gazette* and in one newspaper.

(h)   The Official Receiver must decide whether to call the first meeting of creditors within 12 weeks of his appointment (s 136(4)). The main aim of that first meeting of creditors is to decide whether to appoint an insolvency practitioner as the liquidator in place of the Official Receiver. If the Official Receiver decides not to call the first meeting of creditors, he must tell all creditors of his decision. A quarter (in value) of the creditors can compel him to call a meeting of creditors. The Official Receiver's decision as to whether to call a first meeting of creditors is essentially based on the assets of the company. The Official Receiver knows that a practitioner would not be interested in taking any such appointment unless there were any assets (and therefore fees) in the job.

(i)   The first meeting of creditors must be held not later than four months after the appointment of the Official Receiver.

(j)   After he has completed his work, the liquidator holds a final meeting of creditors (s 146) and explains to that meeting how the assets have been realised and distributed (see **19.5.3.4**).

19.5.3.3 Powers and duties of the liquidator in a compulsory liquidation

The powers of the liquidator in a compulsory liquidation are very similar to the powers of a voluntary liquidator. The only major difference is that if he wants to conduct litigation or to carry on the business he needs the sanction of the court (IA 1986, Sch 4).

Upon the making of a compulsory winding-up order, the Official Receiver is always appointed liquidator of the company.

Directors' powers pass to the Official Receiver and (unlike voluntary liquidations) the directors' appointments are terminated (*Measures Brothers Ltd v Measures* [1910] 2 Ch 248).

All legal actions against the company are stayed.

The Official Receiver is under a duty to investigate the affairs of the company and the reasons for the company's failure (s 132(1)). Once he has investigated the affairs of the company and reasons for failure he may report to the court, if necessary. He must also report to the creditors at least once during the course of liquidation on the results of his investigations.

The Official Receiver has power to call officers of the company for public examination before a court for them to answer any questions regarding the affairs of the company and reasons for the company's failure (s 133). The creditors can compel the Official Receiver to call officers for public examination if half the creditors in value wish public examination to take place.

19.5.3.4 End of the compulsory liquidation

The compulsory liquidation concludes when:

(a) the liquidator sells the available assets;

(b) he distributes the money to the creditors;

(c) he holds a final meeting of creditors (s 146);

(d) the liquidator is released by the meeting or by the court;

(e) the accounts are forwarded to Companies House and the court; and

(f) three months later the company is dissolved by the Registrar of Companies.

19.5.4 Statutory order of payment

During the course of the liquidation a liquidator (whether it be voluntary or compulsory) will ask creditors to send him proof of debt. The liquidator will then approve, or reject, the proof of debt and will rank it in the liquidation.

Once all the assets have been collected in and realised then a liquidator must pay the assets in the following order (fixed charges have been paid out already):

(a) expenses of the winding up (the liquidator's and his professional advisers' fees);

(b) preferential debts ;

(c) monies secured by floating charges;

(d) unsecured creditors;

(e) interest on preferential and unsecured debts;

(f) deferred creditors; and

(g) if there is any surplus it is to be distributed amongst shareholders.

The only preferential creditors who are left after the amendments brought in by the EA 2002 are the employees for their wages, up to a statutory maximum, and occupational pension schemes. The Crown no longer has any rights as a preferential creditor (see **19.5.5** below).

The liquidation could follow an administrative receivership, for an 'old' floating charge granted before 15 September 2003. In that case, the preferential creditors and the floating charge holder may have been paid by the receiver. If so, they drop out of the picture. It should be noted that the previous division of expenses in regard to a floating charge in *Re Barleycorn Enterprises* [1970] 2 All ER 155 has been overruled by *Buchler v Talbot* [2004] UKHL 9. In *Buchler*, the perhaps unsurprising decision was that the expenses of the liquidation process could not be paid out of the proceeds of the floating charge, which were owed to another creditor. However, in contrast to this *administration* expenses can be paid out of assets that are subject to a floating charge (IA 1986, Sch B1, paras 70, 99(3)). The administration expenses could include the costs of administering the estate, making distributions to creditors, eg to ensure the continuance of supplies, and corporation tax liabilities.

A new provision was inserted into the IA 1986 by the CA 2006 on 6 April 2008, allowing liquidation expenses to be paid out of assets subject to a floating charge if the company's other assets are insufficient to meet them (IA 1986, s 176ZA, inserted by CA 2006, s 1282). The ring-fenced fund is still set aside for the unsecured creditors. However, the claims of any preferential creditors and the floating charge holder to the non ring-fenced fund have to cede priority to the liquidation expenses. This change reverses part of the decision in *Buchler v Talbot*.

Secured creditors are not allowed to have access to the ring-fenced fund for any unsecured portion of their debts (*Re Airbase (UK) Ltd v HMRC* [2008] EWHC 124 (Ch)).

The way that the liquidator goes about paying creditors is that where he has funds available he declares a dividend. He then distributes the dividend to those creditors who have proved their debts. He always reserves money for his own fees.

The liquidator may make interim dividends throughout the course of liquidation, and then at the end of liquidation either declare a final dividend or give notice to creditors that no further dividend will be declared.

It is unusual in a compulsory or creditors' voluntary liquidation for unsecured creditors to receive anything more than a few pence in the pound in relation to their debt. So, a very simple example would be:

Funds available to liquidator	£100,000
Owed to floating charge holder	£25,000
Costs and expenses of liquidation	£10,000
Owed to preferential creditors	£15,000
Owed to unsecured creditors	£100,000

In this case, preferential creditors would be paid in full, together with the floating charge holder. However, unsecured creditors would receive only 50p in the pound in respect of their debt (as there is only £50,000 left after paying the costs, the preferential creditors and the floating charge holder).

Winding up is a class remedy. This means it is available to all creditors. Anyone issuing a winding-up petition as a creditor should bear in mind that they will not solely receive the assets of the company. The assets will be distributed equally amongst all of a particular class of creditors.

19.5.5   Abolition of Crown preference and 'ring-fencing' of funds for unsecured creditors

The Crown's status as a preferential creditor was abolished by s 251 of the EA 2002 (which amends IA 1986, s 386 and Sch 6). If matters were left at this, the banks would benefit under their floating charges, as an insolvent company's assets are paid to floating charge holders prior to unsecured creditors. To remedy this, the EA 2002 provides that, in all liquidations, receiverships and administrations, a percentage of a company's net property is 'ring-fenced' for unsecured creditors, rather than being paid to floating charge holders. The percentage subject to the ring-fencing provisions is 50% of the first £10,000 of the company's net property, and 20% thereafter, up to a total ring-fenced amount of £600,000. This represents approximately 20% of £3m. Company net property above £3m will not be subject to ring-fencing (Insolvency Act 1986 (Prescribed Part) Order 2003 (SI 2003/2097)).

It is important to note that only floating charges created after 15 September 2003 are subject to the ring-fencing provisions (IA 1986, s 176A).

19.6   Receivership

A receiver is someone appointed by the holder of a charge, usually a bank, when the company is not complying with the terms of the loan. He will be an insolvency practitioner. The task of the receiver is to take possession of the charged property and deal with it for the benefit of the charge holder, which will usually mean selling it. After this has been done, he has no further interest in the company (though he does also have a duty to pay preferential creditors (IA 1986, s 40)).

A receiver can be appointed under a fixed charge. This is known as an 'LPA receiver' as he would usually be dealing with premises, or fixed plant and machinery. We will not consider LPA receivers further. We will now look at receivers appointed under a floating charge – administrative receivers.

19.6.1 Administrative receiver

Since implementation on 15 September 2003 of the reforms brought in by the EA 2002, administrative receivership can only be used for floating charges created before that date (IA 1986, ss 72A–72H). (There are some minor exceptions which we shall ignore.) This part of this chapter has been left in so that the reader can see how such 'old' floating charges are dealt with. These charges will, however, become increasingly less important with time. The only insolvency route which can be used for floating charges created after 15 September 2003 is administration.

Administrative receivers may be appointed under s 29 of the IA 1986 by a charge holder who has a floating charge over the company's undertaking. Banks will often take such a charge to give themselves this power, even though the floating charge may be of little additional financial value (because they have fixed charges as well). The party appointing the administrative receiver can block the appointment of an administrator. The administrative receiver has wide powers to manage the business and sell assets. (These are normally set out in the loan document, but a set of implied powers is listed in Sch 1 to the IA 1986.) In *Feetum v Levy* [2005] EWCA Civ 1601, the court refused an application to appoint an administrative receiver under s 72A of the IA 1986. There is a general prohibition on such appointments for floating charges created on or after 15 September 2003, and none of the statutory exceptions applied.

19.6.2 Events triggering the appointment of an administrative receiver

Typical events included in loan documentation which could trigger the appointment of a receiver could be:

(a) failure to meet a demand to pay capital or interest;

(b) presentation of a winding-up petition;

(c) presentation of a petition for administration or a CVA (see **19.3** and **19.4**);

(d) levying of distress or execution against the company's assets;

(e) failure to comply with restrictions in the loan documentation, for example by granting a new charge over assets;

(f) the company ceasing to trade;

(g) the assets being in jeopardy; or

(h) inability of the company to pay its debts.

19.6.3 Procedure for administrative receivership

(a) The charge holder (the bank) will appoint an investigating accountant to do a review of the company's financial position and its prospects. Often, the person appointed as a receiver after this investigation is an accountant from the same firm. Once he receives his letter of appointment from the bank, he has until the end of the next business day to accept it (IA 1986, s 33).

(b) Once appointed, the receiver must inform Companies House within seven days. He must also inform all known creditors and the company of his appointment within 28 days (IA 1986, s 46). He must place a notice to the same effect in the *London Gazette* and a local newspaper.

(c)   If the appointment of the receiver is defective for any reason, the court may order removal of the receiver. Both the receiver and the party appointing him could be liable in tort to the company (eg *Rushingdale Ltd SA v Byblos Bank SAL* [1986] BCC 99).

(d)   Section 48 of the IA 1986 requires a receiver to prepare a report within three months of a statement of affairs from the company officers. It deals with the circumstances leading up to his appointment, what he has done and intends to do to about disposing of the company's property, and the prospects for the creditors.

19.6.4   Effects of the appointment of the administrative receiver

Legally, the appointment of a receiver has little effect on the company. The directors remain in office and the company continues to trade. The employee's contracts of employment are not affected (unless disclaimed by the receiver within 14 days of his appointment). Existing contracts remain binding on the company. (A receiver has no power to disclaim contracts, unlike a liquidator.) If the receiver decides not to honour a contract, the other party can sue the company but will rank only as an unsecured creditor (that is, one who does not hold a charge – see **12.3**).

19.6.5   Powers and duties of the administrative receiver

A receiver will carry on the company's business. He will try to sell the business or the assets to satisfy the claim of the bank. He can even petition for the winding up of the company. In any event, once his task of selling assets is completed it may be that the only remaining option is to wind up the company as it is no longer a viable business.

A receiver makes contracts on behalf of the company (for example, to sell premises). He is acting as the agent of the company in doing so (IA 1986, s 44(1)(a)). However, he can incur personal liability on it. He will be protected by an indemnity from the company as far as its assets go. However, he will also contract out of personal liability.

The receiver is under a duty of good faith, primarily to the party appointing him, that is the bank. He also owes a duty of care to the company, and to other third parties such as guarantors. This would include taking reasonable steps to ensure profitability if the receiver continues the business (*Medforth v Blake* [1999] BPIR 712).

19.6.6   End of the administrative receivership

A receivership ends when the receiver:

(a)   has sold all the available assets covered by the charge and has distributed the proceeds;

(b)   resigns; or

(c)   is removed by the court.

19.7   Clawing back money – overturning past transactions

When insolvency is looming on the horizon, it is understandable that the directors (and others) may want to disperse assets of the company to keep them out of the hands of the liquidator. Such behaviour is not novel. There are various provisions in the IA 1986 designed to overturn past transactions. They allow the liquidator or administrator to claw back the money, or other assets. In addition to these provisions, it should also be kept in mind that failure to register a charge under ss 860, 869 of the CA 2006 will register that charge unenforceable against a liquidator or administrator. The loan agreement between the charge holder and the company will still be valid.

The possibilities for voidable transactions are:

(a)   transactions at an undervalue;

(b)   preference;

(c)   extortionate credit transactions;

(d)   avoidance of floating charges;

(e)   transaction defrauding creditors;

(f)   misfeasance;

(g)   fraudulent trading; or

(h)   wrongful trading.

A liquidator or administrator has to obtain the consent of the court before using the 'clawback' provisions (IA 1986, Sch 4, para 3A).

19.7.1 Transactions at an undervalue (IA 1986, s 238)

(a)   Only a liquidator or administrator can pursue a transaction at an undervalue (s 238(2)). It is not a matter which can be pursued by creditors generally.

(b)   The essence of the transaction at an undervalue is contained in s 238(4). A transaction will be one at an undervalue if, at the relevant time (see later), the company makes a gift to someone, or enters into a transaction with someone where the consideration provided by the other person is 'significantly less' than that provided by the company. In short, the company is being swindled.

(c)   For a transaction to be one at an undervalue it must occur within the 'relevant time'. The 'relevant time' for a transaction at an undervalue is two years ending with the onset of insolvency (s 240(1)(a)). The onset of insolvency is basically the date of commencement of winding up. See item (g) below.

(d)   There is a defence in s 238(5) if the transaction was entered into in good faith, for the purpose of carrying on the business and when it was made there were reasonable grounds for believing it would benefit the company.

(e)   A number of orders can be made if a transaction at an undervalue is established. These are set out in s 241 and include returning property to the company; returning proceeds of sale to the company; the discharge of any security, etc.

(f)   When the transaction was entered into, the company must have been insolvent at the time of the transaction or become insolvent as a result of the transaction (see s 240(2)).

(g)   Where the transaction is made with a connected person (see below) then it is presumed that the company was insolvent unless it can be shown otherwise.

If a liquidator alleges that a transaction at undervalue has occurred, then the balance sheet will have to be examined to see whether the company was insolvent at the time of the transaction or as a result of it. Furthermore, other evidence of insolvency will have to be sought. This could be judgments being entered against the company, execution over the company's assets, payment of creditors only upon issue of writ or statutory demand.

'Connected person' is defined in s 249. A person is a connected person if he or she is a director of the company, an associate of a director or an associate of the company. A husband or wife is an associate.

19.7.2 Preferences (IA 1986, s 239)

A preference is where one creditor is 'preferred' by the company in that it has been paid ahead of other creditors, in the following circumstances.

(a)   Only a liquidator or administrator can bring proceedings for preference.

(b)   The definition of preference is contained within s 239(4), but there are a number of things that need to be noted in relation to the definition, as follows:

    (i)   the person preferred must be the company's creditor, surety or guarantor (otherwise there can be no preference);

(ii)   the person preferred must have been put in a better position on liquidation than they would have been had the event not occurred; and

(iii)   the company must have desired to prefer the creditor/guarantor/surety (s 239(5)). The courts have said that desire to prefer is stronger than intention and that a desire means that the company should 'positively wish' to put somebody in a better position (*Re MC Bacon Ltd (No 1); Re a Company (No 005009 of 1987) (No 1)* [1990] BCLC 324).

(c)   Desire to prefer is presumed if the preference is in favour of a connected person.

(d)   The company must have been insolvent at the time of the preference or must have become so as a result, but there is no presumption of insolvency if the preference is to a connected person.

(e)   The preference must occur within a relevant time.

(f)   The orders made are the same as for transactions at an undervalue.

The 'relevant time' for a preference is twofold.

(a)   If a preference is given to a person who is connected with the company then the time period is two years, ending with the onset of insolvency.

(b)   If a preference is given to someone who is unconnected then the relevant time is six months, ending with the onset of insolvency.

Examples of a preference include:

(a)   making an unsecured creditor secured;

(b)   paying one unsecured creditor before other unsecured creditors;

(c)   allowing a supplier of goods to change its terms and conditions to include a retention of title clause where none existed previously; or

(d)   allowing a creditor to enter judgment against the company when the company has a good defence to the claim.

19.7.3   Extortionate credit transactions (IA 1986, s 244)

(a)   A liquidator or administrator can apply to reopen credit transactions made within three years from when the company went into liquidation (s 244(2)).

(b)   They only apply if the credit transaction was extortionate. This is defined in s 244(3). Basically, payments must be 'grossly exorbitant' or the transaction must 'grossly contravene ordinary principles of fair dealing'.

(c)   There is very little case law on this area as it is quite rare in practice. It seems that s 244 is analogous to the equivalent provisions in the Consumer Credit Act 1974.

19.7.4   Avoidance of floating charges (IA 1986, s 245)

Certain floating charges are invalid if the criteria as set out in s 245 are fulfilled. This does not apply to fixed charges.

There does not have to be an application by a liquidator under s 245. If the criteria are fulfilled, the floating charge is automatically invalid. In practice, the liquidator will write to the floating charge holder stating he believes the floating charge to be invalid. Usually, the next step is that the floating charge holder will either seek to enforce the charge and force the liquidator into injunctive proceedings or, more commonly, seek a declaration from the court that the floating charge is valid. The section is primarily designed to invalidate floating charges which have been created for no consideration.

A typical situation is where a creditor has been unsecured and has had the debts secured without giving any consideration. So, for example, if the company has an unsecured overdraft at the bank and the bank, upon hearing that the company is in financial difficulty, requires a floating charge to secure the overdraft then it will be invalid. This is because no consideration has been provided by the bank for the creation of the security.

The floating charge has to be created within the 'relevant time'. This is within two years of insolvency in the case of a connected person, or within 12 months of insolvency for any other person.

If the person is not connected, then the company has to have been insolvent at the giving of the charge or become insolvent by reason of giving it (see s 245(4)).

19.7.5 Transactions defrauding creditors (IA 1986, s 423)

This section is much wider than the other sections we have already looked at. Basically, any 'victim' of such a transaction can make application. Liquidators, etc can also make application.

A transaction is one to defraud creditors if it is at an undervalue (same definition as s 238 is used, see **19.7.1**). However, it will only be a transaction defrauding creditors if the purpose of the transaction was to put assets beyond the reach of someone, or to prejudice the interests of someone in relation to a claim they may make. A classic example is a company engaged in litigation which sees that a substantial judgment will be awarded against it at the end of the day. As a result of this, it siphons off assets to third parties so that the judgment may not be enforced.

Orders the court may make for such transactions are set out in s 435. Section 435 is very similar to s 240 in relation to orders. There is no 'relevant time', so there is no time limit for actions.

19.8 'Phoenix' companies (IA 1986, s 216)

Section 216 prohibits the re-use of a company's name where the company has gone into insolvent liquidation. This is to counter the threat of an unscrupulous trader putting one company into liquidation and then transferring the assets to a new one using the same name, possibly operating on the same premises with the same staff, the debts of the old company having been left behind (see, eg, *R (on the application of Griffin) v Richmond Magistrates Court* [2008] EWHC 84 (QB)). The new company has risen from the ashes like the fabled phoenix, hence the name of the problem. The directors in question can be held personally liable for the debts of the insolvent company under s 216, unless they obtain the consent of the court to be directors of the new company.

19.9 Basic procedure – liquidation

(a) *Compulsory liquidation*

  (i) petition court and advertise petition in *London Gazette*

  (ii) hearing – court makes order

      – Official Receiver becomes liquidator

      – Official Receiver advertises order in *London Gazette* and local newspaper, notifies Registrar and company

  (iii) statement of affairs

  (iv) meetings of members and creditors to nominate liquidator of their choice (creditors' choice takes precedence)

  (v) assets collected in and distributed in required order

  (vi) final meeting of creditors held

  (vii) final return filed with court and Registrar

  (viii) company dissolved three months later.

(b)   *Creditors' voluntary winding up*

    (i)   directors prepare statement of affairs

    (ii)   special resolution to wind up passed by members

        both filed with registrar

    (iii)   members can nominate liquidator

    (iv)   resolution advertised in *London Gazette* within 14 days

    (v)   creditors' meeting held within 14 days of GM

       –   NB notice requirements

       –   creditors' choice of liquidator takes priority over that of members

    (vi)   appointment of liquidator published in *London Gazette* and notified to Registrar

    (vii)   assets collected in and distributed in required order

    (viii)   final meetings of creditors and members held

    (ix)   final return filed with Registrar

    (x)   company dissolved three months later.

(c)   *Members' voluntary liquidation*

    (i)   statutory declaration of solvency by directors

    (ii)   special resolution passed by members within five weeks of statutory declaration

        both filed with Registrar

    (iii)   members appoint liquidator

    (iv)   resolution and notice of liquidator's appointment advertised in *London Gazette* and notice of appointment to Registrar

    (v)   assets collected in and distributed in required order

    (vi)   final meeting of members held

    (vii)   final return filed with Registrar

    (viii)   company dissolved three months later.

19.10 Schemes of arrangement

This is not an insolvency procedure but a procedure used in various circumstances, including by companies which are in financial difficulties, though they may still be solvent. In essence, the company's financial affairs are restructured with the consent of both its creditors and its shareholders. The idea is to sort things out by putting in place some sort of financial compromise, to avoid the company going into administration or liquidation. Approval by the court is needed. At the first hearing, the court will order that separate meetings of the creditors and shareholders take place to approve, or not as the case may be, the scheme being put forward. The court will then sanction the scheme if the relevant approvals are forthcoming and if the court considers that the scheme is fair and equitable. The procedure therefore requires two court hearings and has itself no moratorium to enforce a 'freeze' on creditor actions in the interim (unless it takes place as part of an administration). It therefore has considerable problems, including cost.

Summary of compulsory and voluntary liquidation procedures

This flowchart summarises and compares the compulsory and voluntary liquidation procedures. It shows that although the entry routes are different, the liquidator's functions, conduct and result of the liquidation itself are largely the same, with the Official Receiver's investigatory function being confined to compulsory liquidation.

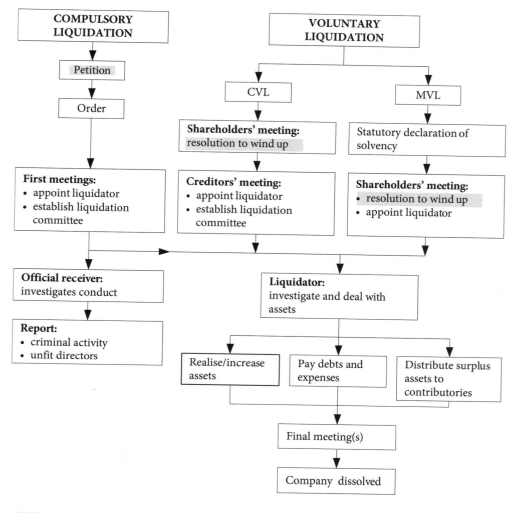

= commencement of winding up

© FL Memo 2009

Distribution of assets

The following flowchart summarises the way in which a company's secured and unsecured assets are distributed to its creditors and contributories in a set order.

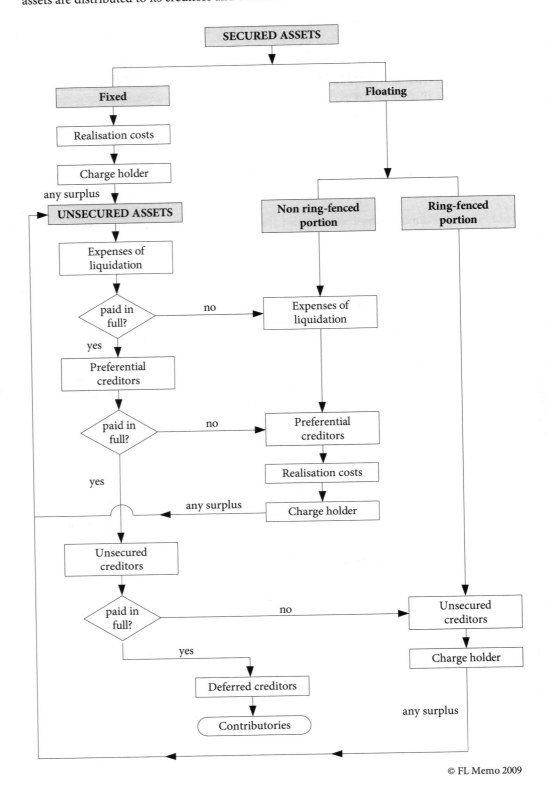

© FL Memo 2009

The following examples illustrate how to use the flowchart:

Examples

1. *Insufficient assets to repay all creditors*

    Jones & Black is in liquidation. Its total assets are worth £100,000. The expenses of the winding up amount to £20,000, and the company's debts are as follows:

bank	£60,000
employees	£1,000
unsecured creditors	£30,000
deferred creditors	£4,000

    The bank holds a fixed charge and a floating charge over certain of the company's assets as security for its debt. Once liquidated, the assets subject to the fixed charge are worth £60,000, and those subject to the floating charge are worth £15,000 (of the assets subject to the floating charge, the liquidator ring-fences £6,000). Therefore, £75,000 of the company's assets are *secured* and £25,000 are *unsecured*. They can be distributed as follows:

    (a)   With the proceeds of the assets subject to the *fixed charge*, the liquidator can pay the realisation costs, which amount to £9,000, as well as £51,000 of the bank's debt. At this stage, the bank is still owed £9,000, and there is no surplus left over from distributing the assets subject to the fixed charge available to add to the unsecured assets to meet the other claims.

    (b)   Out of the unsecured assets, the *expenses of the liquidation* (£20,000) are paid first. The nature of the employees' claims falls within the definition of *preferential debts*, and so they are paid next.

    (c)   Since the preferential debts have been paid in full, the *non ring-fenced* portion of the assets secured by the *floating charge* (£9,000) can be applied to the costs of realising those assets (£1,000) and the rest paid to the bank. The bank is now owed £1,000. There is no surplus in the ring-fenced portion to feed back into the pot of unsecured assets.

    (d)   Only £4,000 of unsecured assets are available to meet the *unsecured creditors'* claims (which now include the bank, for £1,000), which would give them a dividend of 13p in the £1. Since they are not paid in full, they are entitled to be paid out of the *ring-fenced* portion of the assets subject to the *floating charge* (£6,000), which increases their dividend to 33p in the £1 but does not leave any surplus to meet the rest of the bank's debt or to pay the deferred creditors. A distribution cannot be made to the contributories.

2. *Sufficient assets to repay all creditors*

    If the company's *total assets* were worth £140,000 (again, £60,000 subject to the fixed charge and £15,000 to the floating charge; £65,000 unsecured), the liquidator would distribute them as follows:

    (a)   As in 1. above.

    (b)   As in 1. above.

    (c)   As in 1. above.

    (d)   £44,000 of unsecured assets are available to meet the *unsecured creditors'* claims (£30,000), enabling them to be paid in full. Therefore, the *ring-fenced* portion of the assets subject to the *floating charge* (£6,000) is not required to meet the unsecured creditors' claims and can be used to pay the bank. There is a surplus of £5,000, which is added to the remaining unsecured assets, leaving a total of £19,000 left to distribute.

    (e)   The *deferred creditors* (£4,000) can be paid in full, leaving a surplus of £15,000 to be distributed to the *contributories*.

Chapter 20
Personal Insolvency

20.1 Introduction

The term 'bankruptcy' applies to individuals, not to companies. In the context of a business, an individual may be declared bankrupt because an unincorporated business has failed (ie either the business of a sole trader or of a partnership, neither of which has the advantage of limited liability). Alternatively, he may have carried on his business through the medium of a limited company but nevertheless has incurred personal liability in some way. This could happen, for example, where directors are forced personally to guarantee a loan to their company. Equally, bankruptcy could arise through unwise personal extravagance and could be unrelated to the individual's business interests.

The law of personal insolvency has changed quite radically as a result of the EA 2002 which has amended the IA 1986. The aims of the revised regime are to:

(a) *remove the 'one-size-fits-all' approach to bankruptcy* – making the process fairer for the honest majority and making it more stringent for reckless or dishonest bankrupts;

(b) *create 'fresh start' proposals to give entrepreneurs another chance* – including a shorter discharge period of one year;

(c) *create tougher penalties for reckless bankrupts* – a new regime of bankruptcy restriction orders which can last two to fifteen years; and

(d) *remove the Crown's right to be paid ahead of ordinary creditors* – removal of Crown preference.

20.2 What is bankruptcy?

Bankruptcy is a judicial process by which a person (a debtor) is found to be unable to pay his debts. It may be that a debtor may be unable to do this because he has cashflow problems. He could pay all his debts eventually but does not have sufficient available resources to pay those debts which are due to be paid now or in the near future. Alternatively, it may be that the debtor faces a liability which is due to arise at some future point, it being clear that the debtor will not be able to meet that liability when it arises. If a debtor is unable to pay his debts in either of the two ways described above, he is insolvent. If the court makes a bankruptcy order, that debtor will become a bankrupt and his property will vest in his trustee in bankruptcy and be distributed among his creditors. Eventually, even if all of his debts have not been paid in full, the bankrupt may be discharged and he is then free from almost all of his previous debts. Individual voluntary arrangements are an alternative to bankruptcy (see **20.6**).

English bankruptcy legislation was originally devised to deal with business failures. However, today one of the main reasons for bankruptcy is consumer credit, not a failed business.

Under the revised regime, nine out of ten bankrupts make only one visit to the Official Receiver's office. They obtain their discharge within about six months of the bankruptcy order. The remaining one out of ten bankrupts are targeted by the Government as candidates for bankruptcy restriction orders (BROs) (see **20.4.3**). The BRO process is managed by the Government, not the private sector. Even where a private sector appointment is made, the trustee in bankruptcy is only able to sell the bankrupt's matrimonial home on certain conditions (see **20.3.4**). The revised, 'pain-free' bankruptcy regime has caused the number of bankruptcies to rise considerably. For more information on the revised regime, the reader may wish to consult Stephen Davies QC, *Insolvency and the Enterprise Act 2002* (Bristol: Jordans, 2003).

Gambler lost £40k in 10 weeks

North Wales man sold his house to pay off debts – but lost the lot in a 10-week gambling spree.

Stephen Alexander Edge blew more than £40,000 then declared himself bankrupt.

He gambled the money, despite already owing more than £50,000.

The 40-year-old Royal Mail worker was yesterday placed under special restrictions by the Insolvency Service aimed at 'irresponsible, reckless or dishonest bankrupts'.

When he filed for bankruptcy, he had just £148 cash in the bank and owed £61,773.

He was declared bankrupt in July last year.

The Insolvency Service yesterday revealed the delivery manager had given a bankruptcy restrictions undertaking (BRU) for the next six years.

His liabilities include more than £20,000 in credit card debt and more than £38,000 in bank loans.

The 'unfit conduct' which led to the BRU was not disputed by Mr Edge.

(From the *North Wales Daily Post*, 28 January 2005.)

20.3   The bankruptcy process

Bankruptcy is commenced by the presentation of a petition, and is governed principally by the Insolvency Act 1986 (as amended).

In 2008, the Insolvency Service reported that there were 67,428 bankruptcies in England and Wales, and 39,116 voluntary arrangements (see **20.6**). These figures represent an overall increase of about 50% in the total number of personal insolvencies when compared with 2006 and 2007. One reason for the increase would seem to be that the revised regime makes bankruptcy an easier option for a debtor.

20.3.1   The petition

20.3.1.1   Creditor's petition

A creditor can present a petition to the court (IA 1986, s 264) if the debtor owes him £750 or more (the amount owing being a liquidated sum which is an unsecured debt). He must also be able to claim that the debtor is unable to pay the debt or has little prospect of being able to pay it, as evidenced by the fact that he has failed either to comply with a 'statutory demand' (a demand for payment formally served on the debtor by the creditor) or to satisfy execution of a judgment debt. Any creditor who is owed less than £750 cannot present a petition on his own but can join together with other creditors to present a petition, provided the total amount owed to all the petitioners is not less than £750. The petition should be presented to the High Court (if the debtor either lives or carries on business in London) or the county court with bankruptcy jurisdiction for the area where the debtor resides or carries on business (but not all county courts have bankruptcy jurisdiction).

20.3.1.2   Debtor's petition

A debtor may petition for his own bankruptcy. In his petition, he must allege that he cannot pay his debts (IA 1986, s 272). This must be accompanied by a statement of affairs, ie details of all his creditors, debts, liabilities and assets.

A debtor may petition for his own bankruptcy in order to escape pressure from creditors. By doing so, he places responsibility for his financial affairs in the hands of his trustee in bankruptcy. Any existing creditors should then deal with the trustee rather than dealing with the debtor. This can be an enormous relief to the debtor, as can the fact that, once he is discharged as a bankrupt, he is free from virtually all of his current debts, even if such of his assets as are available to his trustee are insufficient to pay them all in full.

20.3.2 The order

Where there is a creditor's petition before the court the bankruptcy order will usually be granted if all the necessary conditions are satisfied.

Where the petition is a debtor's petition, in certain circumstances the court will appoint an insolvency practitioner to investigate the possibility of a voluntary arrangement before reaching a final decision as to whether to make a bankruptcy order (see **20.6**).

Under the changes brought in by the EA 2002, the aim is for the general discharge period for bankrupts to be one year. However, even that period can be reduced if the Official Receiver files a notice stating that further investigation into the bankrupt's conduct and affairs is unnecessary, or has been concluded (IA 1986, s 279).

20.3.3 The trustee in bankruptcy

When a bankruptcy order is made by the court, the Official Receiver (a civil servant) initially takes control of the debtor's property. He may continue to supervise the sale and distribution of the debtor's assets if he assumes the role of trustee in bankruptcy. The debtor must submit a statement of affairs to the Official Receiver within 21 days of the order, who will then decide whether it is necessary to call a meeting of creditors to enable them to appoint an insolvency practitioner of their choice as trustee in bankruptcy. An insolvency practitioner must be licensed (either by the DTI or his own professional body) to act as such. In most cases, an insolvency practitioner is an accountant. Any creditor can demand that such a meeting be called if he and any other creditors supporting him comprise 25% in value of the bankrupt's creditors (IA 1986, s 294). If the creditors do not appoint their own trustee in bankruptcy, or if the Official Receiver decides that a creditors' meeting is unnecessary, then the Official Receiver will continue to conduct the bankruptcy as trustee in bankruptcy.

Under the revised regime, the Official Receiver is no longer required to investigate the conduct and affairs of every bankrupt (IA 1986, s 289), but only where the Official Receiver thinks it necessary.

20.3.4 The bankrupt's property

The bankrupt's estate vests automatically in his trustee in bankruptcy (IA 1986, s 306). The bankrupt's estate is defined in s 283 of the IA 1986 and includes most of the bankrupt's real and personal property. Excluded from the definition of the bankrupt's estate are tools of the trade, clothing and furniture which the bankrupt may retain. However, if, for example, the bankrupt has furniture of high value, then the trustee has power to sell the asset and replace it with something cheaper (see IA 1986, s 308).

Similarly, the bankrupt is entitled to retain any salary he makes subject to his trustee's right to make application for an income payments order if the salary exceeds a sum sufficient to meet the reasonable needs of the bankrupt and his family (see IA 1986, s 310). Under the revised regime, an income payment order can last for up to three years, irrespective of the revised provision that the bankrupt is normally discharged after one year. Income payments can be made by agreement between the bankrupt and the trustee in bankruptcy without the need to go to court (IA 1986, s 310A).

If the debtor owns his own home, his interest in that home passes to the trustee in bankruptcy. However, there may be other legal or equitable interests in the house, and therefore frequently the trustee is not free to realise the value of this major asset immediately. The house may be held in joint names with the spouse of the bankrupt or, even where the house is in the sole name of the debtor, the spouse may have an equitable interest arising from an implied, resulting, or constructive trust (for example where that spouse contributed to the purchase price). The spouse may also have a right of occupation under the Family Law Act 1996 and, where minor children (under 18) live with the bankrupt in his home, that may give the debtor himself a right of occupation. In these situations, the debtor cannot be evicted from his home, so the trustee cannot sell it without a court order. When deciding whether to make such an order, the court will consider the interests of creditors, the financial resources of the bankrupt, the needs of the children (if any) and all relevant circumstances.

After one year, the needs of the creditors outweigh all other considerations, save where exceptional circumstances exist (see IA 1986, s 336(5)). Exceptional circumstances justifying the refusal of an order for sale have been construed narrowly by the courts – see *Re Citro (Domenico) (A Bankrupt)* [1991] Ch 142. Another example of this narrow construction is *Re Raval (A Bankrupt)* [1998] 2 FLR 718, where the bankrupt's wife was a paranoid schizophrenic. A psychiatrist had reported that her condition might be exacerbated by forced rehousing. The court allowed postponement of a possession order for one year only, not for the five years requested. The case of *In re Holliday (A Bankrupt); ex p Trustee of the Property of the Bankrupt v Holliday* [1981] Ch 405 was distinguished, as it now seems to be in recent cases after the harsher judgment in *Re Citro*.

If no spouse or minor children live in the house with the bankrupt (ie where the bankrupt lives alone, with a cohabitee or with adult children), the trustee can sell immediately. When the house is sold, the trustee in bankruptcy can only claim whatever the bankrupt would have been able to claim had he been the seller, ie the trustee can only claim the amount of the debtor's interest in the property.

Section 283A of the IA 1986 provides that the bankrupt's interest in the matrimonial home reverts back to the bankrupt unless, within a three-year period following the bankruptcy, the trustee:

(a)   realises the interest;

(b)   applies for an order of sale or possession in respect of the house;

(c)   applies for a charging order over the house; or

(d)   enters into an agreement with the bankrupt regarding the bankrupt's interest in the house.

Section 313A of the IA 1986 provides that orders for possession or charging of the bankrupt's house cannot be made if the value of the bankrupt's interest in the property is below a value prescribed in regulations, currently £1,000.

The idea behind these changes is that, under the old regime, the bankrupt's matrimonial home vested permanently in his trustee in bankruptcy. The situation could therefore arise that the home had risen in value many years after discharge of the bankruptcy. The bankrupt would have had to apply to the Official Receiver for consent to sell the house, for example, to move location. The Official Receiver could appoint an insolvency practitioner at that stage to sell the house from under the bankrupt and his family. This was felt to be unjust, not least as the insolvency practitioner would be getting fees for the work. The new provisions were agreed late in the Bill's passage through Parliament. They have been referred to as the 'use-it-or-lose-it' right (as regards the trustee's ability to sell the matrimonial home).

20.3.5   Distribution of assets

The task facing the trustee in bankruptcy is to convert the debtor's property into money, and to use that money to pay the bankrupt's debts.

Secured creditors may not be dependent upon the trustee for repayment of the debt due to them. A secured creditor can realise the asset over which he has a charge as security for the debt. If the sale does not produce funds equivalent to the full amount of the debt, the creditor will have to claim the balance as an unsecured creditor. If the proceeds of sale are greater than the sum due to the secured creditor, he must pay over the excess to the trustee in bankruptcy for distribution among other creditors.

The trustee must pay the bankrupt's debts in the order set out below.

20.3.5.1   The cost of the bankruptcy

The first item to be paid is the expense incurred as a result of the bankruptcy, including the professional charges of the trustee in bankruptcy himself.

20.3.5.2   Preferential debts

Schedule 6 to the IA 1986 creates a long list of debts which are designated as 'preferential debts'.

They include:

(a)   accrued holiday pay owed to employees; and

(b)   wages of employees due in the last four months before the bankruptcy order (subject to a current maximum amount of £800 per employee).

If there is insufficient money available to pay all preferential debts, they rank and abate equally. This means that each creditor will receive only a percentage of the amount due to him, that percentage being the same for each creditor.

Under the revised regime, the Crown's preferential status has gone. Preferential status will remain for some other categories, the common one here being payment of employees for the relevant period. It should be noted that there is no equivalent in bankruptcy law of the ring-fencing provisions in regard to corporate insolvency. The very simple reason for this is that it is in general impossible for an individual to grant a floating charge. There is therefore no problem of the money freed up by the absence of Crown preference being grabbed by a floating charge holder.

20.3.5.3   Ordinary unsecured creditors

Ordinary unsecured creditors can only be paid after both of the above categories of debt have been paid in full. If funds are insufficient to pay all debts in this category, they rank and abate equally.

20.3.5.4   Postponed creditors

Certain debts can only be paid once all the ordinary creditors' debts have been paid in full. The main example of a 'postponed debt' is a loan between spouses.

20.3.6   Discharge

When the bankruptcy order is discharged, the bankruptcy comes to an end. The effect of this is that the bankrupt is released from most of his previous debts (IA 1986, s 281) but not necessarily freed from most of the disqualifications which affect a bankrupt (see **20.4**).

A bankruptcy order is discharged automatically one year after the date of the bankruptcy order. At this point, the realisation and distribution of the assets of the bankrupt may not be complete. Any property which has vested in the trustee in bankruptcy remains so, and is not returned to the debtor, and the debtor is still required to assist the trustee with his task. Any property acquired by the debtor after the discharge of the bankruptcy order does not vest in the trustee in bankruptcy but belongs to the ex-bankrupt.

As stated in the previous paragraph, bankrupts are automatically discharged one year after the bankruptcy order was made (IA 1986, s 279, as amended). The period may be reduced if the Official Receiver files a notice at court stating that further investigation of the bankrupt's affairs is unnecessary or has been concluded. This is likely to happen in many cases. However, discharge can be suspended if the bankrupt breaches any of the conditions attached to the discharge.

A brief summary of bankruptcy procedure is given at **20.7.2**.

20.4 Effect of bankruptcy on the bankrupt

When a bankruptcy order is made, the individual who is the subject of that order is subjected to a number of restrictions and disabilities.

20.4.1 Restrictions on business activities

A bankrupt is allowed to retain the tools of his trade and a vehicle, but it is a criminal offence for a bankrupt to obtain credit of more than a prescribed amount (currently £500 in total) without disclosing his bankruptcy. Practically, this may make it extremely difficult for him to carry on his business. It is also a criminal offence for the bankrupt to trade under any name other than that in which he was declared to be bankrupt by the court, unless he discloses to all persons with whom he enters into any business transaction the name in which he was declared bankrupt (IA 1986, s 360). The provision also applies to anyone subject to a bankruptcy restriction order (see **20.4.3**).

If the bankrupt has previously been running a business in partnership with others, his bankruptcy will automatically cause the dissolution of that partnership (Partnership Act 1890, s 33), unless the partnership agreement provides otherwise. The bankrupt's share in the partnership will have to be realised. It is common to find a provision in the partnership agreement by which the bankrupt immediately and automatically ceases to be a partner and the other partners have an option to buy him out, rather than completely dissolving the firm.

If a director of a company is declared to be bankrupt, the articles usually provide that he immediately ceases to hold office as a director (model articles for private companies, art 18), as a bankrupt is prohibited from acting as a director or being involved directly or indirectly in the management of a company (CDDA 1986, s 11).

20.4.2 Personal disabilities

It used to be the case that various jobs and positions were barred to someone who was an undischarged bankrupt. However, the amendments brought in by the EA 2002 have reduced the range of these positions. The principal one that remains is that of insolvency practitioner. A justice of the peace is no longer automatically disqualified if he becomes bankrupt. Other positions are excluded under the IA 1986 only if the debtor is still subject to a bankruptcy restriction order (BRO) (see **20.4.3**). Various professional bodies also impose restrictions on their members if they have become bankrupt.

A solicitor will have his practising certificate suspended. A chartered accountant will have his membership of the Institute of Chartered Accountants in England and Wales terminated.

A bankrupt can operate a bank account. The conditions will depend on the bank concerned but often the restrictions will be that the bankrupt can only have a cashpoint card, and not a cheque book, debit or credit card. In short, he can only draw out money which he has in his account and cannot run up further debts.

20.4.3 Bankruptcy restriction orders and bankruptcy restriction undertakings (IA 1986, s 281A and Sch 4A)

Bankruptcy restriction orders (BROs) are intended to protect the public from dishonest or otherwise culpable bankrupts after they have been discharged (ie after one year). Such orders will be made by the court and will last two to 15 years. An individual voluntary arrangement (IVA) coming into effect to succeed a bankruptcy will not affect any BRO which has been granted, so the bankrupt will still be bound by the terms of the BRO. The bankrupt may offer to give the trustee in bankruptcy a bankruptcy restriction undertaking (BRU) as an alternative to going to court to contest the terms of a BRO. It is estimated that 7% to 12% of bankrupts are culpable, and BROs or BRUs are expected to apply in these cases.

Individuals subject to a BRO or BRU are not allowed to do various things (IA 1986, Sch 4A):

(a) act as receiver or manager of a company's property on behalf of a debenture holder (IA 1986, s 31);

(b) obtain credit above the prescribed limit without disclosing they are subject to a BRO (IA 1986, s 360);

(c) trade in a name other than that under which that person was made bankrupt (IA 1986, s 360);

(d) act as an insolvency practitioner (IA 1986, s 390); or

(e) act as a company director (CDDA 1986, s 11(1)).

Members of Parliament of both houses are disbarred if they have a BRO against them, but not if they are merely bankrupt (IA 1986 s 426A). This is also the situation with members of a local authority. There were some 360 prohibitions and restrictions which could have applied to an undischarged bankrupt under the old regime. The criterion now used under the revised regime is not that of being bankrupt, but of only restricting persons who are subject to a BRO. (A BRU will have similar effect.)

20.5 Increasing the bankrupt's estate

The trustee has a duty to creditors to increase the fund available to pay them, if possible, and to do nothing which would diminish whatever money is available. The following provisions are designed to enable him to do so.

The revised regime provides that the trustee in bankruptcy must have the approval of the creditors or the court before seeking to recover assets under the provisions dealing with antecedent transactions (IA 1986, s 314 and Sch 5, para 2A). These are transactions at an undervalue (IA 1986, s 339), preferences (s 340) and transactions defrauding creditors (s 423).

20.5.1 The collective nature of bankruptcy

Prior to bankruptcy, creditors are in a 'first come first served' position with respect to claims against the debtor. That is to say that creditors who press hardest for their money are likely to be paid first. The presentation of a bankruptcy petition changes this state of affairs and replaces it with a collective regime for the benefit of all creditors. Therefore, even though creditors may have commenced legal action against the debtor prior to his bankruptcy, they cannot necessarily pursue this once the bankruptcy order has been made. A judgment creditor can retain the money realised from enforcement of the judgment only if the process is completed (which means the goods have been seized and sold) before the date of the bankruptcy order (IA 1986, s 346). If a landlord distrains on the goods of the bankrupt for rent due, he can only keep the proceeds equivalent to six months' arrears and must prove in the bankruptcy as an ordinary unsecured creditor if he is owed more (IA 1986, s 347).

A further example of the collective nature of bankruptcy is shown by the fact that any disposition by the bankrupt of any of his property between the date of the presentation of the petition and the appointment of the trustee is void unless the court gives its consent or subsequently ratifies that disposition (IA 1986, s 284).

20.5.2   Onerous property (IA 1986, s 315)

The trustee can disclaim onerous property (IA 1986, s 315), such as land burdened with onerous covenants, or unprofitable contracts. A disclaimer ends all the bankrupt's rights and liabilities in respect of the property in question and discharges the trustee from any personal responsibility for that property. Any person who suffers loss as a result of a disclaimer by the trustee in bankruptcy may prove in the bankruptcy for their loss. Such people are, however, unsecured creditors. To prevent third parties from having to wait a long time to find out whether a trustee intends to disclaim, any person who has an interest in property previously owned by the bankrupt is entitled to serve written notice on the trustee in bankruptcy requiring him to disclaim the property within 28 days, failing which he loses the power to do so (IA 1986, s 316).

20.5.3   Transactions at an undervalue (IA 1986, s 339)

A transaction is at an undervalue where the bankrupt has made a gift, or has received consideration significantly lower in value than that which he provided. If the bankrupt was party to any such transaction in the five-year period prior to the petition, the trustee can apply to the court to have the transaction set aside, provided he can show that the debtor was insolvent at the time of the transaction at an undervalue or became insolvent as a result of it (IA 1986, s 341). If the transaction at an undervalue took place within two years before the bankruptcy, insolvency of the debtor at the time or as a result of the transaction is not a requirement.

Where the transaction at an undervalue is in favour of an 'associate' (broadly, a close relative), the debtor's insolvency at the time is presumed unless the associate can rebut this presumption (IA 1986, ss 341 and 435).

Any transaction at an undervalue, for whatever purpose, is potentially caught by this provision, including, for example, a property adjustment order on divorce, nullity or judicial separation. Motive is therefore irrelevant. In *Hill and Bangham v Haines* [2007] EWCA Civ 1284, the Court of Appeal held that a transfer of property to his ex-wife by the debtor as part of divorce proceedings was not a transaction at an undervalue. The ex-wife could have applied under the relevant matrimonial legislation for a court order for transfer of the property. Forgoing a legal right counted as consideration.

20.5.4   Preferences (IA 1986, s 340)

An arrangement is a preference if it places a creditor or surety in a better position than he would have been in otherwise and the debtor intended (at least partly) to do this (IA 1986, s 340). For example, if the debtor has borrowed money from a friend and, facing imminent bankruptcy, repays that friend in order to ensure that the friend does not lose money, that would be a preference. The trustee must prove that the debtor was insolvent at the time or became insolvent as a result of the preference being granted. The trustee in bankruptcy can make an application to set aside any 'preference' made within the six months prior to the petition, or within two years prior to the petition if the preference is in respect of an associate (IA 1986, s 341).

Where the preference is in favour of an associate, there is a presumption that the debtor intended to prefer that person, unless the contrary can be proved.

20.5.5 Transactions defrauding creditors (IA 1986, s 423)

Where a transaction has been made at an undervalue for the purpose of making the debtor's property unavailable to pay creditors, any 'victim' of the transaction or the trustee or supervisor of a voluntary arrangement can make application to have the transaction set aside. This provision has no time limit, so even a transaction which took place many years ago could be set aside on this basis. However, the greater the time that has elapsed between the transaction and the bankruptcy, the weaker is the evidence that the aim of the transaction was to avoid the asset in question being used to pay creditors (IA 1986, s 423).

Motive is essential here. The trustee must show that the purpose of the transaction was to put assets beyond the reach of creditors. The provision is therefore rarely used by trustees unless the time limit for an application under s 339 has expired (see **20.5.3**).

20.6 Avoiding bankruptcy: individual voluntary arrangements

If a debtor is in financial difficulties, he may attempt to make a voluntary arrangement in order to avoid a bankruptcy order. To do this, he requires professional assistance, so he must find an insolvency practitioner who is willing to assist him in drawing up proposals and to supervise their implementation if they receive the approval of creditors. The insolvency practitioner is known as the debtor's 'nominee'.

If a debtor petitions for his own bankruptcy, under s 273(1) of the IA 1986, the court must consider a voluntary arrangement where:

(a)   the aggregate unsecured debts are no more than £40,000;

(b)   assets are above the minimum amount of at least £4,000;

(c)   the debtor must have not made an arrangement with his creditors within the last five years; and

(d)   it is appropriate to investigate the possibility of an individual voluntary arrangement under s 274 of the IA 1986.

Once he has found someone willing to be his nominee, the debtor must prepare a statement of affairs for that nominee, and should immediately apply to the bankruptcy court for an interim order (IA 1986, s 252). This has the effect of stopping any other proceedings being taken against him while his creditors consider his proposals. While the interim order is in force (usually for 14 days but it can be extended), no bankruptcy petition can be presented or proceeded with unless the leave of the court is obtained. No other proceedings, execution or other legal process can be commenced or continued against the debtor or his property. It creates a moratorium.

The nominee will prepare a report for the court advising whether there are any realistic proposals to be made and therefore whether it is worth calling a meeting of creditors. If a meeting of creditors is called and the meeting approves the proposals (by more than a 75% majority in value), every ordinary, unsecured creditor who had notice of the meeting and was entitled to attend and vote is bound by the decision of the meeting, whether or not he actually did so. Preferential and secured creditors are bound by the voluntary arrangement only if they agree to it (IA 1986, s 260).

If the creditors approve the proposed voluntary arrangement, the nominee (now called a 'supervisor') will implement the proposals. If the debtor fails to comply with the arrangement, or if it transpires that the creditors were persuaded to accept his proposal by means of false or misleading information, the supervisor or any creditor who is party to the voluntary arrangement can petition for the debtor's bankruptcy. This is particularly relevant where it is discovered that the debtor has made transactions at an undervalue (see **20.5.3**) or preferences (see **20.5.4**) immediately prior to the voluntary arrangement, as only a trustee in bankruptcy has the power to apply to the court to set aside these transactions and recover the money which can be used to pay creditors. A supervisor has no power to do this.

The revised regime makes two changes to individual voluntary arrangements. First, it enables Official Receivers to act as nominees and supervisors where the individual voluntary arrangement follows on from a bankruptcy (IA 1986, s 389B). Secondly, it introduces a fast-track procedure for such post-bankruptcy individual voluntary arrangements (IA 1986, ss 263A–263G). Under this procedure, the proposal is agreed with the Official Receiver and filed with the court. No meeting of creditors is held. The Official Receiver will then send out the proposal to creditors on a 'take-it-or-leave-it' basis. The creditors will apply by letter, either agreeing or disagreeing. If the proposal is agreed, the Official Receiver will notify the court, which can then annul the bankruptcy order. The majority required for approval is as before – more than 75% by value of the creditors (Insolvency Rules 1986, r 5.23).

20.6.1 Advantages for the debtor in a voluntary arrangement

If a debtor manages to reach a voluntary arrangement with his creditors, he avoids the stigma of bankruptcy, the accompanying bad publicity, and the trauma of, possibly, a public examination in open court. He also avoids the various disabilities and disqualifications which follow from being declared bankrupt (see **20.2**). A voluntary arrangement is suitable only if the debtor has the means to make a reasonable offer of payment to his creditors. The insolvency practitioner will be able to advise on the likely acceptability of the proposals.

20.6.2 Advantages for the creditor

If the debtor is insolvent (as he frequently will be) then creditors, particularly ordinary unsecured creditors, will have to accept that they are unlikely to be paid the amount due to them in full. They may feel that if they accept a voluntary arrangement proposed by the debtor they will recover a higher percentage of the debt due to them (because the costs involved in a voluntary arrangement may be lower than in a full bankruptcy) or that they will be paid sooner (because the full bankruptcy process can be extremely lengthy). Creditors will also need to judge for themselves whether the debtor can be relied upon to honour the arrangement. They can always instigate bankruptcy proceedings should the debtor prove to have deceived them in the information he has provided or to be untrustworthy.

20.7 Debt relief orders

Debt relief orders (DROs) became available on 6 April 2009 (Tribunals, Courts and Enforcement Act 2007, s 108 and Sch 17). They give respite from creditors for a debtor whose liabilities and assets are small. The DRO is made by the Official Receiver following an on-line application by the debtor and his approved intermediary.

The key criteria are that the debtor must *not*:

(a)   have total unsecured liabilities exceeding £15,000;

(b)   have total gross assets exceeding £300;

(c)   have disposable income exceeding £50 per month, after deduction of normal household expenses;

(d)   have been the subject of a DRO in the preceding six years; and

(e)   be subject to another formal insolvency procedure.

The effects are that the debtor will be:

(a)   protected from enforcement action by his creditors;

(b)   free of the debts at the end of the DRO period (usually 12 months);

(c)   obliged to co-operate with the Official Receiver and provide information; and

(d)   expected to make arrangements to pay his creditors if his financial situation improves.

The debtor is under various restrictions while the order is in place, eg not obtaining credit of £500 or more.

20.8 Summaries and checklists

20.8.1 The bankrupt's home

(a) If house is in joint names of bankrupt and co-owner:

    (i) if co-owner had legal and beneficial interest, trustee needs court order for sale (unless the other co-owner voluntarily agrees to sell).

(b) If house is in sole name of bankrupt:

    (i) an occupier may have beneficial interest (eg by contribution to purchase price);

    (ii) a spouse may have right of occupation under the Family Law Act 1996;

    (iii) if so, trustee needs court order for sale.

(c) If infant children live with the bankrupt in the house:

    (i) gives bankrupt a right of occupation against the trustee;

    (ii) trustee needs court order for sale.

(d) Trustee needs no court order for sale where house in sole name of bankrupt and either:

    (i) he lives alone; or

    (ii) he lives with a cohabitee and/or adult children who have no equitable interest in the property.

(e) Trustee has three years from the end of the bankruptcy to sell the ex-bankrupt's house, otherwise it is returned to the ex-bankrupt.

(f) If the house is of low value, the trustee cannot sell or charge the property.

20.8.2 Summary of bankruptcy procedure

(a) Petition – creditor's or debtor's.

(b) Court hearing – bankruptcy order made.

(c) Official Receiver appointed.

(d) Statement of affairs submitted to Official Receiver within 21 days (unless already done with debtor's petition).

(e) Creditors' meeting held – at discretion of Official Receiver or if sufficient creditors demand it.

(f) Trustee appointed by creditors or Official Receiver continues to act.

(g) Bankrupt's property vests in trustee.

(h) Trustee distributes assets.

(i) Bankrupt discharged (automatically one year after bankruptcy order made).

Part IV Summary – Insolvency

Topic	Summary
Terminology and regulation	The term 'insolvency' is used when referring to companies; 'bankruptcy' applies to individuals. The principal regulations relating to these areas are found in the Insolvency Act 1986.
Insolvency regimes	There are a number of insolvency regimes which can be used to deal with companies in financial difficulties: company voluntary arrangements; administration; liquidation; and receivership.
Company voluntary arrangements	CVAs allow a company's directors to make a proposal to creditors. The proposal will be some alternative means of dealing with the company's financial difficulties as opposed to liquidation or administration. Where a small company is involved, there is also a 28-day moratorium on actions by creditors. An insolvency practitioner, the *nominee*, reports to court on the proposal's viability. If viable, the nominee calls meetings of creditors to seek approval of the proposal. Creditors representing more than 75% in value of the company's debts must approve the proposal. If approved, all creditors, save secured and preferential creditors, are bound by the CVA.
Administration	This is aimed at saving companies in financial difficulties or at least securing a better return to creditors. Administration may be commenced by a company in difficulties, its directors or a qualifying floating chargeholder. Other creditors may also seek an administration order by petitioning the court.
Process	The procedure is based on the appointment of an administrator, whose role is to achieve the aims referred to. The administrator is given statutory powers to deal with the company's property and, effectively, run the company during the period of administration. As with CVAs, creditors' meetings may be held.
Moratorium	The advantage of an administration is that it creates a moratorium on creditor actions, providing the administrator with a 'breathing space' to carry out his duties.
Liquidation	Liquidation is also known as 'winding up'. The most common insolvency procedure, it results in the distribution of assets to creditors and the eventual dissolution of the company. There are different types of liquidation, depending on the company's financial position and who commences proceedings.
Members' voluntary	This is available only where a company is solvent. The directors make a statutory declaration of solvency. The members pass a special resolution to wind up the company and an ordinary resolution to appoint a liquidator. The liquidator gathers in and realises the company's assets, then distributes them to the company's creditors who, given the company's solvency, should be paid their debts in full.

Topic	Summary
Creditors' voluntary	Where a company is insolvent, its directors may decide to call a members' meeting to pass two resolutions: an extraordinary resolution to wind up the company and an ordinary resolution to appoint a liquidator. This liquidator then calls a creditors' meeting at which they may vote, in proportion to the value of their debt, to appoint a different liquidator. The liquidator then, as in a members' voluntary liquidation, gathers in and realises the company's assets, before distributing them to creditors.
Compulsory liquidation	Liquidation can also be commenced by a creditor. This is brought about by court order rather than company resolutions. A creditor may petition for liquidation on the grounds that the company is unable to pay its debts. If the petition is successful, the Official Receiver is appointed. He may call a meeting of creditors, who may then decide to appoint an insolvency practitioner in his place to be liquidator. Again, this liquidator is charged with realising assets and distributing them to creditors.
Statutory order of payment	Liquidators are required to pay out assets in a particular order. First, the expenses of the winding up; secondly, preferential debts; thirdly, monies secured by floating charges; and then unsecured creditors. Following these, interest on preferential and unsecured debts is paid before, finally, any remaining surplus is paid to shareholders. An element of a company's assets is 'ring-fenced' for unsecured creditors.
Receivership	Where a creditor has a fixed charge over a company's assets, then it will be entitled to appoint a receiver to realise these assets if the company becomes insolvent. Prior to September 2003, floating chargeholders could appoint an administrative receiver, who had wide powers. The ability to do so is now reserved to specialised situations, with administration being the main procedure available to floating chargeholders.
Past transactions	Liquidators and administrators are able to take action to overturn certain antecedent transactions in order to claw back assets. These include: • transactions at an undervalue • preferences • extortionate credit transactions • certain floating charges • transactions defrauding creditors. The basic premise behind these rights is that creditors should not be prejudiced where a company, prior to insolvency, has caused assets to be diverted from the creditors who would be entitled to them on insolvency.

Topic	Summary
Bankruptcy	Bankruptcy is commenced by a petition to the court by a creditor or the debtor himself. An order will be made if it is proved a debtor is unable to pay his debts. Where an order is made, all the bankrupt's property – save for tools of the trade, clothing and furniture – will vest in a trustee in bankruptcy. The trustee's job is to convert the property into money and use that money to pay the bankrupt's debts. Similar provisions to those applicable to corporate insolvency allow the trustee in bankruptcy to seek to recover assets where particular antecedent transactions have taken place.
Discharge	A bankruptcy order is discharged automatically one year after the date of order.
Individual voluntary arrangements	An IVA is an alternative to a bankruptcy order. A debtor works with an insolvency practitioner to draw up proposals to be made to creditors. A statement of affairs is prepared and an interim order sought from the court. This prevents proceedings being brought against the debtor – usually for 14 days – whilst creditors consider his proposals. If more than 75% in value of creditors approve the proposals at a meeting, then every ordinary, unsecured creditor with notice of the meeting will be bound. The nominee then becomes the supervisor of the IVA and carries out the proposals.
Debt relief orders	A debt relief order is available for debtors with small debts and little in the way of assets.

Part V

TAXATION

Any business that is run with a view to making a profit should be structured in the light of the tax issues relevant to that business. These issues affect the operation of the business itself, and also the personal financial affairs of those involved in running the business. In the case of a sole trader, this link is obvious, but also applies to the partners in a partnership, the shareholders (and other investors) in a company, and the employees of a business (in whatever form it operates).

The rationale behind, and the operation of, income tax, capital gains tax, inheritance tax and VAT are discussed in *Legal Foundations*, and the impact of those taxes, along with that of corporation tax, is considered further in Part V.

Part V begins (**Chapter 21**) with a description of the method of calculating the trading profits of a business (whether unincorporated or a company) and goes on to analyse how profits are taxed in the context of a company (**Chapters 22** and **23**) a sole trader (**Chapter 24**) and a partnership (**Chapter 25**). **Chapter 26** considers the taxation of employees and company directors, and Part V concludes with a description of the taxation of savings and investment income (interest and dividends) in **Chapter 27**, and an analysis of the capital tax issues relevant to individuals when they dispose of their business interests (**Chapter 28**). It does not deal with provisions relating to trustees or personal representatives.

A summary of the key themes contained in Part V, and of the main rates and allowances for 2009/10, is reproduced at the end of Part V for ease of reference.

The text of Part V is drafted on the assumption that all individuals and companies concerned in a business are UK-resident for tax purposes, and is only intended as a brief introduction to some of the major taxation provisions.

Note: At the time of writing (May 2009), the Finance Bill 2009 has yet to complete its passage through Parliament. The text of Part V assumes that the Finance Bill will be enacted without major amendment.

Chapter 21
Calculation of Trading Profits of a Business

21.1 Introduction

21.1.1 The nature of trading profits

A business may make two kinds of profit: income and capital. In so far as profits are recurring by nature (eg trading, rent, interest), they are likely to form income profits. This chapter concentrates on the calculation of trading profits (which are likely to form the largest source of income profits for most businesses). The way in which trading and other income profits are taxed depends on the format of the business being carried on.

21.1.1.1 Sole trade

A sole trader's income profits form part of his 'total income' for the purposes of income tax (see Step 1 of the income tax calculation described in *Legal Foundations*).

21.1.1.2 Company

A company's income profits (along with its capital profits) are charged to corporation tax (see Step 1 of the corporation tax calculation described in **Chapter 22**).

21.1.1.3 Partnership

The income profits made by a partnership are divided amongst the partners and charged either to income tax (in the case of individual partners) or to corporation tax (in the case of corporate partners).

21.1.1.4 Relevant legislation

The way in which each business format is taxed is considered in more detail in **Chapters 22** and **23** (in relation to companies), **Chapter 24** (in relation to sole traders) and **Chapter 25** (in relation to partners).

The way in which trading profits are calculated is broadly the same for both income tax (relevant to sole traders and individual partners) and corporation tax (relevant to companies). Tax legislation is, however, in the process of being rewritten as part of the Tax Law Rewrite Project (aimed at simplifying the legislation) and, as a result of this, the rules for income tax and corporation tax are contained in different statutes. To calculate trading profits for the purposes of income tax, reference should be made to the Income Tax (Trading and Other Income) Act 2005 (ITTOIA 2005). The ITTOIA 2005 contains provisions on 'Trading Income' in Part 2; this covers various items but the key one is 'profits of a trade'. The corporation tax code is currently contained partly in the Income and Corporation Tax Act 1988 (ICTA 1988) and partly in the Corporation Tax Act 2009 (CTA 2009) where Part 3 also contains rules for 'profits of a trade'. For simplicity, the rules (which are largely the same across the legislation) are referred to below in the context of 'trading profits'.

21.1.2   The accounting period of a business

A business must prepare accounts for an accounting period (usually of 12 months) to show the profit (or loss) made by its trade. Although the profit and loss account for the accounting period will be used as a starting point for ascertaining the figure which is taxable, some adjustment will usually be required as some of the expenses likely to be shown in the profit and loss account (such as entertainment of customers) are not generally allowed as deductions for tax purposes and the calculation must be revised to satisfy the tax rules prior to submission to Her Majesty's Revenue and Customs (HMRC). It is Government policy to encourage the alignment (so far as possible) of the rules for taxable and commercial profits with International Accounting Standards (IAS) and International Financial Reporting Standards (IFRS).

21.1.3   Method of calculation of trading profits

For tax purposes, the trading profits of a business for an accounting period are calculated in the following way:

>   chargeable receipts (see **21.2**)
>   LESS
>   any deductible expenditure (see **21.3**)
>   LESS
>   any capital allowances (see **21.4**)
>   EQUALS
>   trading profit (or trading loss).

21.2   Chargeable receipts

To be chargeable, receipts of the business must derive from its trade and be income rather than capital in nature (ITTOIA 2005, Part 2; CTA 2009, Part 3, Ch 6).

21.2.1   Trade

Despite the frequency with which 'trade' appears in all the major tax statutes, it does not have a full statutory definition (beyond, for example, the rather unhelpful reference in the Income Tax Act 2007, s 989, which confirms that '"trade" includes any venture in the nature of trade'). Many cases have had to address the issue, but each turns on its own facts and so none provides a conclusive test. As a general guideline, however, Lord Reid's comments in the case of *Ransom (Inspector of Taxes) v Higgs* [1974] 1 WLR 1594 may be helpful:

> As an ordinary word in the English language 'trade' has or has had a variety of meanings or shades of meaning. Leaving aside obsolete or rare usage it is sometimes used to denote any mercantile operation but it is commonly used to denote operations of a commercial character by which the trader provides to customers for reward some kind of goods or services.

Receipts of the trade are those which derive from the trading activity rather than from circumstances not directly connected with the trade. Most receipts of the trade, such as money received from sales of goods and services, are easily identified, but some are less so. For example, a sum received on cancellation of a trading contract as compensation would be a receipt of the trade, but a gratuitous sum received on termination of a trading relationship as a token of personal appreciation would not.

21.2.2   Income

There are no clear-cut rules to determine when a receipt is income in nature rather than capital (despite the large amount of case law on the subject). As a general rule, however, if something is purchased for the purpose of resale at a profit (such as stock), the money received from the resale will be of an income nature. In contrast, receipts of a capital nature will generally derive from the sale of an asset which was purchased for the benefit or use of the business on a more or less permanent basis rather than for resale. For example, a trader who purchases some trading premises and who eventually (perhaps many years later) sells them receives a sum of a capital nature.

Some receipts will arise from types of transactions which are different from the sale of goods or services, so that the above principles have to be applied by analogy. For example, a sum received as compensation for cancellation of a contract for the sale of goods is of an income nature because it represents what would have been an income profit if the goods had been sold.

21.3 Deductible expenditure

In calculating taxable trading profits there must be deducted from chargeable receipts of the trade any expenditure which is of an income nature, which has been incurred 'wholly and exclusively' for the trade and deduction of which is not prohibited by statute (ITTOIA 2005, s 34; CTA 2009, Part 3, Ch 4).

21.3.1 Expenditure of an 'income nature'

(a)   If expenditure on an item is incurred for the purpose of enabling the trader to sell that item at a profit, it is of an income nature. Therefore the expense to a trader of buying his stock is of an income nature and deductible from chargeable receipts in calculating trading profits. Conversely the expense to the trader of buying his premises (buying a permanent asset for his business) is of a capital nature and not deductible (but see **21.4**).

(b)   A further relevant (and sometimes more appropriate) test is whether the expenditure has the quality of recurrence, rather than being once and for all expenditure. All expenditure on general overheads like electricity, telephone charges, staff salaries and rent has this quality of recurrence in the sense that the type of expenditure is likely to be incurred repeatedly. Also, interest paid on borrowing (eg on an overdraft) for business purposes will generally qualify as being expenditure of an income nature. Expenditure on the purchase of long-term assets of the business (like premises and furniture) will not recur in the foreseeable future in that the asset has been acquired for the on-going benefit of the trade, and so is not of an income nature.

21.3.2 'Wholly and exclusively for the purposes of the trade'

To be deductible, the expenditure must also have been incurred wholly and exclusively for the purposes of the trade (ITTOIA 2005, s 34; CTA 2009, s 54). Expenditure which has a dual purpose cannot be wholly and exclusively for one purpose. For example, when a taxpayer pays for a meal in a restaurant when working away from home, the greater cost of the meal compared with eating at home was not incurred wholly and exclusively for business purposes; the cost of the meal had a dual purpose which included satisfying a person's basic need to eat (*Caillebotte v Quinn* [1975] 1 WLR 731). Similarly, when a barrister purchases clothing suitable for wearing in court, the greater cost of that clothing compared with casual clothing was not incurred wholly and exclusively for business purposes; the cost of the clothing had a dual purpose, including satisfying a person's basic need to be clothed (*Mallalieu v Drummond* [1983] 2 AC 861). In fact, despite this principle which has been clearly established in case law, HMRC allows some expenses to be apportioned so that part is deductible; for example, where a taxpayer works from home, part of the cost of heating and lighting the home will be deductible for tax purposes (and a right to apportion an identifiable proportion of an expense where that proportion is incurred wholly and exclusively for the purposes of the trade is now included in ITTOIA 2005, s 34(2)).

21.3.3 Common examples of deductible expenditure

Although any given item of expenditure must be checked to confirm that it is of an income nature and incurred wholly and exclusively for the purposes of the trade, the following common examples of expenditure by a business will usually be classed as deductible:

(a)   salaries;

(b)   rent on premises;

(c)   utility charges (eg gas, electricity, and telephone bills);

(d)   stock;

(e)   business rates;

(f)   stationery/postage.

21.4 Capital allowances

As described in **21.3** above, expenditure on capital items cannot, in principle, be deducted from chargeable receipts when calculating trading profits for an accounting period because it is not of an income nature. This can cause severe cash flow problems for a business that needs to invest in expensive capital items to help produce the goods or services in which it deals. To help alleviate this problem, legislation exists to allow a specified amount of the cost of certain capital items or activities to be deducted each year in calculating trading profits. The principal category covered by the legislation is plant and machinery (although allowances may also be available for other specified expenditure, such as research and development). Under the Capital Allowances Act 2001 (CAA 2001), where expenditure is incurred on certain assets or activities, a percentage of the capital expenditure will be allowed as a deduction in calculating trading profits in a given accounting period. These deductions are known as capital allowances.

21.4.1 Plant and machinery

For most businesses, the most common form of capital allowance claimed will be those for plant and machinery.

21.4.1.1 Definitions

'Plant and machinery' is not defined in CAA 2001. In *Yarmouth v France* (1887) 19 QBD 647, it was said that plant includes whatever apparatus is used by the businessman for carrying on his business; this includes all goods and chattels which he keeps for permanent use in his business but not, for example, stock in trade. Examples of plant and machinery are office equipment, computers, tools and manufacturing equipment.

21.4.1.2 The allowance (CAA 2001, ss 52–59)

At present, for most qualifying assets, the taxpayer is allowed, in each 12-month accounting period of ownership of the asset, to deduct a 'writing down allowance' of up to 20% of the reducing balance of the cost of the asset in calculating his trading profits. (Note: there are special rules for calculating the capital allowances given for expenditure on certain types of assets (see **21.4.1.6**).) The reduced balance of the cost at the end of each accounting period is also known as the 'written-down value' of the asset. It is possible to claim part only of the maximum permissible allowance, but all of the examples that follow assume the taxpayer will take full advantage of the allowances available each year.

> **Example**
>
> A builder, owning no other machinery or plant, purchases a JCB (digger) for £15,000. Starting in the accounting period of purchase, and assuming no further purchases (and ignoring the annual investment allowance and first year allowance, for which see **21.4.1.5**), his capital allowances are as follows:

Year 1 – 20% of £15,000 = £3,000	writing down allowance, leaving £12,000 as the written-down value of the asset
Year 2 – 20% of £12,000 = £2,400	writing down allowance, leaving £9,600 as the written-down value of the asset
Year 3 – 20% of £9,600 = £1,920	writing down allowance, leaving £7,680 as the written-down value of the asset

etc.

Suppose that his chargeable receipts of the trade less other deductible expenses are £50,000, £60,000 and £70,000 for Years 1, 2 and 3 respectively. This means (following deduction of the writing down allowance) that his trading profit from this source is as follows:

Year 1: £47,000 (£50,000 less £3,000 writing down allowance)

Year 2: £57,600 (£60,000 less £2,400 writing down allowance)

Year 3: £68,080 (£70,000 less £1,920 writing down allowance).

21.4.1.3 Sale of assets

If, in due course, the item of plant and machinery is sold, it will be necessary to compare the written-down value of the asset at the time of sale with the actual sale price in order to assess whether the sale produces a 'profit' or a 'loss' when comparing these figures. If a 'profit' results, this may (subject to pooling – see **21.4.1.4**) be the subject of a 'balancing charge' and form a chargeable receipt in the accounting period in which the sale takes place; if a 'loss' results, there may be a 'balancing allowance' (ie a deduction from chargeable receipts in that period). The purpose of a balancing charge or a balancing allowance is to ensure that the taxpayer has had tax relief for precisely the amount by which the asset diminished in value.

Suppose that the builder in the Example, at the beginning of Year 4, sells his JCB for £8,000. If so, he has made a 'profit' of £320 compared with its written-down value (£7,680) and the £320 will form part of his chargeable receipts in Year 4.

21.4.1.4 Pooling

In practice, traders will often own more than one item of plant and machinery. To avoid a calculation being required every time an item is sold, all expenditure on plant and machinery is, in general, 'pooled' together and the writing down allowance is given each year on the balance of expenditure within the whole pool. This is expressed in s 55 of the CAA 2001 as being an allowance on the amount by which the 'available qualifying expenditure' ('AQE') exceeds the 'total of any disposal receipts' ('TDR'). If an asset is sold, the sale proceeds are deducted from the value of the pool; generally, therefore, no balancing allowance or charge should occur until the trade is discontinued and the whole pool sold.

Example

Bob, a sole trader, has an existing pool of machinery and plant with a written-down value of £80,000. He sells some machinery for £20,000:

	£
Written-down value of pool at the start of the accounting period (AQE)	80,000
Less: disposal value (TDR)	20,000
	60,000
Less: writing down allowance (on £60,000) for the year of 20%	12,000
Value of pool carried forward to the next accounting period	48,000

If Bob sells the business in the following accounting period and the value agreed for the assets in the pool is, say, £50,000 a balancing charge of £2,000 will be included as a chargeable receipt when calculating Bob's trading profit for the final accounting period of the business under his ownership.

If the written-down value of the pool being used for an accounting period is ever £1,000 or less, the trader has the option of claiming a writing down allowance big enough to eliminate the pool (and so avoid having to submit accounts showing very small writing down allowances for years to come).

21.4.1.5 Annual investment allowance and first year allowance (CAA 2001, ss 51A–51N)

Since 1997, additional capital allowances have been given in the first year of ownership of an asset in certain circumstances. The rules vary from year to year but, at present, every ongoing business now receives an annual investment allowance ('AIA') of a maximum of £50,000 so that the first £50,000 of 'fresh' qualifying expenditure on plant and machinery incurred in an accounting period will be wholly deductible (in effect a 100% allowance). Any additional spending during the accounting period will be eligible for a first year allowance ('FYA') of 40%.

(A group of companies will receive only one AIA for the group in each accounting period but can allocate it within the group as it sees fit.)

Example 1

Riz, a sole trader, owns a manufacturing business. In her current accounting period, she buys some machinery for £37,000. The written-down value of her existing pool of plant and machinery is £80,000. In the current accounting period, she is entitled to the following capital allowances:

		£	£
AIA – entire £37,000 spent on new machinery:			37,000
Writing down allowance:			
Written-down value of pool	80,000 x 20% =	16,000
Total capital allowances for the accounting period			53,000

(The written-down value of the pool for the next accounting period will be £64,000 (£80,000 less £16,000).)

Example 2

Tom, a sole trader, owns a manufacturing business. In his current accounting period, he buys some machinery for £120,000. The written-down value of his existing pool of plant and machinery is £80,000. In the current accounting period, he is entitled to the following capital allowances:

		£	£
AIA – first £50,000 spent on new machinery:			50,000
Writing down allowance:			
FYA on remaining value of new machinery	70,000 x 40%		28,000
Written-down value of pool	80,000 x 20% =		16,000
Total capital allowances for the accounting period			94,000

(The written-down value of the pool for the next accounting period will be £106,000 (£64,000 written-down value of the existing pool plus £42,000 written-down value of the new machinery).)

21.4.1.6 Special rules for particular types of assets

(a) Energy saving assets (CAA 2001, ss 45A–52)

A business may claim an enhanced first year allowance of 100% on assets certified as being energy saving by HM Treasury. This is in addition to the AIA.

(b) Cars (CAA 2001, ss 74–82)

Complex rules apply to expenditure on cars. The detail of these rules is beyond the scope of this book, but under new rules in the Finance Bill 2009 the rate of writing-down allowance will depend on the car's carbon dioxide emissions.

(c) Long-life assets and integral features (CAA 2001, s 33A and ss 90–104E)

Long-life assets are defined as those with an expected working life, when new, of at least 25 years. Again, these rules are complex, but their general effect is to give a less generous writing down allowance (of 10%) for long-life assets.

'Integral features' was a new concept introduced by the Finance Act 2008, and covers plant and machinery that is integral to a building (such as escalators, electrical and lighting equipment, and air conditioning systems). Like long-life assets, such integral features only qualify for a 10% writing down allowance (and are also pooled with them in a separate 'special rate pool').

Both long-life assets and integral features are eligible for the AIA but not the FYA of 40%.

Example

Samuel, a sole trader, owns a high street fashion store. In his current accounting period, he replaces an escalator to the first floor at a cost of £70,000. He has no existing pool of integral features.

In the current accounting period, he is entitled to the following capital allowances:

	£	£
AIA – first £50,000 spent on escalator		50,000
Writing down allowance:		
Remaining value of escalator	20,000 x 10% =	2,000
Total capital allowances for the accounting period		52,000

(The written-down value of the special rate pool for the next accounting period will be £18,000 (£70,000 less £52,000).)

21.4.2 Industrial buildings

The allowance given for expenditure on industrial buildings relates to the *cost of construction* of a building and so is less likely to be of use to most businesses than the machinery and plant allowances. The Finance Act 2008 contained provisions to phase out capital allowances for industrial buildings by 2011, and they are not considered further in this book.

21.4.3 The interrelation of capital allowances and capital gains legislation

Some capital assets (eg plant and machinery) may qualify both for capital allowances and be chargeable assets for the purposes of capital gains legislation. If so, special rules apply to determine exactly how any rise or fall in the value of the asset on its disposal will be taxed. The rules are designed to ensure that where capital allowances have been claimed an adjustment is made so that only the 'true' gain or loss on the disposal of the asset is used in the capital gains calculation.

Example

Some plant and machinery is acquired in Year 1 for £20,000. Two years later, it has a written-down value of £12,800.

(a) If it is then sold for £12,800, there will be no balancing capital allowance or charge, and no gain or loss created for capital gains purposes.

(b) If, instead, it is sold for £12,000, there will be a balancing capital allowance of £800, but no gain or loss created for capital gains purposes.

(c) If, instead, it is sold for £15,000, there will be a balancing charge of £2,200 for capital allowances purposes, but no gain or loss created for capital gains purposes.

(d) Finally, if it is sold for £22,000, there will be a balancing charge of £7,200 for capital allowances purposes (to reflect the difference between the written-down value of £12,800 and the acquisition value of £20,000) plus a capital gain of £2,000 to reflect the rise in value above and beyond the original acquisition value.

Scenario (c) and, particularly, scenario (d) are unlikely to occur frequently in practice because machinery and plant tends to decrease in value and so is unlikely to be sold for more than its written-down value.

21.5 Illustration of trading profit calculation

Dave, a sole trader, runs a business that makes and sells ceramic tiles. In the business's most recent accounting period, the sales from tiles totalled £450,000. Expenditure was £300,000, broken down as follows:

Wages	£80,000
Materials	£140,000
Rent	£40,000
General overheads (telephone, electricity, advertising etc)	£40,000

The business has a pool of general plant and machinery (kilns, etc) with a written-down value at the start of the accounting period of £100,000.

Calculation of trading profits:	£
Chargeable receipts (sales)	450,000
Less	
Deductible expenditure	300,000
Less	
Capital allowances – writing down allowance £100,000 at 20%	20,000
Trading profit	130,000

The written-down value of the pool of plant and machinery carried forward to the next accounting period will be £80,000 (£100,000 less the £20,000 allowance claimed this year).

21.6 Trading losses

The calculation of chargeable receipts, less deductible expenditure, less available capital allowances may produce a negative figure – ie a trading loss rather than a trading profit. In such a situation there will be no trading income from the accounting period of the loss to be taxed. In certain circumstances, relief is given for the trading loss for tax purposes – see **Chapters 22** and **24** for further details.

Chapter 22

Taxation of Companies I – Corporation Tax

22.1 Introduction

Companies pay corporation tax rather than income tax or capital gains tax. This difference between companies on the one hand and individuals (whether sole traders or partners) on the other is not as fundamental as it might appear because, in calculating the company's profits chargeable to corporation tax, income profits are broadly calculated on the principles applicable to income tax and capital gains are broadly calculated on the principles applicable to capital gains tax.

A company is liable to pay corporation tax on its income profits and capital gains and the method of calculation is dealt with in detail at **22.2–22.6**. In short, it involves the following steps:

Step 1: Calculate income profits (see **22.2** and **22.3**)

Step 2: Add chargeable gains (see **22.4**)

Step 3: Deduct any charges on income and capital (see **22.6**)

Step 4: Calculate the tax (see **22.7**)

22.2 Step 1: income profits

A company's income profits chargeable to corporation tax will be calculated under the rules of the appropriate part of the CTA 2009, most notably:

Part 3 – Trading Income

Part 4 – Property Income

Parts 5 and 6 – Loan Relationships

This chapter concentrates on trading income.

22.2.1 Trading income

It will be necessary to calculate the trading profits (or loss) for an accounting period using the rules considered in **Chapter 21**, ie:

chargeable receipts
LESS
any deductible expenditure
LESS
any capital allowances
EQUALS
Trading profit (or trading loss).

22.2.1.1 Chargeable receipts

Examples of chargeable receipts for a company will usually be very similar to those of other businesses, ie money received for the sale of goods and services (for further details see **21.2**).

22.2.1.2 Deductible expenditure

The rules described at **21.3** apply to a company. Particular examples of deductible expenditure in the context of a company are:

(a)   Directors'/employees' salaries or fees and benefits in kind. Occasionally there may be a problem over deductibility if a director is paid a salary that is excessive as remuneration for his services. If the salary is paid for personal reasons and not wholly and exclusively for the purposes of the trade, then it will not be deductible. It has been held (in *Copeman v William J Flood and Sons Ltd* [1941] 1 KB 202) that a substantial salary paid to a director who performed minimal duties should be apportioned into two parts; that part which was reasonable for the duties performed would be deductible in calculating the company's taxable profits and the other excessive part would not. It is unlikely that this problem would arise over a salary paid to a director who works full-time for the company where the salary would be fully deductible for corporation tax purposes.

(b)   Contributions to an approved pension scheme for directors/employees. These are fully deductible.

(c)   Payment to a director/employee on termination of employment. Where a payment is made to a director/employee by way of compensation for loss of office or employment, this will qualify as a deductible expense under the normal rules. Where a payment is made in return for a director's/employee's undertaking not to compete with the company's business following termination of his office or employment, such a payment is deductible under specific provisions (Income Tax (Earnings and Pensions) Act 2003 (ITEPA), s 225, and see **26.3**).

(d)   Interest payments on borrowings. These will generally be deductible under the loan relationships rules (see **27.2.2**).

22.2.1.3 Capital allowances

In calculating its trading profit, a company may also deduct capital allowances claimed on expenditure on machinery and plant and on other qualifying assets. These are available by way of writing down allowances in the way described in **21.4.1**, and the annual investment allowance, first year allowance and balancing charges or allowances also work similarly.

22.2.2 Trading losses brought forward

The company may be able to reduce its trading profit by claiming relief for a loss previously suffered in the trade and 'carried forward' under s 393(1) of the ICTA 1988 (see **22.3**).

22.2.3   Other income

Any income from other sources must be added (eg property income or interest received from investments). (For the corporation tax treatment of goodwill and other intellectual property, see **22.5**.)

22.3   Relief for a trading loss

The calculation of trading income described at **22.2.1** may produce a trading loss for which relief may be available. There are various provisions in the ICTA 1988 that allow a company in effect to deduct a trading loss from other profits in order to provide relief from corporation tax on those profits. Where the circumstances are such that relief could be claimed under more than one of the provisions described below, the company may choose which to claim. It may be that the company's trading loss for an accounting period is greater than can be relieved under just one of these provisions; if so, the company can claim as much relief as is available under one provision and then claim relief for the balance of its loss under any other available provision (although it cannot claim relief for the same loss twice over). Generally a company will want to claim relief under whichever provision is best for cash flow; two of the provisions described below may lead to a refund of tax previously paid, whilst the third acts to reduce the amount of corporation tax that will become payable in future.

22.3.1   Carry-across/carry-back relief for trading losses (ICTA 1988, s 393A)

A company's trading loss for an accounting period can be carried across to be set against profits (income and capital and of whatever description) for the same accounting period. If these are insufficient to absorb (or fully absorb) the loss, the loss (or remaining loss) can then be carried back to be set against profits (income and capital and of whatever description) from the accounting period(s) falling in the 12 months prior to the accounting period of the loss (provided that the company was then carrying on the same trade); in this way, the company may recover corporation tax previously paid.

The Finance Bill 2009 contains provisions intended to assist businesses during the recession by a temporary extension of the carry-back period for some losses. For trading losses incurred during accounting periods ending 24 November 2008 to 23 November 2009 inclusive or 24 November 2009 to 23 November 2010 inclusive, the relief under s 393A is extended. If there is any unused trading loss having applied the relief in the normal way, the excess loss (up to a maximum of £50,000) can be carried back to accounting periods falling in the two previous years (taking later periods first).

> **Example**
>
> A Co Ltd, a company with an accounting period that ends on 30 June each year, makes a trading loss in the accounting period ending 30 June 2010. The company can set the loss against any other profits it makes in the same accounting period (eg investment income and capital gains on the disposal of some premises). If any loss remains unused, it can be carried back and set against all profits in the accounting period ending 30 June 2009. If any loss still remains unused, a maximum £50,000 of that loss can be carried back and set against all profits in the accounting period ending 30 June 2008, and finally the accounting period ending 30 June 2007.

22.3.2   Terminal carry-back relief for trading losses (ICTA, s 393A)

As an extension to the normal carry-back rules, when a company ceases to carry on a trade, a trading loss sustained in the final 12 months of the trade can be carried back and set against the company's profits (income and capital and of whatever description) from any accounting period(s) falling in the three years previous to the start of that final 12 months, taking later periods first. There is no £50,000 cap on the amount of loss that can be carried back under these provisions.

> **Example**
>
> B Co Ltd, a company with an accounting period that ends on 31 December, makes a trading loss in 2009 and ceases trading on 31 December 2009. It could set the 2009 loss against any profits made in 2009, then (if necessary) 2008, 2007, and finally 2006.

Note:

(a)   Where a company's accounting periods do not match exactly with the carry-back period, profits will be apportioned so that profits attributable to any part of an accounting period falling within the carry-back period will be eligible for reduction by available losses.

(b)   A claim under s 393A must usually be made within two years of the end of the accounting period in which the loss was incurred.

22.3.3   Carry-forward relief for trading losses (ICTA 1988, s 393(1))

A company's trading loss for an accounting period can be carried forward indefinitely to be set against subsequent profits which the trade produces. Section 393(1) does not allow relief against non-trading income or against capital gains. Although losses can be carried forward indefinitely, a claim that relief will be used at some stage must be made within four years of the end of the accounting period in which the loss was incurred.

> **Example**
>
> C Co Ltd, a company with an accounting period that ends on 31 March each year, makes a trading loss in the accounting period that ends 31 March 2009, but returns to profit in the following accounting period. The company can deduct the loss from the trading profit made in the accounting period ending 31 March 2010. Any remaining loss can be carried forward to be used against trading profit made in the accounting period ending 31 March 2011, and so on until the loss is fully relieved.

22.3.4   Summary

Section of ICTA 1988	When will the loss have occurred?	Against what will the loss be set?	Which accounting periods are relevant?
s 393A (carry-across/carry-back relief)	Any accounting period of trading	The company's profits (income and capital)	The accounting period of the loss and, thereafter, the accounting period(s) falling in the previous 12 months.*
s 393A (terminal carry-back relief)	The final 12 months of trading	The company's profits (income and capital)	The accounting period(s) of the loss and, thereafter, the accounting period(s) falling in the three years previous to the final 12 months of trading (taking later periods first)
s 393(1) (carry-forward relief)	Any accounting period of trading	Subsequent profits of the same trade	Subsequent accounting periods until the loss is absorbed

* For trading losses incurred in accounting periods ending 24 November 2008 to 23 November 2009 or 24 November 2009 to 23 November 2010 inclusive, up to £50,000 of the loss can be carried back for a further 2 years.

22.4   Step 2: chargeable gains

A company's gains chargeable to corporation tax will be calculated using the same broad principles as for capital gains tax, but with important modifications. The stages to calculate the gain within Step 2 are as follows:

Stage 1: Identify a chargeable disposal (see **22.4.1**).

Stage 2: Calculate the gain (or loss) (see **22.4.2**).

Stage 3: Apply reliefs (see **22.4.3**).

Stage 4: Aggregate remaining gains/losses.

Any gain remaining after the application of reliefs forms part of the company's total profits for the purposes of corporation tax (Taxation of Chargeable Gains Act 1992 (TCGA 1992), s 8).

22.4.1   Stage 1: identify a chargeable disposal

22.4.1.1   General principles

A chargeable disposal by a company can arise on a disposal of chargeable assets by way of either sale or gift. Chargeable assets for corporation tax purposes are defined broadly as for capital gains tax and the most common examples in the context of a disposal by a company are likely to include land and buildings and shares held in other companies (although if the disposal proceeds form part of the company's income stream (eg regular sales of land as part of a property developer's trade) they will normally form part of the company's income profits rather than its chargeable gains – see TCGA 1992, s 37).

22.4.1.2   Plant and machinery

The position for plant and machinery is complicated by the fact that capital allowances may be available in relation to the expenditure incurred on it. If this is the case, the plant and machinery will not benefit from the usual capital gains exemption for 'wasting assets' (assets with a predicted working life of 50 years or less). In practice, however, plant and machinery is unlikely to increase in value and so a chargeable capital gain will not arise (and any decrease in value will have been deducted from trading profits (income) under the capital allowances regime so no allowable capital loss will arise either). For further details on the interaction of the capital allowances and capital gains legislation, see **21.4.3**.

22.4.2   Stage 2: calculate the gain (or loss)

22.4.2.1   Method of calculation

The procedure to follow in order the calculate the gain (or loss) on a chargeable disposal involves the following calculation.

Proceeds of disposal (or market value in the case of a gift or sale at an undervalue)

LESS

Costs of disposal

= Net proceeds of disposal

LESS

Other allowable expenditure (initial and subsequent expenditure)

= Gain (before indexation) or Loss

LESS

Indexation allowance

= Gain (after indexation)

If a company sells an asset at an undervalue, a decision must be made as to what figure to use for the proceeds of disposal. If the sale is merely a bad bargain, the actual sale price will be used, but if there is a gift element then the market value of the asset will be used. If the company sells to a 'connected person', the sale will be deemed to take place at market value. A company is connected with a person if that person controls the company (either alone or with others connected to him). A company is connected to another company if they are both controlled by the same person, or by a combination of that person and others connected with him (TCGA 1992, s 286(5); and see also **28.3.3**).

If the disposal of the asset leads to a loss (ignoring indexation, for which see below), that capital loss can be deducted from the other chargeable gains made by the company in its accounting period, but not from its income profits. Any unused loss can be carried forward to be deducted from the first available chargeable gains made by the company in subsequent accounting period(s) (until the loss is absorbed).

22.4.2.2 The indexation allowance

The indexation allowance is used when calculating the gain on an asset which has been owned for any period between 31 March 1982 and the date of disposal. The purpose of the indexation allowance is to remove inflationary gains from the capital gains calculation so that a smaller gain is charged to tax. Inflation is measured by reference to the Retail Prices Index ('RPI'). The indexation allowance is calculated by applying to the initial and subsequent expenditure the percentage increase in the RPI from the date the expenditure was incurred (or 31 March 1982 if later) to the date of disposal. Tables published by HMRC express this information as an indexation factor for ease of calculation. Once the allowance has been calculated, it is deducted from the 'gain (before indexation)' to give the 'gain (after indexation)'.

There are several other features of indexation to note:

(a)   The allowance is applied to initial and subsequent expenditure but not to the costs of disposal. If different items of expenditure are incurred at different times, different indexation factors will have to be used for each item of expenditure.

(b)   Where a company disposes of an asset which it owned on 31 March 1982, special rules are applied. The aim of these rules is to exclude from the tax calculation the part of the gain that accrued before 31 March 1982, so that no tax is paid on that part of the gain. The indexation allowance for such assets will be based on the market value of the assets on 31 March 1982, rather than actual expenditure.

(c)   The indexation allowance can be used to reduce the gain to zero, but cannot be used to create or increase a loss.

(d)   If the RPI shows an overall fall between the date of the expenditure and the date of disposal, no indexation allowance is available on that expenditure.

Example

Smallco Ltd acquired some premises in June 2004 for £100,000 and sold them in January 2010 for £250,000. The incidental costs of disposal (legal and land agent fees) were £5,000 and the incidental costs of acquisition (legal and surveyor's fees) were £3,000. In August 2006, the company extended the premises at a cost of £30,000. Assume the indexation factor for the period between June 2004 and January 2010 is 0.2 and that for the period between August 2006 and January 2010 it is 0.12.

	£	£
Proceeds of disposal		250,000
Less incidental costs of disposal		5,000
= Net proceeds of disposal		245,000
Less initial expenditure:		
Acquisition cost	100,000	
Incidental costs of acquisition	3,000	103,000
Less subsequent expenditure		30,000
= Gain (before indexation)		112,000
Less indexation allowance:		
On initial expenditure	(103,000 x 0.2)	20,600
On subsequent expenditure	(30,000 x 0.12)	3,600
= Gain (after indexation)		87,800

22.4.3 Stage 3: apply reliefs

The range of reliefs available to companies is smaller than that available to individuals. Examples of some of the reliefs available to a company are described below (other reliefs of less general application are considered in other titles in this series).

22.4.3.1 Roll-over relief on the replacement of qualifying business assets (TCGA 1992, ss 152–159)

This relief is designed to encourage companies to expand and thrive by allowing the corporation tax due on the disposal of a 'qualifying asset' to be effectively postponed when the consideration obtained for the disposal is applied in acquiring another qualifying asset by way of replacement.

(a) Conditions for the relief to apply

(i) Qualifying assets

The principal qualifying assets for the purposes of the relief are land and buildings, although more exotic assets, such as ships, satellites and spacecraft, also qualify. The company must use the asset in its trade (as opposed to holding it as an investment).

(Note:

(a)   company shares are *not* qualifying assets;

(b)   goodwill and other intellectual property is subject to a separate roll-over relief (see **22.5**);

(c)   although *fixed* plant and machinery is a qualifying asset, a sale of such an asset will rarely produce a gain (as most depreciate in value) and any roll-over relief when acquiring such assets will be restricted if they are wasting assets (TCGA 1992, s 154). What constitutes 'fixed' plant and machinery is, in itself, not straightforward. There is no statutory definition, so each case turns on its own facts, but claims are unlikely to succeed if the item in question is moveable and intended to be so to enable changes in the layout of the workplace.)

Provided both the asset disposed of and the asset acquired fall within the definition of qualifying assets, they do not need to be the same type of asset. For example, it is possible to sell a qualifying ship, and roll-over the gain into the purchase of qualifying buildings.

(ii) Time limits

For the relief to apply, the disposal and acquisition must take place within certain time limits. The replacement asset must be acquired within one year before or three years after the disposal of the original asset, unless an extended period is allowed by HMRC.

Example

If a company disposes of a qualifying asset at the start of January 2010, a replacement qualifying asset would need to be acquired at some point in the period stretching from the start of January 2009 to the end of December 2012.

(b) Application of the relief

If a qualifying asset is disposed of and, within the time limits, the consideration from the disposal is applied in acquiring another qualifying asset to be used in the company's trade, then any liability to corporation tax arising from the disposal can be postponed (at least until the disposal of the replacement asset) by rolling-over the gain (after allowing for any indexation) on the disposal of the original asset into the acquisition cost of the replacement asset. This means that the gain (after allowing for any indexation) is notionally deducted from the acquisition cost of the replacement asset to give a lower acquisition cost for use in subsequent corporation tax calculations. Thus a later disposal of the replacement asset may produce a gain that comprises both the rolled-over gain and any gain on the replacement asset itself (TCGA 1992, s 153 contains restrictions on the relief if part only of the value of the consideration on the disposal of the original asset is used to acquire the new asset).

Example

In September 2009 Mediumco Ltd sells some premises that it has owned since 1996 for £70,000. It makes a gain (after indexation) of £30,000. Six months later, the company buys some more premises for £80,000. If the company claims roll-over relief on the replacement of qualifying assets:

(a)   the company will not pay any corporation tax in respect of the gain realised on the disposal of the original premises (as it has been effectively postponed by being rolled-over);

(b)   for the purposes of future corporation tax calculations the replacement premises will be treated as being acquired for £50,000 (£80,000 less £30,000).

Imagine that the company then sells the new premises in 2012 for £125,000. The calculation of its gain will be:

	£	
Proceeds of disposal	125,000	
Less		
Adjusted acquisition cost	<u>50,000</u>	(without the effect of roll-over it would be 80,000)
Gain before indexation	75,000	(without the effect of roll-over it would be only 45,000)

Provided the qualifying conditions were met, the gain from the 2012 sale (after indexation) could itself be rolled-over.

(Note: The roll-over relief contained in TCGA 1992, ss 152–159 is also available to individuals in a slightly different form – see **28.4.1**.)

22.4.3.2   Corporate Venturing Scheme (FA 2000, s 63, Schs 15 and 16)

The Corporate Venturing Scheme is designed to encourage investment by companies in the shares of other small 'enterprise' companies. As an incentive to invest in such (potentially risky) trading companies, the investing company is offered certain tax reliefs. (The rationale behind the Scheme is similar to that behind the Enterprise Investment Scheme open to individual investors – see **28.4.3**.)

The details of the Scheme are complex but, in outline, three types of relief are available:

(a)   investment relief – a deduction from the investing company's corporation tax bill of up to 20% of the amount invested in shares in the issuing company;

(b)   deferral relief – if the shares acquired in the issuing company realise a capital gain when they are disposed of, that gain can be deferred if the investing company reinvests in more qualifying shares;

(c)   loss relief – if the shares acquired in the issuing company realise a capital loss when they are disposed of, that loss can be set against the investing company's other capital gains (in the normal way) or (as an exception to the normal rules) against its income profits.

Both the investing company and the issuing company must comply with numerous conditions for the Scheme to apply; amongst the more important are that the issuing company must be unquoted (shares on AIM are unquoted for these purposes), and the investing company must not own more than 30% of the issuing company's ordinary share capital.

22.4.3.3   Exemption for disposals of substantial shareholdings (TCGA 1992, Sch 7AC)

A company's gains on the disposal (on or after 1 April 2002) of shares it owns in another company are completely exempt from corporation tax if the conditions of the relief are met. In outline, these are:

(a)   both the company disposing of the shares and the company in which the shares are owned must be trading companies;

(b)   the disposing company must have owned at least 10% of the ordinary shares in the other company for a continuous period of at least 12 months in the two-year period leading up to the disposal.

The structure of the relief allows the disposing company to dispose of its shareholding in the other company in more than one 'batch', provided the time limits are met.

Example

Y Ltd has owned 10% of the ordinary shares in Z Ltd for five years. In January 2010, Y Ltd sells half its shareholding in Z Ltd. The gain on this disposal is exempt. In June 2010, Y Ltd sells the remainder of its shares in Z Ltd. This disposal is also exempt because, although Y Ltd did not own 10% of Z Ltd at the time of the June 2010 disposal, it had owned 10% of the shares for at least 12 months in the two-year period leading up to the June 2010 disposal (ie it had owned 10% of the shares from June 2008 to January 2010).

Additional rules apply to disposals involving groups of companies. Although the exemption will benefit companies that make a gain on the disposal of a substantial shareholding, it will be a disadvantage when a loss is made as that loss will not be deductible for capital gains purposes.

22.5   Corporation tax on goodwill and intellectual property (CTA 2009, Part 8)

The Finance Act 2002 introduced a new corporation tax treatment of goodwill and intellectual property (such as patents, trade marks, registered design, copyright and design rights) acquired by companies on or after 1 April 2002. These rules are now incorporated in the CTA 2009. Although such 'intangible fixed assets' are essentially capital in nature, they will generally be taxed as part of a company's income profit/loss calculation. The main features of the new approach are as follows.

22.5.1   The general rule

Receipts from transactions in intangible fixed assets will generally be treated as income receipts and expenditure on intangible fixed assets will generally be deductible in calculating a company's income profits (although not when the expenditure is part of the incorporation of a business – see **31.3**).

22.5.2 Disposals of intangible fixed assets

Any profit on the disposal of intangible fixed assets may be rolled-over into the acquisition of replacement intangible fixed assets (provided the qualifying conditions are met) thus deferring any corporation tax charge arising from the disposal. Otherwise profits and losses on disposal will generally be accounted for in the income profit/loss calculation.

The treatment of intellectual property and goodwill for tax purposes will, in general, reflect the UK Generally Accepted Accounting Practice (GAAP) and so reference will need to be made to a company's accounts to establish the exact effect of that treatment on a company's profit or loss for the accounting period in question.

22.6 Step 3: deduction of charges on income and capital (ICTA 1988, ss 338–339)

A company's income profits and capital gains for an accounting period will be added together to produce the company's total profit for that period. From these total profits may be deducted charges on income and capital (eg qualifying donations to charity).

22.7 Step 4: calculating the tax

22.7.1 Basis of assessment

The series of steps described so far will establish the company's taxable profit for the accounting period and the corporation tax will be calculated on that figure by applying the appropriate rate. Where the company's accounting period is a period different from the corporation tax financial year (1 April to 31 March (see **22.7.2**)) and the rates of tax have changed from one financial year to the next, it will be necessary to apply the different rates to the appropriate portions of the accounting period. If, for example, a company has an accounting period of 1 January to 31 December, one-quarter of the company's profit for 2009 (representing the first three months) will be taxed at the appropriate rate for Financial Year 2008 (ending 31 March 2009) and the remaining three-quarters of the profit will be taxed at the appropriate rate for Financial Year 2009. (This is a different method of assessment from that used for the trading profits of individuals where income tax is assessed by reference to income tax years on the profits of the accounting period which ends in the tax year.)

22.7.2 Rates of corporation tax (ICTA 1988, s 13 and CTA 2009, Part 2)

Corporation tax rates are fixed by reference to financial years, being the period from 1 April in one year to 31 March in the following year (this is different from the income tax year which runs from 6 April to 5 April in the following year). Financial years are described by reference to the period in which they commence, so the corporation tax year running from 1 April 2009 to 31 March 2010 is 'Financial Year 2009' (this is also different from the description of the income tax year which is described by reference to the years in which it begins and ends). The rates for Financial Year 2009 are as follows.

(a)   For companies whose profits do not exceed £300,000, there is a 'small companies' rate of 21% which is applied to all the company's taxable profits.

(b)   If a company's profits exceed £300,000 but do not reach £1,500,000, the first £300,000 is charged at 21% and the excess over £300,000 is charged at a marginal rate of, effectively, 29.75%.

(c)   The 'main' rate of corporation tax is 28%; this only operates where a company's profits reach £1,500,000, and the rate is applied to all of the company's taxable profits rather than just the excess over £1,500,000.

The reason for the marginal rate is to 'smooth' the transition from one tax band to the next. As a company's profits approach the main rate threshold of £1,500,000, the marginal rate has the effect of bringing the total tax bill up towards the same figure as if the main rate had been charged on the entire profit.

> **Example**
>
> Company A has profits of £1,400,000. Its corporation tax calculation is:
>
> | | |
> |---|---:|
> | First £300,000 @ 21% = | 63,000 |
> | Next £1,100,000 @ 29.75% = | 327,250 |
> | Total | 390,250 |

In establishing the *rate* at which the company's profits are liable for corporation tax, it is not only the company's taxable profit that is relevant. The relevant profit figure is the taxable profit *plus* the company's 'franked investment income' (except where that franked investment income is received within a group of companies falling within ICTA 1988, s 13(7)). Franked investment income consists broadly of dividends *received* by the company plus the 10% tax credit. However, in calculating *how much* tax is payable, franked investment income is not actually charged to corporation tax. The effect of the franked investment income is to reduce the amount of the small company rate band available to a company that also receives dividends from other companies.

> **Example**
>
> Company B has profits of £1,400,000 and franked investment income of £100,000. Company B is not taxed on the £100,000 franked investment income but, because the total of its trade profits plus the franked investment income reaches £1,500,000, it will be taxed at 28% on the whole of its trade profits, ie £1,400,000 @ 28% = £392,000.

22.8 Illustration of corporation tax calculation

The accountant of D Co Ltd produces the following figures relevant to calculation of the company's income profits for its accounting period ending 31 March 2010:

(a)   chargeable receipts are £95,000

(b)   £18,000 is deductible in respect of salaries

(c)   £10,000 is deductible in respect of capital allowances

(d)   income from rents (after deductible expenditure) is £48,000.

In addition, the company has sold some land which was surplus to requirements and has made a chargeable gain of £50,000; it has no plans to buy replacement assets.

The company has paid in total £8,000 in dividends to its shareholders (these are not deductible – see **22.9**).

The calculation of the company's corporation tax liability may be summarised as follows:

Step 1 – Calculate income profits:

	£	£
• Trading Profit:		
Chargeable receipts	95,000	
less		
Deductible expenditure (salaries)	18,000	
less		
Capital allowances	10,000	
Trading profit		67,000
• Property Income:		48,000
Total income profits		115,000

50,000
——————
165,000

Step 2 – Add chargeable gains

Step 3 – Deduct charges on income and capital

–

Step 4 – Calculate the tax (on the total profits of £165,000)

The small companies rate applies to the whole of the £165,000 profit and so the corporation tax due is:

£165,000 at 21% = £34,650

22.9   Dividends

Dividends paid by a company are *not* deductible in calculating the company's taxable profit, but are treated as distributions of profit. Similarly, when a company buys back its own shares from shareholders, the payment is not deductible in calculating the company's taxable profit and that part of the price which is over and above the allotment price may be treated in the same way as a dividend (see **27.3**). Neither of these payments reduces the company's profits chargeable to corporation tax (CTA 2009, s 1305).

22.10   Notification to HMRC and payment

22.10.1   Notification

Section 55 of the Finance Act 2004 requires a company to inform HMRC in writing of the beginning of its first accounting period (such notification to be within three months of the start of that period). Thereafter, a notice requiring delivery of a self-assessment corporation tax return will be issued.

22.10.2   Payment

For most companies, the corporation tax due under self-assessment is payable within nine months and one day from the end of the relevant accounting period (TMA 1970, s 59D). The company must make a payment to HMRC within this time limit in relation to its anticipated corporation tax liability for that period, even though the final assessment may not have been agreed with HMRC by that stage (the deadline for the self-assessment return itself is 12 months after the end of the relevant accounting period).

Large companies may, depending on the company's overall corporation tax liability, have to pay the tax in four instalments (TMA 1970, s 59E). A 'large' company for these purposes is one with annual profits of £1,500,000 or over. The instalment due dates are calculated by HMRC as:

First	6 months and 13 days after the start of the accounting period
Second	3 months from the first instalment due date
Third	3 months from the second instalment due date
Fourth	3 months and 14 days after the end of the accounting period

> **Example**
>
> Large Co plc is required to pay corporation tax by instalments for its accounting period ending 31 December 2009. These instalments will be due on 14 July 2009, 14 October 2009, 14 January 2010 and 14 April 2010.

Under the systems for large and other companies, payments are likely to be made based on an estimate of the company's final liability. Any adjustments necessary are made once the final liability is known.

22.11 Companies and VAT

A company which makes chargeable supplies in excess of £68,000 in any 12-month period will be required to register for VAT. Details of the calculation and administration of VAT are contained in *Legal Foundations*.

22.12 Companies and inheritance tax

A company cannot make a chargeable transfer for inheritance tax purposes because a chargeable transfer is defined as being a transfer made by an individual. In certain circumstances, however, gifts made by companies do have inheritance tax implications (see **23.2.4** for further details of the provisions applying to 'close companies').

Chapter 23

Taxation of Companies II – Special Provisions Relating to Companies

23.1 Introduction

In addition to the general rules governing the taxation of companies, special provisions exist within the tax legislation with the aim of preventing the use of a company as a trading vehicle from being significantly more or less attractive (from a tax perspective) than trading as a sole trader or via a partnership.

The rules discussed in this chapter relate to companies controlled by a small number of persons ('close companies') and to groups of companies.

23.2 'Close companies'

23.2.1 Definitions (ICTA 1988, ss 414, 416 and 417)

(a) A 'close company' is one which is controlled by five or fewer participators or by participators (however many) who are directors (or shadow directors) (ICTA 1988, s 414).

(b) A 'participator' is essentially a person owning, or having the right to acquire, shares in the company.

(c) Broadly, 'control' exists in the hands of those having, or having the right to acquire, more than half of the shares or more than half of the voting power. The test for 'control' does not depend on whether particular shareholders whose combined shareholdings represent a majority actually act together, but rather on whether, if they were to act together, the company would be under their control. In establishing who has control, any rights of a participator's 'associate' (defined so as to apply principally to a close relative or a business partner) are treated as rights of that participator.

(Note: although a subsidiary company is controlled by one participator (ie by its parent company), the subsidiary will not normally fall within the definition of close company unless the parent company is also a close company – ICTA 1988, s 414(5).)

Example 1

AB Company Ltd has nine shareholders. This must be a close company because, whatever the distribution of shareholdings, there must be at most five who, between them, own a majority – even if all nine shareholders have equal shareholdings, five of them must hold a majority compared with the other four.

Example 2

CD Company Ltd has 100 shareholders of whom four own between them 51% of the shares. This is a close company.

Example 3

EF Company Ltd has 18 shareholders, consisting of nine married couples. This is a close company because a married couple can be identified as a participator and an associate and therefore only counts as one person in assessing control. Effectively, therefore, there are nine participators for gauging control and five of them must hold a majority of the shares (as in Example 1).

Example 4

GH Company Ltd has 25 equal shareholders, none of whom are 'associates' of one another. They are all directors. This is a close company under the second part of the s 414 definition because, although control is in the hands of 13 participators (being the bare majority), those participators are all directors.

23.2.2 The charge to tax imposed when a close company makes a loan to a participator

23.2.2.1 The company's position (ICTA 1988, s 419)

Subject to exceptions (see **23.2.2.3**), when a close company makes a loan to a participator or to his associate, the company must pay to HMRC a sum equivalent to one-quarter of the loan. For example, it will cost a close company £100,000 to lend £80,000 to a participator or to his associate, because on top of the loan it must pay an additional £20,000 to HMRC.

The sum paid to HMRC is in the nature of a deposit since it will be refunded to the company if, and when, the recipient of the loan (the participator or his associate) repays the loan to the company or if the loan is written off.

23.2.2.2 The borrower's position (ITTOIA 2005, s 416)

From the borrower's point of view, the loan has the advantage that it is a receipt of money which is not taxable in his hands so long as it remains a loan; however, if the debt is written off by the company, it is charged under the income tax Savings and Investment Income provisions (ITTOIA 2005, Pt 4, Ch 6) as if the borrower received a sum net of 10% tax (see **27.3.1**).

Example

In June 2008 A Ltd, a close company, lends £80,000 to B, a participator (shareholder) in the company. In June 2009 the debt is written off by the company so B does not have to repay it.

(a)   At the time of the loan A Ltd must pay £20,000 (one-quarter of £80,000) to HMRC. There are no tax consequences for B at this stage.

(b)   When the debt is written off, HMRC will repay the £20,000 to A Ltd. B is treated as receiving a net payment of £80,000 with a 10% tax credit. The gross sum of

£88,888 (80,000 × $\frac{100}{90}$)

will form part of B's total income for 2009/10.

23.2.2.3 The exceptions (ICTA 1988, s 420)

The charge to tax described does not apply:

(a)   if the loan is made in the ordinary course of a money-lending business (eg a bank loan to someone who happens to hold shares in the company);

(b)   if the loan (together with any outstanding loan to the same person) does not exceed £15,000 and the borrower works full-time for the company and owns no more than 5% of the company's ordinary shares.

23.2.2.4 The reason for the charge

These provisions play an important role in preventing tax avoidance. Without such provisions, a major tax saving could be achieved by the use of close companies, particularly for a participator who is a higher rate income tax payer. Whereas any withdrawal of the company's profits in the form of salary (as employee/director) or dividend (as shareholder) will attract a charge to income tax in the hands of the recipient, money which is borrowed from the company is not income at all and therefore cannot in principle attract income tax.

A clear disadvantage to the borrower is that a loan must normally be repaid, perhaps with interest, but if the company is closely controlled the company may not enforce the obligation to repay for many years, if at all. Therefore, subject to that possible disadvantage, there would be a clear incentive to use the borrowing device to avoid the payment of income tax.

Section 419 of the ICTA 1988 helps to close that loophole, although the use of loans may still help defer the payment of tax for the individual borrower which may have a cash flow advantage. A higher rate taxpayer may also benefit by postponing the time when the payment is treated as chargeable in his hands to some future date when he may no longer be a higher rate taxpayer (eg following retirement).

When loans are made to directors, consideration should also be given to the provisions of s 197 of the CA 2006.

23.2.3 Income tax relief on a shareholder's borrowings (Income Tax Act 2007, ss 383, 392–395)

Not all provisions relating to close companies are aimed at preventing tax avoidance. An individual shareholder who takes out a loan in order to purchase shares in a close company or to lend money to it may be able to claim income tax relief on the interest he pays on his borrowings.

23.2.3.1 The relief

Where a taxpayer pays interest on a loan taken for an eligible purpose, that interest qualifies for tax relief. The interest payments are deductible from the taxpayer's 'total income' at Step 2 of the income tax calculation.

23.2.3.2 Conditions

(a) To be eligible, a loan must be for the purchase of ordinary shares in a close company which carries on a trade, or for the borrower to lend money to such a company.

(b) It is a further condition that the borrower must either:

    (i) control (by personal ownership or through another person) more than 5% of the company's ordinary share capital/assets; or

    (ii) own ordinary shares in the company (with no 5% threshold) and work for the greater part of his time in the management or conduct of the company.

Any shares acquired as a result of the borrowing are counted in applying either limb of this condition if they are owned at the time the interest (for which relief is claimed) is paid.

Example

Clare borrows £20,000 from Bigbank plc in order to buy 10% of the ordinary shares in E Co Ltd (which is a close company). In the tax year 2009/10, the interest payments that Bigbank plc charges Clare total £1,600. Clare can deduct £1,600 from her total income for 2009/10.

23.2.4 Inheritance tax and close companies (IHTA 1984, s 94)

A company cannot make a chargeable transfer for the purposes of inheritance tax because the definition of a chargeable transfer in s 2 of the IHTA 1984 is limited to a transfer of value made by an individual. In order to prevent a company being used as a vehicle for making transfers which would otherwise escape inheritance tax, special provisions apply to gifts made by close companies. These are complex but, broadly, a gift made by a close company is treated as a set of gifts by the participators in that company. This is achieved by apportioning the gift amongst the participators in accordance with their proportionate shareholdings in the company; each participator is then treated as having made a transfer of value of the appropriate fraction of the company's gift. Unless covered by an exemption and/or relief, this is a lifetime chargeable transfer rather than a potentially exempt transfer so that inheritance tax may become payable immediately. It is the company itself that is primarily liable for any tax arising.

The above provisions do not apply if the company's gift is charged to income tax in the hands of the recipient. The main examples of this would be:

(a)   a dividend that is chargeable to income tax as Savings and Investment Income (ITTOIA 2005, Pt 4);

(b)   a benefit in kind provided for a director or employee that is chargeable to income tax under the ITEPA 2003.

23.3 Groups of companies

23.3.1 Introduction

A group of companies may be a useful way of organising a business in terms of minimising risk, running a number of different trades, and streamlining the management structure of the business.

As regards taxation, each company in a group is treated as a separate entity for corporation tax purposes. The tax legislation contains provisions, however, with the aim of ensuring that trading via a group of companies is broadly 'tax neutral' – ie it does not lead to any major advantages or disadvantages when compared with trading via a single company.

The detail of the tax provisions relating to groups is beyond the scope of this book, but some of the more important rules relating to corporation tax are outlined below.

23.3.2 Group Relief

Group relief describes the process whereby certain losses and expenses incurred by a company can be transferred (or 'surrendered') to another company within the same qualifying group (to enable that company to use the loss/expense to reduce its own taxable profits). This relief is available only if both companies are within the definition of a group for these purposes (there are additional provisions applying to consortia).

23.3.2.1 Definition of a group for group relief (ICTA 1988, ss 402–413)

For two companies to be within the same group, one must be the 75% subsidiary of the other, or both must be 75% subsidiaries of a third company. The test for a 75% subsidiary is complicated by anti-avoidance rules, but at its core is the requirement for the holding company to own (directly or indirectly) 75% or more of the subsidiary's ordinary share capital (widely defined in ICTA 1988, s 832).

Example

W and X are in a group together, as are X and Y, but W and Y are not part of the same group as W owns only an indirect shareholding of 60% in Y (80% x 75% = 60%).

23.3.2.2 The effect of group relief

If two companies are in the same group for group relief, certain items (most notably trading losses, charges on income, and management expenses) can be surrendered from the 'surrendering company' to the 'claimant company'. This is possible only to the extent that the loss/expense was incurred in the surrendering company's accounting period (or part period) that overlaps with the accounting period of the claimant company that generated the profit for which relief is sought.

Example 1

Claimant Co and Surrender Co are in a group together for group relief purposes and both have accounting periods ending 31 March each year. In the year ending 31 March 2010, Surrender Co makes a trading loss of £400,000 and Claimant Co makes taxable profits of £1 million. Surrender Co may surrender its loss to Claimant Co which may use it to reduce its taxable profits to £600,000.

Example 2

The facts are the same as in Example 1, except that Surrender Co made its trading loss of £400,000 in the year ending 31 March 2009. This loss can be carried forward to the year ending 31 March 2010 by Surrender Co (using ICTA 1988, s 393), but cannot then be surrendered to Claimant Co in that year.

Group relief does not provide relief for capital losses, and there are further restrictions on the application of the relief where either the surrendering company has other profits and/or the claimant company has losses of its own.

23.3.3 A company's chargeable disposals (TCGA 1992, ss 170–181)

It may be possible for companies within a group to arrange for the disposal of a chargeable asset to be made by the company that will benefit most for tax purposes.

23.3.3.1 Definition of a group (TCGA 1992, s 170)

The definition of a group for chargeable gains purposes differs from that for group relief. Here a group will contain a company (a 'principal company'), its direct 75% subsidiaries and the direct 75% subsidiaries of those subsidiaries (and so on), provided that all of the subsidiaries are 'effective 51%' subsidiaries of the principal company (to pass the 'effective 51%' subsidiary test, the principal company must be beneficially entitled to more than 50% of the available profits and assets of the subsidiary as laid out in TCGA 1992, s 170(7)). A chargeable gains group may have only one principal company.

Example 1

W (the principal company,) X and Y are in a group together for chargeable gains purposes as W owns at least 75% of X and X owns at least 75% of Y, plus W effectively 'owns' 60% of Y (80% x 75%) satisfying the 'effective 51%' test.

Example 2

$$W \downarrow 80\%$$
$$X \downarrow 75\%$$
$$Y \downarrow 75\%$$
$$Z$$

W, X and Y are in a group as before, but Z does not form part of the group as, although it satisfies the first part of the test (as Y's 75% subsidiary) it is not the effective 51% subsidiary of W as W effectively owns only 45% of Z (80% x 75% x 75%).

23.3.3.2   The available relief (TCGA 1992, ss 171–171A)

Where two companies are within a group for chargeable gains purposes, one can transfer a chargeable asset to the other on a tax neutral 'no gain, no loss' basis (so that the disposal is treated as being for such consideration as to give rise to neither a gain nor a loss by the transferor company). This is likely to be useful in two main situations:

Example 1

Company A and Company B are in a group together. Company A owns a building with an unrealised gain of £300,000 which it wishes to sell to a third party. Company B has made a capital loss of £200,000 on the sale of some land and is not likely to make any chargeable gains in the near future. Company B may not set the capital loss against its trading profits, neither can it surrender the loss to Company A using group relief. What can happen, however, is that Company A transfers its property to Company B on a 'no gain, no loss' basis and then Company B sells it, realising the £300,000 gain against which it can set the £200,000 loss, so reducing the chargeable gain to £100,000.

Example 2

Company C and Company D are in a group together. Company C owns some land with an unrealised loss of £400,000. Company D has just sold some premises, realising a £650,000 gain. If Company C transfers the land to Company D at no gain, no loss and Company D then sells it, Company D will make a £400,000 loss which it can set against its own gain of £650,000, so that its taxable chargeable gains for the year will be only £250,000.

In fact, if both companies elect under TCGA 1992, s 171A, the same effect as described in the above examples can be achieved without any actual transfer within the group prior to the third party sale (thus saving, for example, the cost of conveyancing formalities). A similar form of relief is available for assets within the intangible assets regime (see **22.5**). The Finance Bill 2009 contains measures to amend s 171A to simplify the way in which the relief is claimed.

23.3.3.3   Roll-over relief (TCGA 1992, s 175)

When a company within a group for chargeable gains purposes disposes of a chargeable asset outside the group, it can roll-over its gain (if the usual roll-over relief criteria are satisfied – see **22.4.3.1**) into qualifying assets it acquires or, as an alternative, into qualifying assets acquired by another group company.

Example

J Co sells a qualifying asset for £2 million in June 2009, realising a gain (after indexation) of £800,000. In October 2011, K Co (in the same group as J Co) acquires a qualifying asset for £3 million from a third party. If J Co's gain has not been relieved in some other way then it may be rolled over into K Co's acquisition so as to enable J Co to claim a reduction in its corporation tax liability.

Both group relief and the chargeable gains provisions are subject to numerous anti-avoidance provisions, which are beyond the scope of this book but which are designed, for example, to prevent the manipulation of the rules when companies join or leave a group.

23.3.4   Corporation tax rates (ICTA 1988, s 13)

To prevent each company in a group claiming the full benefit of the small companies (21%) and marginal rate of corporation tax, companies that are 'associated' (being under common control, or where one controls the other) must share the available corporation tax bands between them. This is achieved by dividing the upper limit of each tax band between the number of active companies in the group that are associated.

> **Example**
>
> A Ltd, B Ltd, C Ltd and D Ltd are in a group together and are associated. Each company makes a profit of £100,000. Instead of each company benefiting from the 21% small companies rate on its full £100,000 profit, it will only benefit from one-quarter of the small companies rate band (£300,000 × ¼ = £75,000) and its remaining £25,000 profit will fall within the 29.75% marginal rate band (the upper limit of which will have reduced to £375,000, ie £1,500,000 × ¼).

23.3.5   VAT

A qualifying group of companies may be able to obtain a single registration for VAT purposes.

23.3.6   Stamp duty and stamp duty land tax

Provided certain conditions are met, stamp duty or stamp duty land tax will not be charged on transfers of assets between companies in a qualifying group.

Chapter 24
Taxation of Sole Traders

24.1 Introduction

In the course of running a sole trade, an individual must be aware of the impact of several different taxes.

24.1.1 Income profits and losses – income tax

The trading profits of a sole trader's business (calculated in accordance with the rules for trading income described in **Chapter 21**) form part of the sole trader's total income chargeable to income tax. (Other income related to the business, such as rents and loan interest will also form part of the individual's total income.) If the business makes a trading loss in an accounting period this may, in certain circumstances, be offset against the sole trader's other income and (more rarely) capital gains.

24.1.2 Capital profits and losses – capital gains tax

On the disposal of a chargeable asset used in his trade, a sole trader may realise a capital gain or loss. The treatment of capital gains realised by individuals is considered further in **Chapter 28**.

24.1.3 Gifts – inheritance tax

If a sole trader transfers a business asset (usually by gift) that results in a transfer of value for inheritance tax purposes, an inheritance tax charge may arise. Details of this charge and available reliefs are described in **Chapter 28**.

24.1.4 VAT

A sole trader who makes chargeable supplies in excess of £68,000 in any 12-month period will be required to register for VAT. Details of the calculation and administration of VAT are contained in *Legal Foundations*.

24.1.5 National Insurance contributions

As a self-employed person, a sole trader will pay Class 2 and Class 4 National Insurance contributions. If he employs any staff, he will pay Class 1 contributions in respect of their earnings (see **26.7**).

The remainder of this chapter concentrates on the treatment of the trading profit (or loss) of a sole trader's business.

24.2 Basis of assessment of a trading profit

Trading income is one of the components that comprise a person's total income at Step 1 of the income tax calculation (set out in the Income Tax Act (ITA) 2007, s 23). The detail of the steps is described in *Legal Foundations* but, in outline, they are:

Step 1: calculate 'total income'

Step 2: deduct allowable reliefs (to leave 'net income')

Step 3: deduct any personal allowance

Step 4: calculate tax at the applicable rate(s)

Step 5: add together the amounts of tax from Step 4 (to give the overall income tax liability)

(Steps 6 and 7 concern adjustments to the overall liability in defined circumstances and are beyond the scope of this book: see ITA 2007, ss 26 and 30 for further details.)

As described in **Chapter 21**, taxable (trading) profits are calculated with reference to an accounting period (usually of 12 months). This accounting period may not synchronise with the tax year for income tax (running 6 April to the following 5 April) and so ITTOIA 2005, Pt 2, Ch 15 contains rules to ascertain in which tax year a business's trading profit will be assessed. Accordingly income tax on the profits of a trade is assessed under the rules described in **24.2.1** to **24.2.4**.

24.2.1   The 'normal' rule (relevant to the third and subsequent tax years of a business)

Income tax will be assessed on the profits of the 12-month accounting period which ends in the tax year. For example, if a trader prepares his accounts for calendar years, the trading profits of the accounts prepared up to 31 December 2008 will form part of his total income for assessing income tax for the tax year 2008/09.

24.2.2   The first tax year of a new business

In the first tax year (6 April to the following 5 April) in which the trade is carried on, income tax will be assessed on the profits made during that tax year, ie from the date of commencement to the following 5 April. For example, a trader who commences his trade on 1 January 2009 will have his trading profits from 1 January to 5 April 2009 (inc) assessed as part of his total income for the tax year 2008/09.

24.2.3   The second tax year of a new business

In the second tax year in which the trade is carried on, income tax will generally be assessed on the basis of the 'normal' rule so that the profits to be assessed will be the profits of the 12-month accounting period which ends in the second tax year. If the trader in the example at **24.2.2** prepares his accounts on a calendar year basis, his profits for the period 1 January to 31 December 2009 (including those for 1 January to 5 April already taxed) will be assessed as part of his total income for the tax year 2009/10. (In some instances – eg an opening accounting period of less than 12 months – the rule is that the taxpayer will be assessed on the basis of the profits of the first 12 months' trading, even though this will not coincide with the taxpayer's own accounting period.)

24.2.4   The closing tax year of a business

In the final tax year, income tax will be assessed on the profits made from the end of the latest accounting period to be assessed until the date of cessation, less a deduction for what is described as 'overlap profit'. 'Overlap profit' means a profit which is included in the assessment of two successive tax years as, for example, the first and second tax years of a new business (see the example in **24.2.3**).

Example

A trader commences his business on 1 January 2006 and decides to prepare accounts for calendar years. Although the trade never suffers a loss, it is not as successful as the trader had hoped and he closes the trade on 31 December 2009. The accounts show the following trading profits:

	£
2006:	20,000
2007:	30,000
2008:	40,000
2009:	10,000

Income tax will be assessed on the following figures:

	£	
2005/06: (1st tax year)	5,000	(one-quarter of £20,000, representing the three-month period 1 January 2006 to 5 April 2006)
2006/07: (2nd tax year)	20,000	(profits made in the 2006 accounting period which ends in the tax year)
2007/08: (3rd tax year)	30,000	(profits made in the 2007 accounting period which ends in the tax year)
2008/09: (4th tax year)	40,000	(profits made in the 2008 accounting period which ends in the tax year)
2009/10: (final tax year)	5,000	(profits made from the end of the latest accounting period to be assessed less overlap profit, ie

		£10,000	(for 2009)
less		5,000	(overlap profit)
		5,000)	

The information used in the example may be presented in diagram form as follows:

Accounting period:		2006	2007	2008	2009	
Profit:		£20,000	£30,000	£40,000	£10,000	= £100,000
Tax year:	**05/06**	**06/07**	**07/08**	**08/09**	**09/10**	
Amount taxed:	£5,000	£20,000	£30,000	£40,000	£5,000	= £100,000

Note: The purpose and effect of deducting 'overlap profit' in the final tax year in calculating the assessment figure is that the total profit for the lifespan of the business is the same as the total amount assessed to income tax. However, there is still a cash flow disadvantage for the taxpayer in the example who does not receive any credit for the initial double taxation of the 'overlap profit' until the business ceases.

24.3 Date for payment (TMA 1970, ss 59A and 59B, inserted by FA 1994, ss 192 and 193)

A sole trader must register with HMRC within three months of starting the business (even if he already completes a self-assessment tax return).

Income tax assessed on a trading profit forms part of the income tax liability that is payable by two equal instalments, of which the first is due on 31 January in the tax year in question and the second is due on 31 July following the end of that tax year. Since the trader's taxable profit may not be known by the first of those dates, generally he will make his two payments based on the previous year's income. On or before the 31 January following the end of the tax year, the taxpayer will make a tax return on which his actual liability to income tax will be self-assessed and an adjustment (by further payment or by repayment of tax) will be made. (Delaying submission of the tax return until the deadline of 31 January is not possible for taxpayers submitting paper returns. Here, an earlier deadline of the 31 October following the end of the tax year applies.)

No payments on account are required if the amount of tax due under these rules is less than £500 (or if more than 80% of the total tax bill has already been collected by deduction at source/ dividend tax credits).

Example

A trader whose accounts are prepared on a calendar year basis will be taxed on profits for 2009 in the tax year 2009/10. If his total tax due is £12,000 (estimated based on his 2008 profits and assuming no deduction of tax at source), the first instalment of £6,000 will be due on 31 January 2010, the second (also of £6,000) will be due on 31 July 2010, with a balancing payment or rebate due on 31 January 2011 once the return for 2009/10 has been processed under the self-assessment system.

24.4 Relief for a trading loss

The trading income calculations described in **Chapter 21** may produce a trading loss for which relief may be available.

There are various provisions in Pt 4 of the ITA 2007 which allow the taxpayer, in effect, to deduct a trading loss from other income in order to provide relief from tax on that other income. Where the circumstances are such that relief could be claimed under more than one of the following provisions, the taxpayer may choose under which to claim. It may be that the taxpayer's loss is greater than can be relieved under just one of these provisions; if so, the taxpayer can claim as much relief as is available under one provision and then claim relief for the balance of his loss under any other available provision (although he cannot claim relief for the same loss twice over). Generally, the taxpayer will want to claim relief under whichever provision is best for cash-flow; some allow a repayment of tax previously paid, while others act to reduce the amount of tax that will become due in the future.

These losses are allowed for at Step 2 of the income tax calculation, and in some cases the loss is set against 'total income', whereas in others it is only set against a particular component of income. (As older cases and textbooks refer to the provisions under ICTA 1988, those old references are included below for ease of reference.)

24.4.1 Start-up loss relief (ITA 2007, ss 72–81, formerly ICTA 1988, s 381)

If the taxpayer suffers a loss which is assessed in any of the first four tax years of a new business, the loss can be carried back and set against the taxpayer's 'total income' in the three tax years prior to the tax year of the loss. This provision might be particularly useful to a person who starts a new business having previously had a steady income from a former business or employment. While the new business becomes established, it may make losses but the trader may be cushioned by claiming back from HMRC some income tax which he has paid in his previous business or employment in the earlier years. This would be especially beneficial if some or all of the income tax which he paid and is now able to claim back was at the higher rate of 40%.

If the taxpayer elects to use this provision, the loss in question must be set against earlier years before later years – the taxpayer cannot pick and choose which year's income is reduced first.

A claim for relief must usually be made on or before the first anniversary of the 31 January following the tax year in which the loss is assessed (eg by 31 January 2012 for a loss assessed in 2009/10).

Example

Bruno commences a business on 1 January 2009. In the first few months of trading, he incurs a lot of expense in setting up the business but has few customers. As a result, he makes a trading loss in the first tax year of assessment (for the period 1 January to 5 April 2009 inclusive) of £25,000.

Before starting his own business, Bruno had been an employee of a large company, and had the following income:

Tax year	2005/06	£20,000
	2006/07	£25,000
	2007/08	£43,000
	2008/09 (part)	£45,000

If Bruno claims relief under s 72, his £25,000 trading loss will be relieved as follows:

£20,000 will be set against his income for 2005/06, reducing the revised income for 2005/06 to nil (so Bruno will get a tax rebate for that tax year).

The remaining £5,000 will be set against his income for 2006/07, reducing the revised income for 2006/07 to £20,000 (so Bruno will get a partial tax rebate for that tax year).

Note:

(a)   The relief is given against total income at Step 2, ie before deduction of the personal allowance (at Step 3). For 2005/06, Bruno has, therefore, effectively wasted his personal allowance.

(b)   The rule that a loss must be set against income from earlier years before later years means that Bruno has had his income reduced for years when he was a basic rate taxpayer, not when he became a higher rate taxpayer.

24.4.2   Carry-across/one year back relief for trading losses generally (ITA 2007, ss 64–71, formerly ICTA 1988, s 380 and FA 1991, s 72)

24.4.2.1   Set off against income (ITA 2007, s 64)

A trading loss which arises in an accounting period is treated as a loss of the tax year in which the accounting period ends. The loss can be set against:

(a)   the taxpayer's 'total income' in the tax year of the loss (defined as 'the loss-making year'); or

(b)   the taxpayer's total income in the preceding tax year.

If the loss is big enough to reduce total income to nil using method (a) or (b), the taxpayer has the option to set the loss against:

(c)   the taxpayer's total income in the loss-making year with the balance of any unused loss set against total income in the preceding tax year; or

(d)   the taxpayer's total income in the preceding tax year, with the balance of any unused loss set against total income in the loss-making year.

As with start-up relief, if the taxpayer claims this relief, the loss must be set against total income which may result in him having no income left against which to set his personal allowance; this would mean that the personal allowance for that year is wasted since there is no provision for personal allowances to be carried forward to another year.

In the example at **24.4.1**, Bruno may have preferred to claim relief for his trading loss under s 64 rather than s 72. This would have enabled him to set his loss of £25,000 against either his total income of £45,000 in 2008/09 or his total income of £43,000 in 2007/08 (both years when he was a higher rate taxpayer).

The Finance Bill 2009 contains provisions intended to assist businesses during the recession by a temporary extension of the carry-back period for some losses. For trading losses incurred during accounting periods ending in tax year 2008/09 or 2009/10, the relief under ss 64–71 is extended. If there is any unused trading loss having applied the relief in the normal way, the excess loss (up to a maximum of £50,000) can be carried back for a further two tax years (taking later year(s) first) but only to be set against profits of the same trade.

> **Example**
>
> Ben's business makes a large trading loss in the accounting period ending 31 December 2009. Having set the loss against his total income in 2009/10 and 2008/09, he still has some unused loss, and a maximum £50,000 of that loss can be carried back and set against his trading profits in 2007/08 and, finally, 2006/07.

24.4.2.2 Set off against capital gains (ITA 2007, s 71 and TCGA 1992, ss 261B and 261C)

If a claim is made under s 64 and the taxpayer's total income for the tax year in which the trading loss is used is effectively reduced to nil and some of the loss has still to be used then, if the taxpayer does not opt to relieve the excess loss in some other way (eg by using s 72 or s 83), it can be set against the taxpayer's chargeable gains (if any) for that tax year.

This is the only loss relief considered in this chapter which allows relief, in certain circumstances, against a taxpayer's chargeable capital gains as well as against income.

A claim for relief pursuant to s 64 must usually be made on or before the first anniversary of the 31 January following the tax year in which the loss is assessed (eg by 31 January 2012 for a loss assessed in 2009/10).

24.4.3 Carry-forward relief (ITA 2007, ss 83–85, formerly ICTA 1988, s 385)

If a taxpayer suffers a trading loss in any year of a trade, the loss can be carried forward to be set against subsequent profits which the trade produces, taking earlier years first. This has two disadvantages for the taxpayer when compared with relief under s 64 (see **24.4.2**). First, he must wait until future profits of the trade become taxable before he benefits from his loss relief. Secondly, s 83 is more restrictive than s 64 in that it only provides for the loss to be set against profits which the trade produces – it does not provide for relief against other sources of income or against capital gains.

However, the losses carried forward under s 83 can be carried forward indefinitely until a suitable profit from the trade arises to be relieved (although a claim confirming the intention to do this must be made on or before the fourth anniversary of the 31 January following the tax year in which the loss is assessed (eg by 31 January 2015 for a loss assessed in 2009/10)).

> **Example**
>
> Carl's business has an accounting period which ends on 31 December each year. In 2008, he makes a trading loss of £40,000. In 2009 he makes a trading profit of £35,000 and in 2010 he makes a trading profit of £20,000. He has no other income. If Carl makes a claim under s 83, his income tax assessments will be based on:
>
> | Tax year | Profit/(loss) £ |
> | --- | --- |
> | 08/09 | (40,000) |
> | 09/10 | Nil – the £35,000 profit is fully covered by carried forward loss |
> | 10/11 | £15,000 – the £20,000 profit is reduced by remaining £5,000 loss. |

24.4.4 Carry-back of terminal trading loss (ITA 2007, ss 89–94, formerly ICTA 1988, s 388)

If a taxpayer suffers a trading loss in the final 12 months in which he carries on the trade, this loss can be carried across against any profits made in the final tax year and then carried back to be set against his trading profit in the three tax years prior to his final tax year, taking later years before earlier years. He may thus reclaim from HMRC tax which he has paid in earlier years. Note that s 89 does not allow relief against non-trading income or against capital gains (but there is no £50,000 cap on the amount of loss that can be carried back under these provisions). If any loss remains unrelieved, the other reliefs described in **24.4** are available if relevant in light of the taxpayer's situation.

A claim for relief must be made on or before the fourth anniversary of the 31 January following the final tax year of the trade (eg by 31 January 2015 if 2009/10 was the final tax year in question).

Example

After making a profit in its early years, Dee's organic aromatherapy business (which makes its accounts up to 5 April each year) closes on 5 April 2010 making a loss in the final accounting period of £20,000. There is no profit in 2009/10 against which to set the loss but it could be deducted from Dee's trading profit for the accounting period ending in the tax year 2008/09 with any remaining loss carried further back against trading profits assessed in 2007/08 and, finally, 2006/07.

24.4.5 Carry-forward relief on incorporation of business (ITA 2007, s 86, formerly ICTA 1988, s 386)

If the taxpayer has suffered trading losses which have not been relieved and transfers the business to a company wholly or mainly in return for the issue to himself of shares in the company, the losses can (unless otherwise relieved (eg by s 64 or s 89)) be carried forward and set against income which he receives from the company, such as a salary as a director or dividends as a shareholder. In order to be 'wholly or mainly in return for the issue of shares', at least 80% of the consideration for the transfer must consist of shares in the company.

Example

On 30 November 2009, Ella transfers her business to a company wholly in return for shares in the company. Her trading loss from the business at that stage is £10,000. In the remainder of the 2009/10 tax year she receives a small salary from the company of £6,000. In the following tax year, 2010/11, she receives a salary from the company of £15,000 and her shareholding in the company produces dividends of £2,000. She has no other income. If Ella uses relief under s 86:

(a)   her income from the salary of £6,000 in 2009/10 is reduced to nil by the losses carried forward; and

(b)   the remaining loss of £4,000 can be set against her income of £17,000 in 2010/11 (reducing the salary by £4,000).

(Note: the Finance Act 2008, s 60 and Sch 21 contain restrictions on the amount of certain loss reliefs that can be claimed where the sole trader is 'non-active' (in essence where the trader spends an average of less than 10 hours a week on the trade).)

24.4.6 Summary of reliefs for a trading loss

Section of ITA 2007	When will the loss have occurred?	Against what will the loss be set?	Which periods are relevant?
s 72 (start-up relief by carry-back)	The first four tax years of trading	Total income	The three tax years preceding the tax year of the loss
s 64 (carry-across/ carry- back one year relief)	Any accounting year of trading	Total income and (thereafter) chargeable gains	The tax year in which the accounting year of the loss ends and/or the preceding tax year.*
s 83 (carry-forward relief)	Any accounting year of trading	Subsequent profits of the same trade	Any subsequent tax year until the loss is absorbed
s 89 (terminal relief by carry-back)	The final 12 months of trading	Previous profits of the same trade	The final tax year and then the three tax years preceding the final tax year
s 86 (carry-forward relief on incorporation)	Up to incorporation	Subsequent income received from the company	Any subsequent tax year until the loss has been absorbed

* For trading losses incurred in accounting periods ending in 2008/09 or 2009/10, up to £50,000 of the loss can be carried back a further 2 tax years (but only to be set against profits of the same trade).

Chapter 25

Taxation of Partnerships

25.1 Introduction

For most tax purposes, a partnership falling within the definition contained in PA 1890 (see **Chapter 13**) is treated as 'transparent' so that any tax liability arising from the partnership's business is assessed not against the partnership as a whole, but against each of the members of the partnership. This chapter describes how each partner's share of income and capital profits is calculated and the subsequent tax liability that arises from that calculation. The rules governing the calculation differ depending on whether the partnership comprises only individuals or whether one or more of the partners is a company. The chapter concludes with a brief analysis of how a limited liability partnership (LLP) is taxed.

25.1.1 Partnerships comprising only individuals

An individual partner must consider his liability for income tax on trading profits and other income from the partnership, for capital gains tax on capital profits, and inheritance tax on transfers of value made by the partnership as a whole or by the individual partner.

25.1.2 Partnerships where one or more partner is a company

If a company is a partner additional provisions must be considered, given that a company pays corporation tax rather than income tax, capital gains tax or inheritance tax.

25.2 Partnerships comprising only individuals – income tax

25.2.1 General principles

The principles described in **Chapter 24** for the income tax treatment of a sole trader apply, with modifications, to this type of partnership. These principles are:

(a) calculation of trading profits (see **Chapter 21**);

(b) the basis of assessing the taxable profit of a given tax year for each partner;

(c) income tax relief for trading losses.

25.2.2 Application of general principles to partnerships (ITTOIA 2005, Part 9)

As mentioned above, a partnership is not treated as an entity distinct from the partners themselves and so there is no assessment to income tax on the firm as a whole.

The assessment of income tax in the context of a partnership will therefore entail the following steps:

(a)   The trading profit of the business will be calculated in the same way as if the business were run by a sole trader, applying the rules for trading income:

chargeable receipts

LESS

any deductible expenditure

LESS

any capital allowances

EQUALS

trading profit (or trading loss).

(b)   The trading profit will be allocated between the partners according to the way in which income profits were shared under their agreement for that accounting period (eg 'salaries', interest on capital and then profit shares).

(c)   Each partner's income from the partnership will then be included in his tax return and will be assessed in the ordinary way, taking account of whatever reliefs and allowances he is entitled to receive. Each partner is only liable to HMRC for income tax on his share of the profits – he cannot be required to pay income tax on the profits which are allocated to his partners.

Example

W, X, Y and Z started a business on 1 January 2003. They share income profits as follows.

(a)   W, X and Y each receive 'salaries' of £10,000 per annum to reflect the fact that they work full-time whereas Z only works part-time.

(b)   All partners receive interest on capital at 10% per annum; their capital contributions were as follows:

W: £20,000
X: £20,000
Y: £10,000
Z: £50,000

(c)   Profits remaining after 'salaries' and interest on capital are shared equally between the partners.

The firm's accounts are prepared for calendar years and, in the calendar year 2009, the firm makes a taxable profit before allocation between the partners of £100,000. The partners' entitlement is:

	W	X	Y	Z	Totals
'Salary'	10,000	10,000	10,000	—	30,000
Interest	2,000	2,000	1,000	5,000	10,000
Profit	15,000	15,000	15,000	15,000	60,000
	£27,000	£27,000	£26,000	£20,000	£100,000

The figure produced at the foot of each partner's column (eg £27,000 for W) is the figure for inclusion in that individual's total income for the tax year 2009/10 (see 24.2 as to the 'basis of assessment').

In the event of the business making a trading loss, that loss will be allocated between the partners for income tax purposes in accordance with the agreement for that accounting period and the partners then choose individually how they will claim the benefit of income tax relief for their share of the loss. See 24.4 for the possible alternatives for claiming relief for a trading loss. (Note: ITA 2007, Pt 4 contains measures to restrict available loss relief for a non-active partner.)

25.2.3 Change in firm's membership

25.2.3.1 Joiners

Where a new person joins a well-established partnership, he will be assessed to income tax for his first two tax years on the basis described in **24.2.2** and **24.2.3**, because as far as he is concerned this is a new business. The existing partners will continue to be assessed on the basis described in **24.2.1**.

25.2.3.2 Leavers

Where a person leaves a continuing partnership (eg on retirement or on expulsion), he will be assessed to income tax for his final tax year on the basis described in **24.2.4**, because as far as he is concerned the business is coming to an end. The remaining partners will continue to be assessed on the basis described in **24.2.1**.

Example

A, B and C start a business in partnership on 1 January 2006; they prepare accounts for calendar years. On 1 January 2008, D joins the partnership. On 30 June 2009, A retires. Profits for these four years are:

	£
2006	20,000
2007	27,000
2008	40,000
2009	60,000

(a) D's assessments to income tax:

    (i) D's first tax year (2007/08)

        D will be assessed to income tax on his share of the £10,000 profits for the (roughly) three-month period 1 January 2008 to 5 April 2008 (this figure being one-quarter of the profit for the full year 2008).

        Note: For 2007/08, A, B and C will be assessed individually to income tax on their shares of the £27,000 profits made in 2007 (this being the profit for the accounting period which ends in the tax year).

    (ii) D's second tax year (2008/09)

        D will be assessed to income tax on his share of the £40,000 profits for his first 12 months in the business (this being the profit for 2008).

        Note: For 2008/09, A, B and C will also be assessed by reference to this period because it is the accounting period which ends in the tax year.

(b) A's assessment to income tax for his final tax year (2009/10).

A will be assessed to income tax on his share of the profits made from the end of the latest accounting period to be assessed (ie 2008) until the date of his retirement LESS a deduction for his 'overlap profit'. This means that he will be assessed on his share of the £30,000 profits for the six-month period from 1 January 2009 to 30 June 2009 (this figure being one-half of the profit for the full year) LESS a deduction for his share of the £5,000 profits made in the period 1 January to 5 April 2006 which were assessed in both his first and second tax years (2005/06 and 2006/07).

Note: For 2009/10, B, C and D will be assessed individually on their shares of the £60,000 profits made in 2009 (this being the profit for the accounting period which ends in the tax year).

25.2.4 Income tax relief on a partner's borrowings (ITA 2007, ss 383 and 398)

An individual who borrows money (eg from a bank) in order to buy a share in a partnership or to lend money to a partnership can deduct the interest he pays each year (on the money he has borrowed) from his total income. The relief is designed to encourage investment in business and a similar provision exists for investment in certain companies (see **23.2.3**).

> **Example**
>
> Brian borrows £20,000 from Bigbank plc in order to invest in a partnership. In the tax year 2009/10, the interest payments that Bigbank plc charges Brian total £1,600. Brian can deduct £1,600 from his total income for 2009/10.

25.3 Partnerships comprising only individuals – capital gains tax

25.3.1 General principles

Normal capital gains tax principles apply to partnerships (in accordance with an HMRC Statement of Practice (SPD/12, reissued 8 October 2002)). Thus capital gains tax may arise where there is a disposal of a chargeable asset resulting in a chargeable gain.

A partnership as a whole is unlikely to make gifts of the partnership assets and so the likely 'disposal' which is relevant is their sale. Bearing in mind that certain assets are not chargeable assets for capital gains tax, the partnership assets which are most likely to be subject to capital gains tax are land and premises, goodwill and certain investments.

An individual partner may dispose (independently of the other partners) of his interest in an asset, or his interest in the partnership (see **Chapter 28**).

25.3.2 Disposal by the firm

Where the firm disposes of a chargeable asset, this is treated for capital gains tax purposes as being separate disposals by the partners of their individual interests in that asset. These interests are established by applying the terms of the partnership agreement relating to the sharing of capital profits (see **14.7**). The partners may have expressly agreed on the proportions (eg to share the capital profits in the same proportion as their capital contributions). If there is no express or implied agreement between the partners, capital profits are shared equally (PA 1890, s 24(1)).

> **Example 1**
>
> If a firm consists of three partners who have equal shares in capital profits, then each partner is treated as owning one-third of each asset.

> **Example 2**
>
> If the firm consists of three partners (A, B and C) who share capital profits in the ratio of A:2, B:1 and C:1, then A owns half of each asset, B one-quarter and C one-quarter.

25.3.3 Calculation of gain

When calculating the gain made by each partner arising from the firm's disposal of an asset, it is necessary to apportion the disposal proceeds and allowable expenditure (most importantly the acquisition cost) among the partners according to their fractional interest in the asset.

> **Example**
>
> D, E, F and G have been partners for many years and share all profits equally. In 1996 they purchased shop premises, paying £120,000 as the purchase price. In July 2009, they sell the shop premises for £280,000. Each of the partners is taken to have disposed of one-quarter of the chargeable asset (the shop) at one-quarter of the sale price (ie £70,000). To each of them, there will be allocated one-quarter of the acquisition cost (£30,000) and of any other allowable expenditure.

25.3.4   Business reliefs

Once each partner has established whether the disposal of a partnership asset will give rise to a chargeable gain in his hands, he should consider whether that gain can be reduced, or the payment of tax on it postponed, by the use of one or more of the capital gains tax reliefs currently available. In the context of the disposal of a business asset, the most common reliefs are:

(a)   roll-over relief on the replacement of qualifying business assets;

(b)   hold-over relief on gifts (and the gift element of sales at an undervalue) of business assets;

(c)   deferral relief on reinvestment in EIS shares;

(d)   roll-over relief on the incorporation of a business;

(e)   entrepreneurs' relief.

The availability of each of the above reliefs (described in detail in **Chapter 28**) depends on the circumstances surrounding the disposal of the asset and the disponer's own circumstances. It may be, therefore, that one or more of the partners can claim relief(s) that are not available to other partners. If different reliefs are available to different partners, each individual may choose which relief (if any) he claims; there is no need for all the partners to treat their respective share of the gain on the disposal of a partnership asset in the same way.

Example

If D disposes of his share in the shop premises for £70,000, having acquired his share for £30,000 (see previous example), his CGT calculation would be as follows:

In order to show the calculation of D's gain (by way of illustration), the following assumptions will be made:

(a)   there was no allowable expenditure other than the purchase price;

(b)   no relief is available.

	£
Proceeds of disposal	70,000
LESS	
Acquisition cost	30,000
Gain	40,000

D's gain will be aggregated with any other gains and losses he has made in the tax year 2009/10 and, following deduction of the annual exemption of £10,100, those gains will be taxed at 18%.

25.3.5   Payment of tax

Once each partner's chargeable gain and any resultant tax liability have been calculated, the tax is payable by that partner individually; as with income tax on the firm's income profits, capital gains tax can only be assessed on each partner for his own share of the firm's gain.

25.3.6   Capital gains tax on disposals by partners individually

A partner may dispose of his fractional share in each of the partnership assets when the firm is not making a disposal.

25.3.6.1   Retirement

On retirement a partner may sell to his fellow partners (ie they are 'buying him out') or he may sell (or give away) his share to a third party. In these instances, the principles described in **25.3.2** and **25.3.3** will govern the identification of his fractional share, and the calculation of his gain. The reliefs listed in **25.3.4** may be available and any tax due as a result of the disposal will be payable in accordance with **25.3.5**.

25.3.6.2 A partner joins

When a new partner joins an existing partnership, he will usually buy into the partnership and so become entitled to a share in each of the partnership assets (at the value at the date of joining). The other partners are, therefore, each disposing of part of their existing share of the assets, leading to a possible CGT charge.

> **Example**
>
> H and K own partnership assets equally. J joins the partnership in June 2009 and pays to acquire a one-third share in the partnership assets at their June 2009 values. As a result of this, H and K each make a disposal of one-sixth of the overall value of each asset so that H, K and J each end up owning two-sixths (ie one-third) of each asset. H and K have both made disposals on which the gain will need to be calculated (in the way described in **25.3.2** and **25.3.3**) even though the assets have not left the partnership as a whole.

(Note: the above example assumes that there has been a revaluation of the partnership assets when a new partner joins. For other possible accounting treatments in such a situation, and their possible tax consequences, see HMRC SPD/12, para 4 onwards.)

25.4 Partnerships comprising only individuals – inheritance tax

As noted in **25.3.1**, it is unlikely that the partnership as a whole will make gifts of assets. If an individual partner disposes of his share of the partnership asset(s) at less than full value, inheritance tax should be considered and the general inheritance tax rules apply to any transfer of value that a partner makes (eg on a gift of his share to a relative). Exemptions and reliefs which may be available are described in **Chapter 28**.

25.5 Partnerships where one or more of the partners is a company

Most partnerships are formed between individuals, but it is possible for a partnership's members to be companies or a mixture of companies and individuals. Special rules are needed for partnerships where one or more of the partners is a company, given that the income and capital profits of companies are assessed to corporation tax whereas, in the case of individuals, income tax and capital gains tax are the relevant taxes. The detail of these special rules is beyond the scope of this book, but their general effect is described below.

25.5.1 Trading profits (CTA 2009, Part 17)

The trading profit (or loss) of a partnership for its accounting period will be split between the partners according to how the partners have agreed to share such profits (or losses).

The share of the partnership profit attributed to a partner who is an individual is taxed in the tax year in which the partnership's accounting period ends.

The position is more complex for a company. The share of the partnership profit attributed to a partner that is a company is taxed according to the company's own accounting period. This is relatively straightforward when the partnership's accounting period and that of the company synchronise (eg both have yearly accounting periods ending on 31 March). If, however, the accounting periods do not match (eg the partnership's accounting period ends on 31 December, and the company's accounting period ends on 30 June), then the company's share of the profit from the partnership must be apportioned between the company's two accounting periods that overlap with the partnership's accounting period.

> **Example**
>
> X Ltd has an accounting period that ends on 30 June each year. It is a partner in a partnership with an accounting period that ends on 31 December each year. For the partnership accounting period ending 31 December 2009, X Ltd's share of the trading profit is £150,000. Half of that profit will be assessed in X Ltd's accounting period ending 30 June 2009, and the other half in the company's accounting period ending 30 June 2010.

25.5.2 Capital profits (TCGA 1992, s 59)

Where the partnership disposes of a chargeable asset, this is treated as being separate disposals by the partners of their interests in that asset (applying the terms of the partnership agreement as described in **25.3.2**).

The gain or loss arising from the disposal and attributable to a partner who is an individual is assessed in the tax year in which the disposal took place (using the rules for capital gains tax described in **25.3.3**).

The gain or loss arising from the disposal and attributable to a partner that is a company is assessed in the company's accounting period in which the disposal took place (using the rules and applying the reliefs for corporation tax described in **22.4**).

25.6 Limited liability partnerships (LLPs)

As described in **Chapter 18**, the Limited Liability Partnerships Act 2000 (LLPA 2000) was introduced to provide an element of protection from unlimited liability for the members of a partnership formed as an LLP, whilst allowing the LLP to be taxed in the same way as a partnership governed by the Partnership Act 1890 (despite the fact that an LLP is a body corporate).

HMRC has issued guidance to the effect that, where an LLP is used to carry on a trade or a profession (but not if it is used to make investments), it will be treated for most UK tax purposes in the same way as an ordinary partnership. Particular points to note are mentioned below.

25.6.1 Trading profits

Trading profits will be calculated in the same way as for an ordinary partnership. If an ordinary partnership converts to an LLP, this will not trigger a balancing charge or allowance for the purposes of the capital allowances regime, and the partners will not be treated as ceasing one trade and starting another. An individual partner who borrows money to invest in an LLP or lend money to it will be able to claim interest relief on the loan in the same way as a partner in an ordinary partnership. There is, however, a difference in the availability of relief for a trading loss, with available loss relief being restricted in the case of a partner in an LLP in certain conditions (the detail of these provisions is beyond the scope of this book).

25.6.2 Capital profits

Whilst the LLP is trading, capital gains will be assessed in the same way as for an ordinary partnership. If an ordinary partnership converts to an LLP, this will not trigger a disposal for capital gains purposes. A major change occurs, however, when an LLP ceases to trade and in certain situations it may stop being treated in the same way as an ordinary partnership and instead be treated as a body corporate. In advising on such cases, careful reference will need to be made to the provisions of s 59A of the TCGA 1992 .

25.6.3 Inheritance tax

The usual inheritance tax rules apply to individual partners who make transfers of value. When an ordinary partnership converts to an LLP, this does not interrupt a partner's period of ownership for the purposes of claiming agricultural and/or business property relief.

25.7 VAT and partnerships

A detailed discussion of VAT is beyond the scope of this book but it should be noted that, unlike the position for the assessment and payment of income tax, capital gains tax, inheritance tax and corporation tax, VAT registration for a partnership can be in the name of the firm itself.

25.8 National Insurance

Partners (other than 'sleeping' partners) will make Class 2 and Class 4 National Insurance contributions on income earned as self-employed individuals. If the partnership employs staff, Class 1 contributions will be made in respect of those staff (see **26.7**).

Chapter 26

Taxation of Employees and Directors

26.1 Introduction

Income tax produces more revenue for HM Treasury than any other single tax, and the majority of that tax is collected from employees. Staff salaries will usually constitute one of the major expenses of any business and a substantial proportion (sometimes the whole) of the business's trading receipts may be absorbed by paying salaries or fees and other benefits to its employees (and, in the case of a company, also to its directors). As such payments are deductible expenditure in calculating trading profits, this means that a substantial proportion of the business's trading receipts may ultimately attract income tax as the income of its employees rather than being taxed as the employer business's taxable profit. The charge to income tax on employees (and company directors) is under the Income Tax (Earnings and Pensions) Act 2003 (ITEPA 2003).

In respect of the earnings of employees, both the employer and employee must also be aware of the impact of National Insurance contributions.

26.2 The income chargeable generally under the ITEPA 2003

Income tax is charged under the ITEPA 2003 on 'employment' income, 'pensions' income, and 'social security' income. This chapter concentrates on employment income. Employment income includes 'earnings'; that is all benefits received by the director or employee which derive from his office or employment as a reward for his services, whether they are paid by the employer or by a third party. Salaries, bonuses and tips are taxable; a gift on the other hand for purely personal reasons would not be taxable since it is not a reward for services. In relation to non-cash benefits such as company cars, there are particular provisions which require separate consideration.

26.3 Cash payments

A cash salary usually forms the largest part of any remuneration package, but it is not the only cash payment that is taxable. A number of other receipts are chargeable under the ITEPA 2003, for example:

(a) a lump sum received at the beginning of the employment and referrable to future services (a 'golden hello');

(b) a lump sum received at the end of the employment when the employee was entitled to the payment under his contract of employment;

(c) a lump sum received in return for the employee entering into a covenant not to compete with the employer's trade (ITEPA 2003, s 225);

(d)   other payments (ITEPA 2003, ss 401–416). A sum received on termination of office which is not otherwise chargeable to income tax is brought into charge by s 403 of the ITEPA 2003, even though it does not derive from the office or employment as a reward for services. Examples include compensation for unfair dismissal, damages for wrongful dismissal or even a gratuitous payment (a gift) on termination of the employment. However, the first £30,000 of any such sum is exempt.

Any payment on termination which exceeds £30,000 will attract income tax on the excess. Because of the exemption for the first £30,000, it is clear that it is advantageous to the employee from a tax viewpoint if any termination payment is caught by s 403 rather than the ordinary rules of the ITEPA 2003. The ordinary rules, however, take priority over s 403. It may therefore be undesirable, for example, for the employee's contract to provide for a lump sum payment on termination or for payment in lieu of notice, since this would be taxable under the ordinary rules and there would be no £30,000 exemption. On the other hand, if the lack of contractual obligation means the employer chooses to make no terminal payment, the employee may lose the entire payment, not just the tax element of it.

26.4   Non-cash benefits

26.4.1   The general rules

26.4.1.1   Examples of non-cash benefits

Common examples of non-cash benefits provided or paid for by the employer are:

(a)   the use of a 'company' car for private as well as business use;

(b)   the provision of private medical insurance;

(c)   an interest-free or low-interest loan;

(d)   rent-free or low-rent living accommodation;

(e)   an expenses allowance;

(f)   vouchers exchangeable for goods or services (eg a season ticket for a football club).

26.4.1.2   The tax treatment of non-cash benefits

The ITEPA 2003 makes a fundamental distinction in the taxation of non-cash benefits between:

(a)   employees whose earnings are less than £8,500 a year (described as 'lower-paid' employees); and

(b)   other employees and company directors generally.

Often, a director will be an employee of the company in a defined role (eg as sales manager) but this is not always the case. A non-executive director may simply attend board meetings and receive fees for doing so; this is why company directors generally are brought within the legislation. A company director (unless, broadly, he has no more than 5% of the shares in the company and works full-time for the company (ITEPA 2003, s 216)) is treated in the same way as a higher-paid employee irrespective of the level of his earnings.

In assessing whether or not a person is a 'lower-paid' employee, the value (assessed as explained at **26.4.1.3**) of all earnings must be taken into account. Thus an employee with a salary of £7,500 a year plus the unrestricted use of a company car and with private medical insurance paid for by the employer, is bound to have earnings of at least £8,500 a year, because the cost to the employer of providing the company car and insurance will, taken with the salary, reach and exceed the £8,500 limit.

26.4.1.3 The 'normal' rules

Employees and company directors generally are liable to income tax under the ITEPA 2003 on all benefits which derive from the office or employment.

Generally, the taxable value of the benefit is taken as the amount of the cost incurred by the employer in providing that benefit (ITEPA 2003, s 204). For example, where the employer pays premiums for private medical insurance provided for the employee, pays rent for a house provided for the employee and pays for the employee's membership at his local gym, the employee will be assessed to income tax on the benefits valued on the amount of the premiums paid, the rent paid and the cost of the gym membership respectively. If the employee reimburses the employer to any extent (eg paying half of the rent), this reduces the cost incurred by the employer and hence reduces the taxable value of the benefit.

In some instances the taxable value of the benefit is calculated on a different basis; for example if the employer actually owns the asset, there may be no ongoing cost to the employer in providing that asset. In this case, the ITEPA 2003 sets prescribed methods for calculating the value of the benefit to the employee in each year. Particular examples are as follows.

(a) Private use of a 'company' car (ITEPA 2003, ss 114–172): the taxable value of the benefit to an employee from the private use of a car depends on the carbon dioxide emissions of the type of car in question. The minimum charge will usually be 15% of the list price of the car (and accessories), rising to 35% of the list price for cars with the greatest emissions (calculated according to official tables).

(b) Private use of other company assets such as a house or a yacht (ITEPA 2003, s 205): the taxable value of the benefit is its annual value; for a house this will usually be its rateable value, whilst for other assets this will be 20% of the market value of the asset at the time it was first provided as a benefit.

(c) Loans at special rates by the employer (ITEPA 2003, ss 173–191): the taxable value of the benefit is the interest 'saved' by the director/employee as compared with the official interest rate as set from time to time. For 2009/10, the official rate is 4.75% (although this is likely to alter if commercial interest rates change significantly during the year). Thus if a director/employee pays no interest on a loan from his employer in 2009/10, the amount he has saved by not paying interest at 4.75% will be treated as part of his earnings. (However, see the exceptions mentioned in **26.4.2**.)

26.4.1.4 Lower-paid employees (ITEPA 2003, ss 216–220)

The lower-paid category of employee is treated more favourably in relation to non-cash benefits.

Lower-paid employees are generally taxed on a non-cash benefit only if the benefit can be converted into money by the employee. This means, for example, that these employees would suffer no charge to tax on the use of a company car or an interest free loan (provided the total level of earnings in the tax year does not reach the £8,500 threshold). By way of exception, however, lower-paid employees are liable to tax in the same way as other employees on the benefits of rent-free or low-rent accommodation and of vouchers.

For a lower-paid employee, an expenses allowance is not liable to tax unless HMRC can establish that it is a benefit of the employment rather than a genuine expenses allowance. (The position is reversed for other employees who will suffer tax on the expenses allowance unless they can establish that the expenditure to which the allowance relates is deductible (see **26.5**).)

The taxable value of a non-cash benefit on which a lower-paid employee suffers a charge to tax is the amount of money into which it could be converted. Thus if such an employee receives a gift of a suit of clothing from his employer, he will be liable to tax on the second-hand value of the suit; the higher-paid employee would have been assessed on the cost to the employer of providing the benefit (ie the cost of the new suit).

26.4.2   Exceptions

There are exceptions in certain cases, where the charge to tax described above will not apply to either lower- or higher-paid employees. The following are common examples.

26.4.2.1   Certain accommodation (ITEPA 2003, s 315)

In certain instances, employees are not charged to tax (but generally directors are) on the benefit of rent-free or low-rent accommodation. Common examples are caretakers (exemption because occupation is necessary for the performance of the employee's duties) and police and fire officers (exemption because occupation is customary and for the better performance of the employee's duties).

26.4.2.2   Interest-free or low-interest loans (ITEPA 2003, s 180)

There is no charge to tax where the total outstanding on all special-rate loans from the employer does not exceed £5,000 at any time in the tax year.

26.4.2.3   Employer's pension contributions (ITEPA 2003, s 308)

The director/employee is not charged to tax on the benefit of contributions under HMRC-approved schemes.

26.4.3   Share schemes

The employer company may provide the employee or director with non-cash benefits which relate to shares in the company. These can take a variety of forms including a gift of the shares, a sale of the shares at a favourable price, a sale of the shares on terms where payment for them is postponed, an option to purchase shares in the future and various schemes involving the use of trusts. The tax treatment of such benefits requires more detailed explanation than is appropriate here, but it is worth noting that there are possible tax and other advantages to both the company employer and the employee or director in using these schemes. Part 7 of the ITEPA 2003 deals with the taxation of share-related income.

26.5   Deductible expenditure (ITEPA 2003, ss 327–385)

26.5.1   The general test (ITEPA 2003, s 336)

In calculating what is taxable within the ITEPA 2003, an employee or director is generally entitled only to deduct expenditure which is incurred 'wholly, exclusively and necessarily in the performance of his duties'. Travelling expenses and certain other items of expenditure are considered separately below. The 'wholly and exclusively' part of the test is the same as that considered in **21.3.2** in relation to trading income (ITTOIA 2005, Pt 2), where duality of purpose is generally fatal to a claim for deduction.

The ITEPA 2003 test is more severe in two respects:

(a)   it contains the additional requirement of necessity, so that it must be shown that the employee's duties could not be performed without the expenditure in question;

(b)   it contains the additional requirement that the expenditure was incurred in the performance of the duties so that, for example, expenditure incurred when preparing for the duties (eg in finding the job through an agency) is not deductible.

26.5.2   Particular kinds of expenses

The ITEPA 2003 test is so severe that there are few examples of expenditure that will satisfy the test. In a few instances the position is, therefore, modified.

26.5.2.1   Travelling expenses

Deductibility of travelling expenses depends on a slightly different test in that the expenditure must be necessarily incurred in the performance of the duties; it need not be wholly and exclusively incurred. It is clear that the employee/director who incurs expenditure when travelling from one place of work to another can treat that expenditure as deductible. However, this must be distinguished from travelling from home to the place of work; this travel cannot be in the performance of the duties, because the performance will only commence when the employee gets to work.

26.5.2.2   Pension contributions

An employee, or director, is entitled to deduct his contributions to an occupational pension scheme or to a personal pension scheme (although if such contributions exceed certain limits the excess will not be deductible). On the other hand, National Insurance contributions of the employee or director are not deductible.

26.6   Collection of tax on employment income (ITEPA 2003, Part 11)

Tax on most employment income is deducted at source by the employer under the PAYE (Pay As You Earn) system and paid to HMRC on the basis of earnings received in the tax year. This applies to most earnings, whether cash or non-cash (only the tax on non-cash benefits which are not readily convertible into cash is not collected via PAYE). Tax is collected at the appropriate rates (basic and higher). The system works by HMRC allocating to each taxpayer who is a director or an employee a code number based on information relating to his earnings and allowances. This code number is communicated to the employer, who is provided with Tables which enable him to calculate how much tax should be deducted before the director or employee's earnings are paid to him. The tax is then paid by the employer to HMRC. Employees/directors are, therefore, taxed on their income sooner under PAYE than a sole trader or partner who is assessed under ITTOIA 2005, Pt 2 (see **30.2.1**).

26.7   National Insurance

After income tax, National Insurance contributions are the second largest source of receipts in the UK revenue system. Most of these contributions are made by employees and their employers in the form of 'Class 1' contributions on employees' earnings. The rate of payment depends on several factors (including whether the employee stands to benefit from the State Second Pension, 'S2P', formerly known as the State Earnings Related Pension Scheme – SERPS). Contributions from those 'contracted in' to the State Second Pension are higher than for those who are 'contracted out'. The basic (contracted in) rates for 2009/10 are set out at **26.7.1** and **26.7.2**.

26.7.1   Employee (primary) contributions – 2009/10

An employee only has to make National Insurance contributions if his earnings exceed the earnings threshold (currently £110 per week). If that is the case, payment rates on earnings are:

First £110 per week – nil
Between £110 and £844 per week – 11%
Above £884 per week – 1%

26.7.2   Employer (secondary) contributions – 2009/10

An employer only has to make contributions in respect of an employee whose earnings exceed £110 per week. The employer's rate of contribution for all earnings above that level is 12.8%. These contributions are in addition to those paid by the employee.

The employer may deduct its National Insurance contributions in calculating the taxable profit of the business for an accounting period, but an employee is not permitted to deduct his contributions when calculating his taxable income for a tax year. Contributions (like tax on employment income) are collected via the payroll.

Chapter 27

Taxation of Savings and Investment Income

27.1 Introduction

This chapter describes the tax treatment of the income received by those who invest in business, either by way of making a loan to the business, or by buying shares in a company.

27.1.1 Interest received on loans/debentures

Both individuals and companies regularly make loans with a view to receiving interest on the loan. In the case of an individual, the interest forms income chargeable to income tax under Pt 4, Ch 2 of the ITTOIA 2005. For a company, the interest is income chargeable to corporation tax, although the exact tax treatment of the interest depends on the reason for the loan (see **27.2.2**).

27.1.2 Income received by shareholders

A shareholder (whether an individual or a company) could receive payments from the company in which the shares are held (and relating to the shares) in a number of situations. The most common example of such payments are dividends, but other payments (see **27.3.1**) are also charged to tax and are collectively known as 'distributions'. The rules contained in Pt 4, Ch 3 of the ITTOIA 2005 are relevant in order to determine the amount of income tax (in the case of an individual shareholder) due on a distribution. Again, the rules for companies differ from those for individuals.

27.2 Taxation of interest

27.2.1 Income tax (ITTOIA 2005, Pt 4, Ch 2)

27.2.1.1 Interest received

For an individual who receives interest on a loan, Pt 4, Ch 2 of the ITTOIA 2005 charges income tax on interest received in the current tax year. When paid such interest, the lender will receive a sum that is net of income tax deducted at source at the rate of 20% by the borrower. The borrower pays the 20% deducted direct to HMRC. The lender must include the amount of gross interest in his total income for the tax year in question (see *Legal Foundations* for further details).

27.2.1.2 Deductible expenditure

There are no provisions in Pt 4, Ch 2 of the ITTOIA 2005, for expenditure of any description to be deducted in calculating the amount of income that is taxable. For example, an individual lender cannot use his income from this source to obtain tax relief on any pension contributions he may be making (although certain sums may be deductible from the lender's total income when lending to a close company or a partnership – see **23.2.3** and **25.2.4** for details).

27.2.2 Corporation tax (CTA 2009, Parts 5 and 6)

The way in which a company is taxed on the interest it receives varies according to the company's purpose in making the loan, with different treatment for loans made in the course of a trade and loans made by way of investment. The rules are contained in the 'loan relationship' regime introduced by Finance Act 1996. The detail of the rules is beyond the scope of this book but, in general terms, interest paid or received as part of a company's trade is included in calculating the company's trading profit, whereas interest received on loans made by way of investment is assessed under CTA 2009, ss 299–301.

27.3 Taxation of shareholders

27.3.1 Income tax on distributions (ITTOIA 2005, Pt 4, Ch 3)

27.3.1.1 Dividends

For an individual shareholder, Pt 4, Ch 3 of the ITTOIA 2005 charges income tax on company dividends received in the current tax year. The shareholder must include the amount of the gross dividend in his total income for the tax year in question. (The taxation of the gross dividend and the treatment of the dividend tax credit are described in *Legal Foundations*.)

27.3.1.2 Written-off loan to a participator in a close company (ITTOIA 2005, s 416)

When a 'close company' makes a loan to a shareholder, there may ultimately be income tax consequences for the shareholder (see **23.2.2** for details).

27.3.1.3 'Profit' on sale of shares back to a company (ICTA 1988, ss 219–229)

(a) Income tax treatment

A charge to income tax may be made when a shareholder sells his shares back to the company itself. The profit represented by the excess of the sale price over and above the issue price of the shares may be treated in the same way as a dividend (as described at **27.3.1.1**). (Note that it is not possible for the seller to recover the tax credit if he is not liable to income tax.)

(b) Capital gains tax treatment

The income tax treatment of a sale of shares back to a company described above does not always apply and the shareholder's profit may attract capital gains tax instead where certain conditions are satisfied. Broadly these conditions are:

(i)   the buying company must be a trading company and its shares must not be listed on a recognised stock exchange (AIM is not included in the definition of stock exchange for these purposes); and

(ii)   the purpose of the buy-back must not be to avoid tax; it must either be to raise cash to pay inheritance tax arising from a death or be for the benefit of the company's trade (this latter purpose might be achieved, for example, where the selling shareholder is at odds with the other shareholders so that the proper functioning of the company is best served by the dissenting shareholder selling his shares back to the company); and

(iii) the selling shareholder must have owned the shares being sold back for at least five years; and

(iv)   the seller must either be selling all of his shares in the company or at least substantially reducing his percentage shareholding to no more than 30% of the issued share capital of the company. (A 'substantial' reduction in the shareholding is a reduction of at least 25%.)

(Note: It may be difficult to decide whether all of the above conditions are met (especially in cases where the buy-back must be shown to be for the benefit of the company's trade). In such situations it is possible to apply to HMRC for advance clearance of the proposed tax treatment of the buy-back.)

(c) The importance of the distinction between the income tax and capital gains tax treatment of a buy-back

The question of whether the income tax basis or capital gains tax basis will apply to the sale of shares back to a company may be important to the selling shareholder in that a significant difference in his liability to tax may be involved.

If the capital gains tax basis applies, the availability of reliefs and exemptions (such as entrepreneurs' relief and the annual exemption) may significantly reduce his liability to that tax.

Alternatively he may prefer the income tax basis to apply, given that the 10% tax credit attaching to the 'profit' received by the seller will mean that there will be no further liability for a basic rate taxpayer. For a higher rate taxpayer, however, the effective rate at which the seller will pay income tax is 22.5% (the dividend upper rate of 32.5% less the 10% tax credit). This does not compare well with a rate of capital gains tax of 18%.

Which treatment is preferable will depend on the selling shareholder's own circumstances and it may be possible to structure the sale back to the company to ensure that the most favourable tax treatment is obtained. (The position is further complicated where the vendor did not acquire the shares directly from the company but as a result of a subsequent share transfer. In such circumstances, both an income tax and a CGT calculation may be required on the disposal – the detail of the treatment of such a disposal is outside the scope of this book.)

(Note: As the company that buys back the shares must pay stamp duty on the purchase, a buy-back may have tax consequences for both parties and so requires careful consideration. Above the de minimis threshold of £1,000 introduced by the Finance Act 2008, stamp duty on shares is charged at 0.5% of the consideration (rounded up to the nearest multiple of £5).)

27.3.1.4 Tax treatment of 'treasury shares'

Certain companies can (as described at **10.5.1**) hold shares 'in treasury' rather than cancelling them following a sale back to the company by a shareholder. Section 195 of the Finance Act 2003 contains the tax treatment of such shares. In outline, shareholders are governed by the rules described at **27.3.1.3** when selling the shares to the company and the company must pay stamp duty on the purchase; whilst the shares are held in treasury, they are treated as if they do not exist for tax purposes; and a transfer by the company of shares previously held in treasury is treated as if it is an issue of new shares by the company.

27.3.2 Income tax relief for an individual shareholder

There are no provisions in Pt 4, Ch 3 of the ITTOIA 2005, for expenditure of any description to be deducted in calculating the amount of income that is included in the individual shareholder's total income. To encourage individuals to invest in companies, however, the tax legislation does include two important income tax reliefs.

27.3.2.1 Income tax relief for a shareholder's borrowings (ITA 2007, ss 383, 392–395)

When an individual borrows in order to purchase ordinary shares in a close company that carries on a trade, or to lend to such a company, the relief described in **23.2.3** may be available.

27.3.2.2 Income tax relief under the Enterprise Investment Scheme (EIS)

When a qualifying individual invests money in a company whose shares qualify within the terms of the above scheme, a deduction from the individual's income tax liability is given in the tax year of the investment. The relief is described in *Legal Foundations*.

27.3.3 Corporation tax on distributions

27.3.3.1 Dividends (CTA 2009, s 1285)

If a company receives dividends from shares it holds in another UK company, these dividends (and the tax credit that attaches to them) will generally be classed as 'franked investment income'. The effect of such franked investment income on the shareholder company's corporation tax liability is described in **22.7.2**.

27.3.3.2 'Profit' on sale of shares back to a company (ICTA 1988, ss 208 and 219–229)

When a company buys back shares from a shareholder that is another company, it is necessary to decide how any profit on the sale will be treated for the purposes of the selling company's corporation tax calculation. If the buy-back falls within the capital gains rules (using the test set out at **27.3.1.3**), the profit will be taxed as part of the selling company's chargeable gains (see **22.4**). If the capital gains treatment does not apply, the profit will be treated as franked investment income (see **22.7.2**).

Chapter 28

Business Reliefs from CGT and IHT Available to Individuals

28.1 Introduction

Any business, however structured, is ultimately run for the benefit of individuals (although, in the case of sophisticated corporate structures, there may be many layers of ownership including institutional investors such as pension funds between the business and those individuals who stand to benefit from its long-term success).

This chapter considers the tax implications for individuals, with direct involvement in a business venture, when they realise their investment in some way. The relevant taxes in this situation are capital gains tax and inheritance tax and, having identified the possible charge to tax, it is then necessary to identify what (if any) exemptions and/or reliefs may be available to reduce the amount of tax payable.

28.2 The subject matter of a charge to tax

28.2.1 Sole trader

A sole trader may dispose of his business (or a part of it) which will comprise not only his tangible assets such as premises and fixtures but also his intangible asset of goodwill; disposal of these assets may have capital gains tax implications. (The tangible assets will also include trading stock and perhaps machinery and plant, in relation to both of which a disposal may have income tax implications rather than capital gains tax implications; the disposal of trading stock will be relevant to calculation of the final trading profit and the disposal of machinery and plant may result in a balancing charge or allowance for income tax purposes under the capital allowances system.) If the disposal is not a sale at full value, it may also have inheritance tax implications.

28.2.2 Partner

An individual partner may dispose of his interest in the partnership business, comprising his fractional share in each of the assets of the business. This is equally the case if the firm is selling its business in that every partner is then disposing of his interest in the business. In addition, a partner may dispose of a particular asset (most notably the business premises) which is owned by him individually although used by the firm. (The sale of a particular asset by the firm is dealt with in detail at **25.3**.)

28.2.3 Shareholder

An individual shareholder in a company may dispose of his shares in the company and, perhaps, a particular asset owned by him individually although used by the company.

28.3   When and how capital taxation applies: principles

Capital gains tax and inheritance tax are often referred to collectively as 'capital taxes', and this paragraph outlines the main occasions on which they will be chargeable in a business context.

28.3.1   Sale at full value

28.3.1.1   Capital gains tax

Where there is a disposal of assets (whether by a sole trader, an individual partner, partners acting together to sell a partnership asset, or a shareholder) and the disposal is a sale at full value, there may be a charge to capital gains tax in so far as there is a disposal of chargeable assets which have increased in value during the period of ownership. For full details of the steps involved in calculating capital gains tax, see *Legal Foundations*. In outline, the steps are as follows:

Step 1:   *Identify a chargeable disposal*

In a business context, the most common examples of chargeable assets are likely to be land and buildings, goodwill, company shares or the individual's interest in such assets (although, if the disposal proceeds form part of the individual's income (eg regular sales of land as part of a property developer's trade), they will normally form part of the individual's total income rather than be taxed as chargeable gains). Plant and machinery will rarely produce a chargeable gain for the reasons detailed at **21.4.3**.

Step 2:   *Calculate the gain (or loss)*

Proceeds of disposal
LESS
Costs of disposal
= Net proceeds of disposal
LESS
Other allowable expenditure
(eg acquisition cost, other incidental costs of acquisition, subsequent expenditure)
= GAIN or loss

Step 3:   *Apply reliefs*

(If the disponer made gains on more than one disposal during the tax year, the gains should be aggregated before Step 4.)

Step 4:   *Aggregate gains and losses*

Deduct annual exemption

Step 5:   *Apply the correct rate of tax*

28.3.1.2   Inheritance tax

There is no liability to inheritance tax on a sale at full value because there has been no 'transfer of value' under which the value of the disponer's estate is reduced.

28.3.2   Gift during lifetime

28.3.2.1   Capital gains tax

Where an individual makes a gift of a chargeable asset (or of his share in a chargeable asset in the case of a partner), this is a disposal which may give rise to a chargeable gain in the same way as a sale at full value except that in calculating the disponer's gain it is necessary to use the asset's market value at disposal (as opposed to sale price). The logic of this lies in the fact that the tax is imposed broadly on the increase in the asset's value during the period of ownership rather than on any gain in monetary terms that the disponer has actually realised.

28.3.2.2 Inheritance tax

Where an individual makes a gift of an asset, at the same time as being a disposal for capital gains tax purposes this is a disposition which reduces the value of his estate and hence is a transfer of value for inheritance tax purposes. For full details of the steps involved in calculating inheritance tax, see *Legal Foundations*.

In outline, the steps are as follows:

Step 1:   *Identify the transfer of value*

Step 2:   *Find the value transferred*

Step 3:   *Apply any relevant exemptions and reliefs:*

      (a)   spouse/civil partner or charity exemption

      (b)   agricultural property relief and/or business property relief

      (c)   lifetime only exemptions (eg annual exemption).

(Note: If the gift is to an individual (or some types of trusts) there will be no immediate charge to inheritance tax if any value transferred remains after Step 3 because it will be a 'PET', a potentially exempt transfer, and a charge will only arise if the transferor dies within seven years of the gift. In the case of an 'LCT', a lifetime chargeable transfer (broadly, a gift to a company or most types of trusts), tax may become payable immediately and the charge may increase if the transferor dies within seven years of the gift.)

Step 4:   *Calculate tax on a chargeable transfer at the appropriate rate (tapering relief may be available for transfers made more than three years before the transferor's death).*

28.3.3 Sale at an undervalue

Where a sale is at an undervalue, there may be liability to capital gains tax as in **28.3.2.1** on the net increase in the asset's value during the period of ownership and possible liability to inheritance tax on the loss to the disponer as a result of the gift element. The position is different if the disponer has sold at an undervalue merely as a result of making a bad bargain (eg through not recognising how much the asset is really worth). The implications of a sale at an undervalue with a gift element as distinguished from a bad bargain are considered separately below in relation to each of the possible charges to tax.

28.3.3.1 Capital gains tax

The significance of the distinction between a gift and a bad bargain is important to the calculation of the gain. If a sale is at an undervalue with a gift element, the gain, if any, will be calculated by reference to market value at disposal in the same way as with an outright gift; this prevents taxpayers avoiding capital gains tax by fixing an artificially low sale price which would correspondingly produce an artificially low gain. If the sale is a bad bargain, the gain, if any, will be calculated by reference to the actual sale price. The problem of distinguishing between the two is often avoided by provisions in the Taxation of Chargeable Gains Act 1992 on 'connected persons' (TCGA 1992, s 286). A disposal to a connected person will be deemed to be made at market value rather than at the actual sale price; 'connected persons' include the spouse/civil partner of the disponer or other close relatives of the disponer or his or her spouse/civil partner (including parents, grandparents, children, grandchildren and siblings (and the spouses/civil partners of those people) but not, for example, aunts or uncles or nephews or nieces); business partners are also connected persons, but a disposal between such partners which is negotiated on a commercial basis will be taken to be at the actual sale price.

28.3.3.2　Inheritance tax

Section 10(1) of the IHTA 1984 provides that a disposition is not a transfer of value if the transferor had no intention to transfer a gratuitous benefit. Thus if the transferor can prove that he made a bad bargain, having no intention to confer a gratuitous benefit on another person, the loss to his estate resulting from that bad bargain will not have any inheritance tax implications. As with the equivalent capital gains tax point, there may be difficulty in establishing this distinction, although again the concept of a 'connected person' is used. For inheritance tax purposes, the definition of connected person is wider than that for capital gains tax as it is extended to include aunts or uncles or nephews or nieces (or their spouses/civil partners) (IHTA 1984, s 270). If the transaction is with a connected person, the burden on the transferor of proving that there was no 'transfer of value' is heavier because he must show that there was no intention to confer a gratuitous benefit and that the transaction was on the same terms as if it had been made with a person with whom he was not connected.

Example 1

A, a sole trader, has decided to retire and to allow his son B to purchase the business from him. The net worth of the business is £100,000. B can only afford to pay £60,000 even by using all his savings and borrowing as much as he can. A sells to B at £60,000.

Capital gains tax: the fact that B is 'connected' to A is incidental on these facts because it is clearly a sale at an undervalue; A's gains must be calculated by reference to the market value of the chargeable assets of which he disposes.

Inheritance tax: again the fact that B is 'connected' to A is incidental because A is clearly going to be unable to prove that this was merely a bad bargain; A suffers a loss to his estate of £40,000 (the value of the business of £100,000 less the £60,000 paid for it) so that he has made a potentially exempt transfer which will become chargeable to inheritance tax if A dies within seven years (subject to exemptions and reliefs).

Example 2

C, a sole trader, receives an offer from DE Co Ltd (a company with which he has no connection) to purchase his business for £80,000. C accepts the offer and sells at this price without bothering to have the business professionally valued. In fact the business is worth at least £90,000.

Capital gains tax: the company is not 'connected' with C and therefore the transaction can be taken as being merely a bad bargain; the actual consideration will be used for calculation of C's gain.

Inheritance tax: since the company is not a connected person, C should have no difficulty in establishing that he had no intention to confer any gratuitous benefit on the company so that there are no inheritance tax implications.

28.3.4　Death

28.3.4.1　Capital gains tax (TCGA 1992, s 62)

It is a fundamental principle of capital gains tax that there can be no charge to the tax on death; technically, this position is achieved by providing that on death there is no disposal of assets. Also significant is the fact that any increase in the value of assets during the deceased's ownership will not attract any charge to capital gains tax because the personal representatives (and eventually the person who inherits an asset) are deemed to acquire the deceased's assets at their market value at the date of death.

28.3.4.2　Inheritance tax

On death, there is a deemed transfer of value by the deceased of his entire estate immediately before death (IHTA 1984, s 4(1)); also, any potentially exempt transfers made by the deceased in the seven years preceding his death become chargeable transfers as a result of his death.

The charge to inheritance tax is described in *Legal Foundations* but, in brief, is calculated as follows:

(a) inheritance tax will be assessed on any potentially exempt transfers (and reassessed on any lifetime chargeable transfers) made in the seven years preceding death (see **28.3.2.2**);

(b) inheritance tax will be assessed on the death estate using the following steps:

Step 1:   *Identify the transfer of value (the deemed transfer on death)*

Step 2:   *Find the value transferred*

Step 3:   *Apply any relevant exemptions and reliefs:*

     (a)   spouse/civil partner or charity exemption

     (b)   agricultural property relief and/or business property relief

Step 4:   *Calculate tax at the appropriate rates.*

28.4 Capital gains tax – business reliefs

Having established the chargeable gain on the disposal of a chargeable asset, the available reliefs should be considered. The reliefs described below relate to business assets of various kinds, and have been introduced over the years to encourage investment in business. (Other reliefs of less general application are considered in other titles in this series.) The reliefs considered below are:

(a) roll-over relief on the replacement of qualifying business assets;

(b) hold-over relief on gifts of business assets;

(c) deferral relief on reinvestment in EIS shares;

(d) roll-over relief on the incorporation of a business;

(e) entrepreneurs' relief.

Several of the reliefs require that, in order to qualify for relief, assets being disposed of and/or acquired must be used in a 'trade' or, in the case of company shares, be shares in a 'trading company'. For the meaning of 'trade', see **21.2.1**.

Where it exists, the trading requirement is very important as it is designed to deny relief to disposals of assets held for non-trading purposes (typically where assets are held instead as investments).

(Where an asset is described below as being required to be used in a trade, that also includes, where appropriate, use in a vocation or profession.)

28.4.1 Roll-over relief on the replacement of qualifying business assets (TCGA 1992, ss 152–159)

This relief is designed to encourage businesses to expand and thrive by allowing the capital gains tax due on the disposal of a 'qualifying asset' to be effectively postponed when the consideration obtained for the disposal is applied in acquiring another qualifying asset by way of replacement.

28.4.1.1 Conditions for the relief to apply

(a) Qualifying assets (TCGA 1992, s 155)

The principal qualifying assets for the purposes of the relief are land, buildings and goodwill.

The asset must be used in the trade of the business (as opposed to being held as an investment).

(Note:

(a)   company shares are *not* qualifying assets;

(b)   although 'fixed' plant and machinery is a qualifying asset, a sale of such an asset will rarely produce a gain (as most depreciate in value) and any roll-over relief when acquiring such assets will be restricted if they are wasting assets (TCGA 1992, s 154). What constitutes 'fixed' plant and machinery is, in itself, not straightforward. There is no statutory definition, so each case turns on its own facts, but claims are unlikely to succeed if the item in question is moveable and intended to be so to enable changes in the layout of the workplace.)

The relief can apply on the disposal of a qualifying asset owned by:

(i)   a sole trader and used in his trade;

(ii)   a partnership and used in the partnership trade;

(iii)   an individual partner and used in the partnership trade;

(iv)   an individual shareholder and used in the trade of the company in which he owns shares. The company must be the shareholder's 'personal company' (ie the individual must own at least 5% of the voting shares in the company).

Provided both the asset disposed of, and the asset acquired fall within the definition of qualifying assets, they do not have to be the same type of asset. For example, it is possible to sell qualifying goodwill, and roll-over the gain into the purchase of qualifying buildings.

(b) Time limits

For the relief to apply, the disposal and acquisition must take place within certain time limits. The replacement asset must be acquired within one year before or three years after the disposal of the original asset, unless an extended period is allowed by HMRC.

Example

If a sole trader disposes of a qualifying asset at the start of January 2010, a replacement qualifying asset would need to be acquired at some point in the period stretching from the start of January 2009 to the end of December 2012.

28.4.1.2   Application of the relief

If a qualifying asset is disposed of and, within the time limits, the proceeds of sale are used for the purchase of another qualifying asset to be used in a business, then any liability to capital gains tax from the disposal can be postponed (at least until the disposal of the replacement asset) by rolling-over the gain on the disposal of the original asset into the acquisition cost of the replacement asset. This means that the gain is notionally deducted from the acquisition cost of the replacement asset to give a lower acquisition cost for use in subsequent capital gains tax calculations. Thus a later disposal of the replacement asset may produce a gain that comprises both the rolled-over gain and any gain on the replacement asset itself (TCGA 1992, s 153 contains restrictions on the relief if part only of the value of the consideration on the disposal of the original asset is used to acquire the new asset).

Note that when an individual claims this relief the annual exemption cannot be set against the gain before it is rolled-over.

Any claim for relief must be submitted within four years after the 31 January following the tax year in which the replacement asset is acquired (or, if later, the original asset sold).

Example

In September 2009, H, a sole trader, sells some premises that he has owned since 1996 for £70,000. He makes a gain of £30,000 (it is his only chargeable disposal in the 2009/10 tax year). Six months later, H buys some more premises for £80,000. If H claims roll-over relief on the replacement of qualifying assets:

(a)   H will pay no CGT in 2009/10 as the gain on the disposal of the original premises is postponed;

(b)   for the purposes of future CGT calculations the replacement premises will be treated as being acquired for £50,000 (£80,000 less £30,000);

(c)   H will not be able to use his annual exemption for 2009/10.

Imagine that H then sells the new premises in 2012 for £125,000. The calculation of his gain will be:

Proceeds of disposal	125,000	
Less		
Adjusted acquisition cost	50,000	(without the effect of roll-over it would be 80,000)
Gain	75,000	(without the effect of roll-over it would be only 45,000)

Provided the qualifying conditions were met, the gain from the 2012 sale could itself be rolled-over.

(Note:

(a)   Although roll-over relief on the replacement of qualifying assets can apply in theory when a qualifying asset is given away, it would be unusual in practice for a donor to be so generous as to both make a gift and retain the CGT liability relating to that gift. The hold-over relief described at **28.4.2** is likely to be more relevant in these circumstances as liability for any future CGT on a disposal of the gifted asset passes to the donee under the terms of that relief.

(b)   The roll-over relief contained in ss 152–159 of the TCGA 1992, is also available in a modified form to companies – see **22.4.3**.)

28.4.2   Hold-over relief on gifts (and the gift element in sales at an undervalue) of business assets (TCGA 1992, s 165 and Sch 7)

Hold-over relief on gifts is available to an individual who disposes of 'business assets' by way of gift or, to the extent of the gift element, by way of sale at an undervalue. Like roll-over relief, hold-over relief does not exempt any of the chargeable gain, but instead acts to postpone any tax liability. The relief is designed to allow business assets to be given away without a tax charge falling on the donor (who would not otherwise have any sale proceeds to fund the tax).

28.4.2.1   Conditions for the relief to apply

(a)   Gift or gift element. The relief is only available on gifts, or on the gift element on a sale at an undervalue.

(b)   Only the gain relating to chargeable business assets can be held-over. 'Business assets' include the following:

(i)   assets which are used in the donor's trade or his interest in such assets. This applies to the assets of a sole trader or partnership;

(ii)   shares in a trading company which are not listed on a recognised stock exchange (AIM is not included in the definition of stock exchange for these purposes);

(iii)   shares in a *personal* trading company even if listed on a recognised stock exchange;

(iv)   assets owned by the shareholder and used by his *personal* trading company.

(To be a 'personal company', the individual must own at least 5% of the company's voting shares.)

Note: The relief does not apply to a gift of shares if the donee is a company.

(c)   For the relief to apply, both donor and donee must so elect (as the donee is effectively taking on the liability for any capital gains tax that eventually arises from the gift). The election must be made within four years after the 31 January following the tax year of the disposal (eg by 31 January 2015 for a disposal in 2009/10).

28.4.2.2   Application of the relief

To apply hold-over relief, the chargeable gain must be calculated in the usual way (taking market value as the consideration for the disposal) and then this gain will be deducted from the market value of the asset in order to establish an artificially low 'acquisition cost' for the donee.

When the donee eventually disposes of the asset, the artificially low acquisition cost (plus any qualifying expenditure – see **28.4.2.3**) is deducted from the sale price (on a sale at full value) or market value (on a gift) to find the gain of the donee. Thus the donee's gain will include the held-over gain plus any gain attributable to his own period of ownership. Having calculated the donee's chargeable gain, reliefs should be considered (including hold-over relief again if relevant). If the donee dies without having disposed of the asset, all gains then accumulated in respect of the asset will escape capital gains tax altogether.

Note that the donor cannot set the annual exemption against the gain before it is held over.

Example

J gives M, his son, the family business at a time when the business's chargeable assets are worth £100,000 and the total gains on those assets are £20,000. Eighteen months later M sells the business for £110,000 (he makes no other disposals in the same tax year).

(a)   J pays no CGT on the disposal to M.

(b)   J and M elect to hold-over J's gain on the disposal to M, so that M's adjusted acquisition cost is £80,000 (£100,000 less £20,000). J's annual exemption for the year cannot be deducted from the held-over gain.

(c)   on the sale of the business by M, his gain is:

	£
Sale price	110,000
Less: adjusted acquisition cost	80,000
Gain	30,000

M's annual exemption for the tax year of the sale can be used to reduce the gain.

28.4.2.3   Interaction with inheritance tax

In calculating the gain on any subsequent disposal by the donee as described in **28.4.2.2**, there is one item which may be deducted as an expense which would not usually occur. Given that this relief is only relevant to gifts or sales at an undervalue, the original disposal may lead to eventual charges to both inheritance tax on the original disposal (eg if a potentially exempt transfer is followed by the death of the donor within seven years) and capital gains tax (on the donee's eventual disposal) which will include the held-over gain from the original disposal. If a charge to inheritance tax does occur, the inheritance tax paid by the donee can be added to the acquisition cost of the asset, thus reducing the gain on the donee's eventual disposal. (The gain may be reduced to nil following this calculation, but it is not possible to use the inheritance tax charge to produce a loss for capital gains tax purposes.)

As most business assets qualify for 100% relief from inheritance tax (see **28.5.2**), such an inheritance tax charge will occur infrequently. An example of when it might occur is following a chargeable transfer of a minority holding of *quoted* shares (eg a gift followed by the donor's death within seven years). This transfer may qualify for hold-over relief for CGT purposes (as a shareholding of 5% or more of the company's shares) but not for inheritance tax business property relief (as it is not a controlling shareholding).

Example

M gives her 5% shareholding in B plc to her daughter D in September 2009 when the shares are valued at £100,000 (according to the price quoted on the Stock Exchange at the time). M acquired the shares several years previously – they were then valued at £30,000. There was no relevant expenditure to deduct in calculating M's gain. M and D claim hold-over relief on M's gain. M dies in January 2010 and D has to pay IHT of £40,000 in relation to the gift of shares from M (the PET becomes chargeable as a result of M's death within seven years and M's nil rate band had been exhausted by other gifts shortly before that to D).

In July 2010, D sells the shares for £110,000. She had no relevant expenditure to deduct in calculating her gain. Calculations for CGT purposes are as follows:

M's disposal (the gift to D)

	£
Disposal value	100,000
LESS	
Acquisition value	30,000
M's gain held over	70,000

D's disposal (sale)

	£
Disposal price	110,000
LESS	
Acquisition value as reduced by the gain held over on M's disposal (ie £100,000 less £70,000)	30,000
AND	
IHT paid by D as a result of M's PET becoming chargeable on the death of M	40,000
D's gain	40,000

D will be able to use her annual exemption for 2010/11 to reduce the gain further.

28.4.3 Deferral relief on reinvestment in EIS shares (TCGA 1992, s 150C and Sch 5B)

Unlimited deferral of capital gains arising on the disposal, by sale or gift, of any asset is available where an individual subscribes wholly for cash for shares in a company which qualifies under the Enterprise Investment Scheme (EIS). The Scheme is described in more detail in **Legal Foundations**. (Note: as the shares must be acquired for cash, this relief will not usually be available to a partner or sole trader who transfers his business to a company, as the shares acquired following such a transfer are usually issued in return for the non-cash assets of the business.)

28.4.4 Roll-over relief on incorporation of a business (TCGA 1992, s 162)

Where a business is transferred by a sole trader or individual partners to a new or established company in return for shares in the company, a disposal occurs for CGT purposes. Roll-over relief on incorporation is given to allow any gain on the disposal to be deferred. The relief postpones the CGT payable on the disposal given that no cash has been realised with which to pay the tax arising.

28.4.4.1 Conditions for the relief to apply

(a) The business must be transferred as a going concern. This means that the business must essentially be carried on as the same business albeit with a change of owner; if, for example, the business premises are transferred but a different business is then carried on by the company, this is not a transfer as a going concern.

(b) The whole gain can be rolled over only if the consideration is all in shares issued by the company. If, for example, the company 'pays' for the business as to 50% by an issue of shares but as to the other 50% by an issue of debentures (ie this amount is treated as a loan to the company), then roll-over relief can only apply to 50% of the gain.

(c)   The business must be transferred with all of its assets (although cash is ignored for this purpose). If, for example, a sole trader's business is transferred to a company as a going concern but ownership of the business premises is retained by the sole trader who will allow the company to use them, then roll-over relief will not apply.

28.4.4.2   Application of the relief

The gain on the disposal is rolled-over by notionally deducting it from the acquisition cost of the shares.

Note that the annual exemption cannot be used to reduce the gain before it is rolled-over.

Example

X decides to sell his sole trade to Y Co Ltd. The business is valued at £100,000 and X receives £100,000 worth of shares in Y Co Ltd in exchange for the business. If X makes a chargeable gain of £25,000 on the disposal to Y Co Ltd and he rolls-over the gain on incorporation, he will not pay any CGT on the disposal but the acquisition cost of his shares in Y Co Ltd will, for tax purposes, be £75,000 (£100,000 less the gain of £25,000). When X eventually sells or gives away his shares, therefore, he will only be able to deduct an acquisition cost of £75,000 when calculating his gain on the disposal of the shares.

Note: Where the conditions for the relief are met, HMRC will apply it automatically unless the taxpayer elects not to use it. This election must be made within two years after the 31 January following the tax year of the incorporation (eg by 31 January 2013 for incorporations in 2009/10). If, however, the shares acquired as a result of the incorporation are sold before the end of the tax year that follows the tax year of incorporation, the election must be made within one year after the 31 January following the tax year of incorporation (eg by 31 January 2012 for incorporations in 2009/10).

28.4.5   Entrepreneurs' relief (TCGA 1992, ss 169H–169S)

Entrepreneurs' relief was introduced in the Finance Act 2008 as a partial replacement for taper relief (which had applied to disposals between 6 April 1998 and 5 April 2008). The aim of entrepreneurs' relief is to remove part of the gain realised on certain business disposals from the charge to tax, thereby reducing the overall amount of CGT payable. The name 'entrepreneurs' relief' is something of a misnomer as there is no requirement that the business be new, innovative or risky in any way, although not all business interests qualify for the relief.

28.4.5.1   Conditions for the relief to apply

For the relief to apply, there has to be a 'qualifying business disposal'. The conditions for this vary depending on the type of interest being disposed.

(a) Sole trade or partnership interests

(i)   The disposal of the whole or part of a business (whether by a sole trader or an individual partner) may qualify. This includes situations both where:

    (a)   the business (or part of it) is sold as a going concern (not simply the disposal of individual asset(s) used in the business); and

    (b)   assets are sold off following cessation of the business (provided the assets were used in the business at the time of cessation).

(ii)   To be a qualifying disposal of part or the whole of a business, the interest in the business as a whole (as opposed to any one asset comprising it) must have been owned either:

    (a)   throughout the period of one year ending with the date of disposal; or

    (b)   throughout the period of one year ending with the cessation of the business (provided the disposal itself is within three years after that cessation).

(iii)   Where there is a qualifying disposal of a sole trade or partnership interest, only assets used for the purposes of the business carried on by the individual or partnership are eligible for relief. Company shares and securities and any other assets held as investments are specifically excluded from this definition.

Example

Jagat has run a graphic design business for 10 years. He decides to retire, and cannot find a buyer for the business as a whole so stops trading. Two years later he sells the premises from which he traded, realising a chargeable gain. This is a qualifying business disposal for the purposes of entrepreneurs' relief.

(b) Company shares

(i)   A disposal of company shares (including securities) may qualify for relief if:

    (a)   the company is a trading company and is the disponer's 'personal company' (so that he holds at least 5% of the ordinary share capital in the company and that holding gives at least 5% of the voting rights); and

    (b)   the disponer is an employee or officer (such as a director) of the company.

(ii)   For a qualifying disposal, the requirements detailed in (i) above must have been satisfied either:

    (a)   throughout the period of one year ending with the date of disposal; or

    (b)   throughout the period of one year ending with the date the company ceased to be a trading company (provided that the disposal itself is within three years of that cessation).

(iii)   To be a 'trading company', the company must not have activities that include 'to a substantial extent activities other than trading activities'. This will restrict the extent to which the company can hold cash reserves or investments whilst still meeting the definition.

Example

Kevin and Leanne each own 20% of the ordinary voting shares in KLR Optics Ltd, a company that makes precision lenses for scientific purposes. They formed the company together eight years ago and Kevin is the technical director, but Leanne resigned from her role in the company four years ago when she decided to take a career break to look after her children. They each sell their shareholding at a large profit when a competitor offers to buy the company. Kevin makes a qualifying business disposal but Leanne does not.

(c) Associated disposals

(i)   Sometimes assets used by a business are not owned as part of the business but separately by an individual. Disposals of such assets owned by an individual outside of the business may qualify for relief if the asset was used for the purposes of the business run either by:

    (a)   a partnership in which the individual was a partner; or

    (b)   a company in which the individual's shares qualify under '(b) Company shares' above.

(ii)   Disposals of such assets qualify only if the disposal of them is associated with a qualifying disposal of the individual's interest in the partnership or company shares as the case may be, and if the disposal is part of the withdrawal of the individual from the business carried on by the partnership or company.

(iii)   To be a qualifying disposal, the asset in question must have been used throughout the period of one year ending with the earlier of:

(a)   the disposal of the interest or shares to which the disposal of the asset is associated; or

(b)   the cessation of the business of the partnership or company which used the asset.

Example

Miles sells his interest in a doctor's partnership to Neil after 20 years' involvement in the practice. Throughout that period, Miles had allowed the partnership to run its business from a surgery in some land he owns near his home. At the same time as selling his interest to Neil, Miles sells the surgery to the continuing partners. Both the sale of the partnership interest and the associated disposal of the surgery are qualifying business disposals.

(Note: further conditions apply if the shares being disposed of are in a company that is part of a group, or if the business or shares are owned as part of the assets of a trust).

28.4.5.2   Application of the relief

If the conditions for the relief are satisfied, the relief operates to reduce the amount of the gain chargeable to tax following a two-stage process:

(a)   The gains arising from the qualifying business disposal are reduced by any losses made as part of the disposal (for example, a sole trader might sell his business and, in the process, make a gain on the goodwill but a loss on the premises).

(b)   If there is any net gain remaining after (a) above, it is reduced by $\frac{4}{9}$ths. There is, however, a restriction on the relief, in that an individual cannot claim the reduction for more than £1 million of qualifying net gains realised on or after 6 April 2008. This cap is a lifetime restriction, so that only £1 million of net gains can qualify for the relief for each individual, whether those gains arise from just one business disposal or from a number of disposals spread over time.

(Note: there are further restrictions on the amount of gain on an associated disposal that can qualify for relief if the asset in question was not used for the purposes of the business throughout the disponer's period of ownership, if only part of the asset was used by the business, if the individual was involved in the business for only part of the time the asset was in use, or if rent was charged for the use of the asset.)

Example 1

Otis is a sole trader who makes a net gain on a qualifying business disposal of £450,000. He has never made any such disposals before. The gain is reduced by $\frac{4}{9}$ths (£200,000) so that only £250,000 is chargeable to tax. Otis can make a further £550,000 of net gains in future that can qualify for the relief.

Example 2

Petra makes a qualifying net gain of £40 million when she sells her shares in a successful clothing company. She has not made any such disposals before. The first £1 million of the gain is reduced by $\frac{4}{9}$ths (£444,445) so that only £555,555 of it is chargeable. The remaining £39 million remains fully chargeable to tax so that her total chargeable gain is £39,555,555. The relief has been exhausted and will not be available on any future disposals Petra makes.

Any claim for entrepreneurs' relief must be made on or before the first anniversary of the 31 January following the tax year in which the qualifying disposal was made (eg by 31 January 2012 for a disposal in 2009/10).

28.4.6   Annual exemption (TCGA 1992, s 3)

In each tax year, a prescribed amount (the first £10,100 for 2009/10) of an individual's gains is exempt from capital gains tax. If the exemption is unused (in whole or in part) for any year, there is no provision for it to be carried forward and so any unused exemption is lost.

As mentioned above, the annual exemption cannot be used on a gain which is being rolled-over or held-over.

28.4.7   Tax rates and payment

28.4.7.1   Tax rate

The Finance Act 2008 introduced a flat rate of 18% for all taxable gains realised in a tax year.

28.4.7.2   Payment date

Any capital gains tax due in respect of a tax year is normally payable on or before 31 January following the end of the tax year. The instalment option may be available in very limited circumstances (see below).

28.4.7.3   Instalment option (TCGA 1992, s 281)

In limited circumstances, payment may be made by 10 annual instalments, the first being on the usual date for payment of capital gains tax (31 January following the tax year of the disposal), with interest being charged on the outstanding tax.

The conditions are:

(a)   the disposal giving rise to the capital gains tax must have been a gift; and

(b)   hold-over relief must not be available (as opposed to merely not claimed); this means that the instalment option will rarely be relevant to disposal of business interests by sole traders, partners or shareholders in private companies except in relation to assets of the business which are investments; and

(c)   the property disposed of must have been either land, a controlling shareholding in any company, or any shareholding (whether controlling or otherwise) in a company whose shares are unquoted.

> **Example**
>
> L gives away some land (held as an investment) in June 2009. He makes no other disposals during the 2009/10 tax year. His gain is £60,000.
>
> L can deduct his annual exemption of £10,100 from the gain of £60,000 to give a taxable amount of £49,900. Tax at 18% on this amount is £8,982 and the tax can be paid by 10 annual instalments, the first instalment being due on 31 January 2011.

28.4.8   Interrelation between reliefs and exemption

On any given disposal realising a gain it is possible that more than one relief could apply to it and that the disposer's annual exemption is available so that the taxpayer may have to choose which relief(s) to claim.

28.4.8.1   Roll-over relief on the replacement of qualifying assets

If a gain is to be rolled over, that gain cannot be reduced by entrepreneurs' relief (if available) before being rolled-over and nor can the annual exemption be set against it. This roll-over relief cannot generally be used in conjunction with hold-over relief, roll-over relief on incorporation, or EIS deferral.

28.4.8.2 Hold-over relief on gifts of business assets

If a gain is to be held-over, HMRC states that the gain cannot be reduced by entrepreneurs' relief (if available) before being held-over and nor can the donor's annual exemption be set against it. The relief cannot generally be used in conjunction with the roll-over reliefs or EIS deferral.

28.4.8.3 Roll-over relief on the incorporation of a business

To the extent that shares are received in consideration for the transfer of the business, entrepreneurs' relief (if available) cannot be applied to reduce the gain prior to the roll-over, and nor can the annual exemption. The relief in these circumstances cannot be used at the same time as roll-over relief on replacement of qualifying assets (shares do not qualify) nor hold-over relief (there is usually no gift) nor EIS deferral (the consideration for the shares is not in cash).

If, however, part of the consideration is in cash and part in shares it might, in certain circumstances, be possible to use the roll-over relief on incorporation for that proportion of the gain attributable to the part of the business exchanged for shares, leaving entrepreneurs' relief and the annual exemption to be used on the proportion of the gain attributable to the part of the business sold for cash. (EIS deferral may also occasionally be available where cash is received in this way and used to buy shares in an EIS qualifying company.)

28.4.8.4 EIS deferral

It is possible to defer any gain after the application of entrepreneurs' relief by investing it in qualifying EIS shares. The deferred gain cannot be reduced by the annual exemption but, as the entire sale proceeds from the 'old' asset do not have to be reinvested in the EIS shares, it should be possible to hold back sufficient cash from the sale to leave a small amount of the gain 'undeferred' and the annual exemption can be set against this. The interrelation of this relief and the hold-over and roll-over reliefs is set out at **28.4.8.1–28.4.8.3**.

28.4.8.5 Entrepreneurs' relief

From the above it can be seen that entrepreneurs' relief cannot be applied before using any of the hold-over or roll-over reliefs but that it can be applied before any remaining gain is deferred using EIS relief. The annual exemption, if available, can be used to reduce gains remaining after any entrepreneurs' relief is applied.

28.4.8.6 The annual exemption

This is the final point to consider when looking at the various business reliefs and exemptions, and its interrelation with each of the other reliefs is set out above.

Example

Malcolm has run a manufacturing business as a sole trader for 15 years (his only business venture). In June 2009, he gives the business to Patsy, his daughter. Malcolm's accountant advises him that the chargeable gain on the chargeable business assets is £135,000.

Option 1 – Malcolm and Patsy can claim hold-over relief for the £135,000 gain. This avoids Malcolm paying any CGT, but means HMRC will state that he cannot use entrepreneurs' relief or his annual exemption in respect of the gain. Patsy, therefore, effectively takes over liability for the whole £135,000 gain when she disposes of the business in future.

Option 2 – Malcolm could claim entrepreneurs' relief so that the £135,000 gain is reduced by $\frac{4}{9}$ ths (£60,000). The remaining gain of £75,000 could be further reduced by Malcolm's annual exemption of £10,100, leaving a taxable amount of £64,900 to be taxed at 18%. The resulting bill of £11,682 would be Malcolm's liability to pay by 31 January 2011.

Assuming Malcolm is able to fund the tax bill arising from Option 2, he will have a choice of which option to take. The best option overall is likely to depend on whether Patsy will continue to run the business for long enough to qualify for entrepreneurs' relief in her own name. If she does then Option 1 may be most attractive – it will not matter that Malcolm did not claim any entrepreneurs' relief to reduce the gain as Patsy will be able to do so instead (assuming that Patsy is at no risk of breaching her lifetime entrepreneurs' relief threshold).

28.5 Inheritance tax – business reliefs

As described in **28.3.2**, a relief may be available to reduce the value transferred by a transfer of value for inheritance tax purposes. The reliefs should be considered after applying any spouse/ civil partner or charity exemption (see *Legal Foundations*). The reliefs are designed to try to ensure that businesses are not unnecessarily broken up by the burden of inheritance tax following gifts made during the donor's life or on his death.

28.5.1 Agricultural property relief (IHTA 1984, ss 115–124)

28.5.1.1 Sole traders and partners

This relief operates to reduce the agricultural value of agricultural property (as defined) by a certain percentage. The 'agricultural value' is the value of the property if it were subject to a perpetual covenant prohibiting its use other than for agriculture. This will be significantly less than its market value if, for example, the land has development potential (eg for housing). That part of the property's value which is over and above its 'agricultural value' will not qualify for any agricultural property relief, but may qualify for business property relief (see **28.5.1.3**). A reduction of 100% is allowed where either (broadly) the transferor had the right to vacant possession immediately before the transfer or where the property was subject to a letting commencing on or after 1 September 1995. A reduction of 50% is allowed in other cases. Further conditions which must also be satisfied for any relief are either that the property was occupied by the transferor for the purposes of agriculture for the two years prior to the transfer or that it was owned by him for the seven years prior to the transfer and was occupied by someone throughout that period for the purposes of agriculture.

28.5.1.2 Shareholders

This relief is also available where the agricultural property is held by a company in which the transferor of shares had control. The value of the shares may be reduced by the appropriate percentage (100% or 50%) where the value of the shares is attributable to the agricultural value of the company's agricultural property. The company's occupancy or ownership of the land (for two years or for seven years (see **28.5.1.1**)) is treated as that of the transferor of shares and the transferor must also have held the shares for the qualifying two- or seven-year period (as the case may be).

28.5.1.3 Relationship with business property relief

Agricultural property relief is given in priority to business property relief (see **28.5.2**), but any of the value transferred not reduced by agricultural property relief may qualify for business property relief.

28.5.2 Business property relief (IHTA 1984, ss 103–114)

This relief operates to reduce the value transferred by a transfer of value of relevant business property by a certain percentage.

28.5.2.1 Conditions for the relief to apply

(a) Relevant business property

The amount of relief given depends on the type of property being transferred.

(i)   A reduction of 100% of the value transferred is allowed for transfers of value where the value is attributable to certain defined types of 'relevant business property' (meaning that there will be no charge to inheritance tax in respect of those assets). These are:

(a)   a business or an interest in a business (including a partnership share);

(b)   company shares that are not listed on a recognised stock exchange (AIM is not included in the definition of stock exchange for these purposes). Only the value of the shares attributable to business/trading activities is eligible for the relief.

(ii)   A reduction of 50% of the value transferred is allowed for transfers of value of any other assets that qualify as relevant business property. They are:

(a)   company shares that are listed on a recognised stock exchange if the transferor had voting control of the company immediately before the transfer;

(b)   land, buildings, machinery or plant owned by the transferor personally but used for business purposes by a partnership of which he is a member, or by a company (whether quoted or unquoted) of which he has voting control.

Note: Voting control, for these purposes, means the ability to exercise over 50% of the votes on all resolutions. Such control may be denied by a provision in the company's articles of association that gives weighted voting rights on certain matters (eg a *Bushell v Faith* clause on a resolution to dismiss a director). The purpose and effect of such an article will be to prevent, for example, a majority shareholder from exercising his normal voting control on those matters and thus deprive him of control.

In assessing whether or not a person has voting control, separate shareholdings of spouses or civil partners can, in certain circumstances, be taken as one, so that if the combined percentage of the votes gives the couple voting control then the test will be satisfied (IHTA 1984, s 269).

(b) Time limits

(i)   Transferor's ownership

To attract any relief at all, the asset or assets in question must have been owned by the transferor *for at least two years* at the time of the transfer or, broadly, must be a replacement for relevant business property where the combined period of ownership is two years (this would include the situation where a sole trader or individual partner incorporated his business; the shares in the company he received in return would be relevant business property). If property is inherited from a spouse or civil partner, the surviving spouse/civil partner is deemed to have owned the property from the date it was originally acquired by the deceased spouse/civil partner (but this rule does not apply to lifetime transfers between spouses/civil partners).

(ii)   Transferee's ownership

Where there is a lifetime transfer that is followed by the death of the transferor within seven years, the relief given at the time of the lifetime transfer will be withdrawn unless the transferee still owns the business property (or qualifying substituted property) at the date of the transferor's death (or, if earlier, the transferee's own death).

28.5.2.2   Application of the relief

A number of further points must be considered when applying the relief (at 100% or 50% as the case may be).

(a)   The transfer need not be of the transferor's entire interest in the business or his entire shareholding.

(b)   Where a person has entered into a contract for sale of his interest in a business (or his company shares), his interest is then taken to be in the proceeds of sale; since cash is not relevant business property, no relief will be available where there is a binding contract for sale. Examples of when such a situation may arise are:

(i)   partnership – under the terms of a partnership agreement which provides that on a partner's retirement or death, for example, the continuing partners *will* buy and the former partner (or his PRs) *will* sell the share of the former partner (as opposed to there merely being an option to sell/purchase);

(ii)   company – under the terms of a shareholders' agreement which provides that on the occurrence of a given event, for example the shareholder's death, the shareholder's PRs *will* sell to the remaining shareholders who *will* buy those shares. (Again, the problem can be avoided by the use of an option to sell/purchase.)

Example 1

A is a 60% shareholder in XY plc (a quoted company) which he established many years ago. He gives half of his shares to his daughter on her twenty-first birthday. Three years later he gives the other half of his holding to his son on his twenty-first birthday. A dies in the following year.

Providing A's daughter still owns the shares on A's death (when the transfer becomes chargeable), the value transferred will be reduced by 50%. The gift to A's son will not qualify for any business property relief because a 30% holding in a quoted company is not relevant business property.

Example 2

For many years C and D have owned 55% and 25% respectively of the shares in a private company whose articles are in the form of Table A; they have also owned the business premises in equal shares as tenants in common. They are both killed in a road accident and their entire estates are inherited by C's son and D's daughter respectively.

C's shareholding and D's shareholding both qualify for 100% business property relief. C's interest in the premises qualifies for business property relief at 50% because his shareholding gave 'control'; D's interest in the premises does not qualify for business property relief at all.

Example 3

For many years E, F and G have been partners, sharing profits and losses equally; E and F have also owned the business premises in equal shares as tenants in common. There is no provision in their partnership agreement dealing with the purchase and sale of assets on the death or retirement of a partner. E and F are both killed in a road accident and their entire estates are inherited by E's son and F's daughter respectively.

The interest in the business of each partner qualifies for 100% business property relief and also each partner's interest in the premises qualifies for business property relief at 50%. (No business property relief at all would have been available if there was a partnership agreement under which there was a binding contract for the purchase and sale of the partners' interests.)

It can be seen that more favourable treatment is given to partners who own assets used by their business than to shareholders who own assets used by their company.

28.5.3   Instalment option (IHTA 1984, ss 227 and 228)

Provided the requirements described below are met, payment of IHT can be made by ten annual instalments, the first being due when the tax would normally be due.

28.5.3.1   Qualifying assets

The instalment option is only available in relation to tax on the following assets:

(a)   land;

(b)   a business or an interest in a business;

(c)   shares (whether quoted or unquoted) which gave the transferor control;

(d)   in certain circumstances, non-controlling shares which are not listed on a recognised stock exchange, for example:

(i)   where the shares are worth over £20,000 and constitute at least 10% of the nominal value of the company's issued share capital; or

(ii)   where HMRC is satisfied that payment of tax in a lump sum would cause undue hardship; or

(iii) where the IHT attributable to the shares and any other instalment option property in the estate amounts to at least 20% of the IHT payable on the estate following the deemed transfer of value made on death.

28.5.3.2   Application of the relief

The instalment option is only available in certain circumstances, primarily:

(a)   where the recipient of a PET or LCT is paying the inheritance tax. The instalment option applies where IHT is payable on the transfer, or where IHT (or additional IHT) becomes payable as a result of the transferor's death within seven years of the transfer and the transferee still owns the original asset (or a qualifying replacement) at the date of the death. If the asset is later sold, the outstanding tax must then be paid;

(b)   where personal representatives are paying the tax. The instalment option applies where the transfer of value was the deemed transfer on death.

Interest is only charged on the outstanding tax if the asset in question is land which is not business or agricultural land, or is shares in an investment company, except that, if an instalment is in arrears, interest then becomes chargeable on the overdue instalment.

28.6 Summaries and checklists

(1) The occasions for a capital tax charge against an individual are:

CGT	IHT
Disposal by sale	Lifetime chargeable transfer (LCT)
Disposal by gift	PET where death occurs within seven years
[NOT death]	Death

(2) The possible business reliefs include:

CGT	IHT
Roll-over relief on replacement of qualifying assets	Agricultural property relief
Hold-over relief (gifts)	Business property relief
Roll-over relief on incorporation of a business	
Deferral relief on reinvestment in EIS shares	
Entrepreneurs' relief	

(3) When to consider the CGT reliefs:

Depending on the client's circumstances, one or more of the CGT reliefs listed at (2) above may be available on the disposal of a business interest, and a choice as to which relief to use may have to be made. Some examples of common scenarios are given below, along with the reliefs that may apply to the gain.

(a) Sale of sole trade or share in partnership:

   (i)   entrepreneurs' relief (+ annual exemption); or

   (ii) roll-over relief on the replacement of qualifying assets

(b) Gift of sole trade or share in partnership:

   (i)   entrepreneurs' relief (+ annual exemption); or

   (ii) hold-over relief.

(c) Sale of company shares:

   (i)   entrepreneurs' relief (+ annual exemption).

(d) Gift of company shares:

   (i)   entrepreneurs' relief (+ annual exemption); or

   (ii) hold-over relief.

(e) Transfer of sole trade or partnership to a company:

   (i)   roll-over relief on incorporation; or

   (ii) entrepreneurs' relief (+ annual exemption).

Note:

(1) In any of the above scenarios, consideration should also be given to the possibility of EIS deferral relief if the disponer is considering investing cash in a qualifying EIS company within the permitted time period surrounding the disposal.

(2) In scenarios (b) and (d), where gifts are being made, consideration should also be given to IHT and the availability of business property relief.

Summary of Main Rates and Allowances

Value Added Tax

Rates:	Standard rate (before 1 January 2010)	15%
	Standard rate (on or after 1 January 2010)	17.5%
Registration threshold:		£68,000

Income Tax – 2009/10

Rates:

Non-savings/dividend income	below basic rate limit (£37,400)	20%
	above basic rate limit	40%
Savings income	below starting rate for savings limit (£2,440) (applicable only to extent non-savings/dividend income is less than £2,440)	10%
	below basic rate limit (applicable only to extent non-savings/dividend income is less than £37,400)	20%
	above basic rate limit	40%
Dividend income	below basic rate limit (applicable only to extent other income is less than £37,400)	10%
	above basic rate limit	32.5%

Income Tax Allowances:

Personal allowance	£6,475

Capital Gains Tax – 2009/10

Rates:

Individuals: 18% flat rate

Annual exempt amount:

Individuals	£10,100

Inheritance Tax

Rates:	(for transfers on or after 6 April 2009)	
	£0 to £325,000	nil %
	over £325,000	40%

Transfers on death

Full rates apply.

Lifetime transfers

(a) Potentially exempt transfers

Gifts to individuals, and gifts into certain trusts.

(i)   On or within seven years of death

On death, the full rates apply with a tapered reduction in the tax payable on transfers as follows:

Years between gift and death	Percentage of full charge
0–3	100
3–4	80
4–5	60
5–6	40
6–7	20

Note: The scale in force at date of death applies

(ii)   More than seven years before death – gift is exempt therefore NIL tax payable.

(b) Chargeable transfers

Gifts to most trusts and gifts involving companies.

At the time of gift, half the full rates apply. If the gift also falls within seven years of death, (a)(i) above applies but the lifetime tax will be credited against tax due on death.

Corporation Tax (effective rate) – Financial Year 2009

Profits:	£0–£300,000	21%
	£300,001–£1,500,000	29.75%
	Over £1,500,000	28%

Stamp Duty – main rates on sales – 2009/10

Shares and securities	
£0–1,000	Nil
Over £1,000	0.5%
(rounded up to nearest £5)	

Stamp Duty Land Tax

Consideration:

£0–125,000* (residential land), £0–150,000 (non-residential land)	Nil
£125,001*–£250,000 (residential land), £150,001–£250,000 (non-residential land)	1%
£250,001–£500,000 (both residential land and non-residential land)	3%
Over £500,000 (both residential land and non-residential land)	4%

* Before 1 January 2010, the threshold for residential land is £175,000

Note: Special rules apply to leases.

Part V Summary –
Key Business Taxation Principles

Topic	Summary	References
The lawyer's role	A lawyer advising a business on tax matters must, of course, understand the way in which relevant taxes are calculated. This is, however, only a means to an end. The lawyer's wider role is to help enable the business to structure its tax affairs in the most efficient manner possible within the legal framework provided by legislation, case law and professional practice. This summary highlights some of the important reliefs and exemptions that exist for each tax covered in Part V and which assist the lawyer in that role.	
Corporation tax – liability	Corporation tax should be considered in relation to the income and chargeable gains of companies.	
Corporation tax – income profits	In relation to its trading profits, a company will seek to maximise its available deductible (income) expenditure and capital allowances.	**21.3**
	The amount of any capital allowance will depend on the type of expenditure and date of the expenditure.	**21.4**
	It may be possible to set a company's trading losses against other profits of the company, depending on the circumstances surrounding the loss.	**22.3**
Corporation tax – chargeable gains	A company's chargeable gains may be relieved in a number of ways. Reliefs include roll-over relief (on replacement of qualifying assets), Corporate Venturing Scheme and the exemption for disposals of substantial shareholdings.	**22.4**
Corporation tax – special provisions	Companies defined as being 'close' or within a 'group' are subject to anti-avoidance measures but also provide planning opportunities to mitigate corporation tax for the company and/or income tax for shareholders in the company.	**Chapter 23**
Income tax – liability	Income tax should be considered in relation to the income of individuals, including sole traders, partners and shareholders.	

Topic	Summary	References
Income tax – trading income	For a business with trading income, relief may be provided by the capital allowances regime.	**21.4**
	It may be possible to set trading losses made by an individual against his or her other income (and possibly capital gains), depending on the circumstances surrounding the loss.	**24.4**
	The date of payment of tax can be adjusted depending on when a business's accounting period ends. For all individuals, use should be made of any allowable reliefs and the personal allowance for each tax year.	**24.2, 24.3** and **25.2**
Income tax – employment income	For employees, the ITEPA 2003 contains rules on what income is taxable and what deductions are allowable. Payment is largely governed by the PAYE system.	**Chapter 26**
Income tax – savings income	Interest and dividends have special rules, including deduction of tax at source and tax credits.	**Chapter 27**
Capital gains tax (CGT) – liability	CGT should be considered in relation to chargeable disposals made by individuals, including sole traders, partners and shareholders.	
CGT – reliefs	A variety of reliefs exist which may be of assistance depending on the type of disposal in question. All are subject to conditions on availability and application. Key reliefs in a business context include roll-over relief (on the replacement of qualifying assets), hold-over relief (on gifts of business assets), roll-over relief on incorporation (of an unincorporated business) and entrepreneurs' relief. Where possible, use should also be made of an individual's annual exemption for each tax year.	**28.4**
Inheritance tax (IHT) – liability	IHT should be considered in relation to transfers of value by individuals, including sole traders, partners and shareholders.	
IHT – reliefs	The key relief in a business context is business property relief. Its availability depends on the length of ownership of the asset in question by the transferor, the type of asset and its use, and the retention of the asset by the transferee (following a lifetime transfer). Other reliefs which may be of use in transferring business assets include the spouse/civil partner exemption and the annual exemption.	**28.5**

Part VI

CHOOSING THE FORM OF BUSINESS ORGANISATION

Where a person decides to set up a business, consideration should be given to whether to trade as a sole trader or as a limited company. Similarly, where two or more persons decide to set up a business, they should consider whether to trade as a partnership or as a limited company.

Chapter 29
General Considerations: Liability

29.1 Introduction

Often, the differences in tax treatment of the self-employed and of the incorporated business have a significant bearing on the choice of the form of business organisation. Where these differences are not critical, a number of other factors are significant. This chapter considers, first, the factor which is the most important in practice: the scope for the individuals involved to be shielded from the risk of personal insolvency by the limited liability enjoyed through trading as a limited company. The main examples of other factors are then discussed, in outline, although the significance of any of these factors will vary according to particular circumstances.

29.2 Liability for debts

29.2.1 Directors

The general position is that directors are agents of the company, and as such are not normally liable for their actions or for the company's debts.

In a number of circumstances, directors are personally liable for what they have done or failed to do. Examples include the following.

29.2.1.1 Personal guarantees

Personal guarantees may be required, for example, for repayment of the company's overdraft in the event of the company's failure or for satisfying the company's obligations under a lease. In theory, anyone dealing with the company might seek guarantees from the directors in this way, but these two examples are the main ones.

29.2.1.2 Fraudulent trading or wrongful trading (IA 1986, ss 213 and 214)

Directors may be ordered to make a contribution to the company's assets in the company's liquidation.

29.2.1.3 Penalties under the Companies Acts and other Acts

Penalties under the Companies Acts are imposed, for example, for default in filing returns and documents with the Registrar of Companies or in maintaining the company's own records (eg, CA 2006, s 858).

Many other Acts have provisions imposing liability on directors, officers and managers if the company is found guilty of an offence, for example, under s 37 of the Health and Safety at Work etc Act 1974.

29.2.1.4 Breach of duty to the company

Directors may be liable to their company for damages and/or an account for profit if they are in breach of their general ('fiduciary') duties (see **6.6**).

29.2.1.5 Signature of certain documents

A person who signs a document, including a cheque, could be personally liable if it is not clear that they are signing for and on behalf of the company. Often, it will be obvious that the document is a company one, for example a printed invoice with the company's name on it, and that the individual is only authenticating it as a company document (*Badgerhill Properties Ltd v Cottrell* [1991] BCLC 805).

29.2.2 Shareholders

The liability of a shareholder in a limited company is limited to paying the agreed price for his shares and usually this is paid in full at, or within a short time after, allotment by the company. The main, albeit unusual, example of possible personal liability for a shareholder is where he has been a party to fraudulent trading.

29.2.3 Partners and sole traders

Partners and sole traders are fully liable for all the debts of the business. A partner has a right of contribution from his fellow partners, but if they are unable to contribute he is liable without limit. Sole traders and partners live with the threat of bankruptcy on a daily basis, either because of financial misfortune or because of litigation. In the case of a partnership, this could be due to the misdeeds of another partner and not through their own fault.

29.3 Raising finance

29.3.1 Loans

A person lending to any business will usually seek security for repayment of the loan. Companies, partnerships and sole traders can all create fixed charges over their assets as security. However, only a company is able to create a floating charge. Although the floating charge is an inferior form of security compared with a fixed charge, nevertheless it affords the company the opportunity to use, for example, its stock-in-trade and future assets as security for its borrowing. Therefore, a company has greater scope than a partnership or a sole trader for raising loan finance.

29.3.2 Capital

A limited company which asks a person to introduce capital by becoming a shareholder has the benefit of being able to assure the investor of limited liability. A partnership which asks a person to introduce capital and become a partner is asking that person to accept unlimited liability for all the debts of the partnership incurred after he becomes a partner.

29.4 Management structure

A company has a prescribed structure which facilitates the separation of management functions from capital investment in the company. Management functions are exercised, broadly, by the directors and relatively few (albeit major) functions are reserved to the shareholders in general meeting. It follows that shareholders have no authority (actual or apparent) to act in the management of the company's business.

A partnership is at liberty to organise itself in such a way that certain partners exercise management functions and the other partners are only consulted on major issues (as identified in their agreement). However, so far as an outsider is concerned, any partner may have apparent authority to act in management and may therefore bind the firm.

29.5 Status

There may be a feeling on the part of persons dealing with the business that a company is a more substantial business medium than a partnership or a sole trader. Such persons may therefore be more willing to deal with a company.

29.6 Formality in setting up

A partnership can be set up without any formality (or expense) since it is simply a question of applying the definition of a partnership to a business relationship in order to discover whether or not a partnership exists. By contrast, the CA 2006 imposes formalities on the formation of a company, in that prescribed documents must be lodged with the Registrar of Companies.

This difference in formality between companies and partnerships may have less substance than at first appears. The reason is that it will always be advisable for persons entering into partnership to have an agreement drawn up which provides comprehensive treatment of all present and future aspects of their relationship. Failure to do this may lead to problems sooner or later. In practice there may well be a similar degree of formality involved in the formation of both a partnership and a company.

29.7 Publicity of information

A company must make public a range of information about its affairs, its directors and its shareholders by filing returns and documents with the Registrar of Companies. This information includes information as to its year-end accounts, although many companies will qualify as 'small companies' which need only file an abbreviated balance sheet and need not file a profit and loss account.

A partnership is entitled to maintain privacy in all of its affairs, except that the identity of all partners and an address for service of documents must be revealed.

29.8 Statutory obligations and control

Throughout its life, a company must comply with statutory obligations as to maintenance and filing of records and information. Examples include the completion of minutes of meetings and statutory registers, and the filing of an annual return and the year-end audited accounts. These obligations represent both an administrative inconvenience and some expense in professional fees. The CA 2006 also imposes controls on certain activities. For example, a dividend can only be paid out of 'available profit', and the company can purchase or redeem its own shares only if detailed conditions and procedures are observed.

A partnership is not subject to any such controls and is free to organise its affairs as it pleases.

29.9 Alternatives

Alternative forms of business structures now include LLPs, which can offer both the protection of limited liability and the informality and lack of publicity of a partnership.

Chapter 30

Tax Considerations in Choice of Medium

30.1 Introduction

In order to compare the tax treatment of different forms of business organisations, it is necessary to consider not only the year-by-year treatment of the trading profits generated by the business but also the longer-term possibilities of capital taxation. Taxation of trading profits requires a comparison between taxation of the self-employed (ie sole trader or partners) and taxation of the incorporated business where profits may be taxed in the hands of the company, its directors and employees and/or its shareholders. Possible capital taxation involves a comparison between the reliefs available for sole traders or individual partners on the one hand and for a company and/or its shareholders on the other hand.

30.2 Trading profits

Although the trading profits of a company are calculated under broadly the same rules as those of a partnership or a sole trader (applying CTA 2009, Part 3 for a company and ITTOIA 2005, Pt 2 for individuals carrying on a trade – see **Chapter 21**), significant differences arise from the fact that the company is a taxpayer in its own right, quite separate from its directors, employees and shareholders.

30.2.1 Comparing charging provisions and rates of tax

30.2.1.1 Profits withdrawn from the business

If *all* of the company's trading profit is withdrawn as directors' fees/employees' salaries, no corporation tax will be chargeable because the company is left with no taxable profit; the directors' fees/employees' salaries will suffer income tax under the employment income provisions in the ITEPA 2003. If the same business were run by a partnership or a sole trader, income tax would be charged on the income of the individual partners or the sole trader under the trading income provisions in Pt 2 of the ITTOIA 2005. It follows therefore that a comparison of the tax treatment of the income of these businesses becomes a comparison between the application of tax on employment income in the context of the company's directors/employees and the application of trading income rules, in the context of the partnership or sole trader. Particular differences are:

(a) the rules on deductible expenditure are more generous under the trading income rules ('wholly and exclusively for the purposes of the trade') than under the ITEPA 2003 ('wholly, exclusively and necessarily in the performance of the employee's duties');

(b) there are rules under the ITEPA 2003 (but not under the trading income rules) for charging income tax on fringe benefits provided by the company, so that if a director/employee uses assets of the company (eg a dwelling) without payment to the company, there is a charge to income tax;

(c)   the timing of payment of tax is more favourable under the trading income rules (tax in two instalments where calculation is based on profits of the accounting period which ends in the tax year) than under the ITEPA 2003 (tax on a current year basis collected at source under the PAYE system).

30.2.1.2   Profits retained in the business

If a business is run by a company and none (or only some) of the company's trading profit is withdrawn as salaries, the profits retained in the business attract corporation tax. If the same business were run by a partnership or a sole trader, income tax would be charged on the entire profits irrespective of whether or not they were withdrawn from the business as opposed to being 'ploughed back'. A comparison of the tax treatment of the income of these businesses is therefore between the payment of corporation tax and the payment of income tax. Differences arise as to rates of tax payable:

Company Profits		Income of Partners or Sole Trader	
Company's profit	Corporation tax rate (effective rate)	Individual's income	Income tax rate
£	£	£	£
0–300,000	21%	0–37,400	20%
300,001–1,500,000	29.75%	over 37,400	40%
over 1,500,000	28%		

A company can retain profits of up to £300,000 before starting to pay tax at a rate higher than 21%; even above that figure the overall rate of corporation tax will never exceed 28%. Individual partners (or sole traders) will pay income tax on all of the trading profit although they will also have their personal allowances to set against the income. This distinction is more likely to be significant when, in a profitable business, the profits are being ploughed back to finance growth; in a company, the retained profits will not be taxed at a rate higher than 28% (and may well be taxed at no higher rate than 21%) while for an equivalent partnership or sole trader the top rate of income tax (40%) may be applicable.

30.2.2   Reliefs for a trading loss

Although most loss-relieving provisions applicable to companies have an equivalent provision applicable to individual partnerships and sole traders, there are three particular points worth noting.

30.2.2.1   Start-up relief (ITA 2007, s 72)

Start-up relief, which permits trading losses assessable in the first four tax years of a business to be carried back and set against the income of the taxpayer for the preceding three tax years, is only available to individual partners and sole traders (see **24.4.1**).

30.2.2.2   Carry-across reliefs – setting losses against other income or gains

A company's trading losses relieved under s 393A of the ICTA 1988 cannot be set against the income or gains of the persons running the company, whereas the trading losses of an individual partner or a sole trader can be set against that person's other income and, possibly, gains under s 64 of the ITA 2007 (see **22.3.1** and **24.4.2**).

30.2.2.3   Terminal loss relief by carry-back

When a company ceases to carry on a trade, a trading loss sustained in its final 12 months may be carried back and set against its profits of any description (income or capital) for the previous three years (ICTA 1988, s 393A). The position is more restrictive for sole traders or individual partners; for these taxpayers, a trading loss made in the final 12 months' trading has a three-tax-year carry back, but the loss can only be set against previous profits of the same trade (ITA 2007, s 89 (see **22.3.2** and **24.2.4**)).

30.2.3 Pension arrangements

The detail of the rules relating to pension payments is outside the scope of this book. However, the ability to make pension arrangements with the benefit of tax relief is greater for a company and its directors/employees through an occupational pension scheme or through the company contributing to the individual's personal pension scheme because two parties are contributing, both with the benefit of tax relief. Where a partner or sole trader is making pension arrangements, he is the only person contributing, albeit with tax relief.

30.2.4 National Insurance contributions

National Insurance contributions are subject to complex rules, and thresholds are adjusted each year. If a business is structured with employer and employees (almost inevitable in the case of a company whereas a partnership or sole trader may have the option of not employing staff), the Class 1 contributions may be greater than the Class 2 and 4 contributions made by the self-employed.

30.2.5 Relief for interest paid

An individual who pays interest on a loan to enable him to buy a share in a partnership or to lend to a partnership will obtain income tax relief for that interest (see **25.2.4**). An individual who pays interest on a loan to enable him to buy shares in a company or to lend to a company in which he is a shareholder will only obtain income tax relief if certain conditions are met; these conditions are that the company must be a close company and that the shareholder must either own more than 5% of the ordinary share capital or work for the greater part of his time in the management or conduct of the company (however few shares he holds – see **23.2.3**).

30.3 Available reliefs for capital gains

30.3.1 Comparing companies with partners and sole traders

30.3.1.1 Indexation

Companies benefit from the indexation allowance throughout the period of ownership of a chargeable asset, whereas gains made by individuals do not. The flat rate of 18% tax for individuals is, however, lower than any of the corporation tax rates. Which regime is more favourable will depend on a number of factors including the amount of the gain, the rate of inflation and the length of ownership of the asset in question.

30.3.1.2 Roll-over relief on replacement of qualifying assets

The roll-over relief on replacement of qualifying assets is available on disposals by companies and, in a modified form, by individual partners and sole traders.

30.3.1.3 Reliefs available only to companies

(a)   Corporate Venturing Scheme (although the EIS scheme offers a broadly similar relief to individuals);

(b)   exemption for disposals of substantial shareholdings.

30.3.1.4 Reliefs available only to individuals

(a)   hold-over relief on a gift of business assets;

(b)   deferral relief on reinvestment in EIS shares (although the Corporate Venturing Scheme offers a broadly similar relief to companies);

(c)   roll-over relief on incorporation of an unincorporated business;

(d)   entrepreneurs' relief.

30.3.1.5 The annual exemption

The annual exemption is not available to companies.

30.3.2 Comparing individual shareholders with individual partners and sole traders

The details of the available business reliefs were considered in **Chapter 28**. A general difference between the treatment of an individual shareholder on the one hand and individual partners or sole traders on the other lies in the fact that, for the shareholder to obtain relief, additional conditions must be satisfied which do not have to be satisfied by a partner or a sole trader.

30.3.2.1 Roll-over relief on the replacement of qualifying assets

A major difference is that shares do not count as qualifying assets for the purposes of roll-over relief on replacement, whereas a sole trader or partner will have an interest in qualifying assets (such as premises and goodwill). Where a shareholder disposes of a qualifying asset (such as premises) used by the company and acquires another qualifying asset, the company must be the personal trading company of that shareholder.

30.3.2.2 Hold-over relief

If the disposal is of company shares, the company need only be the shareholder's personal company if the shares are quoted (see **28.4.2**). Where a shareholder makes a disposal other than at arm's length of a business asset (eg premises) used by the company, the company must be the personal trading company of that shareholder.

30.3.2.3 EIS deferral

In contrast with the other reliefs, deferral relief when investing in EIS shares favours the shareholder as it is not available where the reinvestment is in an unincorporated business as the investment must be in company shares.

30.3.2.4 Entrepreneurs' relief

Entrepreneurs' relief is available for shareholdings in both quoted and unquoted trading companies, but only if the shareholder is both an employee/officer and holds 5% or more of the company's voting shares. Assets held by the individual and used by the company will qualify for the relief only if the company is a qualifying company by reference to the individual owner.

30.4 Possibility of double taxation of a company's income and capital profits

30.4.1 Distributions

Every pound of profit a company makes is charged to corporation tax at effective rates of 21%, 29.75% and 28% (see **22.7.2**). When that profit, net of tax, is distributed as a dividend to its individual shareholders, it is received as their Savings and Investment income (ITTOIA 2005, Pt 4) (see **27.3.1**). The same profit is thus capable of attracting a double charge.

The effect of the double charge will depend upon the rate of corporation tax payable by the company and the circumstances of the individual taxpayer. For shareholders who do not pay income tax at the higher rate, there is no further liability to pay tax beyond that paid by the company, but higher rate taxpayers suffer the dividend upper rate beyond the amount of the tax credit attaching to the dividend.

30.4.2 Capital gains tax

Because the company has a separate legal personality and therefore is a taxpayer separate from the shareholders who own it, there is a possibility that capital gains on the company's assets may give rise to charges to corporation tax against the company and capital gains tax against the individuals concerned. Suppose, for example, that a company owns some land as an investment. The land has increased in value by £100,000 (after allowable expenditure and indexation) and correspondingly the shares in the company have increased in value by £79,000 (after allowing for a potential corporation tax charge of £21,000). If the company were to sell off the land and the shareholders were to sell some shares, the company would be liable to pay corporation tax on its gain and the individual shareholders would be liable to pay capital gains tax on their gains. Even though the shareholders' gains are at least partly attributable to the gain on the premises which is charged to corporation tax, the shareholders are chargeable to capital gains tax without credit for the corporation tax paid by the company. If, on the other hand, the land in the above situation was owned by a partnership, the individual partners might pay capital gains tax on their disposal of the land, but there would be no equivalent of the second charge to tax which occurred in the company context.

30.4.3 Avoiding the double charge

To avoid the possibility of this double charge to taxation suffered by a company and its shareholders, it may be advisable for an appreciating asset, such as premises, to be owned by a shareholder or shareholders individually rather than by the company; the company may be allowed to use the premises under the terms of a lease or a licence. The advantage of individual ownership of assets used by the company is that, although the individual owner may suffer capital gains tax on a disposal, there can be no second charge to tax as might occur if the company owned and disposed of the asset. There are, however, potential problems with such an arrangement from a tax perspective. For inheritance tax business property relief, a maximum 50% relief will be available and then only if the shareholder has voting control of the company (see **28.5.2**).

30.5 Available reliefs for inheritance tax

The details of the available reliefs were considered in **Chapter 28**. As with capital gains tax reliefs, there are additional conditions imposed on shareholders which may result in their receiving less favourable treatment than a sole trader or individual partner.

30.5.1 Agricultural property relief

For a shareholder to qualify in respect of his shareholding, he must have had control of the company at the time of the transfer; for a sole trader or partner, there is no equivalent of this condition.

30.5.2 Business property relief

For a shareholder, relief at 100% is available on the transfer of unquoted shares and at 50% on the transfer of quoted shares which give the shareholder a controlling interest. For a partner or sole trader transferring an interest in the business or the business, 100% relief is available.

Assets such as land, buildings, machinery or plant used by a partnership but owned by a partner will qualify for 50% business property relief. This relief is only available in the company context if the owner is a shareholder whose holding yields control of the company.

30.5.3 Instalment option for payment of IHT

A business or an interest in a business held by a sole trader or individual partner always qualifies as property in relation to which the instalment option may be available, but a shareholding will only qualify if it is a controlling shareholding or, failing that, if further conditions are satisfied (see **28.5.3**).

30.6 Conclusion

Whether it is preferable to trade as a sole trader, in a partnership, or via a company will depend, from a tax viewpoint, on the exact circumstances of the client's business and the tax regime in force at the time of consideration. It is not possible to say that one way of conducting business will always be more tax efficient than another.

Chapter 31
Conversion and the Immediate Implications

31.1 Introduction

This chapter considers the steps and documentation which would be required to convert from sole trader to partnership, from unincorporated business to limited company and from private limited company to public limited company. The tax implications that might ensue as a direct result of the transactions are also considered. For the individuals involved, the possible implications of being a partner rather than a sole trader or of being a director/shareholder rather than being a partner or sole trader may be appreciated from the topics covered earlier in this book.

31.2 Converting from sole trader to partnership

31.2.1 Formalities

In law, the creation of a partnership is simply a question of whether or not the statutory definition of partnership under s 1 of the PA 1890 is satisfied. It follows that there is no necessary formality to be observed in converting from sole trader to partnership. Nevertheless, certain questions should be considered.

31.2.1.1 To whom will the business assets belong?

It is inevitable that certain assets, particularly stock-in-trade and goodwill, will belong to the partners jointly. In relation to other assets, it will be necessary for the partners to reach agreement as to ownership of assets. Ownership of assets can simply be dealt with by means of a clause in the partnership agreement which declares which assets are partnership assets and which assets used by the partnership belong to a partner individually. In relation to premises, for example, this clause would operate as a declaration of trust, where legal title is to remain in the name of one partner alone but the beneficial ownership is to be shared by all the partners. The partners may prefer a formal transfer of title from the original owner to the partners jointly, in which case a conveyance or transfer of the title will be required.

31.2.1.2 Will there be a formal partnership agreement?

Partners should always have a formal partnership agreement prepared, not only to deal with the question of ownership of assets but also to deal with all other aspects of the relationship as described in **Chapter 14**.

31.2.1.3 Will the CA 2006, ss 1192–1208 apply?

If the name of the business is to differ from those of the partners, it will be necessary to set out the names of the partners, together with an address for each partner for service of documents, on all business stationery and on the business premises.

31.2.2 Income tax implications

The incoming person will be assessed to income tax under the rules described in **25.2.3**.

31.2.3 Capital gains tax implications

Where the sole trader agrees to share ownership of the business assets with his new partner, he will be disposing of a share in those assets. If the assets are chargeable assets for capital gains tax purposes (such as premises and goodwill), there will be a possible charge to capital gains tax on the disponer. Reliefs and exemptions that might be available include:

(a)   hold-over relief if the disposal is by way of gift to the incoming partner;

(b)   entrepreneurs' relief;

(c)   the annual exemption.

31.2.4 Stamp Duty Land Tax (SDLT)

The Finance Act 2004 introduced provisions to charge SDLT on certain transfers into and out of partnerships. For further detail on the structure of SDLT, see **31.3.4**.

31.2.5 Employees

Since the former sole trader continues as an employer, there are no necessary implications so far as the positions of employees are concerned.

31.3 Converting from unincorporated business to limited company

31.3.1 Formalities

Because the conversion from unincorporated business to limited company involves a sale of the business by the present owners (partners or sole trader) to a new owner (the company), there are many more formalities attached to this conversion than to that described in **31.2**.

(a)   The present owners will need to form, or purchase off the shelf, a company of which they will be the sole directors and shareholders and to which they will sell the business. The consideration for the sale will normally consist exclusively of shares in the company but some of the consideration may be in the form of debentures (under which part of the agreed price is left outstanding as a loan to the company) or cash.

(b)   Once the company is ready, it will buy the business from the present owners and it will be necessary for the company to observe the usual formalities on decision-making within the company, on filing returns with the Registrar of Companies and on maintaining the company's own records.

(c)   The sale of the business will be effected under the terms of a contract (a sale agreement); typically this will:

(i)   describe the assets being sold to the company;

(ii)   describe the price and the way in which it will be paid by the company, normally wholly in shares;

(iii)   apportion the price to show the value attributed to the various assets or groups of assets comprised in the business and being sold to the company;

(iv)   contain covenants on the part of the company designed to indemnify the sellers in respect of any liability for the existing debts, liabilities and obligations connected with the business;

(v)   contain the company's acceptance of the seller's title to the premises, for example, to ensure that no claim could be brought by the company against the sellers for a defective title (this might otherwise have been a possibility should the company eventually change hands, eg in liquidation); and

(vi)   contain the company's acceptance of the equipment and stock in its current condition so that no claim can be brought by the company against the sellers on the basis of these items being defective or in poor condition.

The contract so far described is designed to ensure not only that ownership of the business and assets changes hands effectively, but also that the sellers (who will run the company but who will in future be protected by limited liability) obtain maximum protection from the company for any present or future liability. This differs significantly from a contract for the sale of a business to a person with whom the sellers are not connected. In such a situation (an arm's length sale), the buyer will be anxious to obtain maximum protection for its own position, including obtaining from the sellers warranties as to assets (eg that they are in a satisfactory state of repair and unencumbered state), employees (terms of their employment and the existence of any disputes), possible litigation (liabilities revealed to the buyer) and environmental matters (compliance with legislation on environmental matters).

In pursuance of the sale agreement, title to certain assets (notably the business premises) will, if appropriate, be transferred to the company by separate document, whilst the title to other assets may pass under the sale agreement (eg goodwill) or by physical delivery (eg stock).

If, as is common, the company takes over the previous name of the business and this is not the same as the company's name, it will be necessary for the company's stationery and a notice at the company's place of business to state the company's name and address (CA 2006, ss 1202, 1204).

31.3.2 Income tax implications

31.3.2.1 General

When the unincorporated business is sold to the company, this is a discontinuance of the business so far as the partnership (or sole trader) is concerned. The individual partners (or sole trader) will be assessed to income tax under the rules for the closing tax year of a business (see **24.2.4**) up to the date of the transfer of the business. The company must pay corporation tax on profits thereafter.

31.3.2.2 Capital allowances

In so far as the partnership (or sole trader) sells to the company assets on which capital allowances have been claimed (eg machinery and plant), there may be a balancing charge to income tax on any profit identified by comparing the sale proceeds with the assets' written-down value. Suppose, for example, that some machinery cost £16,000 when purchased three and a half years ago and capital allowances have been claimed totalling £7,808, so that the written down value is £8,192. If the value attributed to this machinery on the sale was £9,000, there could be a balancing charge to income tax on the £808 'profit'. In other words, this 'profit' would be taxed as part of the trading income in the closing tax year. Conversely, if there is a loss calculated on the same basis, there will be a deduction from profits for the final year for income tax purposes, known as a balancing allowance. If the company is controlled by the sellers of the business, the company and the sellers can elect within two years that the company shall take over the position of the sellers so that no balancing charge occurs (CAA 2001, ss 266 and 267).

31.3.2.3 Trading losses

If the unincorporated business has made trading losses which have not been relieved when the business is transferred to the company, these losses can be carried forward and deducted from income which the former partners (or sole trader) receive from the company, such as a salary as director or dividends as shareholder. This relief is available only if the business is transferred to the company wholly or mainly in return for the issue of shares in the company (see **24.4.5**).

31.3.2.4 Interest on a qualifying loan – income tax relief for partners

Details of this relief are given at **25.2.4**. If a partnership is incorporated as a close company and the loan remains outstanding following incorporation, relief will continue to be given if the conditions for the relief that apply to close companies are met (see **23.2.3**).

31.3.3 Capital gains tax implications

When the business is transferred to the company there will be a disposal to the company by the individual partners (or sole trader) of any of the assets of the business which do not remain in their personal ownership. In so far as these assets are chargeable assets for capital gains tax purposes, there may be a charge to capital gains tax. Reliefs which may be available include:

31.3.3.1 Roll-over relief on incorporation of a business (TCGA 1992, s 162)

The details of this relief were considered at **28.4.4**. The conditions for the relief to apply include the condition that the business must be sold to the company as a going concern with all of its assets (although cash may be ignored for this purpose). Transferring all the assets may present certain disadvantages including:

(a)   possible stamp duty land tax on the transfer of land;

(b)   various other expenses incurred in transferring assets, such as professional fees;

(c)   possible double charge to taxation in relation to future gains on those assets transferred (see **30.4**);

(d)   availability of those assets transferred for payment of the company creditors.

31.3.3.2 Other reliefs

The taxpayer may not wish to roll-over his gain on incorporation of the business. This may be the case if the taxpayer wishes to use one or more of the following (if available – see **28.4**):

(a)   EIS deferral relief;

(b)   entrepreneurs' relief;

(c)   the annual exemption.

31.3.4 Stamp duty land tax (SDLT)

Stamp duty land tax is chargeable on a 'land transaction' in accordance with Part 4 of the Finance Act 2003, and this would include the acquisition by a company of land included as part of a business. The amount of the charge (if any) will depend on the value of the (usually non-residential) land.

31.3.5 VAT implications

If the company is not registered for VAT purposes before the sale to the company takes place, the sellers must charge VAT on the transaction. This is avoided by ensuring that the company is registered for VAT before the sale takes place (under the Transfer of Going Concern (TOGC) Rules).

31.3.6 Employees

As a result of the sale of the business, the owner of the business and therefore the employer will change. Under the Transfer of Undertakings (Protection of Employment) Regulations 2006 (SI 2006/246), the new employer (the company) is taken to stand in the shoes of the old employer and the rights of the employees are automatically transferred. If no change is made affecting the employees, then there will be no immediate implications of the change of employer.

31.4 Converting from private to public limited company

31.4.1 Procedural requirements

The company must pass one special resolution to re-register as a public limited company which will cover altering its memorandum of association (so that it states that the company is to be public), the name (which must end with the words 'public limited company' or the abbreviation 'plc') and the articles.

The company must satisfy the financial criteria applicable to public limited companies, including the requirement that the company's issued share capital must be at least £50,000 in nominal value and that each share must be paid up at least as to 25% of its nominal value and the whole of any premium.

The company must make an application to the Registrar of Companies which contains (CA 2006, s 94):

(a)   a statement of the new name;

(b)   the company's proposed secretary, if there is not one at present;

(c)   a copy of the special resolution;

(d)   a copy of the amended articles;

(e)   a copy of the balance sheet;

(f)   an auditor's unqualified report and opinion on the value of the net assets; and

(g)   a statement of compliance made by the directors (which does not need to be sworn).

If satisfied, the Registrar of Companies will issue a certificate of incorporation stating that the company is a public limited company.

31.4.2 Implications

Since the company remains the same person, there are no implications for the company in terms of taxation or in terms of the employees. The real implications for the company lie in the realm of the company's ability to raise finance by inviting the public to purchase its shares and by applying to have its shares dealt in on the Stock Exchange.

For the shareholders in the company there may be implications as to the availability or otherwise of capital tax reliefs. For example, some inheritance tax reliefs (such as business property relief and the instalment option) operate less favourably for shareholdings in quoted companies than for shareholdings in unquoted companies. Some capital gains tax reliefs (such as retirement relief) are dependent on the company being a 'personal trading company' which is less likely to be established in a company whose shares are quoted on the Stock Exchange.

Part VII
SOME ASPECTS OF TRADING

Part VII looks at some aspects of trading.

Chapter 32 concerns the basics of sale of goods.

Chapter 33 examines employment and other regulatory concerns in running a business.

Chapter 34 and **35** examine agency and distribution agreements, and **Chapter 36** considers the impact of competition law.

Chapter 32
Sale of Goods

32.1 Formation of the contract

It is important not to lose sight of the basics of contract law. You need to differentiate between an invitation to treat on the one hand, and an offer on the other hand. In a well-publicised problem in the recent past, Argos had an incorrect price on their internet website. The price for one model of television was £3 when it should have been £300. A number of customers 'bought' televisions online at £3. However, Argos refused to supply them stating that the advertisement on their website was only an invitation to treat. Any response from a customer was therefore an offer which they could reject. The aggrieved customers argued that the advertisement was an offer which they were accepting, and that Argos was therefore bound as a party to a contract for the sale of goods. What do you think?

Other aspects of contract law which should be kept in mind are:

(a)   whose standard terms apply? – the 'battle of the forms' (eg *Rimeco Riggleson & Metal Co v Queenborough Rolling Mill Co Ltd* [1995] CLY 798, *Sauter Automation Ltd v Goodman (Mechanical Services) Ltd (in liquidation)* (1986) 34 Build LR 81);

(b)   'prevail' clauses (where one set of terms proclaim that they prevail over any other set of terms) are generally considered not to work;

(c)   timing – were the terms brought to the other party's attention at the time the contract was made?

(d)   signing a document is acceptance of its terms; and

(e)   a collateral contract could be construed to exist between the parties, so include a 'whole agreement' clause in the terms to exclude this possibility.

32.2 Relevant legislation

The sale of goods is governed by the Sale of Goods Act 1979 (SGA 1979). Where goods are supplied along with services, the Supply of Goods and Services Act 1982 applies (SGSA 1982).

The Unfair Contract Terms Act 1977 (UCTA 1977) deals with exclusion clauses, including exclusion of the implied terms under the SGA 1979.

There are also various pieces of legislation aimed at protecting consumers and which we do not consider here, for example the Electronic Commerce (EC Directive) Regulations 2002 (SI 2002/2013), the Consumer Protection (Distance Selling) Regulations 2000 (SI 2000/2334) and the Unfair Terms in Consumer Contracts Regulations 1999 (SI 1999/2083). The Directive on Consumer Goods and Associated Guarantees 1999/44/EC (OJ L171/12) has now been implemented as the Sale and Supply of Goods to Consumer Regulations 2002 (SI 2002/3045). There is a minor amendment to s 12(2) of the UCTA 1977, concerning auction sales which affects non-consumer contracts.

32.2.1   Excluding the provisions of the SGA 1979

Section 55 of the SGA 1979 provides that the terms implied into a contract for the sale of goods by the SGA 1979 can be excluded by the agreement of the parties, subject to the UCTA 1977 (see **32.10.1**). In many non-consumer contracts therefore, the provisions implied into a sale of goods contract by the SGA 1979 are a fallback provision. They would often be unsuitable for a commercial contract and it can be perfectly valid and proper to exclude them.

32.3   What are 'goods'?

Usually it is perfectly obvious whether the subject matter of the contract is goods (eg buying a chocolate bar in a shop). Section 61 of the SGA 1979 defines goods as 'including all personal chattels other than things in action and money'.

One area where there has been uncertainty is computer programs. Are they goods or services? (The point is that the implied terms in the contract would be different for goods and for services.) In *St Albans City and District Council v International Computers Ltd* [1996] 4 All ER 481, it was held obiter that programs were goods when they were supplied on a disk. In the case of *Horace Holman Group Ltd v Sherwood International Group Ltd* [2002] EWCA Civ 170, there was a dispute as to whether software was goods, and *St Albans* was cited as the authority. This does not answer the question if the program is supplied over the internet, and arrives in the computer via a telephone line.

32.4   Sale of goods (SGA 1979, s 2)

Section 2(1) of the SGA 1979, defines a contract of sale of goods as:

> A contract by which the seller transfers or agrees to transfer the property in goods to the buyer for a money consideration, called the price.

Subsection (4) defines a sale:

> Where under a contract of sale the property in the goods is transferred from the seller to the buyer the contract is called a sale.

These subsections indicate how a sale of goods differs, for example, from a contract for hire of goods because the property in the goods changes hands. It differs from a gift of the goods because the buyer pays the seller money for the goods.

32.4.1   Definition of 'price' in s 8 of the SGA 1979

Section 8 provides that:

(1)   The price in a contract of sale may be fixed by the contract, or may be left to be fixed in a manner agreed by the contract, or may be determined by the course of dealing between the parties.

(2)   Where the price is not determined as mentioned in subsection (1) above the buyer must pay a reasonable price.

(3)   What is a reasonable price is a question of fact dependent on the circumstances of each particular case.

The basic position is that the parties are free to fix their own price. The fallback position is that if they fail to do so, the price will be a reasonable one. One problem with s 8 is that it is debatable whether or not the parties have concluded a contract at all, if they have not agreed such a basic term of the contract as the price of the goods. If they have not agreed the price then the price has not been fixed by the contract. Alternatively, the parties may conclude the contract but agree that the price will be fixed at some point in the future. This is an 'agreement to agree', which is usually taken to be unenforceable in English law (see, eg, *Courtney & Fairbairn Ltd v Tolaini Bros (Hotels) Ltd* [1975] 1 WLR 297; cf the older case of *Foley v Classique Coaches Ltd* [1934] 2 KB 1, where there was an arbitration clause if the parties could not agree on the price and the contract was upheld).

In *Cable & Wireless plc v IBM United Kingdom Ltd* [2002] 2 All ER (Comm) 1041, it was held that although the law did not generally recognise agreements to agree, the situation here was different. The fact that the agreement prescribed the means by which dispute negotiation should take place, by the identification of a specific recognised procedure, meant that the requirement for contractual certainty was fulfilled and the agreement was thus enforceable.

32.4.2   Agreeing the price (SGA 1979, ss 8, 9)

In most circumstances, the parties will agree the price (or, if they do not, then s 8 applies). It could be by use of a price list, or it could be by quotation or by negotiation. The contract should provide that the price is fixed, or, if not, how price changes between signing and delivery are to be dealt with.

If the parties leave the price to be fixed by the valuation of a third party and he does not do so, the contract is void (s 9).

32.4.3   Value added tax

A price in a contract is taken as including value added tax (VAT) unless otherwise specified (Value Added Tax Act 1983, s 10(2)). If the prices are to be exclusive of VAT, that must be expressly stated. Failure to do this will result in the seller receiving 17.5% less for his goods than he wanted.

32.5   Duties of the seller

The SGA 1979 implies various duties in to a contract for the sale of goods subject to agreement to the contrary. This section deals with the seller's duties.

32.5.1   Duty to pass a good title (SGA 1979, s 12)

Section 12(1) implies into the contract a term that the seller has the right to sell the goods, that is, he has good title to the goods.

Section 12(2) provides that there is an implied warranty:

(a)   that the goods are free from any charge or encumbrance not already known to the buyer, and

(b)   that the buyer will enjoy quiet possession of the goods.

For example, in *Rubicon Computer Systems Ltd v United Paints Ltd* [2000] 2 TCLR 453 it was held that the seller attaching a time lock to a computer system in order to deny access to the buyer was in breach of the 'quiet possession' term under s 12(2)(b).

32.5.2   Duty to hand over the goods (SGA 1979, s 27–29)

Section 27 of the SGA 1979 requires that it is the duty of the seller to deliver the goods and of the buyer to accept and pay for them, in accordance with the terms of the contract of sale. In this case 'deliver' means to pass the goods voluntarily to the buyer (SGA 1979, s 61). It does not mean 'deliver' in the sense that he is obliged to get on his bike and take the goods round to the buyer's premises (ie, transportation of goods).

Section 28 states that delivery of the goods and payment should happen at the same time. For example, this is the normal case when a customer buys goods in a shop – the customer pays the money to the shopkeeper and is handed the goods then and there.

Under s 29 there is no general duty to dispatch the goods to the buyer. The arrangements for that are a matter to be agreed between the parties.

32.5.3   Time of delivery (SGA 1979, s 10)

The basic position under the SGA 1979 is that time of payment is not of the essence in a sale of goods contract (s 10(1)). However, s 10(2) provides that the parties can agree whether or not time is of the essence with regard to any other term of the contract.

The courts have ruled on various aspects on time of delivery. In *Hartley v Hymans* [1920] 3 KB 475, it was held that in ordinary commercial contracts for the sale of goods the rule is that time is prima facie of the essence with respect to delivery.

If the buyer waives the delivery date before the goods are delivered, the buyer is entitled to give the seller reasonable notice that he will not accept the goods after a certain date. See the case of *Charles Rickards Ltd v Oppenheim* [1950] 1 KB 616 where the buyer waived the original delivery date but then gave the seller reasonable notice of a revised date. The seller failed to meet even the revised date and the buyer was held to be entitled to refuse to accept the goods.

32.5.4   Delivery of the right quantity (SGA 1979, ss 30–31)

The seller must deliver the correct quantity of goods. Section 30(1) of the SGA 1979 provides that the buyer may reject the goods if the quantity is less than the contract quantity. However, if the goods are accepted then he has to pay for them at the contract rate. Section 31(1) provides that the buyer is not obliged to accept delivery in instalments.

32.5.5   Delivery of the right quality – sale by description (SGA 1979, s 13)

Section 13 of the SGA 1979 implies a term that the goods sold should comply with their description. This could apply to goods bought from a catalogue, for example. In *Beale v Taylor* [1967] 1 WLR 1193, the sale was held to be a sale by description even though the buyer inspected the car after having seen the advertisement for it in the local paper.

32.5.6   Delivery of the right quality – satisfactory quality (SGA 1979, s 14(2))

Section 14(2) of the SGA 1979 implies a term that, in a sale in the course of a business, the goods are to be of satisfactory quality. This includes fitness for the common purposes of the goods, appearance and finish, freedom from minor defects, safety and durability. It does not extend to matters specifically drawn to the buyer's attention before the contract is made.

32.5.7   Delivery of the right quality – fitness for purpose (SGA 1979, s 14(2) and (3))

As well as fitness for the common purposes of the goods under s 14(2), s 14(3) implies a term that the goods are fit for any particular purpose which the buyer makes known to the seller either expressly or by implication. (See *Micron Computer Systems Ltd v Wang (UK) Ltd*, QBD, 9 May 1990, where the buyer of a computer system failed to tell the seller of the particular purpose in question and was therefore unsuccessful in its claim.)

In *Jewson v Boyhan* [2003] EWCA Civ 1030, the seller was held by the Court of Appeal not to be liable for breach of the SGA 1979 in the supply of electrical heating equipment. The buyers alleged that the sale was in breach of s 14(2) and s 14(3), as the equipment had reduced the energy efficiency ratings of the flat conversions in question. The Court of Appeal held that:

> Although there was considerable overlap between s 14(2) and s 14(3), the function of s 14(2) was to establish a general standard, and the function of s 14(3) was to impose a particular standard tailored to the individual circumstances of the case.

The equipment did work as heating equipment, so s 14(2) was held not to be applicable. As regards s 14(3), the buyer was held not to have relied on the sellers as regards the question of the 'particular' fitness for purpose of the effect of the heating equipment on the flats' energy efficiency ratings.

32.5.8   Delivery of the right quality – sale by sample (SGA 1979, s 15)

Section 15 of the SGA 1979 implies a term that where the sale is by sample, then the bulk of the goods will correspond with the sample in quality. The goods are also to be free of any defect not apparent on reasonable examination which would render the quality unsatisfactory.

32.5.9   Trade usage (SGA 1979, s 14(4))

Section 14(4) of the SGA 1979 states that an implied condition or warranty about quality or fitness for a particular purpose may be annexed to a contract of sale by usage in the course of a particular trade.

32.6   Duties of the buyer

The SGA 1979 implies various duties into a contract for the sale of goods. This section deals with the buyer's duties.

32.6.1   Duty to pay the price (SGA 1979, ss 27–28)

It is the buyer's duty to pay the price (SGA 1979, s 27). The time for payment is prima facie when the goods are delivered, but the parties may agree otherwise (SGA 1979, s 28). The seller is not bound to accept anything but cash, subject to contrary agreement between the parties.

32.6.2   Duty to take delivery (SGA 1979, ss 27–28)

Under ss 27 and 28 of the SGA 1979 it is the duty of the buyer to accept and pay for the goods. The general rule is that delivery and payment takes place at the seller's premises. A buyer's failure to accept the goods does not by itself allow the seller to sell the goods to someone else but see s 48. Section 37 states that a buyer is liable for costs incurred by the seller due to the buyer's neglect or refusal to take delivery.

32.7   Effects of a sale of goods contract

32.7.1   Transfer of property (SGA 1979, ss 17–18)

The property in the goods, ie the title to the goods, passes when the parties intend it to pass (SGA 1979, s 17). Section 18 contains rules for ascertaining the intention of the parties, subject to their contrary intention.

32.7.2   Passing of risk (SGA 1979, s 20)

Section 20(1) of the SGA 1979 provides that the goods remain at the seller's risk until the property in them is transferred to the buyer whether or not delivery has been made, unless the parties agree otherwise.

This can be an important issue, for example, in the installation of a new computer system. The buyer will not want to pay the whole price until the system is running properly, yet the goods are on the buyer's premises and under his control while they are being installed. In such circumstances, the contract should provide that the risk in the goods passes to the buyer when the goods arrive at the buyer's premises (that is, they are delivered in the legal sense). It is then up to the buyer to insure the goods, for example against theft or fire.

32.7.3   Force majeure clause

A force majeure clause is included in a contract to deal with circumstances beyond the reasonable control of the parties and which would frustrate the contract. The terms of the clause are a matter of negotiation between the parties but would typically include the effects of government action, and extreme adverse weather.

32.8 Rights of the seller

32.8.1 Rights of an unpaid seller (SGA 1979, s 38)

The rights of the unpaid seller are:

(a)   a lien on the goods;

(b)   a right to stop the goods in transit;

(c)   a right of resale;

(d)   an action for the price of the goods; and

(e)   a right to retain title to the goods until paid.

Section 38 of the SGA 1979 defines an unpaid seller. The rights in the SGA 1979 assume that the seller still has control over the goods. If this is not the case then the only possibility is a retention of title clause (see **32.8.7**).

32.8.2 Rights under s 39 of the SGA 1979

Section 39 states that the unpaid seller has:

(a)   a lien on the goods or right to retain them for the price;

(b)   a right to stop the goods in transit if the buyer becomes insolvent; and

(c)   a right of resale of the goods.

32.8.3 Seller's lien (SGA 1979, s 41)

Section 41 states that an unpaid seller who is in possession of the goods is entitled to retain possession of them until paid, where any credit period has expired or the buyer has become insolvent.

The lien is lost when the goods are consigned to a carrier without the right to dispose of the goods, or the buyer has possession of the goods, or waiver by the seller.

32.8.4 Stoppage in transit (SGA 1979, ss 44–46)

Sections 44–46 state that the seller may stop the goods in transit where the buyer has become insolvent, and retain them until paid.

32.8.5 Resale by seller (SGA 1979, s 48)

The unpaid seller who resells the goods to another buyer passes good title to the goods, even where the goods were subject to the unpaid seller's lien or were stopped in transit (s 48).

32.8.6 Action for the price, and damages (SGA 1979, ss 49 and 50)

Under s 49, the unpaid seller can sue the buyer for the price of the goods where the buyer has the property in the goods but has not paid for them.

Under s 50, where the buyer has refused to accept and pay for the goods the seller can sue the buyer for damages.

32.8.7 The seller who is not in possession of the goods (SGA 1979, ss 17 and 19)

The rights in **32.8.2–32.8.5** apply where the seller still has possession, or at least control, of the goods. A more difficult situation is where the goods are in the possession or control of the buyer but the seller has still not been paid. This is a major concern for the seller especially where the buyer is going insolvent. The danger is that the goods will be sold by a liquidator.

The seller would be only an unsecured creditor and would be unlikely to be paid much, if anything, by the liquidator.

There is a right under ss 17 and 19 of the SGA 1979 to reserve title to the goods. This can be done in a contract of sale by inserting a retention of title clause (also called a *Romalpa* clause after *Aluminium Industrie Vaassen BV v Romalpa Aluminium* [1976] 1 WLR 676).

Typically, such a clause will reserve title to the seller until all monies owed to the seller by the buyer have been paid. It will also permit the seller to enter on to the buyer's premises to reclaim the goods, though one might query the efficacy of this if contested by a liquidator. There will be a provision seeking to trace the proceeds of onward sale of the goods through the buyer's bank account. There is also an exception. This is where the goods have been sold on to an innocent third party then s 25 of the SGA 1979 states that the third party gets good title.

There will be a requirement to keep the seller's goods identifiable, for example by separate storage.

A problem area is where the goods have been incorporated into other products. Generally, the original goods are considered to have been subsumed into the new products and the seller has no right to the new products. However, where the goods are readily detachable, then it is appropriate to have a clause reserving the right of the seller to detach his goods and remove them. For example, in *Hendy Lennox Ltd v Graham Puttick Ltd* [1984] 1 WLR 485, it was held that the sellers were entitled to detach their diesel engines from electrical generating sets.

If the clause has the effect of the buyer creating an equitable charge over the goods, rather than being a retention of title, then it is likely to be void for want of registration, as such charges are registrable under ss 395 and 396 of the CA 1985. Retention of title clauses are generally not registrable as they are considered to operate by preventing the property in the goods from passing to the buyer in the first place, see *Clough Mill Ltd v Martin* [1985] 1 WLR 111.

32.9 Rights of the buyer

32.9.1 Right to reject the goods (SGA 1979, ss 15A, 35–36)

A buyer's primary right for breach of contract by the seller is to reject the goods and repudiate the contract of sale. The seller's breach would have to go to the root of the contract to justify repudiation. The Sale and Supply of Goods Act 1994 made changes to this area of law including by introducing the new s 15A into the SGA 1979.

Section 15A limits the right to reject the goods for breach of ss 13–15 of the SGA 1979. It provides that the right to reject is lost where the sale is not a consumer sale and the breach is so slight that it would be unreasonable for the buyer to reject the goods. Note that s 15A only applies to breach of ss 13–15 and not, for example, to breach of a stipulation concerning time of delivery.

Section 35 deals with the loss of the right to reject. So, for example, the buyer loses the right where he tells the seller that he has accepted the goods, or does something inconsistent with the seller's ownership after the goods have been delivered to him. He also loses the right to reject if he retains the goods beyond a reasonable period of time (s 35(5)). In *Clegg v Olle Andersson (t/a Nordic Marine)* [2003] EWCA Civ 320, the Court of Appeal held that the Sale and Supply of Goods Act 1994 allowed the buyer to have time to ascertain the actions needed to modify or repair the goods. The case concerned an ocean-going yacht. The buyer took three weeks to assess the situation before rejecting the goods. This was in fact many months after delivery, as the seller was slow to respond to requests for information.

Section 36 of the SGA 1979 states that, where the goods have been delivered to the buyer and the buyer rejects them, he is not obliged to return them to the seller.

32.9.2   Action for damages (SGA 1979, s 53)

The buyer can sue for breach of a contract term, either express or implied (s 53). This is either where the term in question is classified as a warranty, or where it is a condition but the buyer has elected not to reject the goods.

Section 51 lays down the principles for calculating damages for non-delivery of the goods, and in particular s 51(3) states:

> Where there is an available market for the goods in question the measure of damages is prima facie to be ascertained by the difference between the contract price and the market or current price of the goods at the time or times when they ought to have been delivered or (if no time was fixed) at the time of the refusal to deliver.

In other words, the buyer's loss is any increase in the price of equivalent goods obtained from another source.

A problem area is consequential loss. This is dealt with on the principles in *Hadley v Baxendale* (1854) 9 Exch 341. That is, that the damages allowed are those that are considered either as arising naturally from the breach of the contract itself, or such as may reasonably be supposed to have been in the contemplation of the parties at the time they made the contract.

Limitation clauses in sale of goods contracts are often aimed at limiting or excluding consequential loss, subject to being disallowed under the UCTA 1977. The seller does not want to take on liabilities that might far exceed his profit on the sale.

32.9.3   Specific performance (SGA 1979, s 52)

The buyer's right to specific performance is regulated by s 52. The right is only for specific or ascertained goods, that is goods identified and agreed upon at the time the contract is made. The right applies whether or not the property in the goods (title to the goods) has already passed to the buyer.

The right under s 52 does not extend to unascertained goods. These are goods which are not identified and agreed upon at the time a contract of sale is made. They may be divided into the following categories:

(a)   a quantity of a type of goods in general, eg 5 kilos of potatoes;

(b)   future goods, goods which are not yet in existence, eg next year's potatoes; or

(c)   part of a larger quantity of ascertained goods, eg 5 kilos of potatoes out of the 2 tonnes in the Tesco shop in Chester.

In each case, the identity of the individual potatoes in question is not known.

However, there are some cases where an order for unascertained goods has been granted, albeit in exceptional circumstances. For example, in *Worldwide Dryers Ltd v Warner Howard Ltd and Others* (1982) *The Times*, 9 December, the buyer's business would have collapsed pending the full trial if the seller had cut off supplies of the goods which were imported from the United States. These would be 'future goods' under the classification above.

32.9.4   Rescission for misrepresentation

This is now controlled by the Misrepresentation Act 1967. Section 1(a) of the Act states that the fact that a pre-contractual representation has become a term of the contract does not necessarily stop the buyer from rescinding. Rescission is now possible for innocent misrepresentation (s 1(b)).

Rescission for misrepresentation is barred by affirmation, lapse of time, inability to restore the parties to their original position, or the goods being acquired by an innocent third party.

Damages for misrepresentation are also a possibility but there can be no double recovery.

32.10 Exclusion of seller's liability

Exclusion clauses have to be incorporated into the contract in order to be relied upon by the seller. (See, for example, the problems of a 'shrink-wrap' licence for computer software on the difficulties with incorporation – *Beta Computers (Europe) Ltd v Adobe Systems (Europe) Ltd* [1996] FSR 367.) The exclusion clause also has to apply to the facts of the particular matter in dispute.

32.10.1 The effect of the UCTA 1977 on contractual terms

The UCTA 1977 is the main item of legislation dealing with exclusion clauses. Some provisions of the UCTA 1977 apply only to consumer contracts. Also, the Unfair Terms in Consumer Contracts Regulations 1999 (SI 1999/2083) apply only to consumer contracts, perhaps not surprisingly.

The following is a brief synopsis of the main points of the UCTA 1977 and, at **32.10.2**, the 1999 Regulations.

32.10.1.1 Void clauses under the UCTA

Note that although the word 'void' is used here to describe the effect of the relevant sections of the UCTA 1977 on exclusion clauses, and is a convenient shorthand description, none of the sections of the Act actually uses this word. Instead, each section provides that the relevant liability cannot be excluded or restricted.

Section 2(1)

By s 2(1) of the UCTA 1977, a person cannot, either by reference to a contract term or a notice, exclude or restrict his liability for personal injury or death resulting from negligence.

Section 6(1)

By s 6(1) of the UCTA 1977, liability for breach of the implied condition of title under either s 12 of the SGA 1979 or s 8 of the Supply of Goods (Implied Terms) Act 1973 cannot be excluded or restricted by reference to any contract term.

Section 6(2)

By s 6(2) of the UCTA 1977, as against a person who deals as consumer, liability for breach of the implied conditions in ss 13–15 of the SGA 1979 or ss 9–11 of the Supply of Goods (Implied Terms) Act 1973 cannot be excluded or restricted by reference to any contract term. The expression 'deals as consumer' is defined in s 12 of the UCTA 1977; the Court of Appeal has held, perhaps surprisingly, that in certain circumstances, a company can deal as consumer (*R & B Customs Brokers Co Ltd v United Dominions Trust Ltd* [1988] 1 All ER 847). The point arises when a company enters into a transaction which is not in the regular course of its business. (Note that s 7 of the UCTA 1977, which applies to miscellaneous contracts under which goods pass, eg work and materials contracts, contains provisions similar to those in s 6.)

32.10.1.2 Clauses subject to the reasonableness test

The two ways in which the contractual reasonableness test is most likely to apply are as follows.

Section 3

Section 3 of the UCTA 1977 applies either where one party deals as consumer, or, significantly for commercial contracts, where one party deals on the other party's written standard terms of business. It imposes the reasonableness test on a wide variety of clauses.

Section 6(3)

An attempt to exclude the liability mentioned in s 6(2) of the UCTA 1977 (see **32.10.1.1**) against a person who does not deal as consumer is subject to the reasonableness test.

32.10.2 The Unfair Terms In Consumer Contracts Regulations 1999

These Regulations provide (in certain circumstances) a further important statutory control on drafting exclusion clauses.

32.10.2.1 Introduction

The original version of these Regulations (the Unfair Terms in Consumer Contracts Regulations 1994 (SI 1994/3159)) came into force on 1 July 1995, and implemented Directive 93/13/EEC (OJ L095/29) on unfair terms in consumer contracts. However, it subsequently proved necessary to make a number of changes to the Regulations and, as a result, the 1994 Regulations were revoked and replaced (with effect from 1 October 1999) by the Unfair Terms in Consumer Contracts Regulations 1999 (SI 1999/2083).

Note that the Regulations do not apply to a contract between two commercial parties; however, for the commercial client entering into standard-form contracts for the supply of goods and/or services to consumers, their impact is likely to be significant.

32.10.2.2 The Regulations in outline

Regulations 1 and 2 deal with the commencement of the 1999 Regulations and the revocation of the old Regulations; the definitions are found in reg 3. The definitions of 'consumer' and 'seller or supplier' require that a consumer must be a natural person who is not acting for business purposes, and that a seller or supplier must be acting for business purposes. Regulation 4 provides that the Regulations apply 'in relation to unfair terms in contracts concluded between a seller or supplier and a consumer', and also indicates a number of terms to which the Regulations do not apply.

'Unfair term' is then defined by reg 5(1):

> a contractual term which has not been individually negotiated shall be regarded as unfair if, contrary to the requirement of good faith, it causes a significant imbalance in the parties' rights and obligations arising under the contract to the detriment of the consumer.

An 'illustrative and non-exhaustive list of terms which may be regarded as unfair' can be found in Sch 2. Regulation 6 describes how unfair terms are to be assessed. The effect of an unfair term is that it 'shall not be binding on the consumer' (see reg 8).

Regulations 10–15 give power to the Director General of Fair Trading (DGFT) and 'qualifying bodies' (specified in Sch 1) to consider complaints that contract terms drawn up for general use are unfair, and to take action. Under the old regulations, these powers were reserved to the DGFT, but this was an obvious defect in implementation of the Directive, and the 1999 Regulations also give these powers to bodies such as the Consumers' Association.

32.10.2.3 Relationship with the UCTA 1977

The Regulations apply in addition to rather than instead of the UCTA 1977. Thus, a solicitor will have to advise on situations where a term is subject not only to the UCTA 1977 reasonableness test, but also the test of fairness under the Regulations.

32.10.2.4 The requirement of 'plain, intelligible language'

By reg 7, a seller or supplier 'shall ensure that any written term of a contract [to which the Regulations apply] is expressed in plain, intelligible language'. This concept is not further defined in the Regulations, nor is it clear from the Regulations what will happen if a term is not expressed in plain, intelligible language. Perhaps the most appropriate conclusion is that it is one of the factors which may render a term unfair. Regulation 7 also provides that 'if there is doubt about the meaning of a written term, the interpretation most favourable to the consumer shall prevail'; compare the normal *contra proferentem* rule.

32.10.3 Drafting for reasonableness: general principles

32.10.3.1 The contractual reasonableness test

In practice, when the UCTA 1977 applies to a commercial agreement, most (if not all) of the agreement's exclusion clauses will be subject to the reasonableness test, so it is usually against this test that the solicitor will need to assess a clause.

Section 11(1) of the UCTA 1977 states that:

> In relation to a contract term, the requirement of reasonableness ... is that the term shall have been a fair and reasonable one to be included having regard to the circumstances which were, or ought reasonably to have been, known to or in the contemplation of the parties when the contract was made.

It is, therefore, a test of reasonableness of incorporation, not reasonableness of reliance. If (in the light of the actual and constructive knowledge of the parties at the time) it is reasonable to include a particular clause when the contract is made, it should pass the reasonableness test: the court should not look at whether it was reasonable for the 'guilty' party to rely on the clause in the light of the events which actually happened (although it has to be said that it is not uncommon in practice for courts to do this). It is for the party claiming that a term satisfies the reasonableness test to show that it does (s 11(5)).

32.10.3.2 The Schedule 2 guidelines

The guidelines include: the relative bargaining power of the parties; whether the buyer was offered any inducement to accept the clause; whether any choice was available (could the buyer have acquired the goods elsewhere without the clause?); and the extent of the parties' knowledge of the existence and effect of the terms. The list is not intended to be exhaustive and, strictly speaking, only applies when the court is assessing reasonableness under ss 6(3) and 7(3) of the UCTA 1977. However, the courts often apply the guidelines when considering the reasonableness test in relation to other sections (notably s 3; see, for example, *Flamar Interocean Ltd v Denmac Ltd (formerly Denholm Maclay Co Ltd) (The 'Flamar Pride' and 'Flamar Progress')* [1990] 1 Lloyd's Rep 434). This approach was confirmed as appropriate by the Court of Appeal in *Overseas Medical Supplies Ltd v Orient Transport Services Ltd* [1999] 2 Lloyd's Rep 273. This case also contains a useful discussion and summary of the factors which are generally relevant to assessing the reasonableness of a clause.

32.10.3.3 Is the contract a consumer or a commercial contract?

In determining whether a clause will survive the application of the UCTA 1977, the crucial factor is often whether the contract is a consumer or a commercial contract. For example, a clause which excludes liability for breach of s 14(2) or (3) of the SGA 1979 is only subject to the reasonableness test against a commercial buyer, but is void against a buyer who deals as consumer. Even if a clause is subject to the reasonableness test whatever the status of the 'victim' (eg under s 3), the courts are often prepared to be stricter in applying the test where that person is a consumer. The clause may in fact be less likely to pass the test for that reason alone. If the client deals with both commercial and consumer buyers, it is important for the solicitor to recognise this when drafting. There may be several different ways of dealing with the problem, depending on how the client does business and the other relevant circumstances. For example, the solicitor may decide to draft two different forms of contracts, with the 'consumer' version either omitting certain exclusion clauses, or containing only modified versions. However, this may be risky; it would then be necessary to ensure that those operating the contract are able to distinguish between the two versions (perhaps print them on different coloured paper). A simpler solution (where possible) is to have one contract for all customers, but to draft any exclusion so that it will apply only to commercial customers.

32.10.3.4   No guarantee of success

Because of the way in which the contractual reasonableness test is worded, the factors which are relevant when drafting for reasonableness (see **32.10.3.1**) are often specific to the circumstances of each individual contract. The solicitor must therefore advise the client that even the best-drafted clause cannot be guaranteed to work in all circumstances. However, careful drafting can often significantly increase the likelihood of the clause passing the reasonableness test.

32.10.3.5   An example of reasonableness

In *SAM Business Systems Ltd v Hedley & Co* [2002] EWHC 2733, a computer supply company was held to have acted reasonably in excluding liability, not least as this was standard practice in the industry. The parties were of equal size and bargaining power. This also goes to indicate reasonableness. Computer supply companies will try to exclude most of their liability both for the implied terms under the SGA 1979 and the consequences of breach of contract, eg by capping their total liability to a specified amount. In this case, they succeeded. It is a typical UCTA type of dispute.

Chapter 33

Employment and Other Regulatory Concerns in Running a Business

33.1 Introduction

The new business will require personnel. The owner(s) of the business will need to be aware of statutory responsibilities and duties when recruiting employees, when acting as their employer and eventually, perhaps, when terminating their employment. Arrangements will have to be put in place for paying income tax (and corporation tax if the business is run by a company), for paying National Insurance contributions and for collecting and paying value added tax, if appropriate. Also, the product must be considered. Does the business need any licences, should the business carry insurances, or is there a need to protect the intellectual property rights of the business? There may be further matters to consider in relation to the business premises, such as planning consents, although these are not considered further in this book.

33.2 Employees

33.2.1 Recruitment

There is a statutory duty, under the Sex Discrimination Act 1975 and the Race Relations Act 1976, not to discriminate directly or indirectly on the grounds of sex, race or married status in advertising or offering employment. Under the Disability Discrimination Act 1995, it is also unlawful to discriminate against a disabled person in the recruitment of employees. A person should not be refused employment on the ground of his trade union membership (Trade Union and Labour Relations (Consolidation) Act 1992).

The UK has also outlawed discrimination on the grounds of race or ethnic origin, religion or belief, sexual orientation and age, according to the European Framework Equal Treatment Directive 2000/78/EC (OJ L303/16).

There is a further statutory duty under the Equal Pay Act 1970 for an employer to provide equal pay for men and women who are employed by him to do the same or comparable work.

33.2.2 Written statement of terms

By s 1 of the Employment Rights Act 1996 (as amended by the Employment Act 2002), the employer must, within two months of employment commencing, give the employee a written statement of terms and conditions relating to the following particulars:

(a)   identity of the parties;

(b)   date employment began;

(c)   date continuous employment began (taking into account any relevant employment with a previous employer);

(d)   scale or rate of remuneration and intervals of pay;

(e)   hours of work;

(f)   any terms relating to:

    (i)   holidays and holiday pay;

    (ii)   sickness and sick pay;

    (iii)   pensions and pension schemes;

(g)   length of notice required to determine the contract;

(h)   in the case of non-permanent employment, the period for which it is expected to continue or, if it is a fixed term, the date it is to end;

(i)   job title or a brief description of work;

(j)   place or places of work;

(k)   particulars of any collective agreements which directly affect the terms and conditions of employment;

(l)   where employees are required to work outside the UK for a period of more than one month, the period of such work, currency in which payment is made, benefits provided and terms relating to the return to the UK;

(m)   details of the disciplinary and dismissal rules and grievance procedures;

(n)   whether a contracting out certificate is in force (under the Pension Schemes Act 1993).

33.2.3   Dealings with employees

An employer should understand that he has certain statutory obligations towards his employee during the course of the employment in addition to those matters already described. These include:

(a)   allowing employees time off work for:

    (i)   ante-natal care;

    (ii)   trade union duties and activities;

    (iii)   public duties (eg those of magistrates); and

    (iv)   maternity and parental leave;

(b)   not discriminating on the grounds of sex, race, married status, religion or belief, disability or age in offering or refusing promotion or training etc to an employee and dismissal;

(c)   allowing an employee to return to work after maternity leave; and

(d)   taking reasonable care for the employees' health and safety at work.

An employer should also understand the general rights and remedies of an employee whom he may wish to dismiss.

33.2.4   Informing and consulting employees

The Information and Consultation of Employees Regulations 2004 (SI 2004/3426) were enacted in response to an EC Directive. The Directive gives employees in a relevant undertaking the right to be informed about the undertaking's economic situation, informed and consulted about employment prospects, and informed and consulted with a view to reaching agreement about decisions likely to lead to substantial changes in work organisation or contractual relations, including, but not limited to, collective redundancies and business transfers. The detail of the rights is beyond the scope of this book. They apply to undertakings employing 50 or more employees.

33.2.5 Dismissal of employees

An employer should understand the possible rights and remedies of an employee whom he wishes to dismiss. In addition to the discrimination claims mentioned at **33.2.1**, but which apply equally to dismissal (see **33.2.10**), there are three potential claims: the common law claim for wrongful dismissal and two statutory claims — the complaint of unfair dismissal and the claim for a statutory redundancy payment.

33.2.6 Wrongful dismissal

This is a common law claim which is based on the fact that the contract has been terminated by the employer in a manner which is a breach of the contract of employment. This is likely to be so if the employer terminates a contract for an indefinite term with no notice or with inadequate notice, or if a fixed-term contract is terminated before its expiry date.

Most employment contracts are for an indefinite term and terminable by either side giving the correct contractual notice. If the employer gives the proper period of notice, then no breach will have occurred and there will be no claim for wrongful dismissal whatever the reason for the termination. In a fixed-term contract, the contract is not usually terminable by notice. In the case of a fixed-term contract without a break clause, termination of the contract prior to its expiry date will be a breach of contract and the employee may claim wrongful dismissal.

The applicable notice period will usually be expressly agreed in the contract, and if the employer gives no notice or short notice he will be in breach. If an expressly agreed notice period is shorter than the statutory minimum period required by s 86 of the Employment Rights Act 1996 (ERA 1996), then the longer statutory period of notice must be given. In the absence of an expressly agreed period of notice, there is an implied term that the employee is entitled to 'reasonable' notice. What will be a reasonable period will depend on the facts of the case. For more senior employees, a longer period will be implied. In any event, any such implied period is again subject to the statutory minimum period stipulated by s 86.

Where a contract of employment can be ended by notice, s 86 of the ERA 1996 provides for the following statutory minimum periods of notice (which prevail over any shorter contractual period, express or implied). The statutory minimum is:

(a)   one week's notice after one month's continuous employment;

(b)   two weeks' notice after two years' continuous employment;

and thereafter one additional week's notice for each year of continuous employment up to a maximum of 12 weeks' notice after 12 years' continuous employment.

It should be appreciated that the claim for wrongful dismissal requires a dismissal in breach of contract. Where an employee simply resigns, he will have no claim, since it is he, the employee, who has then terminated the contract. He, the employee, will be in breach of contract if he does not give the notice that he was required to give under the contract to end it, or, in the case of a fixed-term contract, he terminates it before the expiry date. (In indefinite contracts, the only statutory minimum notice required to be given by an employee is one week's notice after one month's continuous employment.) However, if the employer had committed a repudiatory breach of an express or implied term of the contract, the employee is entitled to treat the contract as discharged. In this case, the employee is entitled to leave, with or without notice and he can bring a claim of wrongful dismissal. Although he has not been actually dismissed by the employer he has been 'constructively dismissed' in breach of contract. However, in such a case, the employee must leave within a reasonable time of the employer's breach, otherwise he will be deemed to have affirmed the contract. Such a repudiatory breach may occur where the employer unilaterally alters the employee's contract or breaks the implied duty of good faith owed to employees (eg by humiliating him in front of colleagues or clients, imposing unreasonable work demands on him, etc).

It should be noted that even where there is a prima facie wrongful dismissal, the employer will have a defence if the employee had committed a repudiatory breach of an express or implied term of the contract, such as revealing confidential information or trade secrets, wilfully disobeying the employer's lawful orders or other serious misconduct. The employer can still use this defence even if he did not know of the employee's breach at the time he terminated the contract, but only discovered it afterwards.

Damages for wrongful dismissal are damages for breach of contract and the normal contractual rules apply. The aim is to put the employee in the position he would have been in, so far as money can do this, had the contract not been broken. Thus, in the case of an indefinite contract, the starting point for the calculation is the net salary or wages the employee would have earned during the proper notice period. In the case of a fixed-term contract, it is the net salary for the remainder of the fixed term. In addition, the employee may claim damages for loss of other benefits he would have been entitled to for the relevant period (eg lost commission or 'fringe' benefits such as pension rights or use of a company car). Damages can usually be claimed for pecuniary loss only, so they will not generally be awarded for loss of future prospects or for injured feelings.

The employee is under a duty to mitigate his loss. Once his employment has been terminated he will be expected to take reasonable steps to obtain suitable employment and he will not be awarded damages in respect of any loss which has been mitigated or would have been mitigated but for his breach of the duty to mitigate. Note that where an employer has made a payment in lieu of notice, this will be deducted from any damages.

The claim for wrongful dismissal can be brought in either the High Court or the county court or in the employment tribunal.

33.2.7 Unfair dismissal

Under s 94 of the ERA 1996 an employee has the right not to be unfairly dismissed. The claim is brought before the employment tribunal. The employee must prove that he is a 'qualifying employee'. The employee must have one year's continuous employment starting when that employment began and ending with the dismissal.

The employee must prove that he has been dismissed. This includes actual dismissal and constructive dismissal. Actual dismissal is dismissal by the employer with or without notice. Constructive dismissal has been discussed at **33.2.6** in the context of wrongful dismissal. (There is another type of dismissal for the purposes of the statutory claim. This is where the contract was a fixed-term contract which was not renewed on its expiry.)

The burden of proof then moves to the employer. He must show the principal reason for the dismissal and that such reason is one of the six permitted reasons. If he can establish that, the employment tribunal must decide whether the employer acted reasonably in treating that reason as a sufficient reason for dismissing the employee. If either the employer cannot show one of the reasons or the tribunal considers that the employer acted unreasonably, then the employee will win. The potentially fair reasons are:

(a)   the *capability or qualifications* of the employee for doing work of the kind he was employed to do (this could include incompetence, or inability to do the job by reason of illness or injury);

(b)   the *conduct* of the employee (this must generally relate to conduct within the employment – outside behaviour will only be relevant if it has a direct bearing on the employee's fitness to do the job);

(c)   the employee was *redundant* (in this case the employee will be entitled to a redundancy payment (see below));

(d)   the employee could not continue to work in the position held without *contravening some statutory enactment* (eg where a lorry driver loses his driving licence);

(e)   *some other substantial reason* justifying the dismissal of an employee holding the position which the employee held (it is not possible to give a comprehensive list of such reasons, but this category has been held to include dismissal where the employee refuses to accept a reorganisation affecting his working hours and a dismissal arising out of a personality clash between employees); and

(f)   *retirement* – if it takes place at or after 65 (or a lower age which is objectively justified by the employer) and it meets procedural requirements, such as complying with a duty to inform the employee of the intended retirement date and of the employee's right to request to work beyond that date.

If the employer has demonstrated that the dismissal was for a fair reason, under s 98(4) of the ERA 1996 the tribunal must decide whether 'in the circumstances (including the size and administrative resources of the employer's undertaking) the employer acted reasonably or unreasonably in treating it as a sufficient reason for dismissing the employee [having regard] to equity and the substantial merits of the case.' The tribunal will see whether the employer had a genuine and reasonable belief in the facts based on a reasonable investigation and procedure leading to a reasonable decision. It will look at the size of the business — for instance, an employer with many employees may have found it more easy to cope with an employee who has considerable sickness absence. In particular, the employer may be held to have dismissed unfairly if there are procedural defects.

Thus, in 'capability' cases, the employer should normally have warned the employee about his standard of work and given him the chance to improve, and, perhaps additional training and supervision. Perhaps a reasonable employer would have moved the employee to a job within his competence rather than dismissing him. In dismissal for long-term sickness, the employer should consult with the employee as to the likely duration of the illness and its nature.

In 'conduct' cases, the employer should carry out a thorough investigation and allow the employee to state his case. He should not dismiss unless the misconduct is gross or persistent. Guidance on how to deal with misconduct is given by an ACAS Code of Practice, which in particular recommends a system of warnings for less serious misconduct. The Code does not have the force of law, but will be taken into account by the tribunal to see if the employer acted reasonably.

In cases of redundancy, the employer should warn and consult the affected employees or their representatives and adopt a fair basis of selection for redundancy ('Last in, first out' is often used as a basis for selection.) A fair employer would also consider the possibility of redeployment of affected employees within the business.

The employer should generally give the employee the correct notice due under the contract (or payment in lieu of notice). Failure to do so (other than in cases of gross misconduct) may well lead to a finding of unfair dismissal (as well as exposing the employer to a claim for wrongful dismissal).

If the defence is based on the employee's misconduct, unlike wrongful dismissal, the employer cannot rely on misconduct which he only discovered after the dismissal (although, if such misconduct had occurred, the tribunal may reduce any compensation). The remedies for unfair dismissal are as follows.

33.2.7.1   Reinstatement (getting the old job back) or re-engagement (being given another comparable or suitable job with the same or an associated employer)

It is for the employee to ask for such remedies and few such orders are made.

33.2.7.2   Compensation

This consists of two awards:

The basic award

This is calculated by reference to a statutory formula which reflects the employee's age, his pay and length of service. This formula remains untouched by age discrimination legislation. The statutory formula works by multiplying the employee's final gross week's pay (subject to a current maximum of £350; this is reviewed on 1 February each year) by the following factors:

(a)   his length of service (the maximum period taken into account is 20 years);

(b)   a multiplier (as below) depending on the employee's age during those years' service (working backwards from the end of the employment):

for years worked when not below the age of 41 = 1½

for years worked when below 41 but not below 22 = 1

for years worked when below 22 = ½

Example

Ernie starts work for A Co Ltd on his thirtieth birthday. His employment ends on his fifty-seventh birthday. His final gross week's pay is £360. On the basis of 20 years' service (the maximum), his basic award will be:

16 × 1½ × £350	8,400
4 × 1 × £350	1,400
	9,800

The compensatory award

In addition to the basic award, the tribunal will award such amount as it considers to be just and equitable having regard to the loss sustained by the employee in consequence of the dismissal in so far as that loss is attributable to the action taken by the employer. The award is subject to a maximum of £66,200 and is calculated under the following heads:

(a)   immediate loss of net wages from the date of the dismissal to the date of the hearing, assuming the employee has not at that date got another job;

(b)   future loss of net wages – based on an estimate as to how long it might take the employee to get another job (assuming he has not yet done so);

(c)   loss of fringe benefits; and

(d)   loss of statutory protection. In any new job, the employee will have to start building up as against a future employer his statutory rights to a redundancy payment and unfair dismissal protection and a statutory minimum notice.

The tribunal will deduct from the compensatory award any payment in lieu of notice or ex gratia payment received from the employer. Both the basic award and the compensatory award can be reduced due to the employee's contributory fault.

In addition, if either party unreasonably failed to follow ACAS's recommended Code on discipline and grievance before the tribunal proceedings were started, the compensatory award may be adjusted. If the failure to comply is wholly or mainly the employee's, it may be reduced by up to 25%. If it is deemed to be wholly or mainly the employer's fault, it may be increased by up to 25%.

33.2.8   Redundancy

The person primarily liable to pay a redundancy payment is the employer, and in most cases he pays it without dispute. Where he does not, or the employee disputes the calculation, the employee may refer the matter to an employment tribunal. There is a six-month time limit.

To claim a statutory redundancy payment, an employee must be 'qualified'. The factors are very similar to unfair dismissal, but the employee must have two years' continuous employment.

As in unfair dismissal, the employee must prove that he has been dismissed (actually, constructively or by failure to renew a fixed-term contract on expiry).

Once the above has been proved, a presumption arises that the employee has been dismissed for redundancy. The employer may be able to show a reason other than redundancy, but this may open the door to a claim for unfair dismissal. At this point, it is vital to consider whether or not the reason for the dismissal fits into the statutory definition of redundancy (contained in ERA 1996, s 139). The s 139 definition covers three situations:

(a)   *complete closedown* (the fact that the employer has ceased or intends to cease to carry on the business for the purposes of which the employee was employed by him);

(b)   *partial closedown* (the fact that the employer has ceased or intends to cease to carry on that business in the place where the employee was so employed); and

(c)   *overmanning or a change in the type of work undertaken* (the fact that the requirements of the business for employees to carry out work of a particular kind, or for employees to carry out work of a particular kind in the place where the employee was employed by the employer, have ceased or diminished, or are expected to cease or diminish).

At this point, the employee may have a prima facie entitlement to a redundancy payment. However, it should be noted that an employee may lose his entitlement if he unreasonably refuses an offer of suitable alternative employment made by his employer.

The statutory redundancy payment is calculated in general in the same way as the basic award for unfair dismissal.

33.2.9   Overlapping claims

The employer should appreciate that a dismissed employee may have more than one potential claim against him. If the dismissal is unfair and without proper notice (or within a fixed term) the employee may claim both wrongful dismissal and unfair dismissal. Should the employee succeed in both claims, the basic principle is that compensation will not be awarded for the same loss twice. Immediate and future loss of wages form a substantial part of the compensatory award for unfair dismissal, and this would substantially reduce any damages awarded for wrongful dismissal.

An employee may have a claim for a redundancy and also for unfair dismissal. This could arise where an employee is unfairly selected for redundancy. The redundancy payment will be set against the unfair dismissal award and usually it simply offsets the basic award (since the two are calculated according to a similar formula). However, if the redundancy payment exceeds the basic award (as it might if the basic award were reduced because of the employee's own conduct) the balance will reduce the compensatory award.

33.2.10   Discriminatory dismissals, etc

If an employer discriminates on the unlawful grounds mentioned at **33.2.1** in dismissing an employee, the employee will be entitled to claim compensation from the employer. This also applies to subjecting the employee to any of the other detrimental treatments mentioned at **33.2.1** and **33.2.3**. This compensation is similar to the unfair dismissal compensation award. It is not subject to any maximum and can include compensation for injured feelings. Again if claimed in addition to other claims, compensation will not be awarded twice for the same loss.

33.2.11   Compromise agreements

Many complaints are agreed without a hearing before the employment tribunal, usually because the employer pays the employee a sum in settlement.

However, under s 203 of the ERA 1996, any provision in an agreement is void in so far as it purports to exclude or limit the operation of any of the provisions of the ERA 1996, or to stop someone bringing proceedings before an employment tribunal. The caveat is that this can be done if a conciliation officer has taken action under s 18 of the ERA 1996, or a compromise agreement has been entered into.

A compromise agreement is an agreement entered into by the parties. For it to be binding, it has to do the following:

(a)   it must be in writing, identify the adviser, relate to the particular complaint and state that the relevant statutory conditions are satisfied;

(b)   the employee must have received advice from a relevant independent adviser as to the terms and effect of the proposed agreement and, in particular, its effect on his ability to pursue his rights before an employment tribunal; and

(c)   there must be in force, when the adviser gives the advice, a contract of insurance, or an indemnity provided for members of a profession or professional body, covering the risk of a claim by the employer or worker in respect of loss arising in consequence of the advice.

The compromise agreement must relate only to the matter in dispute. It cannot purport to exclude all possible claims (see ERA 1996, s 203).

Section 267 of the CA 2006 provides that a company cannot pay compensation to a director for loss of office without particulars of the proposed payment being disclosed to the members and approved by them in ordinary resolution.

33.2.12   Directors and members

A director or a member (ie a shareholder) can also be an employee of the company – see *Secretary of State for Trade and Industry v Bottrill* [2000] 1 All ER 915.

33.3   Accounting records for tax purposes

There is no statutory form of accounts which must be maintained, unless the business is run by a company, and only a company is required to have its accounts audited (see **8.1**). Nevertheless, it is necessary to maintain accounts which are sufficient to give a true and fair view of the affairs of a business so that the profits which are liable to tax can be ascertained.

33.4   National Insurance

A sole trader or partner will pay Class 2 National Insurance contributions which are at a flat rate and may also pay Class 4 National Insurance contributions which are calculated as a percentage of taxable profits. A limited company will pay the employer's National Insurance contributions in relation to each of its employees (including directors) and will collect and pay the employee's own Class 2 National Insurance contributions.

33.5   Value added tax

If the annual turnover of the business is expected to exceed £58,000 in the ensuing 30 days, the proprietor must register for VAT. This will mean that VAT must then be charged and accounted for on the output of goods or services by the business.

33.6   Licences

33.6.1   Consumer Credit Act 1974

If the business involves offering credit or hire facilities, the proprietor may require a licence under the Consumer Credit Act 1974 which may be obtained by application to the Office of Fair Trading.

33.6.2   Other licences

Particular types of businesses require a licence to operate obtained from the appropriate local administration office. Examples include licences for liquor sales (from the local authority), for food manufacture (from the environmental health department) and for children's nurseries (from the social services department).

33.7   Insurance

A range of possible insurances should be considered, two of which (employer's liability insurance and third party liability motor insurance) are compulsory. Examples of non-compulsory but advisable insurances include fire, theft, product liability, public liability and motor insurance (for more risks than the compulsory third party liability).

33.8   Intellectual property

The business may be using brand names, inventions, designs or products which can be protected from copying by competitors by registration. A patent may be granted for an invention which is capable of industrial application following an application to the Patent Office. A design (ie the outward shape or decorative appearance of a product) may be registered at the Patent Office. A trade mark is a brand name or logo which distinguishes the product in the minds of the public (eg 'Coca-Cola' for soft drinks, or 'Honda' for motorcycles). It may be registered at the Trade Marks Registry, which is part of the Patent Office.

33.9   Terms and conditions of trading

A business will want to set up the terms of the contracts it uses. These contracts could be for the provision of services or for the sale of goods, or a combination. Some aspects of trading are dealt with in **Chapters 32, 34** and **35**.

Chapter 34

Introduction to Agency and Distribution Agreements

34.1 Introduction

This chapter will look at differences between agency and distribution agreements and compare them with other types of commercial contracts, such as licensing and franchising agreements. **Chapter 35** will examine which factors are relevant in deciding whether to go for an agency or a distribution agreement.

34.2 Agency

Suppose Latham Ltd, a furniture manufacturer, decides to sell its furniture in France. However, what if Latham has little or no experience of the market conditions in France? It is likely that any marketing exercises it might undertake over there would be, at best, ill-informed. If Latham is still determined to sell in France, one solution is to find someone who does know the market in question, and enter into an arrangement whereby that person markets the furniture on Latham's behalf.

One way of marketing the goods would be for Latham to appoint a French company as its agent for the selling of the furniture. The agency agreement is likely to be one of two main types.

34.2.1 'Sales' agency

Latham may authorise the agent (the French company) to enter into contracts with customers on its behalf; Latham will be 'the principal' under this arrangement. As a result, Latham will be in a direct contractual relationship with the French customers through the agent's actions. This is sometimes called a 'classical sales agency'.

34.2.2 'Marketing' agency

However, Latham may not be very happy with the idea of being bound into a contractual relationship with a customer whom it has never met. It may therefore prefer to give its agent a more limited type of agency authority, where Latham merely authorises the agent to find potential buyers, carry out preliminary discussions and put them directly in touch with Latham. This type of agency is sometimes known as a 'marketing', 'solicitation' or 'introducing' agency.

34.2.3 'Del credere' agency

This describes the situation where the agent agrees to guarantee the customer's performance of the contract in return for an additional commission. This is exceptional, since an agent is usually not liable at all on any contract which he negotiates on the principal's behalf.

34.3   Distribution agreement

Another marketing possibility for Latham would be to sell the furniture to the French company, to enable that company to sell on to customers in France.

However, assume that, rather than simply selling the furniture to the French company and then leaving everything up to them, Latham wants to control the way in which the French company markets the furniture in France. For example, it wants to ensure that the French company exercises its best endeavours to sell as many of the products as possible, and that it uses advertising material which is appropriate to the products and accords with Latham's image. It also wants to ensure that the distributor will carry enough items of furniture to satisfy customer demand so that its goodwill in France will not be damaged by failure to make furniture available to customers. The French company agrees to all these conditions in return for the exclusive right to sell Latham's furniture in France. In other words, the parties enter into a distribution agreement, and both parties have accepted terms which limit their commercial freedom.

34.3.1   The nature of a distribution agreement

The basis of a distribution agreement is that one party (the distributor) buys goods from the other (the supplier) in order to resell them to the distributor's own customers. Thus, there is a contract between Latham and the distributor for the sale and purchase of the furniture, and a contract between the distributor and its customers (also for the sale and purchase of furniture), but no contract between Latham and the distributor's customer.

When goods are being marketed via a distribution agreement, there may be a number of levels of distribution between the producer of the goods and their ultimate consumer. For example, assume that a manufacturer of goods enters into a distribution agreement with a wholesaler. The wholesaler then enters into a distribution agreement of its own with one or more retailers. A supplier at any level of distribution may enter into a number of separate but identical agreements with different distributors, so that the goods can be marketed as widely as possible. The number of distributors appointed by each supplier is likely to increase as the goods move down the 'marketing chain'.

34.3.2   Distribution contrasted with agency and sale of goods

The relationship of supplier and distributor depends on the law of contract. A supplier and distributor will normally enter into a formal distribution agreement, which sets out the terms of their relationship. Central to this will be the terms on which the supplier sells the goods to the distributor (compare this with an agency agreement, where the principal is not selling the goods to the agent but there may be similar provisions relating to the terms upon which the agent contracts). These terms will cover matters such as the goods to be sold, price, payment, delivery and quality. Unlike an agent, a distributor will not receive commission in respect of goods sold. A distributor makes its profit from the margin between the price it pays for the goods and the price at which it sells them.

Although a distribution agreement is essentially a sale of goods contract, it is normally much more than that. In our example, of equal importance with the transfer of ownership in the furniture in return for payment (terms which characterise a sale of goods agreement) are the terms indicated at **34.3** under which the French company accepts certain obligations and restrictions in relation to its advertising and selling of the products and Latham agrees to give it exclusive rights to sell in the relevant territory.

34.3.3   Types of distribution agreements

The form and substance of distribution agreements can vary considerably, depending on the nature of the products being marketed and the level of distribution which has been reached.

Despite this variety, however, agreements tend to fall into a number of broad categories. For example, some are classified as 'selective distribution' agreements. In this case, the supplier attempts to control the sales which its distributor makes. A classic way in which this is done is by a manufacturer putting a term into its agreement with a wholesaler that the wholesaler can only sell the goods to persons who meet the manufacturer's suitability criteria. This may happen, for example, where the goods are luxury items and the manufacturer wants to ensure that any retail outlet to which the wholesaler sells has the appropriate ambience, or where the goods are highly technical and retailers need properly trained staff both to sell the goods and to provide effective after-sales service. In either case, the agreement must provide a set of clear and objective criteria for suitability, and even then, there may be problems with competition law (the impact of competition law on commercial agreements generally is considered in **Chapter 36**).

Another significant category of agreement is 'exclusive distribution'. Usually, this means that the supplier appoints a distributor as its only authorised representative in a certain area (eg in the UK), agreeing not to appoint any other distributors for that area and also not to supply customers in the area itself. This is probably what Latham and the French company have in mind when they agree that the French company is to have 'exclusive rights' to sell in France. It is also possible for the parties to enter into a 'sole distribution' agreement, where the supplier agrees not to appoint any other distributors for the area, but reserves the right to supply customers direct. It is normally a good idea, however, to avoid using these terms in the drafting of an agreement without further explanation, as businesses do in practice use the terms to mean different things. In our example, it would be important to check what the parties understood the expression 'exclusive rights' to mean.

34.3.4 Distribution agreements and competition law

Great care has to be taken in drafting distribution agreements as, without proper thought and advice, the parties may include terms which fall foul of competition law. This will be considered further in **Chapter 36**.

34.4 Other types of marketing agreements

Agency and distribution agreements are not the only types of marketing agreements available. The remainder of this section will briefly consider three other possibilities:

(a)   licensing agreements;

(b)   franchising agreements; and

(c)   joint ventures.

The various types of agreements are by no means mutually exclusive. For example, a distributor may also need some access to the intellectual property rights of the manufacturer to enable him to market the product to potential customers. The distribution agreement may therefore include a licence to the distributor of some of the manufacturer's rights (eg the right to use the manufacturer's trade mark).

34.4.1 Licensing

Example

An inventor has come up with a revolutionary new product with great sales potential. There may be various reasons why he does not want to manufacture and distribute that product himself:

(a)   he may not have the facilities to manufacture or distribute the product. He may not be a manufacturer at all, or he may be a small manufacturer with insufficient resources to meet the costs involved in developing, advertising and supplying a sufficient quantity of the product in question;

> (b)   he may want to market the product in a particular territory and be compelled or encouraged by local laws in that territory to arrange for the product to be manufactured in the territory itself, rather than to manufacture it himself and sell it to a distributor in the usual way.
>
> In such cases, the inventor may consider granting a licence to a third party to manufacture and market the product on his behalf.

34.4.2 Franchising

The essence of a franchising agreement is that the franchisor establishes what is usually known as a 'uniform business format' and then authorises the franchisee (often known as the satellite business) to use it.

> **Example**
>
> A restaurateur opens up an American-style restaurant in a large provincial town. The food is good, the atmosphere is agreeable and the decor distinctive. Before long, he is so busy he is turning customers away.
>
> He begins to have a vision of many other similar restaurants in other large provincial towns, all with the same name, the same decor, the same menu and the same ambience. However, he feels that he will not have the capacity to run these restaurants himself, and he does not want to employ managers to run them. He feels that someone with a financial stake in such a business is more likely to make a go of it.
>
> The dilemma is one of control. The restaurateur does not want to be responsible for the satellite restaurants, but he does want to be able to control them, in the sense of ensuring that they retain the same format as the original restaurant. One solution to this problem would be to grant franchises to set up the new restaurants.

34.4.2.1 Advantages of a franchise

The restaurateur benefits since he can extend his business system without having to raise capital to do so. Also, since the franchisee is an independent owner-operator, the restaurateur:

(a)   can usually count on a higher level of performance and profitability; and

(b)   incurs less risk of legal liability to customers and staff.

The franchisee benefits because:

(a)   he can use a business format or product already tested in the market which carries a name familiar to customers and suppliers;

(b)   he can usually count on the franchisor's assistance and training during the risky start-up period (eg advice on the provision of equipment and stock); and

(c)   he will often find it easier to raise the necessary bank and other finance to get the business off the ground.

34.4.2.2 Disadvantages of a franchise

The restaurateur may find it difficult in practice to maintain consistently high standards in the franchise and this may damage his reputation with third parties.

The franchisee may find the franchise frustrating because:

(a)   the uniform business format leaves little room for individual initiative;

(b)   the goodwill of the business remains in the franchisor (however hard the franchisee works to build up clientele); and

(c)   the sale of the business therefore remains within the franchisor's control.

34.4.2.3 Conclusion

In practice, many shops, restaurants and other outlets are franchised, including many fast-food restaurants.

34.4.3   Joint ventures

The joint venture agreement commonly occurs where two or more businesses collaborate on a particular project or business enterprise. They may be similar businesses which are, in effect, pooling their resources. Alternatively, they may operate in different spheres and be collaborating on a project which involves the application of both of their areas of expertise.

Often, the parties involved will form a joint venture company and much thought will need to be given as to what powers each party has in respect of that company. However, there are other structures for joint ventures (see **Appendix 1**).

34.4.4   Impact of competition law

Licensing agreements, franchising agreements and joint venture agreements are normally all capable of being affected by competition law. The main provisions of EC competition law (and the main ways of avoiding its impact) are considered in outline in **Chapter 36**.

34.4.5   Other forms of agreement

There are many other forms of commercial agreements; however, further consideration of this area is outside the scope of this book.

Chapter 35
Choosing a Marketing Agreement

35.1 Introduction

This chapter looks in outline at the various factors which might be relevant in choosing between an agency or a distribution agreement.

Before considering the choice between agency and distribution, note that a commercial client may not always require outside assistance in marketing its goods. For example, a large manufacturer intending to market a new line of goods may already be established (eg in the form of a subsidiary company) in its chosen market. It may then be appropriate to let the subsidiary handle the marketing (this can have competition law advantages: see **Chapter 36**).

However, where a client does need a 'trading partner' to help it find buyers and make sales, both agency and distribution agreements are potentially suitable. The client will naturally wish to market the goods as cheaply and efficiently as possible, as well as to promote demand for the goods in the chosen market. The best way of doing this will have to be assessed individually in each case, but the factors described in the following paragraphs should always be considered. Some of these factors may suggest whether an agency or distribution agreement is more suitable; others should always be borne in mind when considering marketing agreements generally.

35.2 Commercial factors

Commercial factors play an important part in making the right choice of marketing agreement for a client. They may vary from case to case, but certain points are always worth considering.

35.2.1 Size and organisation of the client's business

A large business with considerable resources may be able to use existing subsidiaries, or set up new ones to handle marketing. In this way, it may be able to create an integrated marketing system which runs more efficiently than one in which goods are sold on down the marketing chain between different, independent businesses.

This may, however, not be possible for many clients; setting up a subsidiary (especially overseas) may be too expensive and time-consuming, in which case the client should consider appointing an independent agent or distributor. Bear in mind that a sales agency will need more supervision than a marketing agency or distribution agreement, because a sales agent binds its principal. A client which lacks the time or resources to keep a close check on its marketing operations should choose either a marketing agency or a distribution agreement.

35.2.2 Location and nature of proposed market

If the client is trying to penetrate an unfamiliar market (especially overseas), a distribution agreement is likely to be preferable to an agency agreement. Under a distribution agreement, the client does not have the risk of operating in the market itself (or direct responsibility to customers: see **35.2.4**), and can rely on the distributor's knowledge of local trading conditions and rules. This may be particularly helpful if there is a language barrier to be overcome. As an independent entrepreneur, a distributor may also have more incentive to exploit the market to the full; a distributor is acting for itself, and keeps the profit it earns.

35.2.3 Nature of goods to be marketed

If the client's goods are relatively easy to market (eg they are standard in specification, do not vary greatly according to customer requirements and do not require repackaging before they can be sold to customers) a distribution agreement is particularly suitable. If, however, it is essential for the client to be in touch with customers to give them the products they need (eg tailor-made goods, or goods requiring substantial modifications to suit individual customers) an agency agreement is more appropriate.

35.2.4 Client's responsibility to customers

In an agency agreement, the principal will have a contractual relationship with customers (ie the ultimate buyers of the goods); the agent will have either made the contract on the principal's behalf (sales agency) or found and introduced the customers to the principal (marketing agency). In a distribution agreement, the supplier is only liable in contract to the distributor, not to the ultimate customers. If the goods are defective, customers sue the distributor. The supplier's liability to the distributor will be subject to the terms of their agreement and the law governing that agreement, but it may be possible to define and control this liability more strictly than liability to customers. A supplier may, however, be liable to the distributor's customers in other ways (eg in certain circumstances under the Consumer Protection Act 1987 in the UK or parallel provisions in other Member States of the European Union (EU)).

35.3 Overseas operations

If the parties to a marketing agreement are to be based in different countries (eg a UK supplier appoints a French distributor to market the supplier's goods in France), they should consider a number of points concerning the law which applies to the agreement.

35.3.1 Governing law

If the parties to an agency or distribution agreement are in different countries, they will have to decide what law they wish to govern the agreement. For example, the UK supplier and French distributor are likely to choose either English law or French law. If, however, they cannot agree on the law of one of the parties, they should find an acceptable compromise, such as the law of a neutral third country.

As far as the UK and most of the countries of Western Europe are concerned, contracts made on or after 1 April 1991 are governed by the 1980 Rome Convention relating to contractual obligations. Under the Convention, the general principle is that the parties have complete freedom to decide which law governs their contract. However, this will not prevent certain mandatory rules applying to the contract.

For instance, where all the elements of the contract apply to one country only, the mandatory rules of that country cannot be excluded by merely choosing the law of a different country. For example, if both parties were resident in England and the contract were to be performed in England, the parties could not avoid the impact of English law on, for example, restraint of trade, by opting for Swiss law. Even where some of the elements of the contract apply to a different country, certain mandatory rules protecting consumers and employees may be non-excludable.

The best advice must be to examine the terms of the Convention before committing the client to a particular choice of law.

35.3.2 How will local law affect the agreement?

Local law (ie the law of the place where the agreement is performed) may be relevant even if the parties have chosen a different law to govern the agreement. Although detailed consideration of this aspect of the parties' relationship is beyond the scope of this chapter, the solicitor should be aware that, in some jurisdictions, provisions of local law may purport to exclude or override parts of the agreement.

35.3.3 Agency agreements

In drafting an agency agreement which is to operate within the EU, it is important to be aware of the impact of the Directive 86/653 on the Co-ordination of the Laws of Member States relating to Self-Employed Commercial Agents ([1986] OJ L382/17). The Directive attempts to harmonise national laws on commercial agency, and in particular provides for the way in which agents are to be remunerated and for the compulsory payment of sums of money by way of compensation or indemnity to an agent on termination of an agency agreement in certain circumstances. The UK implemented the Directive by the Commercial Agents (Council Directive) Regulations 1993 (SI 1993/3053). Detailed consideration of the Regulations is beyond the scope of this chapter, but it is important to note that their provisions on remuneration, termination and compensation considerably strengthen the agent's position under an agency agreement. Significantly, there is some evidence that, since the Regulations came into force, businesses which might in the past have appointed agents have tended to choose other forms of marketing arrangements, as they are concerned about the high level of protection which the Regulations give to agents. In this sense, the Regulations must now be counted as a factor in the choice between agency and distribution.

35.3.4 Specialist advice

If the client's agreement has an overseas element, it will usually be necessary to take the advice of a local lawyer. Local factors may affect the choice of agreement (eg in some countries, foreign businesses are not permitted to act as principals; they can trade only through a locally-run office). Specialist advice may also be needed on other matters, including the effect of local taxation. In addition, if the proposed agent is an individual, local employment or social security laws may apply to the agreement.

35.4 UK taxation

If both parties to an agency or distribution agreement are based in the UK, there are no particular tax advantages or disadvantages to either type of agreement. However, it may be important to advise a client on taxation when the principal or supplier is based overseas, with the agent or distributor in the UK, because the principal or supplier could in some circumstances be liable to pay UK corporation tax.

The detailed rules in this area are beyond the scope of this chapter; broadly speaking, however, if an overseas business trades in the UK through a branch or agency, it can be liable to UK corporation tax. For example, if a sales agent makes regular contracts on its principal's behalf here, the principal may become sufficiently established in the UK for tax purposes and the agent may have to account to the Revenue for tax on the principal's profits on the principal's behalf. In a distribution agreement, the important factor in deciding whether a non-resident supplier can be liable for corporation tax is whether the supplier has established a sufficient business presence within the UK.

Other features of the agreement between the parties may also require special care from the tax point of view; in particular, whether there is any liability on either party to pay VAT. It may be necessary to take specialist advice on this matter.

35.5 Competition law

The impact of EC competition law on both agency and distribution agreements is dealt with in **Chapter 36**.

For the purposes of this chapter, it is sufficient to note that genuine agency agreements are unaffected by EC competition law. This means that Article 81 EC (Article 85 prior to the renumbering of the EC Treaty by the Treaty of Amsterdam) cannot apply to the agreement (see further **36.8.2**).

Distribution agreements may run into difficulties with EC competition law. Many distribution agreements contain terms which could affect trade and competition (eg the supplier appoints the distributor to be its distributor for a defined territory, and then agrees to appoint no other distributors for that territory: see further **36.4.2**). It is often possible, however, to arrange matters so that the practical effect of competition law on the agreement is minimal. The EC competition law authorities are relatively sympathetic in their treatment of distribution agreements (especially those between smaller businesses), believing that such agreements may facilitate trade between Member States and help reinforce the single market.

As far as English competition law is concerned, s 2 of the Competition Act 1998 contains a general prohibition on agreements and certain other business arrangements which may affect trade within the UK and have as their object or effect the prevention, restriction or distortion of competition within the UK. This is known as the 'Chapter I prohibition', and is almost identical in its wording to Article 81 EC. It is unlikely that this provision will apply to agency agreements, but it may affect some distribution agreements.

35.6 Making a choice

The choice of marketing agreement must depend on the circumstances of each case. However, the following examples show how the choice might work in practice:

Example 1: Distribution agreement

Tea Time Ltd was set up five years ago. It is a small company which manufactures jams and pickles. The directors believe that the company's products will sell very well in France, but are not confident about conducting business abroad and in a foreign language. They can spend some time on developing their overseas business, but feel that they need to concentrate on manufacturing. The jams and pickles can be easily exported in a form suitable for immediate resale.

These facts strongly suggest that a distribution agreement is the right choice. The company needs a trading partner, and wants to trade overseas in an unfamiliar market. The expertise of a local trading partner will help to overcome the language barrier, but the company will not be able to spare the time or resources to supervise that partner very closely. The goods can easily be marketed in the form in which they leave the company. One possible disadvantage of a distribution agreement when compared with an agency agreement is that EC competition law is more likely to apply, but if the trading partner is also a small business, this is unlikely to be a major problem (see **36.8.3**).

Example 2: Agency agreement

Wood Magic Ltd is a medium-sized company based in Chester. It has traded successfully for nearly 20 years, making luxury fitted furniture from woods such as yew and cherry. Its operations have so far been confined to northern England, but it now wishes to expand into the rest of the UK (and possibly into continental Europe). The company has up to now handled its own marketing, because of the need to make each piece of furniture to each customer's exact requirements. However, its directors feel that they will require outside marketing assistance in making the planned expansion. They are happy to spend time working with and supervising their chosen trading partner; they feel that this will be necessary to maintain the excellent reputation of their products.

These facts suggest that an agency agreement is appropriate. The company is experienced in running its business, but needs a trading partner. Customer contact is absolutely vital. It may be a case where agency is appropriate for the projected overseas operations as well as those in the UK; the factor of customer contact may outweigh the drawbacks of operating an agency agreement abroad. Either sales or marketing agency may be suitable, although marketing agency does have the advantage of requiring less supervision. This may not, however, be crucial if Wood Magic Ltd is prepared to set aside plenty of time to keep a check on the agency.

Chapter 36
Competition Law

36.1 Introduction

This chapter builds on and develops the basic principles of EC competition law which were introduced in *Legal Foundations*, placing particular emphasis on the application of EC competition law to individual commercial agreements. In order to prepare for this, a reminder of those basic principles is likely to be helpful.

36.2 Principles and sources of EC competition law

36.2.1 Direct effect

Articles 81 (formerly 85) and 82 (formerly 86) of the European Community Treaty (also known as the Treaty of Rome; this chapter will refer to the Treaty as the 'EC Treaty') have direct effect and are directly applicable in all Member States. EC law takes precedence over the law of Member States where there is a conflict between the two. Thus, if the law of a Member State permits a trading practice, but EC competition law prohibits it, the practice is unlawful.

As noted briefly in **35.5**, most Articles of the EC Treaty were renumbered by the Treaty of Amsterdam, which came into force on 1 May 1999. The remainder of this chapter uses only the post-Amsterdam numbers for these Articles. Note that if the Treaty of Lisbon (the Reform Treaty) does ever come into force (which is still uncertain following the Treaty's rejection in Ireland's referendum in June 2008), the Article numbers will change again. Articles 81 and 82 will become Articles 101 and 102 of the Treaty on the Functioning of the European Union. However, their wording will not change.

36.2.2 Sources

There are four main sources of EC competition law:

(a)   the relevant Articles of the EC Treaty (see **36.5**);

(b)   secondary legislation issued under the authority of the Treaty by the Council of Ministers or European Commission (eg Regulation 2790/1999 on the application of Article 81(3) EC to vertical agreements ([1999] OJ L336/21): see **36.8.7**);

(c)   case law (created by decisions of the Commission and judgments of the Court of First Instance and the European Court of Justice);

(d)   notices issued by the Commission indicating policy (eg the Notice on Agreements of Minor Importance: see **36.8.3**).

36.2.3   Operation of EC competition law: the institutions

36.2.3.1   The European Commission

The Council of Ministers has delegated power to the Commission to supervise the operation of EC competition law. The Commission, through its Competition Law Directorate-General, is therefore responsible for developing competition policy, investigating suspected infringements of competition law, issuing Decisions on most points of competition law and taking action against infringements if necessary. For more detail on the enforcement of EC competition law, see **36.6**.

36.2.3.2   The Court of First Instance and the European Court of Justice

Appeals against Decisions of the Commission are heard by the Court of First Instance. Appeal from the Court of First Instance is to the European Court of Justice.

The European Court of Justice also has jurisdiction under the general Article 234 EC reference procedure to give preliminary rulings on points of interpretation of EC competition law referred to it from national courts.

36.3   Other systems of competition law

36.3.1   Systems of Member States

It is important to note that most Member States have their own domestic systems of competition law and that, depending on the circumstances, it may be necessary to consider this domestic law in addition to EC law. Alternatively, domestic competition law may apply where EC law does not (eg where there is no effect on trade between Member States). Competition law in the UK underwent major changes as a result of the Competition Act 1998. This Act repealed a number of existing UK competition law statutes (notably the Restrictive Trade Practices Act 1976 and the Resale Prices Act 1976), and replaced them with a system much closer to Articles 81 and 82 EC. The emphasis of English competition law is now on prohibiting business arrangements which may affect trade within, and have the object or effect of preventing or distorting competition in, the UK and also on prohibiting abuse of a dominant position within the UK. Further detailed consideration of UK competition law is outside the scope of this book, although the following sections will make some brief comparisons where appropriate.

36.3.2   US competition law

It is worth noting that probably the most developed system of competition law in the world is that of the USA. Like EC competition law, it shows the strong influence of political theory (although it lacks the EC dimension of being used as a means of creating a single internal market between different, independent countries) and has been even more heavily influenced by economic theory. The competition authorities of the USA and EC frequently liaise with each other and so developments in US policy may influence EC thinking. Briefly, US competition law in its present form began with the Sherman Act 1890. This was designed to combat the anti-competitive practice by which trustees took control of independent companies, and then used that control to eliminate competition. US competition law is therefore known as 'anti-trust' law, although the term has come to refer to any action taken against anti-competitive practices. Its development has seen a number of different approaches to regulating the struggle between small and large businesses; each type of business has had periods of being in and out of favour with the law. By contrast, EC competition policy has always tended to favour smaller businesses.

36.4   EC competition law and commercial agreements

36.4.1   Vertical and horizontal agreements

For competition law purposes, agreements are often classified as either 'vertical' or 'horizontal'. As a general principle, the EC competition authorities treat vertical agreements more leniently than horizontal agreements; broadly speaking, the same principle applies to English competition law.

36.4.1.1   Vertical agreements

Broadly speaking, a vertical agreement is an agreement between parties at different levels of the marketing 'chain', although it is important to note that EC law has its own precise definition of 'vertical agreement' (see **36.8.7**). Examples include supply, distribution, agency and franchising agreements. The parties to a vertical agreement may wish to use terms in that agreement which potentially restrict competition. Assume, for example, that a manufacturer and a wholesaler entering into a distribution agreement agree that the wholesaler will buy all its goods for resale from the manufacturer, and that the manufacturer will sell to the wholesaler and no one else. This ties them to one another, and potentially reduces competition in the market in which the parties operate (eg other potential wholesalers may find it harder to break into the market because they cannot easily acquire suitable goods for resale). However, it is arguable that the potential restriction of competition may be beneficial to consumers of the goods in question, rather than harmful. The parties are secure in their relationship, which may encourage greater availability of the goods and more efficient supply.

As a result, EC competition law deals fairly leniently with most types of vertical agreements; see further **36.8.6**.

36.4.1.2   Horizontal agreements

A horizontal agreement is one between parties at the same level of supply; for example, where competing manufacturers agree to fix the prices at which they will sell their products, or to share out product markets between themselves. This type of agreement (often referred to as a 'cartel') is likely to operate in a way which seriously reduces competition and harms consumers (eg prices are kept artificially high). EC law rarely permits such restriction of competition.

36.4.2   Drafting vertical agreements: likely problem areas

Competition law may have a considerable effect on commercial agreements. It may, for example, influence the choice of agreement, as an agency agreement is less likely to infringe Article 81(1) EC than a distribution agreement (see **36.8.2**). This chapter is, however, primarily concerned with the effect of competition law on the drafting of an agreement. The following examples are based on the application of EC competition law: note that the position should be broadly the same in each case under the Competition Act where an agreement is capable of affecting trade and competition within the UK.

36.4.2.1   Grant of territory

Assume that a UK company ('the supplier') is appointing a distributor to sell its goods in France. In order to get the distributorship firmly established, the supplier is prepared to offer the distributor some protection from competition. What the distributor wants in this respect is for the supplier not to appoint any other distributors to sell in France, and also for the supplier not to sell direct to French customers. Will it cause competition law problems if the supplier agrees to this? The term which the parties are contemplating (often referred to as the grant of 'exclusive territory') is a potential restriction on competition. It cuts down the sources from which consumers can buy the goods and, as a result, may keep the price artificially high. It may stop other sellers coming into the market. However, although this is a potential infringement of Article 81(1) EC, it should be permissible under the vertical agreements block exemption (see **36.8.7**).

36.4.2.2   Export ban

Assume that the grant of territory which has just been described is lawful. In return for giving this concession, the supplier wants to ensure that the distributor concentrates on the French market by providing that the distributor will sell the goods only in France and not export them to Belgium. Because one of the aims of EC competition law is to ensure that goods can circulate freely around the entire common market, a term in the agreement which restricts or bans exports will cause problems. It will artificially partition the common market along national lines. It may prevent consumers from being able to buy goods more cheaply from other Member States than they can at home, by impeding 'parallel imports'. Typically, these happen when a trader buys goods in a part of the EU where those goods are cheap, and resells in higher-priced areas, undercutting the higher prices and making them difficult to maintain. The Commission encourages parallel imports as a means of consolidating the single market; an export ban is therefore seen as a serious infringement of Article 81(1) EC and is unlikely to be permitted.

36.4.2.3   Unsolicited requests from outside the territory

Assume that the supplier wants to include a term in the agreement forbidding the distributor from selling the goods in response to sales requests from Italy, believing that the distributor should concentrate its efforts on exploiting its exclusive territory (ie France). The term is likely to impede the free flow of goods around the common market, and potentially cuts off a source of goods for parallel imports. It is a potential restriction of competition and infringement of Article 81(1) EC. However, EC law will probably allow some compromise. The client may be able to stop the distributor actively seeking orders from outside France (making 'active' sales), but may not be able to stop it meeting unsolicited requests (making 'passive' sales). The point is considered further at **36.8.7**.

36.5   The relevant Articles of the EC Treaty

36.5.1   Articles 2 and 3 EC: general principles

Article 2 EC sets out the Community's general aims of establishing a common market and approximating the economic policies of Member States. Article 3 EC lists activities of the Community which are intended to achieve this, including at Article 3(1)(g), 'the institution of a system ensuring that competition in the common market is not distorted'. The Commission and Courts often refer to Articles 2 and 3 EC in their decisions on Articles 81 and 82 EC, using the general principles as a starting point for the interpretation of the specific Articles.

Note that Articles 2 and 3 will be reworded if the Treaty of Lisbon comes into force; in particular there will be no equivalent of Article 3(1)(g). It remains to be seen what impact this will have in practice.

36.5.2   Articles 28–30 EC: free movement of goods

Articles 28–30 EC deal with import and export restrictions on the free flow of goods around the common market, and so are indirectly relevant to competition. Broadly, Article 28 EC prohibits measures enacted by Member States which impose total or partial restraints on imports (eg rules requiring import licences or inspection of imports). Article 29 EC does the same thing for export restraints (eg export licences). The emphasis is therefore on government restrictions on trade, rather than on arrangements between businesses. Article 30 EC, however, sets out circumstances in which such controls may be permitted. For a more detailed discussion of how Articles 28–30 EC operate, see ***Legal Foundations***.

The Treaty of Lisbon will renumber Articles 28–30 as Articles 34–36 of the Treaty on the Functioning of the European Union, but their wording will not change.

36.5.3   Article 81 EC: principle, effect and exemption

Article 81(1) EC prohibits as incompatible with the common market agreements between undertakings, decisions by associations of undertakings or concerted practices which may affect trade between Member States and which have as their object or effect the prevention, restriction or distortion of competition within the common market. It also sets out a non-exhaustive list of business operations or practices which infringe this general principle (eg an agreement to share markets or to fix prices). By Article 81(2) EC, such agreements, decisions or practices are void. Article 81(3) EC, however, allows exemption from the Article 81(1) prohibition in certain circumstances (see **36.8.9**). Article 81 EC is reproduced in ***Business and Company Legislation*** and discussed in detail in ***Legal Foundations***.

36.5.4   Article 81 EC: a brief reminder of the key points

36.5.4.1   Agreements between undertakings

'Agreements' may be formal or informal, written or oral; for example, a formal written contract between two companies for one to distribute the other's products would be an 'agreement', but this would also be the case if nothing were put into writing. This chapter is largely concerned with the effect of Article 81 EC on agreements.

36.5.4.2   Decisions by associations of undertakings

A common example of this is where a trade association (ie an 'association of undertakings') makes a decision to fix the prices of products sold by its member businesses, instead of those businesses fixing their own prices in individual agreements with buyers. The price-fixing is likely to be well-organised and widespread, and so may be a potentially serious restriction of competition.

36.5.4.3   Concerted practices

'Concerted practices' can cover virtually any type of co-operation between undertakings (the basic test is whether the undertakings involved have knowingly substituted co-operation for competition). The concerted practice is most often found in relation to manufacturers, but possible examples in relation to vertical agreements include:

Informal co-operation

Two undertakings draft an agreement which does not infringe Article 81(1) EC, then abide by different, informally agreed, terms which do restrict competition (in practice, this sort of situation may constitute an informal agreement rather than a concerted practice; however, the precise classification is not usually significant for the purposes of Article 81(1) EC).

Networks

In a network of distribution agreements, one supplier enters into a number of agreements with different distributors. Even if none of these agreements contains any terms which directly restrict competition, the effect of the network of agreements may be to close off a market to new businesses trying to enter; it may mean that no new suppliers or distributors are required for that market.

36.5.4.4   Undertakings

The term 'undertakings' covers any entity which is engaged independently in economic activity, including (in the UK) sole traders, partnerships and companies.

36.5.4.5   May affect trade between Member States

The basic test is whether the relevant agreement, decision or practice alters or has the potential to alter the natural flow of trade between Member States. The effect on trade must be appreciable, but the agreement does not necessarily have to be between undertakings based in different Member States. An agreement between parties based in the same Member State and which appears at first sight only to concern that domestic market may have the potential to 'affect trade' in the way required by Article 81(1) EC. For example, two large UK-based businesses which enter into a distribution agreement relating only to the UK market may be able to close off that market so that competitors based elsewhere in the EU find it difficult to enter. It is also possible that an agreement where one party is based outside the EU (or European Economic Area) and one within it may affect trade within the EU, especially where there is a strong trading relationship between the EU and the non-EU country involved.

36.5.4.6   Object or effect

'Object' means that Article 81 EC applies to agreements containing terms such as price-fixing or export bans without any need for a market analysis; ie, by their very nature, they are assumed to fall within Article 81 EC. 'Effect' means that it also applies to agreements which, following analysis, have the effect of restricting competition. This gives the Commission an enormously wide discretion when applying Article 81 EC.

36.5.4.7   Prevention, restriction or distortion of competition within the common market

The Commission gives these words their natural meaning. If an agreement has already been found to affect (or have the potential to affect) trade, it will normally be straightforward for the Commission to demonstrate the necessary effect on competition.

36.5.4.8   Article 81(2) EC

As far as individual commercial agreements are concerned, the effect of Article 81(2) EC may be to render the whole agreement void if it contains provisions which infringe Article 81(1) EC. However, it may be possible for a national court applying Article 81 EC to sever the offending provisions (in accordance with the severance rules of the national law governing the agreement) leaving the rest of the agreement valid. It can prove difficult for the court to do this in a distribution agreement, where the offending provisions (eg those relating to exclusive territory) are often part of the consideration offered to induce the potential distributor to accept the agreement (see **36.4.2**), and are therefore so central to the agreement that they cannot be severed.

36.5.4.9   Article 81(3) EC

Article 81(3) EC applies where an agreement, decision or practice infringes Article 81(1) EC but is worthy of exemption from the prohibition (so Article 81(2) EC does not apply). Exemption under Article 81(3) will be possible only if the agreement etc is essentially pro-competitive (broadly, it must promote or improve trade, give consumers some benefit and not contain unnecessary restrictions of competition). For more detail of how this works in practice, see **36.8.9**.

36.5.5   Article 82 EC: the principle

Broadly, Article 82 EC prohibits as incompatible with the common market the abuse by one or more undertakings of a dominant position within the common market or a substantial part of it in so far as that abuse may affect trade between Member States. The Article is reproduced in **Business and Company Legislation**.

36.5.6   Article 82 EC: key points

36.5.6.1   One or more undertakings

The activities of one undertaking can infringe Article 82 EC. Unlike Article 81 EC, it is not necessary to have an agreement between undertakings (this would normally also be covered, although exactly when two or more unconnected undertakings can be 'collectively (ie jointly) dominant' in a market is still to some extent unclear; for guidance, see *Re Italian Flat Glass* [1990] 4 CMLR 535).

36.5.6.2   Dominant position

Broadly speaking, an undertaking enjoys a dominant position in a market when it is able to behave independently of its competitors and customers, to stop effective competition against itself and to maintain that state of affairs. There is no conclusive arithmetical test of 'dominance'; very broadly, the larger a business's market share, the more likely it is to be dominant, but the conditions of the relevant market must always be taken into account.

36.5.6.3   Market

The word 'market' includes both product and geographic markets. See **Legal Foundations** for a discussion of how to define and identify these markets.

36.5.6.4   Substantial part

Each Member State of the EU is likely to be a 'substantial part' of the common market. Smaller divisions may be possible.

36.5.6.5   Abuse

Abuse is essentially behaviour by a dominant undertaking which is not normal commercial behaviour in the relevant markets and which is detrimental to competitors or consumers. Examples include:

(a)   a dominant undertaking exploiting its customers by charging very high prices which bear no relation to the commercial value of goods, or charging very low prices in order to drive competitors out of the market ('predatory pricing');

(b)   a dominant undertaking refusing to supply a customer for no commercially justifiable reason.

36.5.6.6   May affect trade

This is the same requirement as in Article 81 EC (see **36.5.4.5**).

36.5.7   Application of the Articles

Article 81 EC is more likely than Article 82 EC to be relevant to an individual commercial agreement (eg a distribution agreement). However, both Articles can apply to the same set of facts; equally, the fact that Article 81 EC does not apply will not rule out the application of Article 82 EC (and vice versa).

36.6   The Commission's powers of investigation and enforcement

36.6.1   Attitude of the Commission

Both Articles 81 and 82 EC are expressed in wide terms, and the Commission is prepared to interpret them flexibly. It is unsafe to assume that the Commission will be unable to discover an infringing agreement or practice; it takes enforcement of the competition law rules very seriously and is endowed with considerable powers to track down infringements.

36.6.2   Regulation 1/2003

The way in which EC competition law is enforced underwent major changes in 2004 as a result of Regulation 1/2003 ([2003] OJ L1/1). The Regulation came into force on 1 May 2004, replacing Regulation 17/62, the previous competition law enforcement provision. The changes made by Regulation 1/2003 were intended to modernise and streamline the way in which EC competition law is enforced; in particular the Regulation confers greater powers and responsibility on national courts and national competition authorities to enforce EC competition law. Under the Regulation, the Commission still enjoys significant enforcement powers itself, but some commentators have noted that, in future, its role is likely to be more concerned with policing EC competition law than regulating this area. The main changes made by the Regulation are dealt with at **36.8.9**.

36.6.3   Obtaining information

The Commission receives a considerable amount of unsolicited information about possible infringements. For example, information may come to the Commission from a party to an agreement which feels that it is being unfairly treated by the other party, or from a business claiming that a competitor is abusing a dominant position and driving it out of business. The Commission can also obtain information by request. Most requests are informal: the Commission can make a formal request, but this is uncommon. In both cases, the Commission can fine any undertaking which refuses to supply the information requested.

36.6.4   Investigations

When representatives of the Competition Law Directorate-General investigate an undertaking, they have power to inspect its premises, examine its books and records, and demand immediate explanations of 'suspicious' material or practices. Investigators can seek out information which they believe to be useful but which was not previously known to them (subject to the rules of privilege). The Competition Law Directorate-General can make both informal and formal investigations (the latter is usually known as a 'dawn raid'). An undertaking must submit to a dawn raid, which usually happens unannounced and at all the undertaking's premises; refusal to comply will usually result in a fine. Before the Commission makes a decision on the merits of a case, the undertakings concerned have the right to a hearing (the details of the procedure are outside the scope of this chapter).

36.7   Consequences of infringement

36.7.1   Fines

The Commission can impose heavy fines in respect of infringements of both Articles 81 and 82 EC. By Article 23 of Regulation 1/2003, an undertaking which is found to have infringed either Article 81 or Article 82 can be fined a sum not exceeding 10% of its total turnover in the preceding business year. In deciding on the appropriate level of fines, Article 23 provides that the Commission will have regard to the gravity and duration of the infringement. In practice, the Commission will also look at matters such as the size of the undertakings involved, their market share, and (if relevant) how much the parties to the infringement have profited by keeping others out of their market. Note that the Commission can and will fine in respect of unintentional infringements or behaviour which the Commission has not previously punished, although such fines are likely to be smaller than for deliberate infringements. Co-operation with the Commission during an investigation may be a mitigating factor.

36.7.2   Actions in national courts

It is possible for undertakings to bring actions in their national courts if they have suffered loss due to infringement of either Article 81 or 82 EC (both Articles are directly effective). The remedies available for infringement will vary between different Member States because they will be national remedies. In the UK, there is House of Lords authority suggesting that it should be possible to claim damages for breach of statutory duty or obtain an injunction (*Garden Cottage Foods Ltd v Milk Marketing Board* [1984] AC 130: a case on the old Article 86, but still relevant). An injunction was obtained in *Cutsforth v Mansfield Inns Ltd* [1986] 1 All ER 577, giving the applicant a remedy in circumstances where he would have had none under English law. Damages for breach of Article 81 EC were awarded by the Court of Appeal in *Crehan v Inntrepreneur Pub Co (CPC)* (2004) *The Times*, 28 May. The case was subsequently appealed to the House of Lords, which confirmed that damages were in principle available for such a breach. However, the House of Lords ruled that, on the facts, there had been no such breach, and so damages were not available to this claimant (the citation for the House of Lords judgment is [2006] 4 All ER 465).

36.7.3 Other consequences

Infringement can also have less tangible consequences. For example, a large manufacturer may impose on a small distributor an agreement which it knows to be suspect under Article 81 EC. If the distributor realises that the agreement may infringe Article 81 EC, it may be able to win concessions from the manufacturer by threatening to notify the Commission of the potential infringement. The manufacturer may then be forced to renegotiate the agreement from a position of weakness. Obviously, any undertaking which notified the Commission in these circumstances would itself be running risks, but it is possible that the distributor would be prepared to use the threat as a bargaining counter, significantly altering the normal balance of bargaining power.

36.8   Avoiding infringement of Article 81 EC

36.8.1   Difficulty of avoiding infringement

Subject to what is said at **36.8.8**, infringement of Article 81 EC cannot be avoided simply by using a particular form of agreement. The ways in which Article 81 EC may apply can sometimes be difficult to predict, and it may be impossible to advise a client with certainty on whether a particular agreement or practice is likely to amount to an infringement. However, depending on the nature of the agreement, it may be possible to take steps to minimise the risk.

36.8.2   Article 81(1) EC does not apply

It is sometimes possible to argue that an agreement containing potentially restrictive terms falls outside Article 81 EC altogether. This is particularly likely where the parties to an agreement cannot be described as two separate undertakings. Two important examples of this are: agreements between parent and subsidiary companies, and agency agreements.

36.8.2.1   Parent and subsidiary companies

An agreement between a parent and a subsidiary company is unlikely to infringe Article 81 EC; the Commission normally regards this sort of agreement as nothing more than allocation of business within a group of companies. The parties would never have been potential competitors, and so an agreement between them cannot have an effect on competition.

36.8.2.2   Agency agreements

Many agency agreements will fall outside the scope of Article 81 EC as a result of the Commission Notice of May 2000 which sets out guidelines in relation to vertical restraints and, in particular, on the application of the Vertical Agreements Block Exemption (see **36.8.6** for more explanation of how this block exemption works). Paragraphs 12–20 of the Notice deal specifically with agency agreements.

Paragraph 12 defines an agency agreement for this purpose. Broadly speaking, it is an agreement where one person (the agent) is 'vested with the power to negotiate and/or conclude contracts on behalf of a specific person (the principal)' for the sale or purchase of goods or services by the principal. Paragraph 13 indicates that 'genuine' agency agreements do not fall within the scope of Article 81 EC, and that the determining factor in assessing whether Article 81 EC is applicable is the 'financial or commercial risk' accepted by the agent.

Paragraphs 14–17 discuss in more detail the types of financial or commercial risks which are material to assessing whether or not an agency agreement is 'genuine'; the implication is that if the agent accepts such risks to a significant degree, the agreement will not be a 'genuine' agreement, and Article 81 EC will apply. Paragraph 16 gives particular indications of situations where an agent will *not* be accepting such risks. These include where the agent does not contribute to the supply of goods or services, is not required to invest in sales promotion, does not maintain at its own risk stocks of the contract goods, and does not offer after-sales services unless it is fully reimbursed by the principal. In other words, in these circumstances, an agency agreement is likely to be 'genuine', and therefore to fall outside Article 81 EC.

36.8.3 The Notice on Agreements of Minor Importance

Even if an agreement is made between two independent undertakings, and could affect trade between Member States, its effects may in practice be so small that the Commission will ignore the existence of the agreement. There are two main reasons for this. The Commission has the resources to investigate only the most seriously anti-competitive arrangements; in addition, it is prepared to encourage comparatively small undertakings by allowing them to make agreements which may in theory restrict competition, but which do not have an appreciable impact on market conditions. The Notice on Agreements of Minor Importance sets out guidelines as to when these 'small' agreements will not appreciably restrict competition. Broadly, the Notice can apply to all types of agreements as long as the agreement satisfies an appropriate guideline (the 'thresholds').

The Notice ([2001] OJ C368/07) was last updated in December 2001. In point 7, it provides that the Commission 'holds the view' that agreements which affect trade between Member States do not in fact appreciably restrict competition within the meaning of Article 81(1) EC in two particular situations; each situation has a different market share threshold for the application of the Notice. These are:

(a) if the aggregate market share held by the parties to the agreement does not exceed 10% on any of the relevant markets affected by the agreement where the agreement is made between undertakings which are actual or potential competitors on any of these markets (agreements between competitors); or

(b) if the market share held by each of the parties to the agreement does not exceed 15% on any of the relevant markets affected by the agreement where the agreement is made by undertakings which are not actual or potential competitors on any of these markets (agreements between non-competitors).

Although the Notice does not say this as such, 'agreements between competitors' are likely to be horizontal agreements, and 'agreements between non-competitors' are likely to be vertical agreements.

Thus, if an agreement satisfies the appropriate market share threshold, Article 81 EC will not apply to the agreement: the Commission will, in effect, ignore it. However, the effect of point 11 of the Notice is that this de minimis exemption will not apply to agreements containing various hard-core restrictions (eg price-fixing); the list is essentially the same as the list of hard-core terms in the vertical agreements block exemption (see **36.8.7**).

In cases where it is difficult to classify the agreement as being between competitors or non-competitors, the 10% threshold applies.

Note that in point 8 of the Notice, provision is made for what is called the 'cumulative foreclosure effect of parallel networks of agreements having similar effects on the market'. This is where competition in a relevant market is restricted by the cumulative effect of agreements for the sale of goods or services entered into by different suppliers or distributors: in this case, the market share thresholds under point 7 are reduced to 5% both for agreements between competitors and non-competitors. Such an effect is unlikely to exist if less than 30% of the relevant market is covered by parallel networks of agreements having similar effect.

Point 10 of the Notice provides some guidance on the potentially difficult question of how to determine the relevant market (so that in turn, market share can be calculated); in particular, it refers to the Commission's Notice on definition of the relevant market for the purposes of EC competition law. This Notice is also used, for example, to determine the relevant market for the purposes of Article 82 EC.

36.8.4   Effect of the Notice

Point 4 of the Notice provides that in cases covered by the Notice, the Commission will not institute proceedings (ie for infringement of Article 81 EC). It also provides that where undertakings assume 'in good faith' that an agreement is covered by the Notice but this turns out not to be the case, the Commission will not impose fines. Finally, it notes that although the Notice is not binding on the courts and (competition) authorities of the Member States, it is intended to give guidance to them on the application of Article 81 EC.

Note also the existence of the Commission Notice ([2004] OJ C101/07) containing guidelines on the 'effect on trade' concept (which is common to both Articles 81 and 82 EC). This Notice is usually known as the 'NAAT' Notice, and works on similar principles to the Notice on Agreements of Minor Importance; there is deemed to be no appreciable effect on trade where the aggregate market share of the parties on any relevant market within the Community does not exceed a certain level. There are, however, two substantial differences from the Notice on Agreements of Minor Importance: the NAAT Notice will apply only if the market share does not exceed 5%, and it can apply even if the agreement contains hard-core terms.

36.8.5   Agreements likely to infringe Article 81(1) EC

In the case of an agreement between substantial independent undertakings which is likely to have an appreciable effect on trade and competition within the common market, there is a serious possibility that it will infringe Article 81(1) EC. This is particularly likely with distribution agreements, which often contain provisions (eg exclusive territory) considered by the parties to be essential to the workings of the agreement, but which have the potential to restrict competition. At this stage, the parties should consider whether the agreement could be redrafted to get the benefit of a block exemption.

36.8.6   Block exemptions

Block exemptions work by exempting defined categories of agreement from the prohibition in Article 81(1) EC. They are given in the form of Commission Regulations, and have been designed to ensure that the Commission does not have to investigate agreements which potentially infringe Article 81(1) EC, but do not in fact impose serious restrictions on competition, and which may actually benefit consumers. The exemption is granted under the provisions of Article 81(3), which permits exemption for agreements which can be shown to have these characteristics (for more detail on Article 81(3), see **36.8.9**). Currently, there are block exemptions covering a variety of commercial agreements, including vertical agreements (see **36.8.7**) and agreements for the transfer of technology (eg the licensing of certain types of intellectual property, such as patents). Although there are some differences in format and presentation, block exemptions tend to follow a similar pattern; first, the Regulation states, in a preamble, the Commission's policy in allowing block exemption for the type of agreement concerned, and then outlines the conditions on which block exemption will be granted to that type of agreement.

36.8.7 An example of a block exemption in outline: Regulation 2790/99

The block exemption granted by Regulation 2790/99 ([1999] OJ L336/21) (commonly known as the 'vertical agreements' or 'vertical restraints' block exemption) was adopted by the Council on 22 December 1999, and has applied to vertical agreements (as defined in Article 2) since 1 June 2000. Broadly speaking, a vertical agreement is one of the supply of goods or services where the parties are at different levels of the supply chain (eg, a distribution agreement between manufacturers and wholesaler, or a franchise agreement).

It is important to note that Regulation 2790/99 took a different approach from its three predecessors. Unlike those block exemptions, Regulation 2790/99 does not contain a 'white list' of permitted terms: instead, it simply lists terms which are not permissible or situations which will prevent the block exemption applying. Anything not listed in this way in Articles 4 or 5 (see below) will normally be permissible, creating what is commonly referred to as a 'safe harbour' for agreements which do not contain hard-core terms. In addition, the block exemption is subject to a market share threshold; by Article 3, the block exemption only applies to an agreement if the supplier's share (or in some cases the buyer's share; see Article 3.2) of the relevant market does not exceed 30%; this has been seen as an attempt to bring some economic reality into the operation of the block exemption by restricting the benefit of exemption to small and medium-sized undertakings. The main provisions of the Regulation are as follows.

Preamble:	explains the philosophy behind the grant of block exemption to vertical agreements.
Article 1:	defines various important phrases (eg 'non-compete obligation', 'exclusive supply obligation').
Article 2:	grants exemption to vertical agreements (as defined in Article 2.1).
Article 3:	sets out the market share threshold above which the block exemption will not apply.
Article 4:	'hard-core' restrictions; notably most forms of price-fixing (Article 4(a)) and certain territorial and customer restrictions (Article 4(b)). Use of such terms will prevent the block exemption applying to the agreement at all.
Article 5:	provides further restrictions of the exemption in certain cases of selective distribution or non-compete clauses. Such terms will not have the benefit of the block exemption, but their use in an agreement will not stop the block exemption applying to the rest of the agreement.

Note that by Articles 6–8, the block exemption may be withdrawn; either selectively by the Commission or Member States (Articles 6 and 7) or by the Commission in relation to particular markets (Article 8).

36.8.8 Advantages of block exemption

It is desirable to take advantage of block exemption wherever possible, as it is likely to be cheaper, quicker and safer for the parties concerned. If an agreement is drafted in a way which closely follows any relevant block exemption, it is unlikely that the Commission will take an interest in the agreement unless circumstances change.

36.8.9 Article 81(3)

As noted at **36.5.4.9** above, Article 81(3) provides for the possibility that an agreement may be exempted from the prohibition in Article 81(1) if it satisfies the conditions in Article 81(3). These are that the agreement:

(a)   improves distribution or technical progress;

(b)   allows consumers a fair share of the resulting benefits;

(c)   does not impose restrictions that are not indispensable to achieving those benefits; and

(d)   does not substantially eliminate competition.

As well as allowing for categories of agreements to be exempted from the prohibition (ie allowing block exemptions to be made by the Commission), Article 81(3) can also be used to exempt individual agreements. Until Regulation 1/2003 came into force on 1 May 2004, only the Commission could grant exemption under Article 81(3) to individual agreements. This type of exemption was known as 'individual exemption', and could only be granted after the parties had notified the details of their agreement to the Commission.

This system of individual exemption had a number of disadvantages:

(a)   it was time-consuming and expensive;

(b)   very few individual exemptions were ever granted;

(c)   the notification system greatly increased the Commission's workload, as there was no other body which could grant individual exemption.

Under the system brought in by Regulation 1/2003, the following changes were made:

(a)   notification of agreements to the Commission has been abolished;

(b)   instead, parties to an agreement are responsible for assessing whether or not their agreement satisfies the conditions laid down in Article 81(3);

(c)   in cases of dispute, national competition authorities or national courts have the power to decide whether or not an agreement does satisfy the conditions, and to grant exemption (see further **36.8.10**).

However, it is important to note that the Article 81(3) conditions themselves have not changed.

In practice, the Regulation 1/2003 system is often being referred to as 'self-assessment' rather than under the old name of 'individual exemption'.

Note that under the old system, notification of an agreement to the Commission could result in outcomes other than the grant of individual exemption. Two of the main possibilities were:

(a)   negative clearance: a declaration by the Commission that the agreement did not infringe Article 81 at all (rather than being an infringing agreement which deserved exemption);

(b)   comfort letter: a non-binding pronouncement from the Commission on the status of the agreement.

Negative clearance in its previous form is no longer relevant under the new system, and the former comfort letter system has ceased to exist. However, the Commission has the power under Regulation 1/2003 to pronounce informally on the status of agreements, although this is limited to difficult or novel cases, and there is little evidence of its use so far.

36.8.10   National courts and national competition authorities

A novel feature of Regulation 1/2003 is that it devolves some of the power to enforce EC competition law to national courts and to national competition authorities (NCAs: essentially, these are the bodies in each Member State which enforce national competition law).

Note that although national courts previously had the power to apply Articles 81 and 82 EC where appropriate, they were unable to apply Article 81(3) to grant exemption to agreements, as this power was reserved to the Commission.

The Commission aims to provide guidance via a further regulation dealing with procedural issues and a series of Notices covering such matters as co-operation between NCAs, co-operation between the Commission and national courts, and Commission guidance for courts and NCAs on how to apply Article 81(3).

It appears that, under English law, parties to an agreement would be able to apply to court for a declaration as to the status of an agreement (although it is thought that courts will be reluctant to grant such declarations). In addition, the Office of Fair Trading gives informal guidance on the status of agreements via guidelines on its website. Note that this is general guidance only rather than relating to specific agreements.

36.8.11   Practical impact of Regulation 1/2003

As the system under Regulation 1/2003 has been in force for a comparatively short time, there are inevitably still some areas in which its operation is unclear. However, the following points may be made:

(a)   as the system did not attempt to change the way in which block exemption or the Notice on Agreements of Minor Importance applies, parties may be well advised to rely on these where appropriate (at least until the operation of the 'self-assessment' system becomes fully clear);

(b)   parties who want to rely on the self-assessment exemption under Article 81(3) will need to assess their agreement carefully, and it may be advisable to take detailed legal advice on whether exemption will be possible;

(c)   as noted at **36.8.9**, there are ways in which parties can get informal guidance from the Commission (possibly also from NCAs) or a declaration from a court as to the status of their agreement under Article 81(3). However, this is of limited availability and use, and the burden will primarily fall on undertakings to assess their own agreements;

(d)   if the parties have decided that Article 81(3) applies to their agreement, this conclusion may be challenged by a third party (possibly also by an NCA);

(e)   if a challenge is made, the parties will be able to apply to an NCA or court (as appropriate) for determination of the issue of whether Article 81(3) applies or not.

36.9   Applying the Articles to specific commercial agreements

Although it is not always easy to predict the operation of Articles 81 and 82 EC in relation to a commercial agreement, it is worth considering certain points when drafting or reviewing an agreement. In particular, the solicitor should try to establish two important points: are the Articles likely to apply, and how, if at all, can this be prevented? Bear in mind, however, that the answers may not be clear-cut, and that the following paragraphs provide guidance only on the points to consider.

36.9.1   Article 81 EC: agency agreements

When drafting or reviewing a client's agreement, consider the following points.

(a)   Article 81(1) EC may not apply at all because one or more of the following statements is true.

(i)   The agreement is within the Commission's Guidelines in relation to vertical restraints because the agreement is a 'genuine agency agreement': the agent is not acting independently in relation to the contract goods and, for example, accepts no financial risk under the agency agreement.

(ii)   The principal and agent are parent and subsidiary companies and therefore count as one undertaking.

(iii)   The agreement is otherwise incapable of affecting trade and competition within the common market (eg it does not contain any restrictive terms).

(b)   The parties' market shares may be small enough to fall within the Notice on Agreements of Minor Importance. If so, the Commission is unlikely to take an interest in the agreement.

If neither (a) nor (b) is relevant, the agency agreement will probably have to be treated in the same way as a distribution agreement (see below). Bear in mind, however, that there are no block exemptions which apply to agency agreements.

36.9.2   Article 81 EC: distribution agreements

When drafting or reviewing a client's distribution agreement, consider the following points.

(a)   Article 81(1) EC may not apply because either (or both) of the following statements are true.

    (i)   The parties are parent and subsidiary companies and therefore count as one undertaking.

    (ii)   The agreement is otherwise incapable of affecting trade and competition within the common market (eg it does not contain any restrictive terms).

(b)   Does the Notice on Agreements of Minor Importance or the NAAT Notice apply? (See (b) at **36.9.1**.)

(c)   If neither (a) nor (b) is relevant, consider the terms which the client wants to include in the agreement. If they are likely to restrict competition, it is probably best to assume that Article 81(1) EC applies, and then decide if it is possible to avoid infringement.

(d)   (i) If drafting a new agreement, draft to get the benefit of the relevant block exemption (Regulation 2790/99) wherever possible.

    (ii)   If reviewing an existing agreement, consider whether it could be redrafted to bring it within the block exemption.

(e)   If none of the above is appropriate, consider whether Article 81(3) will apply to exempt the agreement.

36.9.3   Article 82 EC

Article 82 EC is far less likely to apply to individual commercial agreements than Article 81 EC. However, it must not be ignored, especially if one of the parties has a large market share (eg if a supplier with a large market share refused to supply a distributor and there was no good commercial reason for the refusal, it could in certain circumstances be abusing a dominant position). Bear in mind that if Article 82 EC does apply, there is no way of avoiding infringement. Consider the following questions.

(a)   Does the agreement involve one or more undertakings?

(b)   Does the agreement involve an undertaking with a dominant position in the relevant markets?

(c)   Is that dominant position within the common market or a substantial part of it?

(d)   Does the conduct of the dominant undertaking amount to abuse of a dominant position?

If the answer to all of these questions is 'Yes', Article 82 EC prohibits the abuse in so far as it may affect trade between Member States.

Appendix 1
Joint Ventures

1 Reasons for joint ventures

Reasons for setting up a joint venture (JV) of whatever structure include the following.

(a) **Cost savings:** the costs of research and development, or capital investment programmes can be shared, especially in industries when there are high investment costs such as electronics or pharmaceuticals.

(b) **Risk sharing:** a similar rationale is the objective of sharing the significant financial risks in a speculative or capital intensive project (eg the PFI and PPP projects in the public sector to build, and often to operate, major infrastructure projects such as a new power station, roads, prisons, hospitals).

(c) **Access to technology:** a JV may provide a way to gain access to the other parties' technology skills.

(d) **Extension of the customer base:** international JVs can provide an effective route for one party to utilise the other party's strength in different geographic markets and/or use the other party's distribution or a sales network in another territory.

(e) **Entry into new geographical markets:** a JV with a local entity may provide the only realistic route for entering emerging markets such as eastern Europe or Asia.

(f) **Entry into new technical markets:** the rapid pace of technological change produces new markets, and the best way of 'hitting the ground running' is to collaborate with another entity which has a technical start in that field.

(g) **Pressures of global competition:** the merger of similar business between two or more entities may establish economies of scale, wider access to customers throughout the world, better purchasing power or a pooling of capital investment resources needed to meet international competition (eg the proposed alliance between American Airlines and British Airways, but which is now defunct due to competition law issues).

2 Types of joint ventures

Joint ventures come in all shapes and sizes and can include those below.

(a) **Short-term collaborations,** for example to undertake a particular project.

(b) **'Limited function' joint ventures,** for example to build a new production facility for the supply of components to the joint venture parties.

(c) **'Full function'** start-up business ventures based on new technology.

(d) **Full-scale worldwide mergers** of existing businesses (eg Shell and Texaco have merged their industrial lubricants businesses in the US to produce 'Equilon' to deal with these types of products).

3 Problems with joint ventures

(a) **Sharing management**: a JV needs to have management input from each of the JV parties. However, one party may dominate the management structure causing tensions within the JV.

(b) **Differences in culture**: JVs require the various parties to work together. There can be a consequent difference in approach within the JV management, which can affect the harmony and speed of operations.

(c) **The 'Trojan horse' problem**: the fear is that the other party in a JV may use the JV to 'steal' the technology or market knowledge of the other party, and then compete independently.

(d) **Different commercial objectives**: the parties may have different objectives for the same JV.

(e) **Who is in charge?** Is it the management of the companies which are the parties to the JV, or is it the management team of the JV itself?

(f) **Disagreements**: these will need to be resolved by the senior management.

(g) **Extra management time**: the management of the parties will need to devote time and energy to managing the JV.

(h) **Long and costly negotiations**: these add to the costs of setting up the JV.

(i) **Competition law problems**: it may be anti-competitive and may be struck down by the Monopolies and Mergers Commission or the EU Commission.

(j) **Exit**: all JVs come to an end some day, so each party needs to have an eye on the exit route.

4 Structures for joint ventures

Possible structures are:

(a) contractual JV;

(b) collaboration agreements;

(c) corporate JV;

(d) partnership (general or limited liability) which can be:

  (i) for a fixed term;

  (ii) 'at will' (continues until dissolved); or

  (iii) for a specific project;

(e) European Economic Interest Grouping 'EEIG'. This is a creation of the EU. It is not suitable for ordinary profit-making businesses. It has been used for cross-border alliances of, for example, accountants and for research collaboration between existing companies in different jurisdictions. It has a separate legal identity, rather like a company.

5 Advantages/disadvantages of a partnership structure for a joint venture

5.1 Advantages

(a) **Flexibility and simplicity**: there are no formalities for formation of a partnership; the governing rules will be contained in a partnership agreement agreed by the parties themselves (ie there is no equivalent of Table A articles).

(b) **Tax transparency**: tax relief can be readily obtained for capital expenditure, or losses incurred in the early stages of trading.

(c) **No public filings**: the lack of any need to incur the publicity or expense of making submissions to any regulator, eg Companies House, can be a major advantage. There is also no need for public audited accounts.

5.2 Disadvantages

(a) **Liability**: there is joint and several liability of partners for liabilities incurred by a partnership, or by any of the partners acting within the express or implied authority of a partnership.

(b) **Absence of a corporate identity**: contrast this with a corporate structure which would own the assets, and contain the liabilities, independently of shareholders.

(c) **External finance**: there are fewer places to obtain the external finance. A company can borrow money on the security of a floating charge, or could sell its shares to an investor. This cannot be the case with a partnership. A partnership cannot create a floating charge, nor can it issue shares.

(d) **The Partnership Act 1890**: this implies certain terms into a partnership which the partners would often wish to exclude by including contrary terms in the partnership agreement.

(e) **Imprecise structure**: there does not have to be any written partnership agreement.

6 Particular issues with partnership: the Partnership Act 1890

(a) **Starting date**: remember that the partnership comes into being when the s 1(1) criteria are met, which is not necessarily when the parties would like it to (eg as stated in the partnership agreement).

(b) **Liability**: each partner is an agent of the partnership and can bind the partnership in the usual course of business. Each partner has unlimited liability for the debts and obligations of the partnership (ss 9, 10).

(c) **Management**: the management structure will depend on contractual agreement between the parties.

(d) **Variation by agreement**: s 19 provides that the partners can vary their rights and duties, including those under the PA 1890, by consent of all the partners. Such consent may be express or inferred from a course of dealing. (Note that the articles of a company cannot be altered in a manner inconsistent with the CA 1985.)

(e) **Profits and losses**: the agreement should provide rules for calculating division of profit and any losses, otherwise each will be allocated equally to the partners (s 24(1)).

(f) **General implied terms**:

  (i) loans from the partners to the partnership bear interest at 5% per annum (s 24(3));

  (ii) a partner is not entitled to interest on capital payments made to the firm (s 24(4));

  (iii) every partner is entitled to take part in the management of the partnership (s 24(5));

  (iv) no new partner can be introduced without the consent of all existing partners (s 24(7)); and

  (v) a change in the nature of the business requires consent of all the partners (s 24(8)).

(g) **Termination**: if the partnership has no fixed term, a partner may terminate it by notice (s 26).

(h) **Fiduciary duties**: partnership is a fiduciary relationship. Every partner is bound to render accounts and information to any other partner (s 28), including profits from a competing business of the same nature as the firm, unless the firm has consented to him running that business (ss 29, 30).

7 Exit routes

7.1 Dissolution under the PA 1890

(a)   Section 32 provides that a partnership dissolves (subject to contrary agreement between the parties):

    (i)   if a partnership for a fixed term, by expiry of that term

    (ii)   if for a single venture, then when that venture is terminated or

    (iii)   if for an unlimited time, then when a partner gives notice to the others of his intent to dissolve the partnership.

(b)   Section 35 – dissolution by the court, especially (c) breach of the agreement, and (f) just and equitable grounds.

    See also ss 33, 34 on other grounds for dissolution under the PA 1890, which are very unlikely to apply to JVs.

7.2 Dissolution under the partnership agreement

There will usually be a JV agreement between the parties which will provide for dissolution of the partnership, and an exit route before that. Just how those rights are formulated will depend on the agreement itself. The general rule would be that a party's interest cannot be transferred without the consent of the other party or parties to the JV.

Sometimes, there is a need for a detailed procedure rather like the transfer of shares in a private company. This is often dictated in a partnership JV by the regulatory regime in which the JV operates, eg the licences from the UK government for North Sea oil exploration.

7.3 General exit clauses

Two general examples of exit clause that can be used in JVs are known as 'Russian roulette' and a 'Texas shoot-out' clauses.

7.3.1 'Russian roulette' clause

(a)   Party A wants to terminate the JV.

(b)   Party A serves a notice on Party B offering to sell its shares (or share in the partnership) for a price set out in the notice.

(c)   Party B is obliged either to:

    (i)   accept the offer; or

    (ii)   reject it, whereupon Party B becomes obliged to sell its shares (or partnership share) to Party A for the price specified on the original notice.

7.3.2 'Texas shoot-out' clause

(a)   Party A wishes to terminate the JV as above.

(b)   Party A serves a 'buy notice' on Party B offering to buy Party B's share for a specified price.

(c)   Party B then serves a counter notice that either:

    (i)   it is prepared to sell its interest to Party A; or

    (ii)   it wishes to buy Party A's interest at a higher price than that in Party A's notice.

(d)   A sealed bid system is used if both parties want to buy the other's interest.

7.3.3 Miscellaneous exit events

There can also be compulsory termination events in the JV agreement, eg for material default by one party, or insolvency.

8 Role of the lawyer in the joint venture

Various areas which are relevant in JVs include corporate, regulatory, tax, pensions, employment and IP. The role of the lawyer will normally be to:

(a) help structure the JV in line with the client's business objectives;

(b) alert the client to important legal issues and the solutions available;

(c) carry out legal due diligence;

(d) obtain any regulatory clearance or consents;

(e) draft the JV documentation so that it accurately encapsulates the commercial instructions; and

(f) manage the legal and other steps necessary to establish the joint venture.

Appendix 2

The Destination in the Companies Act 2006 of some Commonly-used Sections of the Companies Act 1985

Section(s) in Companies Acts 1985/89	Section(s) in Companies Act 2006	Summary of main changes
1–3 and 10,12,13 (incorporation, memorandum, forms)	3, 4 and 7–10,12,13–16	• The memorandum of association becomes a far simpler document and becomes of historical significance only. Articles become much more significant. • No need for detailed objects – they will be unrestricted; so no need for resolutions to change them. • No need for authorised share capital. 'Statement of Capital' and of initial shareholdings (s 10) must be delivered on incorporation but can be varied later.
25–27 (company names)	53–74	• Easier to form a company online. • Procedure for incorporation (registration of memo, articles, statement of capital and initial shareholdings, registered office, details of proposed officers, statement of compliance) appears to be similar. • No substantive change to restrictions on use of names. • Indications – 'plc' or 'limited/ltd' remain the same (ss 58, 59).
28 (change of name)	77–81	• Articles may provide for change of name by *board* resolution as opposed to special resolution (s 77(1)(b)). Companies House must still be notified.
7 (articles)	18, 19 and 20	• Prescribed model articles for plcs (for first time) and private limited companies (probably reasonably similar to Table A) will be published and be the default provisions.
9 (alteration of articles)	21 and 22	• A company must still use special resolutions to amend articles.

Section(s) in Companies Acts 1985/89	Section(s) in Companies Act 2006	Summary of main changes
		• A company may provide that certain provisions cannot be altered or removed other than by unanimous consent (known as 'entrenching'). • Ordinary resolution is now statutorily defined (s 282) as one passed by a simple majority.
369, 378, 381A (notice periods, short notice, written resolutions)	281–287 288–300 301–303	• For *all* meetings 14 clear days' notice required irrespective of resolution. (21 days still required for AGM of plc.) • Requisite majority (now termed 'requisite percentage') for meetings on short notice of a private limited company (not a plc) is 90% (not 95%) of shareholders having right to attend and vote. • For members' requisitions of meetings the requisite percentage is reduced in certain circumstances to 5% (currently 10%). • There will be two sorts of written resolutions so the requisite majority (100% currently) is reduced to: (a) 75% where a special resolution is proposed; or (b) 50% where an ordinary resolution is proposed (ss 282, 283). • The rules for written resolutions become more detailed depending whether directors or members propose the relevant written resolution. • The need to give notice of meetings to auditors appears to have been repealed (s 310, cf Table A, Art 38). It may be reinstated in secondary legislation.
317 (declarations of interest)	175, 182, 183 and 185	• The basic requirement to *declare* an interest remains. • There are wider provisions as to what constitutes a conflict of interest. • Unconflicted directors may authorise such transactions (opt in for plcs; opt out for private limited companies).

Section(s) in Companies Acts 1985/89	Section(s) in Companies Act 2006	Summary of main changes
320, 322, 346, 730 (substantial property transactions)	190–196 and 252, 253 and 1163	• Essentially remains the same, but with the following relaxations: (a) substantial property transaction may be entered into *conditional* upon shareholder approval; (b) de minimis threshold is £5,000 (currently £2,000). • Definition of 'connected' person is widened but would still include spouse.
375 (Corporate representatives)	323	• No substantial change for appointment of corporate representatives.
283, 288, 289 (register of directors, secretary)	162 and 270	• Private limited companies are no longer *required* to have a company secretary. • There are consequential amendments for registration particulars of secretaries but a register of directors is still required. Form numbers will change. Directors can file a service address rather than a home address.
312–316 (payments for loss of office)	215–222	• Essentially no fundamental change.
330–334, 341, 342 (loans to directors)	197–214	• The prohibitions now apply to all companies – the former private/plc division is repealed. • Criminal penalties are repealed. • Shareholders are empowered to approve (ordinary resolution) but there is an uplift in monetary values for de minimis transactions.
80 (authority to allot)	550	• Private limited companies with only one class of shares (eg £1 ordinary) no longer need shareholders to give directors authority to allot – directors are given power.

Section(s) in Companies Acts 1985/89	Section(s) in Companies Act 2006	Summary of main changes
88–95 (pre-emption rights)	561–557	• Essentially no change to pre-emption rights (eg 21 days' written notice of offer required (s 562(5)) and do not apply where consideration is 'non-cash' (s 565)); *but* • Again, private limited companies, with only one class of share may empower (in articles or by special resolution) directors to allot without complying with pre-emption rights. (s 583).
121–123 (allotment of shares)	554–557	• Directors empowered to allot if given authority (ordinary resolution still required or power in articles). • Administration as now (return within 1 month + statement of capital (s 555)). • NB: authorised share capital is abolished (see above); so is Form 123.
318, 319 (directors' service contracts)	188, 189, 227–230	• Essentially no change except period is two (not five) years. • NB: copies of service contracts must be kept and open for inspection for one year after expiry (s 228(3)).
395, 401 (registration of charges)	860, 861, 869, 870, 874 and 876	• No change – registration still required within 21 days or void (against usual parties). • Register of charges to be kept by company.
324, 325 (disclosure of directors' interests in shares)		• Rules about disclosure of directors' interests in shares have been repealed.
22 (membership)	33, 112, and 113	• As currently, members (other than subscribers) become such on registration. • Register of members to be kept.
162–177 (purchase of own shares)	690, 693 694–708 (general provisions) 709–723 (payment out of capital by private limited companies)	• Essentially no change to the current regime.

Section(s) in Companies Acts 1985/89	Section(s) in Companies Act 2006	Summary of main changes
151–158 (financial assistance by company for purchase of its own shares)	677–683	• Essentially the restrictions are abolished for private limited companies *only*. • The rules, substantially unamended, remain for plcs (whether listed or unlisted).
303, 304 (removal of director)	168, 169 and 312	• Essentially no change (ordinary resolution and special notice still required).
384, 385 (appointment of auditors)	485, 487 and 488	• Directors of private limited companies may dispense with appointment of auditors if reasonably unlikely that company will need to prepare audited accounts. Essentially, small companies (as currently defined) will be exempt. • Auditors of private limited companies are *deemed* to be reappointed each year unless shareholders holding 5% give notice otherwise.

Appendix 3

Company Accounts

1.1 The form of company accounts

1.1.1 The profit and loss and appropriation account

The profit and loss account of a company, like that of a partnership, contains an appropriation section which shows the purposes for which the profit will be used.

A company's legal nature differs from that of an unincorporated business and this is reflected in the way in which items are divided between the profit and loss section and the appropriation section of the account.

Note particularly:

(a) **Directors' salaries**

A director may, in fact, be a shareholder in the company but a director is regarded as an employee. Hence directors' remuneration (unlike a 'salary' for a partner) appears as an expense on the profit and loss account.

(b) **Debenture interest**

Such interest is always shown as an expense on the profit and loss account even if it is payable to a shareholder.

Example

PROFIT AND LOSS A/C FOR YEAR —

		£m	£m
Turnover			3,000
Less			
Cost of Sales			(2,700)
Gross Profit			300
Less			
Expenses (inc directors' fees)		(100)	
Debenture interest		(50)	
			(150)
			250
Profit Before Tax			150
Appropriations			
Less	Tax on Profit		(40)[1]
Profit After Tax			110
Less	Dividend		(30)[2]
	Profit Retained (Reserves)		80[3]
Add	Profit brought forward from previous years		2,420[4]
			2,500[5]

Notes

(1)   Tax is not yet payable. It will be paid nine months after the end of the accounting period. The provision on the appropriation account merely makes it clear that this amount is not available for distribution to shareholders.

(2)   The dividend has not yet been paid. It must be authorised by the shareholders at the annual general meeting.

(3)   The remaining profit is retained by the company.

(4)   This represents profit retained in previous years.

(5)   The total is the amount by which the company's successful trading has increased its assets.

1.1.2   The balance sheet

The Capital Employed section will show amounts owed to shareholders ('shareholders' funds') separately from amounts owed to outsiders.

As is usual on any balance sheet liabilities repayable within 12 months will be shown as current liabilities. Other liabilities will be shown as long-term liabilities.

Example

BALANCE SHEET AS AT—

	£m	£m
ASSETS EMPLOYED		
Fixed Assets		2,600
Current Assets		
Stock	200	
Debtors	600	
Cash	100	
	900	
Less **Current Liabilities**		
Creditors	(130)	
Tax	(40) [1]	
Dividends	(30) [1]	
	(200)	
Net Current Assets		700
		3,300
Debenture		(200)
		3,100
CAPITAL EMPLOYED		
Share Capital		200
Share Premium		400 [3]
Profit and Loss Reserve		2,500 [2]
		3,100

Notes

[1]   These items have not been paid at the end of the accounting period, but will be paid within the next 12 months. Hence they are current liabilities.

[2]   The item 'Profit and Loss Reserve' is an amount owed to shareholders in undistributed profits.

[3]   This is also an amount 'owed' to shareholders. If a share is issued for more than its original value the excess over nominal value must be recorded separately. The combined consideration is 'owed' to shareholders and is regarded as capital not normally distributable to shareholders during the lifetime of the company.

1.2   The limitations of accounts

You must be able to understand what is in the accounts, but looking at accounts alone may provide a misleading picture of the state of a business. Accounts are produced only *after* events have occurred.

Furthermore, accounts can produce information of only a financial nature. Thus, a Balance Sheet will only list assets and liabilities of the business. It will not indicate the health or otherwise of labour relations, despite the fact that many people would regard good staff relations as a very important asset. A poor trade reputation would be regarded by many people as a liability, but it has no place on a financial statement.

There may also be matters entirely beyond the control of management, such as a declining market for the firm's products. In other words, the accounts provide only part of the information needed in the analysis of the position of a business.

1.3   What information do you need?

It is important to have a general picture of the firm that you are investigating:

(a)   It is large or small?

(b)   Is it growing or contracting?

(c)   What is the nature of its business?

(d)   Does it operate in an expanding or declining market?

(e)   Does it depend heavily on a particular product or products?

The questions which you should ask depend on the circumstances and are largely a matter of common sense.

1.3.1   Public companies

A public company must prepare an annual report. The report has two main purposes:

(a)   It complies with the requirements of the Companies Act 1985 to produce certain information and accounts.

(b)   It gives the company an opportunity to promote itself, to its shareholders, to prospective investors and to analysts.

As you read any company's report, be very aware of the need to question and check everything:

(a)   Are any of the figures in the accounts not clear? Is there an explanation in the Chairman's Statement or the Directors' Report? Do the notes help?

(b)   Is the chairman expressing over-optimistic hopes in his statement? Do they look as though they can be supported by the company's current financial position? Do they look sensible in the light of the economy here and abroad?

It is unlikely, although not impossible, that you would find a direct lie in a company's report, but you should always look at the information critically to see whether a particular proposal or intention looks as if it can be justified.

Some of the items in a report are included because they must be, while some are included because the company wants to include them. The following must be included in any public company's report:

(a)   Directors' Report.

(b)   Auditors' Report.

(c)   Balance Sheet – company and group.

(d)   Profit and Loss Account – company or, if there is a group, then group only.

(e)   Cash Flow Statement – company or, if there is a group, then group only.

(f)   Notes giving the required information.

(g)   Details of directors' interests.

Other items are optional, but you would generally be surprised if the following were not there in some form:

(a)   Chairman's Statement. What is there to hide?

(b)   Ten-year record missing? Has the company not been performing consistently in the long term?

In a sense, reading a company report is something that lawyers are well trained to do – you check and question everything before accepting it as true.

Remember, when you are reading the report, that there are other sources of information as well. Keep an eye on newspaper reports, television news, etc.

1.3.2 Partnerships and sole practitioners

There will be no published accounts for partnerships and sole practitioners, though there will be for LLPs. Even so, you should get copies of the accounts they produce and study them.

Be aware that the requirements as to the format and content of reports which apply to companies do not apply to unincorporated bodies to anywhere near the same extent.

In these circumstances, you must get as much information about the business as you can. Find out the following:

(a)   Are its premises in a suitable area?

(b)   Does it seem to be busy?

(c)   Is it dealing in something which is going to provide an income in the long term?

(d)   What sort of reputation does it have locally?

(e)   What can you find out about the proprietors?

You can then look at the accounts in the light of that information. When your analysis raises further questions, you can get down to detailed discussions of the problems with the proprietors or their advisers.

Obviously, the amount of information you can get will depend on what your relationship is, or is to be, with the business.

1.4 Preliminary steps

As well as obtaining as much general information about the business as you can, there are a number of preliminary steps you should take before launching into a detailed analysis of the accounts. These involve, in part, checking the accuracy and reliability of the figures presented and, in part, building up a general picture of the business and the market in which it operates, so that the information extracted can be considered in a proper context. What might be normal for a small business might be very unusual for a large one. A particular level of profitability may be commendable in a time of recession but disappointing in a period when business generally is 'booming'.

Common preliminary steps are as follows.

(1)   *Obtain the accounts for several years.* If you are going to make a realistic assessment of a business, it is important that you obtain its accounts for several years rather than for the previous year alone. One year's accounts will reveal important information – the extent of borrowings, the value of fixed assets, the amount of unpaid bills, the value of stock in hand – but it is difficult to reach reliable conclusions without making comparisons with earlier years.

(2)   *Check the date of the Balance Sheet.* A business can choose a Balance Sheet date to suit itself. If the business is seasonal, then a Balance Sheet drawn up at one date could include figures which would show the business in a much more favourable light than a Balance Sheet drawn up at another date.

> **Example**
>
> A business manufactures Christmas decorations. It sells the decorations to department stores in September. A Balance Sheet drawn up in September would show a healthy cash balance and probably substantial debtors. By contrast, a Balance Sheet drawn up in July would show substantial stock, a high creditors figure and, probably, a large overdraft.

Always consider whether you have to take the date of the Balance Sheet into account when you are analysing the figures.

(a)   Check the method of valuing fixed assets.

(b) When were the assets last valued? Freehold premises purchased 20 years earlier for £5,000 may still be shown in the Balance Sheet at that value. Their current value will probably be quite different.

(c) Has provision been made for depreciation? If so, what method has been used? In the case of a company, you will be looking for the answers to these and other questions in the notes and the statement of accounting policies included in the company's published accounts. If you are dealing with a partnership or sole trader, you should ask for that information from the partners or proprietor.

(3) *Check how the closing stock is valued.* The normal method is to value stock at the lower of cost or current market value. If you want to do the job thoroughly, you should inspect the stock. It may be that it includes items which are no longer readily saleable. For example, in the fashion trade, a business may have purchased items some months ago, which are now out of fashion. They could still be appearing in the accounts under 'Stock' at cost price, when in fact their current market value is little or nothing.

(4) *Analyse the figure given for debtors.* Will all the debts really be paid? Has a provision been made for bad debts? It is quite possible for a business not to write off bad debts so that the debtors figure appears larger than the amount of cash which the business can readily expect to receive.

(5) *Look for unusual or exceptional items or major changes.* The picture given by the Profit and Loss Account and Balance Sheet for a particular year can sometimes be distorted because of some exceptional event or major change either in circumstances or in accounting policy.

Example

A business may have borrowed a substantial amount to invest in new plant or machinery. In the short term, profit may be reduced because there has been no time to use the new machinery to increase profits, yet interest charges will already have been incurred. However, in the long term, there may be prospects of rapid growth in future years.

Fixed assets such as land and buildings may have been revalued for the first time in many years. This will make the Balance Sheet look quite different, but in reality nothing has changed.

You will have to take all these matters into account, particularly if you are going to make comparisons with previous years.

1.5 Some general considerations

1.5.1 Profitability, solvency and liquidity

The two main questions which people ask when reading the accounts of a business are:

(a) Is the business profitable?

(b) Is the business solvent?

Profitability is not the same as solvency. The Profit and Loss Account shows whether the business has made a profit. The Balance Sheet shows whether it is solvent (ie, whether its assets exceed its liabilities).

The fact that the accounts reveal that a profit has been made does not necessarily mean that the money is in the bank.

The Trading and Profit and Loss Accounts of a business will record sales or levels of professional charges which in turn will determine the amount of profit, but, although the goods may have been sold or bills issued, payment may not yet have been received. Thus, although the Profit and Loss Account may show a large profit, the Balance Sheet may record a high figure under debtors and there may be no cash in the bank.

Alternatively, the business may have sold goods or delivered bills and been paid; however, it may have purchased expensive new premises paying cash. The result is that while the Profit and Loss Account will show a profit, there is no money in the bank.

In either example, if the proprietors relied on the Profit and Loss Account to try to withdraw large amounts of cash, they would find they could not because there was no money in the bank.

It is therefore a misconception to think that if a business is profitable it must be solvent (ie, able to pay its debts). This is not so. Obviously, a business which is unprofitable is not likely to be solvent for long, but just because a business is profitable does not necessarily mean that it is able to pay its debts at once. A profitable business may be driven into liquidation if it is unable to pay its debts as they fall due.

Liquidity is an even more important issue for a business. A business can only use current assets to meet its liabilities if it is to continue in business. If it has to sell fixed assets to meet liabilities, it will eventually be unable to continue trading. It is, therefore, important that the business does not run short of current assets. Cash is the most liquid of current assets. Debtors are also liquid as, even if they are not yet due for payment, the business can always turn them into cash quickly by selling them on to someone else to collect. Stock is less liquid as it may be difficult to sell quickly. Some items can only be sold at certain times of year.

1.5.2 Treatment of bank overdrafts

It is necessary to decide how to deal with a bank overdraft, particularly if this is substantial. It will normally appear in the Balance Sheet as a current liability because, in theory at least, it is repayable on demand. The reality may be quite different. The business may maintain a high overdraft indefinitely and finance its activities from it. Unless the business runs into difficulties, the bank will not take steps to call in the money owing.

As a current liability, the bank overdraft will not appear as part of the capital employed in the business. Instead, it will be deducted from the current assets. If, however, it is a source of long-term finance, it should be treated as such in calculating the return on capital which the business is achieving. Again, in calculating whether a business can pay its debts by examining the ratio of current or liquid assets to current liabilities, a totally misleading picture may emerge if no distinction is made between the bank overdraft and ordinary trade creditors.

1.5.3 The impact of inflation

It is necessary to make allowance for the impact of inflation. If profits are increasing at the rate of 2% pa when inflation is running at 4% pa, then in real terms profits are falling.

1.6 Ratio analysis

1.6.1 Why use ratio analysis?

Ratio analysis relates two figures together. The result can be expressed as a percentage or as a ratio. Once you have a percentage or ratio, it is easy to compare the results of different years or of different businesses. You can use ratio analysis to check the profitability and efficiency of a business and also the liquidity.

1.6.2 Profitability and efficiency

1.6.2.1 Return on capital

When looking at a set of accounts, the first thing you are likely to want to know is whether or not the business is making a profit. However, you will then want answers to some further questions:

(a)   Is the amount of profit made satisfactory when compared with the amount of capital invested in the business?

(b)   Is it more or less than the amount of profit similar businesses make from their capital?

To answer these questions, you need to relate the amount of profit produced to the amount of capital used to produce it. This is referred to as the 'return on capital'. It is normally expressed as a percentage:

$$\frac{\text{Net Profit}}{\text{Capital}} \times 100 = \%$$

You can calculate the return on the amount of capital the proprietor has invested or the amount of capital provided from all sources (for example, from bank loans). A proprietor will consider whether the return on capital is satisfactory by reference to the return that could be obtained on other investments.

When calculating the return, you may choose to take the capital figure at the start of the year, the end of the year or an average figure. It is normally easiest to take the figure at the end of the year, although arguably it is more accurate to take the figure at the start of the year as that was the amount invested during the relevant trading period.

Example

The balance on the proprietor's capital account at the end of the accounting period is £200,000; net profit for the accounting period was £40,000. The return on capital is:

$$\frac{£40,000}{£200,000} \times 100 = 20\%$$

This compares very favourably with putting the money in a bank or building society account. How does it compare with other similar businesses?

1.6.2.2   Net profit percentage

If the return on capital is unsatisfactory, a proprietor may want to increase net profit. There are only two ways to make more profit. You can increase income or reduce expenses. To increase income you can either sell more items or make more profit on each item sold. The 'net profit percentage' shows the amount of profit made on each item sold.

$$\frac{\text{Net Profit}}{\text{Sales}} \times 100 = \%$$

A business can improve profit by putting up prices. However, a business will usually try to avoid putting up prices as this may drive away customers. It will prefer to reduce expenses or sell more items.

Example

A business has sales of £400,000 and a net profit of £40,000. The net profit percentage is:

$$\frac{£40,000}{£400,000} \times 100 = 10\%$$

This means that out of every £1 of sales, 90p goes in expenses and 10p is profit. We would need figures from comparable businesses to decide whether or not the business was performing satisfactorily.

1.6.3   Liquidity tests

1.6.3.1   Current ratio

The current ratio compares current assets with current liabilities. The result is normally expressed as a ratio.

$$\frac{\text{Current assets}}{\text{Current liabilities}} = ?{:}1$$

A cautious business will want a current ratio of at least 1.5:1. However, many retail businesses manage with current ratios which are much lower. This is because they buy goods on credit but sell mainly for cash. Each day, they know that large amounts of cash will be injected. In general, therefore, they can meet liabilities due on a particular day from cash received on that day and need only a small amount of additional liquid funds in reserve.

1.6.3.2   Acid test

As we saw earlier, stock may not be quickly saleable. Also, there may be doubts as to whether it is saleable at all. Changes in fashion and technology may make stock obsolete. The acid test is the ratio between current liabilities and current assets excluding stock. (In a non-trading business, we would exclude work in progress as it is uncertain how quickly it can be turned into cash.) These assets are referred to as 'liquid assets':

$$\frac{\text{Liquid assets}}{\text{Current liabilities}} = ?{:}1$$

An acid test of 1:1 means that the business has £1 of liquid assets for every £1 of current liabilities. The lower the ratio, the greater the risk of the business being unable to meet its debts as they fall due.

Example

The following is an extract from a Balance Sheet:

Current Assets		
Stock	65,000	
Debtors	50,000	
Cash	4,000	
Prepayments	1,000	
		120,000
Current Liabilities		
Creditors	(40,000)	
Accruals	(10,000)	
		(50,000)
Net Current Assets		70,000

The current ratio is:

$$\frac{£120,000}{£50,000} = 2.4{:}1$$

The acid test is

$$\frac{£55,000}{£50,000} = 1.1{:}1$$

There are an enormous number of other ratios which can be applied to a set of accounts. However, these are sufficient to show the way in which ratio analysis can give insight into the true position of a business.

Index